# HELLENIC ARMY GENERAL STAFF
## ARMY HISTORY DIRECTORATE

# AN ABRIDGED HISTORY OF THE GREEK-ITALIAN AND GREEK-GERMAN WAR 1940-1941

## (LAND OPERATIONS)

THE ARMY HISTORY DIRECTORATE EDITIONS
ATHENS 1997

ISBN 960-7897-01-3

DEDICATED TO THOSE
WHO PARTICIPATED
IN THAT WAR

TO:   HAGS/AHD         MINISTRY OF NATIONAL DEFENCE
       HARPO          HELLENIC ARMY GENERAL STAFF
                       TRAINING DIVISION/3a
INFO: HAGS/TD/3a      TEL. (ext.) 3187
       HAGS/2o-7o SO    F.205/11/120650
       HAGS/SUPDIV     D.N.2346
       HAPO/C SUBD      ATHENS, 24 Dec. 97

SUBJ:     <u>Military History</u>
REF:      a. Standing Order 9-1/1984/HAGS
         b. Standing Order 9-26/1993/HAGS
         <u>c. F.205.5/6/239114/DN.310/8 Aug 97/HAGS/AHD/5</u>

     1. Taking into consideration the above references
**we ratify**
the Concise History of AHD/HAGS «Concise History of the Greek-Italian and Greek-German War 1940-41» in the English language and command its publication.

     2. Printing will be performed by the Hellenic Army Printing Office (HARPO) in five thousand (5000) copies on VELVET 70x100 type paper; the binding will be performed commercially with cover of hard plastic.

     3. Distribution will be effected care of HAPO/C Subdivision.

     4. Supervision of the publication, correct printing and distribution is entrusted to AHD/HAGS.

     5. All expenses will be charged to the budget of AHD/HAGS for the year 1997.

                               Apostolos-Athanassios Tsohatzopoulos
         True Copy              Minister of National Defence


       Signed-Sealed
    Nikolaos Koimtzoglou
       LTC (Inf)

# THE ARMY HISTORY DIRECTORATE
(for the Greek Edition)

DIRECTOR:    Lieutenant - General  NIKOLAOS KEFALAS

ASSISTANT DIRECTOR
AND PROJECT CO-ORDINATOR:
        Major - General  DIMITRIOS BECHRAKIS

DIRECTOR  OF  5TH  OFFICE  (History Presently Written):
        Major - General  EVANGELOS FLOROS

AUTHORS  OF  THE  PRESENT  VOLUME  (in part):
        Colonel (Infantry)  KONSTANTINOS POLYZOIS
        Major - General  GEORGIOS TOURKANTONIS
        Major - General  DIMITRIOS ADAMOS
        Brigadier General ATHANASIOS PAPADIMITRIOU

EDITOR:    Colonel (Inf.)  KONSTANTINOS  POLYZOIS

TRANSLATED INTO ENGLISH BY: MARIA HAKA

EDITION COMMITTEE:
        Major - General DIMITRIOS GEDEON
        Lieutant - Colonel PANTELIS GEORGIOU
        Historian  ANGELIKI DIMAS - DIMITRIOU
EDITOR (for the English edition):
        Historian ANGELIKI DIMAS - DIMITRIOU

# PREFACE
## (of the Greek Edition)

*The History of the Greek - Italian and Greek - German War of 1940 -
1941 has been published by the Army History Directorate of the Hellenic Army
General Staff (HAGS) in a series of eleven (11) volumes, including four (4)
monographs for a more complete historic presentation of this period.*

*This extensive and voluminous series which includes a large number of
sketch maps, is intended and offered for study mainly by the Armed Forces and
historians. The History Directorate of the HAGS, intent on making the main
events of this period of Modern History known to the general public and in
particular to the younger generations, proceeded to the writing and publication
of the present abridged history, hoping that this will offer an exact yet concise
picture of the main events of the war of 1940 - 1941.*

*It is beyond all doubt that this war constitutes a significant point in the
recent History of Greece and one of the most glorious periods in the history of
the Nation. This is why knowledge of both the war operations as well as the
conditions under which they took place are considered particularly instructive
and essential.*

*Greece, as is well known, had decided to remain neutral and made
great efforts to this end. However, when duty called, Greece unhesitantly
opposed the expansionist tactics of the Axis and became involved in a fight on
two fronts against two mighty armed forces of Europe, in order to maintain its
freedom and territorial integrity. Greece's refusal to submit to the still
undefeated of Rome-Berlin Axis, reflected both asense of National duty and the
unswerving determination of the Greek people and its leaders to the
'Struggle Above All'.*

*Despite the unfavourable weather and terrain and the overwhelming
superiority of the enemy in men and material, the Greek Army fought, for six
months, approximately, a victorious war against the Italians in Northern Epirus
and put up heroic resistance against the Germans in Macedonia and Crete,
earning the admiration of the Allies as well as that of its enemies. Greece was
forced to capitulate to the almighty German war machine, only after every hope
of resistance had been lost.*

*The attainments of the Greek Army were by no means fortuitous. They
were the result of well made preparations and high morale. All possible
strategic and tactical options of the enemy had been examined and responsibly
dealt with, while the mobilization and operations plans were distinguished by*

*simplicity and realism. An order of a few words was enough to bring the entire country's war mechanism into action. During the operations, the enemy's superiority in tanks and air forces was negated by our nation's belief in the rights of the struggle and the everlasting values of our Nation. Thus the Greek Army fulfilled the Nation's expectations. The Army and the People, together as an almighty National force,. wrote down the most heroic pages of Modern Greek History.*

*We also ought to praise the heroism displayed by the troops of the British Commonwealth, both in mainland Greece as well as on the island of Crete. The amazing discipline, their excellent training but above all their spirit of sacrifice, gave the impression that they were fighting for their very own native land.*

*Lastly, it is essential that we note the great contribution of Greece to the fight of the Allies against the Axis. It is a well known and widely acknowledged fact that the delay of the German invasion of Russia, by at least one month, as a result of the offensive against Greece, was fatal for the Germans and decisively altered the outcome of World War II.*

*On 27th April 1942, the first anniversary of the entry of the Germans into Athens, the Radio Station of Moscow stated:*

*'Greeks, you fought unarmed against the fully armed and won. You, the small against the mighty, and carried the day. It could not have been otherwise, for you are GREEKS. We gained time to defend ourselves. As Russians and as human beings we are grateful'*

*The Foreign Secretary of Great Britain at that time also made his statement:*

*'... Had Hitler's unsuccessful - thanks to the Greek resistance - Mediterranean plan succeeded, Germany's assault on Russia would have had a different result ...'.*

*Beyond all military achievements, however, there is no doubt that the Greek fighters on the inaccessible rocky and snow-covered Mainland mountains, at the impregnable forts of the Beles and Nestos defensive area and lastly on the heroic island of Crete, won immortal glory, thus contributing to the history of the Greek Nation, through the centuries.*

*ATHENS*
*FEBRUARY 1984*

*NIKOLAOS KEFALAS*
*LIEUTENANT-GENERAL*
*(for the Greek Edition)*

# INTRODUCTION

*The present volume, 'AN ABRIDGED HISTORY OF THE GREEK - ITALIAN AND GREEK - GERMAN WAR 1940-1941 (LAND OPERATIONS)' refers to war operations as well as the main political and diplomatic events which decisively influenced the beginning as well as the conduct of the war. It is based on the eleven (11) volume history published by the Army History Directorate of the HAGS which preceded the present publication and which refers to the period 1940 - 1941. It consists of four (4) main parts, namely:*

*- PART ONE, includes the main political military and diplomatic events, which preceded the Italian attack against Greece, as well as the operations in Epirus and in North West Macedonia from October 28th until November 13th 1940. Greece, thanks to its appropriate preparation and the timely military measures it took, managed during this period not only to repulse the Italian surprise attack, but also to take the initiative in the operations to come, which in their first phase sought to restore the integrity of the national borders.*

*- PART TWO, refers to the Greek counter-attack, the advance of the Greek Army into the northern mainland territory (approximately 30-80 km in) and the great 'PRIMAVERA' ('Spring') attack of the Italians from 9th to 26th March 1941, which despite its good preparation, failed completely.*

*- PART THREE, refers to the German assault into Greece on April 6th 1941, the heroic defence of the Greek forces in Eastern Macedonia and Western Thrace, the combined operations of the Greeks and the British in Central and Western Macedonia, the withdrawal of the Greek Army from Albania and its capitulation, the retrograde operations of the British Expeditionary Force up to the last embarkation ports and, lastly, the occupation of the country (except for the island of Crete) by the enemy.*

*- PART FOUR, refers to the battle of Crete during the period of 20th to 31st May 1941 and the occupation of the island by the Germans. The battle of Crete constituted the last heroic act of the war drama and inflicted upon the German parachutists such a great number of casualties that Germany never mounted such an operation again.*

*At the end of this volume there are summary tables of figures pertaining to casualties of the Greek Army from October 28th 1940 until May 31st 1941, as well as tables of names of the commanders of the Greek and British large units in mainland Greece and Crete during the same period. In addition, the present volume has been enriched with the necessary sketch-maps and photographs in order to provide the reader with material as complete and understandable as possible.*

*The events and the conditions under which they took place are stated concisely, without comments. Comments and conclusions are left to scholars and future historians, who may also resort to the unabridged volumes published by the Army History Directorate of the HAGS as well as other relevant sources of information and archives.*

*It must be noted that the Historian Ms. Margarita Tsibouxi - Tassopoulou of the Army History Headquarters contributed to the editing of the Greek Edition.*

<table>
<tr><td>*ATHENS*</td><td>*Major-General EVANGELOS FLOROS*</td></tr>
<tr><td>*FEBRUARY 1984*</td><td>*Director/Head of 5th Office*</td></tr>
</table>

# EDITIONS (in Greek) OF THE ARMY HISTORY DIRECTORATE

## 'The Greek Army in World War II'

1. *The Causes and Pretexts of the Greek - Italian War 1940 - 1941.*
2. *The Italian Invasion (28th October - 13th November 1940).*
3. *The Greek Counter-attack (14th November 1940 - 6th January 1941).*
4. *Winter Operations - The Italian Spring Attack (7th January - 26th March 1941).*
5. *Operations in Eastern Macedonia and Western Thrace (6th - 10th April 1941).*
6. *The End of an Epic War (27th March - 30th April 1941).*
7. *The Battle of Crete (20th - 30th May 1941).*

## *Related Monographs of the ARMY HISTORY DIRECTORATE*

8. *The War Preparation of the Greek Army (1923 - 1940).*
9. *Army Supplies in Armament and Ammunition of Infantry and Artillery during the War of 1940 - 1941.*
10. *The Fortification of the Frontier Zone 1936 - 1940 (Confidential).*
1 1. *The Army Medical Service during the War of 1940 - 1941.*

# TABLE OF CONTENTS

*XV*

# PART TWO

## THE SECOND AND THIRD PERIODS OF THE GREEK - ITALIAN WAR
### (November 14 - March 26, 1941)

## CHAPTER III

### THE GREEK COUNTER-ATTACK AND THE ADVANCE OF THE ARMY ON THE NORTHERN EPIRUS TERRITORY (November 14, 1940 until January 6, 1941)

## CHAPTER IV

### THE GREEK ARMY WINTER OPERATIONS AND THE ITALIAN GREAT "PRIMAVERA"(SPRING) ATTACK ( January 7 until March 26, 1941)

# PART THREE

## THE GERMAN ATTACK AGAINST GREECE AND THE FINAL PERIOD OF THE GREEK - ITALIAN WAR

### CHAPTER V

#### THE GERMAN ATTACK AGAINST GREECE AND THE FIGHTING IN EASTERN MACEDONIA AND THRACE (April 6 to 9, 1941)

# CHAPTER VI

## THE BATTLES IN CENTRAL AND WESTERN MACEDONIA-
## THE WITHDRAWAL AND THE CAPITULATION OF THE EPIRUS ARMY-
## THE WITHDRAWAL OF THE BRITISH AND THE COMPLETION
## OF THE OCCUPATION OF GREECE BY THE GERMANS
### (April 9 until May 8, 1941)

# PART FOUR

## THE BATTLE OF CRETE (May 20 to 31, 1941)

## CHAPTER VII

### THE PREPARATIONS AND THE PLANS OF OPERATIONS OF
### THE ADVERSARIES

# CHAPTER VIII

## THE CONDUCT OF THE BATTLE - THE COLLAPSE OF THE DEFENCE AND THE EVACUATION OF THE ISLAND OF CRETE

## TABLES

## SKETCH MAPS

## PICTURES

*XXI*

Picture 1
A Typical Greek Soldier

# PART ONE

# THE FIRST PERIOD OF THE GREEK - ITALIAN WAR

# CHAPTER I

## CAUSES AND PRETEXTS FOR WAR-DEFENCE MEASURES IN THE GREEK TERRITORY UNTIL THE EVE OF THE ITALIAN ATTACK

*The Military and Political Situation in the Balkan Peninsula in the Beginning of 1939 and the Expansionist Aspirations of Italy*

1.    In July 1923, after the Treaty of Lausanne, Greece strove to organise the country and restore it from the ruins of the First World War and the Asia Minor Expedition. The enormous problem of the reception, relief and rehabilitation of approximately one and a half million expatriate refugees from Eastern Thrace and Asia Minor demanded an immediate solution. Furthermore, other vital issues that needed to be dealt with, were the reorganisation of the army, the economic recovery and the restoration of order in internal political affairs.

The primary concern of the foreign policy was to secure the territorial integrity and to safeguard the national independence. Initially, Greece sought to fulfil this aim within the bounds of the general guarantees, offered by the charter of the League of Nations (LoN). However, when the collective security system and the LoN mechanisms proved powerless to guarantee the right of national inviolability, the rendering of justice and peace to the smaller countries, Greece was forced to resort to the old-fashioned practice of balance of forces and to the direct communication among the countries. Thus, after a five-year diplomatic isolation, Greece began to exercise a policy that sought to broaden the co-operation with its neighbours, in order to solve existing differences and pending issues. These acts led to the reinforcement of the bipartite ties between states and a series of friendship pacts were signed with Balkan and non Balkan states, as follows:

- The Greek-Rumanian 'Pact of non-Offence and Arbitration' that was signed on March 23, 1928.
- The 'Pact of Friendship, Compromise and Judiciary Settlement' that was co-signed by Italy on September 23, 1928, and was intended to be valid until October, 1939. This pact, that essentially drew Greece out of its

international isolation, constituted a wide-range political agreement and bordered on being a diplomatic alliance against any Balkan or non-Balkan threat.

- The Greek-Yugoslavian 'Pact of Friendship, Compromise and Judiciary Settlement' that was signed on March 27, 1929, and restored relations between the two countries, which had been disturbed since 1924 due to the dispute about the Free Zone of Thessaloniki. This pact was limited in nature and weaker than the previous Greek - Italian one.

- Two friendship pacts with Turkey, that were concluded after settling the problems which had arisen from the exchange of populations. These were the 'Pact of Friendship, Neutrality, Compromise and Arbitration', that was signed in Ankara on October 30, 1930, and the 'Pact of Cordial Understanding', that was also signed in Ankara on September 14, 1933. Later, on April 27, 1938, an additional agreement was signed, which complemented these bipartite pacts and extended their validity until June 1948.

While being defensive in principle, these bipartite pacts were not accompanied by any relevant military agreements. In general, the pacts offered a mutual guarantee for the common mainland borders against any Balkan or non-Balkan intruder attempting to invade Eastern (Turkish) or Western (Greek) Thrace. In any other event of unprovoked war, the one country was obliged to remain favourably neutral towards the other, so that its territory would not become a base of operations against its ally that had been drawn into war. Furthermore, there was a mutual obligation to communicate beforehand on all international issues of mutual concern and they could both be represented internationally by common representatives, whenever this was possible or necessary.

No pact of friendship was signed with Albania, however certain bipartite issues were settled down through the agreements signed in Athens on October 13, 1926.

2.   After 1933, when the international situation had begun to deteriorate and the inter-European oppositions were assuming alarming proportions, the Balkan countries directed their efforts towards a broader organisation, seeking co-operation and a multi-partite interstate agreement. Thus, after long, laborious and subtle negotiations, in order to reconcile the diverse viewpoints and to remove any feelings of mistrust, the renowned 'Balkan Agreement Pact' was finally signed in Athens between Greece, Yugoslavia, Turkey and Romania on February 9th, 1934. This was defensive in nature and sought to consolidate peace, secure the respect for the already existing conventional obligations and to preserve the territorial status-quo in the Balkans. It was intended to remain in force until February 1941. In February 1940 it was renewed for 7 more years, that is to say until

February 1947. The Pact was accompanied by the relevant military agreements.

According to this Pact, the four countries offered their mutual guarantee for the border safety of each of the contracting member-states against any threat that might arise from another non-member Balkan state. The guarantee would also be in force in the event that this Balkan state was to collaborate with a non-Balkan power as well, under the following two conditions:

- If the collaboration with the non-Balkan state occurred before the mobilisation of the other ally Balkan states was declared, then the pact would not be in force.

- If the collaboration occurred after the mobilisation was declared, then the Balkan allies would be obliged to aid their partner, yet only against the assailing Balkan country and not against the non-Balkan power.

Greece and Turkey both expressed reservations, claiming that they would remain neutral, the former in the event that the assailing non-Balkan country happened to be Italy and the latter, if it were to be Russia. These reservations diminished the validity of the Pact and established precedent for its subsequent debilitation.

Albania and Bulgaria did not participate in the Balkan Pact. Albania had already been under Italian protection and Bulgaria refused to recognise the territorial status-quo in the Balkans as non-revisable.

After this entire framework of bi- and multi- partite agreements and the abovementioned Bulgarian position, Greece, having no offensive aspirations, saw Bulgaria as the only potential adversary likely to satisfy every condition in which the agreements could be enforced, provided also that the latter would initiate offensive operations against Greece or any other Balkan State.

3.    As for Bulgaria, while it had taken no part in the Balkan Pact for the abovementioned reasons, it nevertheless pursued some form of agreement with its neighbours, seeking above all to have the sanctions imposed on it by the treaty of Neuilly after the First World War removed.

Thus, on January 29, 1937, Bulgaria signed a secret pact of friendship with Yugoslavia, which essentially undermined and weakened the effectiveness of the Balkan pact. It proceeded thereafter, benefiting from the desire of the other Balkan countries to smooth down their differences, to sign a non-offensive pact with those states in Thessaloniki in July, 1938, whereby promised not to resort to violence against the states of the Balkan pact. In return for this harmless reassurance, the Neuilly treaty stipulations, which had imposed armament restrictions on Bulgaria, together with the abolishment of disarmed zones on both sides of the borders in Thrace. The fact is that, the restrictions' removal was a mere formality, given that Bulgaria had already violated them in the years before.

In 1939, the war potential of Bulgaria was estimated at 60 Infantry regiments, 190 Light Artillery batteries and 35 Heavy Artillery batteries. Moreover, it had two motorised divisions, 70-80 tanks and various armoured vehicles. Its air strength comprised 100 fighter, 120 reconnaissance and bomber and 90 observation aircraft.. Furthermore it had 40 antiaircraft batteries of 88, 37 and 20 mm.

The above forces had been organised into five armies, which, in the event of war were intended to be supplemented with 40 additional battalions, that could be organised from the reserves.

The Bulgarian Army, by taking advantage of the terrain configuration and the rail and road network of its country and having taken the initiative for the operations, managed to gain a few days ahead of the Greek Army in the mobilisation and assembly of its troops.

4.    Albania, which had not taken part in the Balkan Pact either, was not regarded by Greece as a considerable military power. This country had been established as a state in 1913 with the support of Italy and Austria, in order to serve the expansionist aspirations in the Adriatic sea and the Balkan Peninsula. Since that time, it had led a pro-Italian policy and had remained under Italian guarantee and protection and did not, therefore, take the side of any international alliance.

The forces that Albania could mobilise, were estimated at about six divisions comprising six battalions each and a few artillery pieces. This limited military strength and its overall fighting capability ruled out a unilateral intervention - on its part - against the other Balkan countries. Besides, the possibility of a joint Italian - Albanian intervention against Greece was excluded due to the Greek-Italian friendship treaty of 1928. This treaty had served to erase the bad past that prevailed in the relations between the two countries and safeguarded Greece against the Italian peril, at least until 1939.

5.    Italy, after becoming an independent kingdom, had aspired to rule supreme over the Mediterranean and expand its influence in vital areas of the Balkan peninsula. Thus, its policy had long since been unfavourable towards Greece.

During the Italian - Turkish war of 1910-1912, Italy set foot on the Dodecanese islands, under the pretext of liberation and temporary occupation, holding on to them later, although it was bound by the treaty of Ussy to evacuate them. Thus, the liberation of the Dodecanese islands by the Greek Fleet during the Balkan Wars was foiled. After the unfortunate outcome of the Asia Minor Campaign, in particular, the

Italians sought to alter the ethnological character of the islands by persecuting and pressing the Greeks.

During the Balkan Wars, 1912-1913, and the Northern Epirus Liberation Struggle 1914, Italy opposed the occupation of Avlonas by the Greek Army. Upon a later occasion, when an international committee was entrusted with the task of defining the southern borders of Albania, it supported the Albanian position to the expense of Greece, causing the intrinsically Greek areas of Koritsa, Erseka, Premeti, Leskoviki, Delvino, Argirokastro and Himara to be handed over to Albania, by virtue of the Florence Protocol (17-12- 1913).

In October 1914, after the declaration of the First World War, Italy took advantage of the anarchy prevailing in Albania and seized the islands Sasson and, in December 1914, the port of Avlonas and its mainland, seeking to gain control over the Adriatic sea.

Later on during the War, it led an opportunistic policy, pulling away from the Triple Alliance and entering the Triple Agreement (Entente) after having managed to secure promises of abundant trade-offs through the secret London Agreement (April 1915). Among other trade-offs, came the recognition of the Italian sovereignty in Avlonas and Sasson island, while Albania was placed under Italian protection, which meant that it was turned into an Italian protectorate. The straits between Kerkira (Corfu) and the Mainland coastline were neutralised, while the Dodecanese islands were annexed to Italy, which had already been possessing them 'temporarily' since 1912. Furthermore, Italy was offered the opportunity of colonial expansion in Asia Minor.

In September 1916, after the Macedonian front had opened, Italy seized Agii Saranda and Argirokastro with the blessings of the Entente and reached as far as Ioannina, so as to be in a position to safeguard the allied transport from the port of Agii Saranda towards Koritsa by way of Kakavia and Kalpaki. Despite the vigorous Greek protests, it made no attempt to leave the triangle it had created in Epirus until only much later, in November 1919.

After the end of the First World War, the abovementioned secret agreement of London was regarded by the Entente Powers as 'non-existent', because the international situation had by then been altered.

In spite of all that , Italy managed to gain control over the entire area of South-western Asia Minor without ceasing to have aspirations towards the coastal area of Western Asia Minor as well, including Smyrni. Therefore, it reacted to the mandate of the Allied Council, in May 1919, for the occupation of Smyrni by the Greek Army.

Dissatisfied with its own failure, it began to lead a pro-Turkish policy, causing friction with the Greek Army along the neighbouring zone of occupation in the valley of Maeandros river, while simultaneously instigating raids by Turkish irregulars from its own zone. At the same time, it reinforced and in every way assisted Moustafa Kemal in his struggle against Greece.

In November 1921, Italy managed to achieve the invalidation of the Venizelos - Titoni agreement, of June 1919, according to which the area of Northern Epirus and the islands of Dodecanese would be handed over to Greece. During the same month, it succeeded in securing a statement, signed in Paris by the Governments of Great Britain, France, Italy and Japan, by which, Italy was granted the right to intervene, if need arose, for the protection of the territorial integrity and independence of Albania.

On August 31, 1923, Italy bombed and temporarily seized and held the unfortified island of Kerkira (with 15 civilians dead and 35 wounded), under the pretext of the assassination, by a group of irregulars of unknown nationality, of General Tellini, an Italian representative in the committee for the settlement of the Greek - Albanian borders. The assassination took place at the pass of Kakavia on August 27 and Italy held the Greek Government responsible, without possessing any evidence for such an allegation.

**6.** Since 1926, fascist Italy began to employ new methods to infiltrate and prevail in Albania. On November 27, 1926, the treaty of Tirana was signed in Tirana between Italy and Albania, projected to be in force for five years and placing the territorial and political status quo of Albania under the Italian guarantee and protection. In November, 1927, an Italian - Albanian treaty of defensive alliance was signed, projected to last for twenty years.

Thus, Italy managed to infiltrate into Albania and to gradually place under its control the entire financial, political and military life of the country, through various financial organisations, technical companies and numerous technical and military advisors. The final objective of this infiltration was to employ Albania as a base of operations, in order to satisfy its own further expansive aspirations.

In August 1937, Ciano, the Foreign Minister of Italy wrote in his diary, 'it is necessary to create fixed bases for the Italian interests in Albania and we ought to be prepared to take advantage of the opportunities that may rise for our expansionist policy'.

Italy found itself internationally isolated, after the sanctions imposed by the League of Nations due to its aggression to Ethiopia. Thus, it shifted its focus to Germany, to accomplish its expansionist aspirations. These two totalitarian regimes began preliminary negotiations about their close collaboration, which was officially secured in the end of 1936. On November 1, 1936, Mussolini mentioned the Berlin-Rome 'Axis' for the first time, stressing that 'this does not constitute a dividing line, but an axis

joining the two nations and on which other states may rely, inspired by the will for peace and co-operation'.

Hungary and Bulgaria were the first countries to join this new European order. In December 1936, the Prime Minister of Rumania Antonesko declared that 'he is seeking to consolidate close friendly relations with all powers, especially Germany and Italy'.

Yugoslavia, after these developments, that had rendered its position precarious, signed, in January, 1937, a secret pact of friendship with Bulgaria and a similar pact with Italy in March of the same year. The result of these actions was the weakening of the existing Balkan Pact.

In November 1936, a pact was signed in Berlin between Germany and Japan to seal their close collaboration in the fight against the Communist International and in September, 1940, Germany, Italy and Japan signed the tripartite pact.

In the beginning of Spring, 1939, Mussolini presented to his ally Hitler his plans to conquer the Balkan Peninsula. Hitler, who was also seeking to conquer Europe, accepted the views of the Italian dictator and recognised the Mediterranean as an Italian sphere of influence. Therefore, the political and military leadership of Greece began to apply all its energy to confront the imminent danger that threatened the security and integrity of the country.

### The War Organisation of the Country in the Beginning of 1939

7.    Until the beginning of March, 1939, Greece, which had no offensive intentions, as mentioned previously, regarded Bulgaria as its principal potential adversary and its military preparation in general was thus mainly focused on that direction. To that end, two plans of operations had been drawn up by the Hellenic Army General Staff (HAGS) before 1939, which were the following:

- Plan of Operations B3, which was set in force after October 28, 1937, and dealt with the eventuality of war with Bulgaria, provided that it would have the initiative of its commencement.

- Plan of Operations SM, which fulfilled obligations arising from the military agreements of the Balkan Pact. This was set in force on April 18, 1938, and dealt with the following eventualities as regards the possible threat posed to one of the allies of the Balkan Pact by means of military actions or preparations:

- Bulgaria and Albania unilaterally or both

- Either one of the above countries with Hungary (which had already joined the 'Axis')
- All three countries in common.

Both plans depicted a defensive position, which was to be adopted initially, to cover the mobilisation and to create the necessary conditions for the subsequent undertaking offensive operations. An interesting part of these two plans of operations was the 'Plan of Alert and Reinforcement of the Covering Force'. This provided for the reinforcement of the screening force without any mobilisation taking place, even on a highly limited scale. Thus, it avoided challenging the enemy and offering a pretext for relations to be strained, a situation that could gradually lead to conflict. Such a possibility was definitely to be avoided, without however endangering the security of the country. In the particular event that Plan SM would be applied, the declaration of mobilisation bound all contracting Balkan states as mentioned previously. Therefore, after the declaration of mobilisation, Greece would be forced to take action if a non-Balkan force sided with the enemy. Otherwise delay allowed Greece to retain the freedom of decision and action.

**8.** With view to the confrontation of the threat from Bulgaria, intensive fortification works began in the Greek frontiers to Bulgaria from 1936. This project had made significant progress, so that by the end of 1939, nearly all forts could be considered in full combat readiness.

At the same time, field fortifications continued to be constructed, reinforced with concrete pill-boxes between the forts as well as in other parts of the defensive area in Eastern Macedonia and Thrace.

This fortification sought to cover the mobilisation and the strategic concentration of the field army and also the fortified positions would be used as a base for further operations.

The system of fortifications that had been opted for, included a line of independent forts to block the main axes and various field defences or semi-permanent fortifications to block the secondary axes. Permanent forts of this kind, that were interconnected with field fortifications, had been constructed from mount Beles to the pass of Volakas in the north of Drama. Further east, and as far as the Turkish borders, various field or semi-permanent fortifications had been constructed. In particular, the detached Forts of Echinos and Nymphaea had been constructed in order to block off the carriage roads that led from the borders to Xanthi and Komotini, respectively.

Field fortifications, many of which had been made of ironbound concrete, were also constructed along the western bank of Nestos river, as well as on the bridgeheads of Toxotes (east of Kavala), Papades (Northeast of Drama), Alexandroupolis and Pythion (Southeast of Didimotiho). The latter bridgehead - that of Pythion - was, according to the Agreement of Balkan Understanding, intended to cover the crossing of Turkish forces to the west of Evros river, with view to the undertaking of offensive action towards Bulgaria.

**9.** As regards the military potential, Greece comprised, during the period of peace, 5 Army Corps Commands (A', B', C', D', E'), 14 Infantry divisions of limited strength with the following orientation: 3 towards the borders with Albania and Yugoslavia (VIII, IX, X), 5 towards the Bulgarian borders (VI, VII, XI, XII, XIV) and 6 in the mainland and the islands (I, II, III, IV, V, XIII). More specifically, in the frontier area towards Albania there were the VIII Division, with its Headquarters at Ioannina, which answered directly to the Army General Staff, and the IX, with its Headquarters at Kozani, under the command of the B' Army Corps (Larissa) and covered part of the Yugoslavian borders as well. The strength of the Greek Army according to the peace establishment ranged from 60 to 70 thousand men.

In the event of war, the number of Large Units was to be increased on the basis of the Mobilisation Plan of 1939 to 16 Infantry divisions and 4 Infantry brigades and 1 Cavalry division.

The required supplies, means and ammunition for the armament of the above mobilised Large Units and for certain additional non-divisional units, were almost all in existence.

Furthermore, the required war stock (stocks of general reserve) in ammunition, food, forage and liquid fuel had been provided for and were secured through local resources or from abroad. The only shortages were in mortar shells.

According to the relevant calculations there were food and flour supplies for 15 days, forage for 30 days and liquid fuel for 15 days. The existing ammunition sufficed more or less for a three and a half month combat.

Their replenishment, according to the Industrial Mobilisation Plan, would be undertaken by the local industry, which was in a position to fully respond to all the ammunition requirements of the infantry and, to a large extent, to those of the artillery, the raw materials being imported from abroad.

## The Occupation of Albania by Italy

**10.** From the first months of 1939, the Italian policy began to apply unbearable pressure upon Albania, while simultaneously it sought to subjugate it financially, through the Italian companies, installations and financial organisations. Attempts on the part of Albania to renew the existing Alliance Treaty with Italy, in order to safeguard its position as an independent state, ended in failure. Parallel to this, the Italian press began to inflate various unimportant incidents and disturbances, which were deliberately caused by the Italians at Tirana and at the Albanian ports. At the same time, those telegraph agencies controlled by the Axis, spread information that Italy was concentrating military and naval forces in the ports of Bari and Brindisi in order to occupy Albania. Strong rumours, circulating abroad, presented the abovementioned action as imminent, coupled also by a similar one that was planned against the Greek islands of the Ionian Sea.

The Greek Government and the European diplomacy began to experience uneasiness due to this series of coinciding information and the Italian Government, in order to allay their alarm, hastened to contradict the latter, through the official communique of March 7 and April 2, 1939, labelling it as 'malicious and false'.

**11.** Despite these disclaims on the part of the Italian Government, on April 6, 1939, an Italian ultimatum was delivered to the Albanian Government, containing terms that were both humiliating and unacceptable to Albania, including a request to temporarily station Italian troops in the country and to increase the number of Italian subjects immigrating there.

The Albanian Government called an emergency meeting under King Zog and the ultimatum was declined.

On the following morning (April 7), Italian war and transportation ships, which had already set off the day before, appeared before the Albanian ports of Agios Ioannis of Medoui, Dirrahio, Avlonas, Agii Saranda and Pali north of Dirrahio. At 0600 hrs on the same day, Italian bombers attacked the above mentioned ports and, simultaneously, the Italian Army commenced the landing operation. The Albanian forces offered but little resistance, which was bowed shortly after. Thus, the Italians, continuing to advance virtually undisturbed, occupied Tirana, on April 8, where they established a pro-Italian Government under Prime Minister Verlacci. On April 9, King Zog of Albania, accompanied by the Albanian Prime Minister and other personages, took refuge with his family in the Greek territory. The Greek Government, wishing to avoid any provocation, designated Pilion as his place of residence and advised him to avoid any political action, requesting that he should leave Greece as soon as possible, in order to protect the Greek neutrality.

The Italian forces that had landed in Albania, amounted to approximately three divisions and were provided with many light armoured vehicles. The military occupation of Albania was completed within a few days, with no resistance on the part of the Albanians, save for the minor skirmishes that occurred during the Italian landing.

12.    The occupation of Albania by Italy caused great concern to the Governments of England and France, which demanded appropriate explanations to be given by the Italian Government. The Italian Foreign Minister Ciano, continuing the line of misleading statements, replied that the Italian occupation of Albania was only temporary and that the Italian troops would withdraw once order was restored, a government favourably disposed towards Italy was formed and the Italian interests in Albania were considered secure. Similar explanations were given by Ciano to the Ambassador of the United States, in Rome. Nevertheless, these explanations were not considered sufficient to rule out any other similar occurrences in the area of the Balkan Peninsula. Thus, on April 13, 1939, the Prime Ministers of England and France hastened to guarantee the independence and territorial integrity of Greece and Romania with official statements.

Germany considered the Italian invasion of Albania to be both just and legitimate and was therefore opposed to any notion of the Western Powers of potential intervention on their part.

Greece was placed in a very difficult position after the abovementioned Italian actions. Intelligence reports from various sources presented Italy as having decided to take action for the occupation of Kerkira and the area of Tsamouria within the month of April 1939. Under those circumstances, Greece had the fundamental and sacred duty to prepare the defence of its territorial integrity, national independence and freedom against any enemy and focused all of its attention in that direction.

## The First Measures for the Defence of the Greek Territory

13.    In the beginning of March 1939, when concern was just beginning to grow about an Italian offensive action, which was planned not only against Albania but which also included the Greek islands of the Ionian Sea as well, the Army General Staff briefed the Large Units (Formations), situated in the frontier to Albania, accordingly and issued instructions for dealing

with any situation of this nature. Parallel to this, as of April 3, it proceeded to reinforce the latter with units from the interior. More specifically, the B' Army Corps (Larissa) was provided with an Infantry battalion and a Pioneer company and the VIII Infantry Division (Ioannina) with an Infantry battalion.

Immediately after the landing of the Italian forces on Albania on April 7 and their rapid advance towards the Greek borders, the Army General Staff issued detailed orders and instructions to the Commander of the B' Army Corps and the Commanders of the VIII and the IX Divisions, regarding the increase of vigilance measures and the need to avoid any incident or friction with the Italian forces. Furthermore, it defined the position that was to be maintained and it authorised the Commanders of the VIII and IX Divisions to declare the mobilisation within the zone of their responsibility, in the case that it became necessary to secure the inviolability of the Greek territory. Similar instructions and orders were also given to the Garrison Commander of Kerkira following existing intelligence concerning an imminent landing on the island.

After the completion of the occupation of Albania and the confirmation of the continuous reinforcement of the Italian forces that had landed there, the Army General Staff defined the general guidelines on April 24 and issued its instructions, ordering the Deputy commanders and the Offices of the General Staff to proceed to the development of a Campaign plan on the basis of the new conditions. Simultaneously, it ordered a series of first measures to be taken, to deal with the new situation, the most important of which were the following:

- The B' Army Corps and the VIII Division were assigned the mission of preparing demolition along the main routes that led from Albania to Western Macedonia and Epirus.

- Class of 1939 was called to report for military service.

- The A', B', C' and D' Army Corps were allocated antiaircraft weapons for the protection of the vulnerable areas and the VIII and IX Divisions were reinforced with a small number of antitank weapons, which were removed from the armament of the Forts.

**14.** The new Campaign Plan, that was drawn up by the Army General Staff on the basis of the abovementioned directives, was named IB, after the initials of the two adversaries it dealt with: Italy and Bulgaria. On May 4th, it was made known to the interested parties, the Large Units the Navy and Airforce. This plan was based on the following assumptions:

- The initiative and provocation of war were left to Italy and Bulgaria.

- After the guarantees of England and France, their assistance was regarded as certain, though of unknown extent.

- Turkey was a potential ally of Greece.
- Yugoslavia would probably remain neutral and, if forced to, could perhaps allow the passage of Italian or even Bulgarian troops through its territory.
- At sea, the supremacy of the English-French Fleet was regarded as indisputable, although this did not exclude the action of Italian submarines or even surface speed boats.
- The Italians, by virtue of having already placed five divisions ready for combat in Albania, were in a superior position with regard to the concentration of forces and could operate rapidly against Greece.
- The most probable Italian course of action was considered to be the one of an attack, that would be launched from Koritsa and would be directed against Thessaloniki and Thessaly, in order to achieve considerable results. The simultaneous invasion of Epirus was also considered, although it would only be a secondary effort, owing to the limited local importance of such an action.
- As regards Bulgaria, it was taken into consideration that if it entered the war, its attitude towards Greece would either be offensive or defensive, depending on the Turkish attitude.

Campaign Plan IB was essentially defensive, in order for Greece to be in a position to face a two-fronted war, against two Powers simultaneously.

On the western flank, that is to say the Albanian Theatre of Operations, the Greek Army would follow the dictates of the war conditions and would retire from the whole of Epirus, as far as the river Arahthos, and in Western Macedonia, from the area that extended as far as mount Vermion in order to gain the time required for the completion of the preparations and the mobilisation and in order to defend the mainland on the naturally stronger position Arahthos-Zigos Metsovo-Aliakmonas-Vermion, where the Greek Military Leadership estimated that it would be possible to concentrate almost the entire force and conduct the defensive struggle under more favourable conditions.

On the eastern flank, the Bulgarian Theatre of Operations, the Plan sought to secure the strongly fortified position of Beles-Nestos (which covered the ports of Thessaloniki and Kavala). Further to the east, with the exception of the Alexandroupolis and Pythion bridgeheads and Forts Echinos and Nymphaea, the Plan covered the whole area with weak forces, which could conduct delaying actions as far as the river Nestos, and the two abovementioned bridgeheads.

15. The general disposition of forces and the command organisation with view to the implementation of the abovementioned manoeuvre, were planned as follows[1]:

- Albanian Theatre of Operations: Three commands under the orders of the Commander in Chief, namely:

• The VIII Division Command, stationed at Ioannina. The B' Army Corps Command, stationed at Larissa. The B' Army Corps included under its command the IX and I Infantry Divisions, the V Infantry Brigade and a Cavalry Brigade.

• The C' Army Corps Command, stationed at Thessaloniki. This Corps included under its command the X and XI Infantry Divisions and the IV Infantry Brigade.

- Bulgarian Theatre of Operations: Two commands under the orders of the Commander in Chief, namely:

The Command of the Kavala Field Army Section, stationed at Kavala. The Field Army Section included under its command the Division Group, that comprised the XVII and the VI Infantry Divisions and the Cavalry Division for the passage of the river Axios; as well as the D' Army Corps that was stationed at Kavala and comprised the VII, XIV Infantry Divisions and the VII and XVI infantry Brigades.

• The Command of the E' Army Corps, that was stationed at Alexandroupolis and had the XII and XIII Infantry Divisions under its command.

- General Reserves of the Commander in Chief:

• The A' Army Corps, that was stationed at Athens and the II and III Infantry Divisions, which had been deployed in the area of Thessaly and the IV Infantry Division, in the area of Plati.

• The V Division and the III Infantry Brigade in the area of Thessaloniki.

• The Cavalry Division, which had been temporarily placed under the orders of the Kavala Field Army Section.

In total, the above Large Units, (Divisions-Brigades) that were included in the IB Campaign Plan, amounted to fifteen Infantry divisions, one Cavalry division, five Infantry brigades and one Cavalry brigade.

16. Within May, the Large Units had completed the relevant parts of the Campaign Plan, which were later approved by the Army General Staff. Parallel to this, the appropriate war preparations were carried on, owing to the continuing reinforcement of the Italian troops in Albania and their advance near the Greek - Albanian borders, where, by mid-August, 1939,

---

[1]    Sketch-map no.1

the greatest part of their forces was concentrated, under the pretext of conducting large scale exercises.

The Army General Staff, estimating that a surprise Italian attack against the two Greek divisions, VIII and IX, was possible to occur, recommended to the Government that these two Divisions should be completed according to their war establishment through preliminary mobilisation. The proposal was approved by the Government and, on the eve of August 24, a mobilisation order was issued, regarding the VIII Division in Epirus - including the Garrison of Kerkira - the IX Division (Kozani) and the IV Infantry Brigade (Florina). There was a gradual mobilisation of some of the Cavalry Division units as well as of certain non-divisional units from the B' and C' Army Corps. Parallel to this, a High Command was organised under the name 'Western Macedonia Field Army Section' (WMFAS) and was stationed at Kozani, with the B' and C' Army Corps under its tactical control.

**17.** After conducting the abovementioned mobilisation of the VIII and IX Divisions and the IV Infantry Brigade and the planned orderly concentration of those forces in the frontier position of the IB delaying manoeuvre, the Army General Staff prepared the first alternative to the IB Mobilisation Plan, having assumed that the strict neutrality of Yugoslavia was certain. The alternative plan was signed on September 1, 1939, under the code name IBa, and was immediately disseminated to the Large Units and the Field Army Sections, as well as to the General Staffs of the Navy and the Airforce.

According to this Plan, there was virtually no territory left uncovered in Western Macedonia beyond the main defensive area, which, at that point, was situated close to the borders, its fortification having begun about four months earlier. In Epirus, the largest part of the territory had been covered, save for a frontier strip of land, between the borders and Kalamas river, that was 20-25 kilometres deep. There too, the construction of fortifications, mainly in the Elea-Kalamas area, had commenced about four months earlier.

The Large Units (Divisions-Brigades), included in Plan IBa, were the same as those of Plan IB and were deployed as follows[1]:

a. Albanian Theatre of Operations

In Epirus, the VIII Infantry Division.

In Western Macedonia, the Western Macedonia Field Army Section which comprised from north to south:

---

[1]   Sketch-map no. 2

- The C' Army Corps, with the IV Infantry Brigade on a first echelon in the area of Florina and the X Division on a second echelon in the area of Edessa.

- The B' Army Corps, with the IX Division on a first echelon in the area of Kastoria and the I Division and V Infantry Brigade on a second echelon in the areas of Larissa and Grevena respectively.

- The Pindos Detachment, comprising one Infantry regiment and one Artillery battery, stationed at Eptachori.

- Reserve, under the direct command of the WMFAS, the XI Infantry Division in the area of Yiannitsa and one Cavalry brigade in the area of Kalambaka.

b. Bulgarian Theatre of Operations

The Kavala Field Army Section with:

- The Division Group, comprising the VI and XVII Infantry Divisions in the areas of Kilkis and Serres respectively.

- The D' Army Corps, comprising the VII Division in the area of Drama, the XIV Division in the area of Xanthi and the VII and XVI Infantry brigades in the area of Kavala.

- The E' Army Corps, comprising the XII and XIII Infantry Divisions in the areas of Komotini and Alexandroupolis respectively.

c. General Reserve of the Commander in Chief

- The A' Army Corps, with the III and IV Infantry Divisions in the area of the Kozani highland and the II Infantry Division in the area of Kalambaka.

- The V Infantry Division and the III Infantry Brigade in the area east of Florina.

- The Cavalry Division in the area of Edessa - Yiannitsa.


18. Meanwhile, and by September 17, the Italian troops in Albania had retired twenty kilometres behind the Greek - Albanian borders, towards the interior, in an Italian gesture of goodwill towards Greece. After this, the Greek Government proceeded to the gradual demobilisation of all forces that had been mobilised and all units returned to their stations.

Thus ceased the state of war readiness of the Large Units in the area near the Albanian borders, though the terrain organisation and supplementary measures continued at a rapid pace and with an undiminished intensity for the better preparation of the country for war.

### The Outbreak of the Second World War
### and the Diplomatic Position of Greece

**19.** On September 1, 1939, Germany attacked Poland. The main cause for this invasion was the Polish Corridor towards the Baltic Sea, known as the Danzig Corridor, which traversed the German territory, dividing Eastern Prussia from the rest of Germany. The British Government, having placed Poland under its guarantee, demanded the immediate suspension of the German war operations. However, Germany did not accept this demand, whereupon, on September 3, England and France declared war against Germany and thus the Second World War began.

Russia had been inclined to lead pro-German foreign policy after the failure of the English-French-Russian negotiations of Moscow in the summer of 1939, and the German Soviet pact of non-offence was signed in the Kremlin on August 23, 1939. Taking advantage of the German attack, it also invaded Poland and occupied the country's eastern regions.

Italy, regardless of the fact that it had not yet entered the war, intensified the psychological warfare against Greece and promoted its own war preparations in Albania.

During that time the Greek position could be outlined as follows.

- There were one sided guarantees by the Western Powers, which nevertheless failed to specify the type, extent and duration of the aid to Greece.

- The Greek - Italian Pact of 1928 was about to expire.

- There were political commitments with Turkey, by virtue of the pacts of 1933 and 1938 which, however, did not bear any explicit military obligations.

- In principle, the Balkan Agreement Pact of 1934 was still in force, although each state had a different general approach to the European policy.

**20.** Under these circumstances and owing to the crisis that arose in the autumn of 1939, the diplomatic efforts of Greece mainly focused on two matters:

- Firstly, on clarifying and defining the important issue of the allied aid that was expected by Greece and which it could count on, for this aid, although certain, continued to remain unspecified in terms of its amount and duration. Nevertheless, this uncertainty did not affect the Greek decision to resist all acts of aggression against the country. Greece, that had freely arrived at that decision without relating it to the realisation of allied aid, naturally, greeted the British-French promises for help with satisfaction. However, as the specification of the said aid was considered of military necessity to some extent, and as it was believed that the essential element with view to success was the preparation and co-ordination of the joint allied efforts in the theatre of operations, it requested that an agreement should be made with the Allies, always assuming that an offensive action against Greece was impending.

- Secondly, on promoting the issue of a common and timely defensive organisation of the Balkan Agreement states in the case of an attack. The Greek Government, during that period, had not ceased to remind the above states regarding the need for this common and timely defensive organisation. In parallel, on November 29, 1939, it sent a draft for a military agreement to the Chief of the Turkish General Staff, via the HAGS in which they had foreseen all that ensued and proved to what extent, a common and well organised defence of the four Balkan states, based on the reinforcement and aid of the two Powers, Great Britain and France, which had guaranteed the independence and territorial integrity of those states, would have had the power to reverse the offensive intentions of Italy and Germany.

The above mentioned efforts of Greece were not well received by the two Great Powers, nor by the other Balkan states, owing mainly to their hesitation to be exposed to any decisive and courageous action, that could provoke misunderstandings and incur the disfavour of Germany and Italy.

Initially, France and Britain, especially France, attempted to create a new Macedonian Front by establishing an allied force in Thessaloniki, to no avail however. Besides, Britain was never convinced that this front could be finally created and thus focused its attention on Turkey. That is to say, it believed that the reinforcement of the Turkish defence would cover Egypt, the Suez canal and the Eastern Mediterranean, where the British interests principally focused. The subsequent events were destined to prove the error of this military evaluation. For the Axis by-passed the Turkish defence and advanced towards the Suez canal, without any Turkish involvement in the conflict.

Thus, the obligations of the Balkan countries towards Greece, on the basis of the Balkan Pact, remained as follows:

- If Greece were attacked by Italy, the Balkan Pact would not apply and consequently the Balkan Allies would not be obliged to come to its aid.

- If Bulgaria joined the Italian attack against Greece, either concurrently or subsequently, again the Pact would not apply.

- If Greece were attacked by Bulgaria, the Pact would be fully in force.

- If Greece were attacked by Bulgaria and Italy joined in the attack afterwards, yet before the mobilisation of the allied forces against Bulgaria had been declared, the Pact would not apply and therefore the Allies would not be obliged to support Greece against Bulgaria.

- If Greece were attacked by Bulgaria and Italy joined in the attack later, after the mobilisation of the allied Balkan forces against Bulgaria had been declared, then the Pact would be fully in force and the allies would be obliged to aid Greece against Bulgaria.

Lastly, the bipartite agreements, which had been contracted between Greece and Turkey, resulted in the following obligations:

- If Greece were attacked by Italy, Turkey would be obliged to preserve and defend its own neutrality, to make every effort to resolve the situation and to examine the latter under a favourable light regarding Greece.

- If Greece were attacked by Bulgaria, Turkey would be obliged to support it in the struggle against Bulgaria.

However, it is noted again at this point that, this obligation of Turkey did not stem from any military agreement but was only a moral commitment that resulted from the treaties, which had been contracted between the two countries.

### The Entrance of Italy into the War and its Position towards Greece

**21.** On April 7, 1940, Germany attacked Norway and, by May 2, it had occupied almost the whole of that country. On May 10, the Germans invaded Belgium, the Netherlands and the Duchy of Luxembourg. The Netherlands were the first to submit at the end of a four-day struggle. On May 11, the Belgian resistance was bowed and, on May 19, Antwerp was taken. The German troops proceeded to enter France and forced the English to turn towards Dunkirk and the French to withdraw westwards and southwards.

Mussolini was astounded by this unforeseen and rapid development of the situation and, fearing that the war might end before Italy had the chance to take part in it, on June 10, 1940, declared war on England and France, the latter being on the verge of collapse. At the same time, he declared once more, officially, that he would respect the territorial integrity and independence of Greece.

**22.** In attempting to cover up the expansive aspirations of its policy, Italy not only assured the Greek Government of its so-called good intentions but proceeded to demand assurances on June 11, through its ambassador to

Athens, regarding the Greek position towards Italy, which was at war. The Greek reply was that Greece would remain strictly neutral, provided that the war was not shifted to the Balkans.

Despite its outwardly peaceful intentions towards Greece, Italy did not cease to oppose it and to try to find various ways and pretexts, in order to claim that the Greek orientation towards England and France would occasion a future Italian intervention.

On June 18, Anfuzo, head of the personal office of Italian Foreign Minister Ciano, representing the Minister who was not present in Italy, urgently summoned the Greek Ambassador to Rome and informed him that, it had come to the attention of the Italian Admiralty, through reliable sources, that a number of British warships were present at the harbours of Souda and Iraklio for a period of time exceeding the twenty-four-hour limit accepted by the international law. After the Greek denial on the matter and the reminder that Greece had decided to remain neutral, the Italian Foreign Ministry acknowledged on the following day that the issue concerning the presence of English warships in Crete had ceased to exist.

**23.** After the collapse of France and the truce signed between France and Germany on June 22, 1940, and between France and Italy on June 24, Italy began to appear as an increasing threat to Greece.

On June 26, Anfuzo summoned the Greek Ambassador to Rome and informed him that the Greek Ambassador to Ankara was working against the Axis which was contrary to the declared Greek policy.

On July 3 the Italian Foreign Minister Ciano once more summoned the Greek Ambassador and informed him, outraged, that he had proof that English warships were using the Greek ports and territorial waters for attacks against the Italian naval forces, that the situation was unacceptable, and that, if it was not brought to an end immediately, Italy would take action. In reply to the protestations of the Greek Ambassador that no such violation had been committed by the English, the Italian Minister stated that the Greek position was already well-known, from some French records which had come into the hands of the German authorities, and that this, in conjunction with the Greek aid to the British Fleet, meant war on Italy and Germany. An official negative and well documented Greek reply was delivered on July 6, by the Greek Ambassador to Rome, to the Italian Foreign Minister. Nevertheless, the latter repeated that he had every reason to believe the information to be reliable and that he (Ciano) had made great efforts not to involve Greece in the war, although he feared that Greece had not acted similarly.

**24.** At 0630 hrs, on July 12, three Italian bomber aircraft hit the 'Orion', an auxiliary vessel of the Greek Navy lighthouse service, using bombs and machine-guns, during the resupply of the Gramvoussa lighthouse at the bay of Kissamos in western Crete. The same aircraft proceeded to attack the destroyer 'Hydra', which had been ordered to assist the above mentioned vessel.

At 0650 hrs, on July 30, an Italian aircraft that was flying from the direction of the Dodecanese islands, over the Corinthian bay, dropped four bombs on the Greek destroyers 'King Georgios' and 'Queen Olga' as well as on two Greek submarines, that were inside the bay of Nafpaktos. The chemical analysis conducted on fragments of these bombs proved that were the same type as the ones that had hit the destroyer 'Hydra' on July 12, 1940.

On August 2 an Italian aircraft dropped six bombs on the A6 smuggler-patrol vessel between the isles of Aegina and Salamis.

**25.** The Greek Government issued a series of proceedings to the Italian Government, regarding all the abovementioned incidents, failing however to receive any Italian reply. Following this, on August 7, the Greek Prime Minister summoned the Italian Ambassador to Athens, Grazzi, in order to define the Greek position on the issue of Greek -Italian relations. Grazzi replied by declaring that, Mussolini and Ciano were both amicably disposed towards Greece.

On the same day, August 7, the Greek Ambassador to Rome met with Bennini, the Italian Deputy Minister of Albanian affairs. During the course of this meeting they examined all incidents that had occurred up until that point, along with the charges that the Italian Government had brought against the Greek Government on account of the Greek alleged violation of the neutrality.

On August 11, four days after the abovementioned diplomatic talks, the Italian diplomacy, by using various methods, attempted to exploit internationally the murder of Daut Hodja, an Albanian from Tsamouria, a common law criminal who was being presented as a great national patriot of Albania. According to the Italians, it was an act of assassination committed by Greek agents which was considered to be a provocation on the part of Greece against the Italian Government.

On August 14, the polemics of the Italian press reached their peak. Greece was accused of always having led an anti-Italian policy, not having appreciated the Italian guarantee, and of exercising a policy of provocation against the Axis Powers heedless of the misfortunes of Czechoslovakia, Poland, Norway, the Netherlands, Belgium and France.

**26.** At 0830 hrs, on August 15, 'Elli', the cruiser of the Greek Fleet, of a capacity of 2,115 ton and a crew of 232 men, was suddenly struck by torpedoes in the bay of Tinos, the island it had visited to render honours on the anniversary of the Assumption of the Holy Virgin. The ship sank at 0945 hrs, on the same day and the casualties comprised eight crew members dead and 26 wounded.

A detailed examination of the torpedo fragments proved that the submarine that had fired the said torpedoes was Italian. The register number and the origin were inscribed on fragments belonging to two of those torpedoes, so there was no doubt as to its origin. Nevertheless, the Greek Government did not reveal the nationality of the submarine, wishing to avoid any Greek involvement in the war. It was only later that it did so, on October 30, by which time the war had already been declared.

This criminal Italian act brought grief to the whole of Greece and gave rise to feelings of patriotism, national honour and dignity and, at the same time, stirred up hatred against the criminals, who had chosen that particular day of the great feast of Christianity for their sacrilegious deed. Parallel to this, the torpedoing of 'Elli' roused the international press, which stigmatised the action. Even the German newspapers expressed their sympathy towards Greece. The Italian Government was alarmed by the uprising of the international public opinion and attempted to relieve the burden by presenting the torpedoing as an act of England, which was allegedly seeking to cause upheaval in the Balkan Peninsula and to poison the Greek -Italian relations.

The fact that Italy was responsible for the torpedoing of 'Elli' was later also confirmed by Italian sources after the war. Count Ciano wrote in his diary, in the entry of August 15, 1940. 'A Greek warship has been sunk by a submarine of unidentified nationality. I believe this operation to have been planned by that lunatic De Vecci[1]'.

Furthermore, Grazzi, the Italian Ambassador to Athens, published an article in the Roman newspaper 'Giornale di Matino' on August 19, 1945, where he wrote in regard to the torpedoing: 'This act cannot be simply attributed to an initiative of the General Commander of the Dodecanese', De Vecci, as claimed by count Ciano in his diary entry of August 15, 1940.

'The initiatives of that member of the fascist group of four, could not go as far as to issue an order for the torpedoing of an aged warship in a Greek port, which no seaman could possibly mistake for an English one. The torpedoing of 'Elli' was a direct result of orders issued by Rome.'

27.    The month of September and the early days of October went by without any serious acts of provocation. However, the Italian press continued to bring charges against the Greek Government. During the same time, all information from the Greek diplomatic delegations to Rome and other European capitals, reported that Italy was advancing its forces in

---

[1]    The Italian Commander of Dodecanese.

TURKEY

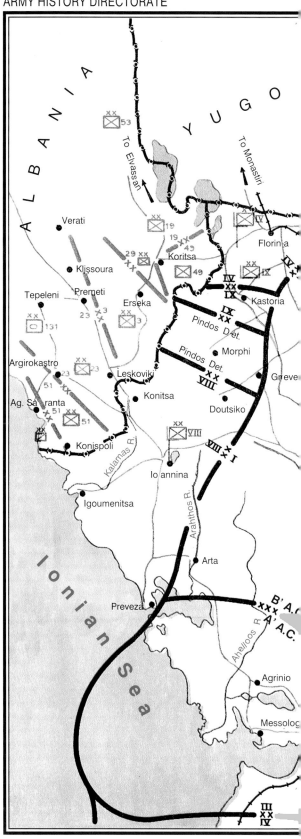

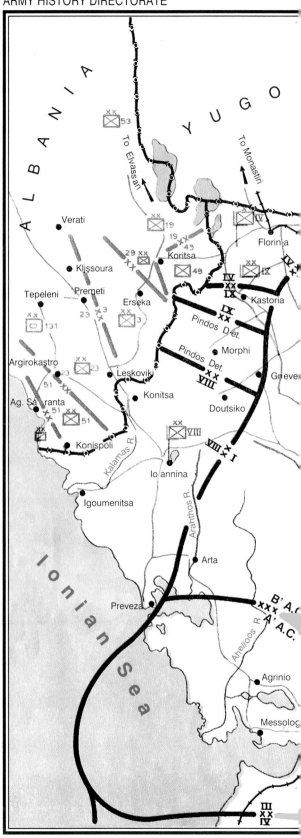

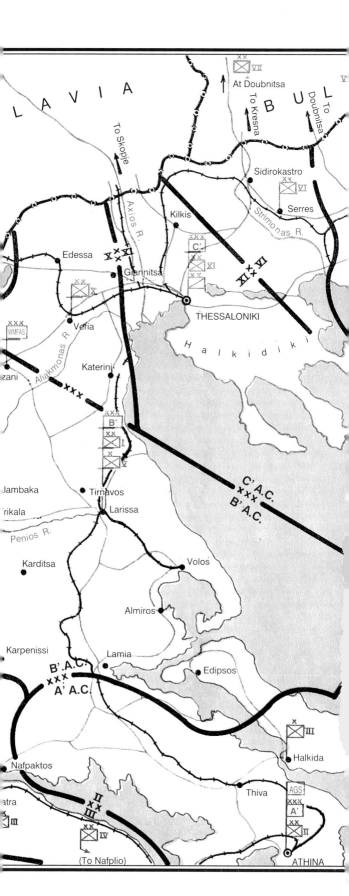

ARIA

At Philipoupolis

To Philipoupolis
To Philipoupolis

At Haskovo

To Varna

Ard

Kirtzali

VII

Drama

Xanthi

Komotini

E'

VII XIV

D'

XIII

Kavala

Alexandroupolis

E'A.C.
xxx
D'A.C.

D'A.C.
xxx
A.C.

Aegean Sea

E' A.C.
xxx
A'   A.C.

DISPOSITION OF THE ENEMY FORCES ON
OF 28TH OCTOBER 1940

Scale: 1 : 2.000.000

0      20      40      60   km

Greek Large Units

Greek Large Units partially mobilized

Greek Large Units fully mobilized

Italian Offensive disposition

Bulgarian covering disposition

V

(At Crete)

Albania towards the Greek borders and that the war was only a matter of a few days.

During the second and third ten-day period in October, intelligence reports indicated an increase in the concentration of Italian troops along the Greek -Albanian frontier, while there was almost daily violation of the Greek airspace by the Italian aircraft.

On October 26, the Stefani News Agency announced that, on that morning, a Greek band had launched an attack, shooting and firing hand grenades against Albanian posts near Koritsa. Another communique, issued on the same day, claimed that, three bombs had exploded near the offices of the Italian Port-Master of Porto-Enda (Agii Saranda), with two victims slightly wounded, and that, either Greek or British agents were wanted for this incident.

After a brief investigation, these incidents were disproved by the Athens News Agency on October 27, through repeated statements by the Greek Government. These statements contained evidence which proved that, the above mentioned incidents were completely false and had been staged by the Italian Government, in order to provoke an incident that would offer them the pretext for declaring war against Greece.

According to certain official Italian records that came to light on July 2, 1944, the final decisions regarding the attack against Greece had been taken on October 15, 1940, during the course of a meeting attended by the higher echelons of the political and military Leadership of Italy, in Mussolini's personal office at the Palazzo Venezia.

The attack had been scheduled for October 26, although for technical reasons and after the insistence of the General Staff, as Mussolini himself revealed in a public speech on June 10, 1941, a last minute decision was taken to postpone it for 48 hours and launch it on October 28.

### New Measures for the Military Confrontation of the Italian Threat

**28.** The deterioration of the situation in Europe and the continually increasing incoming information from abroad concerning an impending Italian attack on Greece, forced the military leadership of the country to adopt with the approval of the Government, a series of new measures to safeguard the defence of the country, in the Spring of 1940.

The most important of these measures were the following:

- The reminder, in the beginning of April, to the Garrison Commander of Kerkira (Corfu) and to the V and XIII Divisions, of the relevant orders since 1939 pertaining to the defence of the islands of

Kerkira, Limnos, Mytilini, Samos and Crete, since intelligence reports from various sources indicated an impending Italian landing on these islands. At the same time, authorisation was given to declare immediate mobilisation on these islands in the event that the threat became imminent.

- The decision, during the month of April, to call the reserve officers of the Infantry, Artillery, Cavalry, Engineer, Vehicle and Medical Corps of the classes of reservists provided by the mobilisation plan, to the arms and to retrain them in successive monthly training courses, starting with the older classes, which were in need of such training. The call-up of the reserve officers aimed at their training in the use of new weapons and machines and mainly at securing the uninterrupted presence of a sufficient number of officers under arms in order to conduct a possible mobilisation and also in order to man the new units that were to be formed. The first series of reserve officers, from the classes of 1921, 1922, 1923 and 1929 of all Arms, presented themselves for the abovementioned retraining on May 15.

- The study and preparation, at the end of April, of the variable IBb of Plan IB, which was immediately disseminated to the Large Units concerned. This Plan dealt with a possible offensive action, on a wider sea front, by the Italian Navy, since the fighting capacity of the British in the Eastern Mediterranean had been diminished and there were intelligence reports on an impending Italian attack on Thessaloniki as well.

According to Plan IBb, the surveillance and defence of the Epirus coastline and Thessaloniki was assigned to forces designated by Plans IB and IBa. The defence of the coastlines of Attica, the Peloponnese and Akarnania was assigned to the A' Army Corps, Crete was assigned to the V Division and the archipelago (Aegean) to the XIII Division.

In order to secure the area of Thessaloniki-Stavros from the sea, the Kavala Field Army Section was provided with the Cavalry Division.

As resistance area of the land front, the plan designated area IBa or IB, depending on the specific conditions prevailing.

- The decisioh, in the beginning of May, to call successively all reserve classes of trained infantry soldiers to the arms, beginning from 13 May, and starting with the class of 1935, for a 45-day retraining course, and for the same reasons that had led to the abovementioned call-up of the officers, as well as the first step in the development of the antiaircraft system.

- The warning, on June 2, to the Army Inspector General and the officers that had been assigned to command the Large Units, which were formed during the mobilisation ('Division Group', XVII Division, III, XVI Infantry Brigades). These officers, who served in other units during peacetime, had to be ready to move to their positions with the first echelon of their Staff within 12 hours of receiving the departure order. The same procedure was also repeated for other officers, who had been intended to reinforce the mobilising Large Units.

- The re-organisation, on June 3, of the Staff of the Western Macedonia Field Army Section (WMFAS), with Lieutenant General Pitsikas as Commander and Colonel Georgoulis as Chief of Staff.

**29.** The months of June and July went by, witnessing the completion of the tasks designated for the Large Units by Plan IBb, the issue of supplementary co-ordinating directives by the HAGS and the conduct of reconnaissance missions on the basis of plan IB and its variables IBa, IBb.

Furthermore, by implementing previous decisions concerning the periodic retraining of reserve officers and trained reserve soldiers, the reserve officers of all Arms, classes of 1920 and 1930, were called under arms on June 15th, and the reserve soldiers, class of 1934 were called on June 25th. On July 16th, the reserve officers, classes of 1932 and 1933 and on July 22rd, the soldiers, class of 1933. The latter remained under arms until October 28, due to the gravity of the situation.

Similarly, the warrant officers, class of 1935, were ordered to remain under arms, as reservists, after completing their service and the reserve soldiers with special key skills (pioneers, radio and telegraph operators etc.) were called up in secret.

All the above mentioned measures were being taken under conditions of utmost secrecy, so as to avoid offering any pretexts to Italy, that were likely to cause political disputes and misunderstandings regarding the preservation of the Greek neutrality.

**30.** As of the second ten-day period in August, 1940, strong Italian forces began to move from the mainland of Albania towards the Greek borders. These movements, coupled with the abovementioned unjustified affronts on the part of Italy together with the information on an impending Italian invasion, forced both the Greek Government and the Greek Army High Command to adopt a series of new significant military measures.

The most important of these measures, the adoption of which began after August 23, were:

- The reinforcement of the Albanian theatre of operations. Thus, the Headquarters of the WMFAS and the B' Army Corps were completed, and similarly the VIII and IX Divisions as well as the IV Infantry Brigade were also completed and reinforced with additional units beyond their organic ones. The Detachment of Pindos was organised under the command of the officer of the permanent reserve, Infantry Colonel Konstantinos Davakis and there was a partial mobilisation of the I Division and the V Infantry Brigade.

- The completion of the state of war synthesis of the XIII Division and its transfer to the area of Alexandroupolis.

- The mobilisation and organisation of a considerable number of units, mainly of infantry and artillery, in the mainland, and the forwarding of those units to Epirus and Western Macedonia, in order to reinforce the Large Units.

- The issue of instructions by the HAGS and the Large Units for the implementation of the existing plans.

Together with the abovementioned pre-mobilisation measures, the training of reserve officers and soldiers continued during the same period. Thus, on August 16, the reserve officers, classes 1919 and 1934, were called up for a one-month training, at the end of which they were not discharged but remained under arms due to the critical nature of the situation. On August 25, the trained soldiers of all Arms, class of 1932, were called up and remained under arms for the abovementioned reasons. On September 11, another series of reserve officers of all Arms, classes 1924 and 1928, were called up. On October 5th trained soldiers of all Arms, class 1930, were also called up.

Within the bounds of the brief outline of the military preparation of the above, it is deemed necessary to praise the attitude of the Greek People, who remained remarkably tranquil and dignified, despite their fiery temperament. Nevertheless, beneath the apparent composure, the soul of the nation was ablaze with the desire to avenge the affronts to its national and religious faith. The abominable acts of the Italian Leadership, far from daunting and defeating the Greek Nation, became the strongest leverage that served to uplift the souls and steel the determination with view to the victorious confrontation of the impending Italian invasion.

# CHAPTER II

## THE SITUATION AND THE PLANS OF ACTION OF THE OPPONENT FORCES - THE COMMENCEMENT OF THE GREEK - ITALIAN WAR AND THE OPERATIONS IN EPIRUS AND NORTH-WESTERN MACEDONIA

### ( 28 October to 13 November 1940 )

*Political and Military Situation on the Eve of the Italian Attack*

**31.** By October l940, Belgium, Luxembourg, the Netherlands, Denmark, Norway and Poland, had already been occupied by the Powers of the Axis.

Britain, which had managed to save, after the disaster of Dunkirk, only the manpower of its expeditionary force in France, had been left to fend for itself and the threat of an invasion on its home territory had not been fully averted, despite the resistance and victories of the British Airforce.

In Africa, the Italians were pressing the British. British Somalia had been taken, while, along the borders of Abyssinia and English-Egyptian Sudan, the Italians had important successes.

Furthermore, the entrance of Italy in the war, on the side of Germany, and the capitulation of France, had rendered the Allied transportation network in the Mediterranean both unsafe and difficult.

Neither Russia, nor America had yet got involved in the conflict. On October 12, 1940, President Roosevelt had defined the two fundamental principles of the United States foreign policy, namely, the protection of the entire Western Hemisphere by American forces and the continuation of all types of aid towards Britain, except for the dispatch of troops.

The entrance of America into the war would lead to the enforcement of the Tripartite Pact, which had been signed by Germany, Italy and Japan in Berlin, on September 27, 1940, and to the spreading of war on a world scale.

**32.** In the Balkans, the Yugoslavian policy was, as previously presented, rather pro-Axis.

Romania had foregone the English guarantee, since the summer of 1940, and had expressed the intention of a political co-operation with Italy and Germany.

Bulgaria was exercising a cautious and opportunistic foreign policy.

The Balkan Pact was not in force in the event of a Greek - Italian clash, and furthermore, a member of the Balkan Agreement, Romania, where German troops had entered on October 7, 1940, wâs politically co-operating with the Axis.

The bipartite Greek - Turkish Agreements and especially the 'Cordial Agreement' of September 14, 1933, were fully applicable, according to the Greek viewpoint, in the event of a Bulgarian intervention. The Turkish attitude, however, was both unknown and uncertain, since the above pacts were not accompanied by any corresponding military treaties.

The aid of Britain had been taken for granted after the guarantees of April 13, 1939, although it was expected to be rather limited, due to the serious problems that the above country had also been faced with.

This was the general outline of the political and military situation in Europe on October 28, 1940, on the day that Greece declined the Italian ultimatum and began the uneven yet honourable struggle for its national independence and freedom. In keeping with its past history, Greece entered the struggle armed with faith, depending mainly on its own strength and well aware of the enormity of the trial and the amount of sacrifices, which would be required of the country.

### The Situation of the Opponent Land Forces
(Sketch-map no. 3)

**33. Italian Forces.** The Italian forces in Albania, on the eve of the Italian attack against Greece comprised an Army High Command under the command of General Visconti Prasca. This HC included the XXV Army Corps of Tsamouria, under the command of General Carlo Rossi, the XXVI Army Corps of Koritsa, under the command of General Gabrielle Nassi and the 3rd 'Giulia' Alpine Division, under the command of General Girotti.

The XXV Army Corps of Tsamouria, was oriented towards the Epirus Section of the Theatre of Operations. This comprised the 23rd 'Ferrrara' Division under the command of General Giannini, deployed in the areas of Mertzani-Premeti, the 51st 'Sienna' Division under the command of General Gambutti, deployed in the areas of Konispoli-Delvino-Agii Saranda, the 131st 'Centaurs' Armoured Division under the command of General Mali, with a limited strength, deployed in the areas of

Tepeleni-Argyrokastro and the Cavalry Division under the command of General Rivolta, which was stationed in the area of Konispoli and had been reinforced with infantry and artillery units.

The total strength of the XXV Army Corps amounted to approximately 42,000 men.

The XXVI Army Corps, was oriented towards the North-western Macedonia Section of the Theatre of Operations and the Yugoslavian frontier area. This comprised the 49th 'Parma' Division under the command of General Grattarola, deployed east of Koritsa, the 29th 'Piedmonte' Division under the command of General Naldi, deployed west of Koritsa, the 19th 'Venezzia' Division under the command of General Bonnini, deployed from Lake Prespa to Elvasan and the 53rd 'Arezzo' Division under the command of General Ferone, in the area of Skodra.

The total strength of the XXVI Army Corps amounted to approximately 44,000 men.

The 3rd 'Giulia' Alpine Division, was deployed between the two ˜abovementioned Army Corps, opposite the sector of Pindos, in the area of Erseka and Leskoviki. Its total strength amounted to approximately 10, 800 men.

The Italian forces in Albania totalled 59 Infantry battalions, 135 batteries (23 of which heavy artillery), 150 tanks, 18 Cavalry companies, 6 Mortar battalions and 1 Machine-gun battalion.

**34. Greek Forces.** On the eve of the Italian attack, opposite the above mentioned Italian forces, in Epirus and Western Macedonia, the Greek forces were the following:

In Epirus, the VIII Division deployed under the command of Major General Haralambos Katsimitros, stationed at Ioannina. The VIII Division had been fully pre-mobilised and was reinforced with the Headquarters of the III Infantry Brigade under the command of Infantry Colonel Dimitrios Yiatzis[1] and with some additional infantry and artillery units. In total, it comprised 4 Infantry regiment commands, 15 Infantry battalions, 16 batteries, 5 Escort Artillery platoons, 2 Self-propelled Machine-gun battalions, 1 Heavy Machine-gun company and 1 divisional reconnaissance unit. In addition, one Infantry regiment -the 39th Evzones Regiment of the III Infantry Division (Patra)- had been pre-mobilised and, on October 27 was moving from Aetoloakarnania to Epirus.

In the area of Western Macedonia from mount Smolikas (not included) to the Prespa Major lake, the forces of the Western Macedonia

---

[1]  The III Infantry Brigade did not operate as a large unit because both its regiments had been allocated from the beginning, one to the I Division and the other, along with the Headquarters of the Brigade, to the VIII Division.

Field Army Section (WMFAS) under the command of Lieutenant General Ioannis Pitsikas stationed at Kozani. These included:

-The B' Army Corps under the command of Lieutenant General Dimitrios Papadopoulos, with its Headquarters at Larissa and comprising the I Division under the command of Major General Vassilios Vrachnos, the IX Division under the command of Major General Christos Zygouris, the V Infantry Brigade under the command of Infantry Colonel Anastassios Kalis and the IXa Frontier Sector. The first echelon of the B' Army Corps comprised the IX Division and the IXa Frontier Sector, which came under it and was of battalion strength, while the second echelon comprised the I Division and the V Brigade.

The IX Division, with its Headquarters at Kastoria, had been gradually pre-mobilised and reinforced, since August 23, 1940, and comprised 10 Infantry battalions and 14 1/2 batteries, occupying position IBa from Skala height of mount Grammos to Ieropigi.

The V Infantry Brigade was a reserve (mobilisable) unit, which had been partially pre-mobilised after August 29, 1940, and was with its Headquarters at Larissa, having deployed the greater part of its forces in the areas of Servia and Amyndaeon (at IB area) and the rest in Larissa.

The I Division was an active unit, from which one regiment had only been pre-mobilised (the 51st Infantry Regiment), with its Headquarters in Larissa.

-The C' Army Corps, under the command of Lieutenant General Georgios Tsolakoglou, stationed at Thessaloniki and comprising the X Division under the command of Major General Christos Kitsos, the XI Division under the command of Colonel (ARTY) Georgios Kotsalos, the IV Infantry Brigade under the command of Major General Agamemnon Metaxas and the IX, X and XI Frontier Sectors. Among the above mentioned units, the frontier units constituted the first echelon of the Army Corps, equivalent to three battalions in strength. In addition, the IV Brigade had also advanced to IBa area, on a first echelon, from Ieropigi to Prespa, having been a reserve unit which had been gradually pre-mobilised since August 23, 1940. This Brigade was stationed at Florina and, apart from its two organic regiments (the 28th and the 33rd), it had been reinforced with six additional Infantry battalions, of limited strength, from the X and XI Divisions. By having the IX Frontier Sector also under its tactical command, the total strength of the brigade amounted to twelve Infantry battalions and eight batteries.

From the remaining forces of the C' Army Corps, the X Division, with its Headquarters at Veria, had most of its units in their peace installations in Veria, Edessa and Yiannitsa, whereas the XI Division, with its Headquarters at Thessaloniki, had the bulk of its forces in the area of Thessaloniki.

-The Pindos Detachment, under the command of Colonel (Inf.) of the regular reserve Konstantinos Davakis, its Headquarters in Eptachori and with its forces deployed along a nearly thirty-seven kilometre front, in the section of the defensive area between the right flank of the VIII Division on mount Smolikas and the left flank of the IX Division on Northern Grammos mountain. The Detachment of Pindos was a reserve unit, which had been pre-mobilised since August 29, 1940, and comprised the 5lst Regiment (minus), a pack battery of 75 mm, an Escort Artillery platoon of 65 mm and a Cavalry platoon.

The Greek forces that had been mobilised and, on the eve of the Italian attack, were deployed along the Albanian borders, amounted to 39 Infantry battalions and 40 1/2 batteries of various calibers and numbered approximately 35, 000 men.

**35.**    In comparison, the opponent forces, deployed in the Albanian Theatre of Operations on the eve of the Italian attack, were as follows.

In Epirus, against the 22 Infantry battalions, 3 Cavalry regiments, 61 batteries (18 heavy artillery) and 90 tanks of the XXV Italian Army Corps, there were 15 Infantry battalions, 1 Reconnaissance squad and 16 batteries (2 heavy artillery) of the VIII Division.

In Pindos, against the 5 Infantry battalions, 6 batteries and 1 Cavalry company of the Italian Alpine Division, there were 2 Infantry battalions, 1 Cavalry company and 1 1/2 battery of the Pindos Detachment.

In Western Macedonia, against the 17 Infantry battalions, 1 Cavalry company, 24 batteries (5 heavy) artillery and 10 tanks of the XXVI Italian Army Corps there were 22 Infantry battalions, 2 Reconnaissance squads and 22 batteries (7 heavy artillery) of the WMFAS.

The above forces constituted the first echelons of adversaries which could be gradually reinforced a few days later. A successful initial action on their part, would seriously affect the subsequent development of operations, as was indeed proved later by the events that ensued.

By comparing the above opponent forces, it becomes evident that, in the area of Epirus, the superiority of the Italian Infantry forces was only slight, whereas concerning the artillery it was overwhelming. The presence of the 131st Armoured Division with 90 tanks seriously increased the offensive potential of the Italians. This superiority was partially counter-balanced by the defensive works in the area of Elea-Kalamas, although these mainly comprised field defences. In the sector of Konispoli- Filiates, the Italian superiority was also overwhelming.

In the area of North-western Macedonia, from Nestori to Krystallopigi, the Greek forces were slightly superior to the corresponding Italian forces which were deployed around Koritsa. This superiority was also increased by the reinforced concrete fortifications which had been constructed in that area.

In the area of Pindos, the Italians outnumbered the Greeks twofold in Infantry and fourfold in Artillery.

Regarding the organisation of the opponent forces, the situation was as follows.

The Italian division included two organic Infantry regiments as opposed to the Greek division which included three, although the multiple reinforcements of the Italian divisions with battalions of Albanians, Blackshirts and Bersaglieri, increased the division strength to eight or more battalions compared to the nine Greek battalions.

The Italian Infantry regiment had six mortars of 81 mm and 54 of 45 mm, whereas the Greek regiment had only 4 mortars of 81 mm. Furthermore, the Italian division had 48 mortars of 81 mm, organised in a mortar battalion.

The Greek battalion was superior in machine-guns, having been provided with twelve machine-guns as opposed to the eight Italian ones.

The Italian division included a Pack Artillery regiment with nine batteries, whereas the Greek division included only one regiment with six batteries.

**36.** The rest of the Greek Armed Forces were at their peace installations from Evros to Crete, with the exception of the **XIII Division** which had been mobilised in the Aegean islands on August 31, 1940 and had been transferred to the area of Alexandroupolis since September 24, 1940.

. Against Bulgaria, there was a first echelon comprising the Fort garrisons, semi-mobilised since peacetime, and the covering forces.

East of the river Axios, the VI Division ( from the C' Army Corps) under the command of Major General Nikolaos Markou, with its Headquarters at Serres, the D' Army Corps under the command of Lieutenant General'Georgios Kosmas, with its Headquarters at Kavala and the E' Army Cops under the command of Lieutenant General Konstantinos Bakopoulos, with its Headquarters at Alexandroupolis. The D' Army Corps had two divisions, the VII under the command of Major General Christos Zoiopoulos, with its Headquarters at Drama, and the XIV under the command of Major General Konstantinos Papakonstantinou, with its Headquarters at Xanthi. The E' Army Corps also had two divisions, the XII under the command of Major General Anastasios Roussopoulos, with its Headquarters at Komotini and the XIII under the command of Major General Georgios Razis, with its Headquarters at Alexandroupolis.

The Bulgarian forces deployed against the Greek forces, amounted to three divisions, the X Division with its Headquarters at Kirtzali, the II Division with its Headquarters at Philipoupolis and the VII Division with its Headquarters at Doubnitsa (south of Sofia), which had been partially oriented towards Yugoslavia as well.

Inland, there were four Infantry divisions and one Cavalry division. Among these three divisions, the II Athens Division under the command of Major General Georgios Lavdas, the III Patra Division under the command of Major General Tilemahos Papadopoulos and the IV Nafplion Division under the command of Major General Leonidas Stergiopoulos, subordinate to the A' Army Corps under the command of Lieutenant General Panagiotis Demestihas and with Headquarters in Athens. In Crete, there was the V Division, under the command of Major General Georgios Papastergiou and subordinate to the B' Army Corps, and in Thessaloniki there was the Cavalry Division under the command of Major General Georgios Stanotas. These forces constituted the reserve of the Commander-in-Chief.

The total number of Large Units of the Greek Army on October 28 was five Army Corps, fourteen Infantry Divisions, one Cavalry Division and three Infantry brigades.

**37.** The situation of the Greek Army, regarding the availability of war material in October, 1940, was the following:

The problem of war supply of the country had been dealt with, almost in its entirety, after combined efforts of the competent authorities in the Ministry of the Army from 1923 to 1940 and mainly since 1935. The expenditure for this purpose was enormous and reached a total of approximately 18.7 billion drachmas, of which three billion was allocated during the period 1923 - 1935 and the rest from 1936 to 1940.

The procurement of war materials from abroad and the successful exploitation of interior resources resulted in the adequate arming of the 16 divisions and the 6 independent brigades included in the mobilisation plan and in the formation of certain artillery units subordinate to the General Headquarters and of 5 Army Corps.

Shortages in mortars, antiaircraft and mainly in antitank artillery still existed.

These shortages were mainly due to the failure in finding supply sources abroad, because of the problems that the supplier countries faced during this period. Fourteen 6 to 7 ton tanks had been ordered in total, which, however, had not been received by the time the war was declared, due to the abovementioned reasons. The great problem of the ammunition had been dealt with satisfactorily, though without being completely resolved. Yet no significant shortage was apparent during the six month struggle that ensued, thanks to the measures that were applied in time, such as the increase of the Greek industrial production, the limitations imposed on consumption and the reuse of ammunition originating from the spoils of war.

As regards the reserve stock for the other supplies, the situation during the same period was the following:

On the basis of a special plan of the Army General Staff, the Central Committee for the protection of local wheat production maintained at the disposal of the Army a supply of wheat to suffice for 50 days. Similarly, there were stocks of the other foods for 15-17 days and forage for 30 days.

Regarding fuel, the country had entered into war with 45-day reserves, except for the aircraft gasoline which was sufficient for 25 days.

The authorised number of horses, pack animals and animal drawn vehicles (carriages), for the needs of the Army field forces, was completed with the commandeering that had been conducted during the mobilisation. The needs of the Army field force demanded a large number of motorised vehicles, amounting to approximately 7,000 as opposed to the 600 available to the Military Service. The problem was partially dealt with by commandeering private trucks of all types.

## The Situation of the Opponent Naval Forces

**38. Italian Naval Forces.** The strength of the Italian Fleet, at the time of the declaration of the Greek - Italian war, amounted to 8 battleships, 8 heavy cruisers, 26 light cruisers, 61 destroyers, 96 torpedo boats and 119 submarines, with a total displacement of 658,398 tons. Most of these ships were newly-built and were equipped with all the latest devices and armament.

The greatest problem of the Italian Fleet at that time was that in parallel with the operations against Greece, it was also expected to support the transportation of troops to Libya, an operation to which special priority had been given by the Italian Leadership.

**39. Greek Naval Forces.** Against this imposing force of the Italian Fleet, Greece arrayed 1 battleship (the veteran cruiser of the Balkan Wars 'GEORGIOS AVEROF'), 10 destroyers, 13 torpedo boats, 2 motor torpedo boats, 6 submarines and approximately 30 small and medium sized auxiliary vessels. An addition was to be made to the latter, in the event of war, of an equal number of merchant navy ships, which had been predetermined and equipped with the appropriate devices and also with a number of guns. These vessels were to be used for mine sweeping, anti-submarine search and patrolling. The total displacement of the Greek Fleet amounted to 14,602 tons. Many of the Greek ships were old and were approaching their life expectancy limit.

The superiority of the Italian Fleet to the Greek Fleet was overwhelming and, consequently, the protection of the country against a possible occupation attempt with sizeable landing forces, depended on the cover offered by the British Fleet in the Mediterranean, which had the added task of protecting the supply lines of Greece from abroad.

Nevertheless, the protection of the Greek coastline from surprise attacks, launched from the naval bases of Tarantas, Brindisi and the Dodecanese isles, could not be solved by the permanent presence of the British naval forces in the Greek waters. Yet, nor did the Greek Fleet suffice to provide immediate protection to all coastal areas. Thus, the most vital areas of the Greek coasts needed to be fortified, so as to enable the repulsion of the enemy forces until the intervention of the British Fleet.

The organisation and command of the coastal defence were assigned to the Coastal Defence Higher Command.

The effort, made by the abovementioned Command to this end, was enormous and resulted in the organisation and command of the naval Strongholds of Araxos river, Rion, Aegina island (North and South), Fleves isles, Evoikos bay (North and South) and Great Emvolon (Thermaikos bay), as well as the Gun-emplacements of Punta and Keramos.

All strongholds and gun-emplacements were armed with guns, taken from old ships. The coastal strongholds had also been combined with minefields and antisubmarine booms for the protection of the most important naval bases and harbours against submarines and surface ships.

Such minefields were lay in the bay of South Evoikos in an area extending for two miles, Preveza for three quarters of a mile and Fleves isles for eight miles. Anti-submarine booms were installed in the North and South Evia bay, in the bay of Corinth between Rion and Antirrion and in the bay of Saronikos between Piraeus - the isle of Psyttalia and Kynosouras on the isle of Salamis.

The Strongholds on Aegina and Fleves safeguarded the area of Piraeus harbour and the Naval Arsenal of Salamis in the bay of Saronikos, against any hostile surface ship or submarine attack.

The stronghold on Araxos river covered, in conjunction with a gun emplacement situated across in the lagoon of Messolongi, the bay of Patra and the approach routes to the bay of Corinth.

The Northern Stronghold of Evia bay protected the northern approach lanes to the straits of Orei as well as the greater area of the northern Sporades isles, while the Southern Stronghold of Evia bay blocked off the bay from the south.

Lastly, the Stronghold of Great Emvolon (Karabournou) safeguarded the bay of Thermaikos and the area of Thessaloniki.

## The Situation of the Opponent Air Forces

**40.   Italian Air Forces.** The strength of the Italian Airforce in Albania, at the beginning of the Greek - Italian war, amounted to approximately 400 active aircraft, which were grouped into 8 bomber squadrons, 9 fighter squadrons and 3 observation squadrons.

The Italian Airforce had a large number of trained flying personnel and could replace any loss at any moment. Furthermore, its personnel had the earlier experience of the previous wars in Abyssinia, Spain and Northern Africa.

There were airfields in Agii Saranda, Avlonas, Verati, Argyrokastro, Koritsa and Tirana. These airfields along with the ones from Bari to Brindisi in south-eastern Italy were situated near the front, had been brought fully up to date and provided all the facilities necessary for the operation of the Italian Airforce.

**41.   Greek Air Force.** During the same period, the Greek Airforce had 143 aircraft (45 fighters, 33 bombers, 65 reconnaissance), which were old, of low capacity, and inferior to the Italian ones.

According to the requirements of the war plans, the Greek Airforce was organised into the following three large commands:

-The Army Aviation High Command, under the General Headquarters, which included: The Fighter Airforce (4 squadrons), the Bomber Airforce (3 Squadrons) and the Army Co-operation Airforce (one reconnaissance squadron for each of the A', B', C', D' Army Corps and the WMFAS, as well as a independent observation flight for the VIII Division).

-The Naval Aviation High Command, under the orders of the Fleet Admiral and having at its disposal three maritime patrolling squadrons and the Faliron Air Base.

-The Airforce of the Ministry of Aviation which included: The Air Bases of Tatoi and Elefsina, the Aviation Academies and Training Centres, the Central Aircraft Industry, the Airforce General Supply Depot and a fighter squadron.

There were Air Bases in Sedes, Larissa, Tatoi (Dekelia), Faliron, Nea Anhialos and Elefsina.

Apart from those bases, 23 alternative airfields had also been organised as well as another 22 airfields which serviced the confidential communications network. Some of these airfields were rendered unusable in wintertime, especially during the months of December and January owing to the rain and the snow, which meant that the aircraft were immobilised on the ground and could not carry out their missions.

The personnel was in excellent condition with regard to the training and morale, although the flying personnel barely sufficed to cover the existing needs. Replacement was very difficult, due to the lack of adequate means to train new personnel.

## The War Plans of the Adversaries

**42.    The Italians:** The Italian War Plan against Greece provided for a first-stage simultaneous surprise seizure of Epirus, Kerkira and the other Ionian islands. At a second stage, Western Macedonia would be taken. After securing the above areas, a rapid advance towards Thessaloniki and Athens would follow, with new forces which would land on the Epirus coast and the islands with view to the occupation of the entire country.

On the basis of the above War Plan, the General Plan of Operations was drawn up by General Prasca and was approved by the Italian General Staff. The latter plan anticipated that during the first period, the forces in the area east of Koritsa should remain on the defensive and that an attack should be launched in the general direction of Kalpaki-Ioannina-Preveza, with simultaneous cover and support of this main effort in both the direction of Leskoviki-Samarina-Metsovo and along the Epirus coastal zone. At the same time, the island of Kerkira would also be occupied. During the second period, an attack had been planned to be launched in the direction Koritsa-valley of Aliakmonas river-Thessaloniki, as well as a continuation of the effort from Arta to Athens, with a secondary activity, at the same time, from Metsovo towards the Thessaly plain.

More specifically, the Plan of Operations included the seizure of the fortified junction of Elea (Kalpaki) in the course of the first four days, by frontal attack of the main effort divisions, the 'Ferrara' and the 'Centaurs' (Armoured), which would be assisted by the 'Sienna' Division. The latter would operate in the general direction Delvino-Filiates and would then turn east towards the area of Ioannina.

On the right and left of the main effort, two divisions would be operating, the Cavalry Division and the 3rd 'Giulia' Alpine Division. The Cavalry Division would move along the coastal Epirus zone and would cover the main effort from the south-west. The 'Giulia' Division would move through the mountain-area of Pindos, cover the main effort from the north and seize the area of Metsovo. Thus, it would be interposed between the Greek forces which were deployed in Thessaly, Macedonia and Epirus.

The flank of the entire Italian offensive effort towards Epirus, would be covered from the north by the forces which were deployed in the area of Koritsa and which would maintain a stands of active defence in the event of any Greek attack against this flank. The planned occupation of Kerkira would secure from the west the right flank of the forces that would be advancing towards Paramythia and further to the south.

The Italian Fleet, according to the above Plan, was to carry out the seizure of Kerkyra and, possibly, other Ionian islands as well and was to concurrently secure the transport sealines in the Adriatic and the Ionian sea. In the end, however, the landing did not take place due to the priority given to the support of the transport sealines to Libya and Albania.

The Italian Airforce would support the maneuver of the ground forces in the entire front with reconnaissance and bombings, both in the battlefield as well as inland on the Greek territory. The inland bombings would be directed against the most important towns and road junctions and would aim at the frustration of the Mobilisation and Concentration Plan of the Greek Army.

The success of the above General Plan of Operations against Greece was generally based upon the surprise element of the invasion with the use of motorised means of transport before the mobilisation and concentration of the Greek Army were carried out. The Italians were entering the war under the conviction that, they were about to strike one of those quick successes that the world had come to expect of the German war operations. General Soddu, Minister of the Army on the eve of the war, had reassured Mussolini that, it would only take one week for the Italian Army to reach Ioannina and fifteen to twenty days, at the most, to get to Preveza and commence right away the second stage of operations, the advance towards Thessaloniki and Athens.

In conclusion, out of the nine Italian divisions in Albania, according to the abovementioned plans there were two divisions for the covering operations towards Yugoslavia and two in the area of Koritsa for the active defence against the Greek forces of the area Kastoria-Florina. Three divisions (that comprised a third of the total Italian forces in Albania) were provided for the main effort against Epirus and the remaining two had been assigned to cover the flanks of that effort. The covering forces of the main effort during the onset of war, were twice the size of the Greek forces deployed against them. The forces of the main effort were stronger insofar as the artillery was concerned, though only slightly superior in the infantry, which would be of primary importance in the mountainous terrain of Epirus. In addition, ninety tanks from the 'Centaurs' Armoured Division had been provided for the main effort towards Epirus, although these would be forced to operate against a fortified position and move within narrow lanes along the carriage roads.

Thus, although the directions of action had been wisely chosen by the Italian Leadership, insufficient support had been given, especially to the main effort towards Epirus, since nearly half of the available divisions had been assigned to conduct covering missions in Northern and Central Albania. This was probably determined by two main factors, the underestimate of the adversary, regarding the material strength and morale, and the overestimate of the capabilities of the tanks and the airforce.

**43.    The Greeks.** The Greek War Plan had been drawn on the basis of the political-military situation prevailing in the Balkans, in conjunction with the superiority of the possible adversaries in airforce and armoured vehicles. The Plan aimed at:

-Initially, the defence of the national territory in the fortified frontier areas, with the existing forces deployed there, regardless of whether it was attacked by Italy or Bulgaria, simultaneously or separately.

-At a second stage, after the implementation of mobilisation and strategic concentration of the forces and depending on the prevailing situation, the undertaking of offensive actions.

The Plans of Operations in force on October 28, 1940, were the Campaign Plans, which had been drawn after the seizure of Albania by the Italians and were called IB and IBa.

According to these plans, the Theatre of War designated was the part of the Greek territory north of the line Maliakos bay-Amvrakikos bay. This area was conceptually divided by the river Axios into the Albanian and Bulgarian Theatres of Operations.

The Albanian Theatre of Operations was divided into two Sections, the Epirus and the Western Macedonia Sections. The two Sections were connected through the Pindos Sector.

The above mentioned Plans for Operations were fundamentally defensive. It was only in the Albanian Theatre of Operations that there was provision for the undertaking of offensive operations against the Italian forces in the sector of Koritsa, in the event that the appropriate favourable conditions should arise, whereupon the plan would be adapted to the new situation.

**44.** As regards the mobilisation and strategic concentration of the Greek forces on October 28, 1940, the Mobilisation Plan of 1940 was in force, providing for the organisation of a General Headquarters, two Field Army Sections -the Western Macedonia (WMFAS) and the Eastern Macedonia (EMFAS)- as well as a Division Group. Furthermore, in addition to the Large Units existing since peacetime, the following new Large Units would be formed: the XVII Infantry Division in the area of Thessaloniki, the VII Infantry Brigade in the area of Kavala, the XVI Infantry Brigade in the area of Lamia and òne Cavalry brigade in the area of Kalambaka. Moreover, a considerable number of new infantry and artillery units were included, which were required to complete the war establishment of the field army.

The mobilisation and concentration of the Greek forces was estimated to be completed within twenty-two days for the Albanian Theatre of Operations and fifteen days for the Bulgarian Theatre of Operations.

The Greek Fleet would be allocated, upon the declaration of war, in accordance with the Fleet Plan of Action of 1939 as follows:

-The destroyers and the battleship 'GEORGIOS AVEROF' would remain under the direct command of the Fleet Commander, Rear Admiral, Epaminondas Kavadias.

-The torpedo boats, motor torpedo boats and mine-sweepers would be allocated to the coastal defence under the command of the Rear Admiral Oikonomou.

-The submarines, under the orders of Captain Alexandros Xiros, and the Naval Aviation would be directly answerable to the Chief of the Navy General Staff, regarding operations under his personal direction.

Furthermore, a detailed Plan for the Military Sea Transportation and Concentrations had been drawn up. According to this plan, the military transportation from Attiki would be conducted through the ports of Halkida and Oropos and not through Piraeus, for it was certain that, the latter would be bombed by the Italians as early as the first days of war.

The Greek Airforce had been assigned the following missions:

-Intelligence, with priority given to the collection of military information regarding the disposition, composition and activity of the enemy in the zone between the frontier and the general line Agii Saranda-Tepeleni-Pogradetz.

-Bombings, in the following sequence of priority: the enemy airfields in Albania, the concentrations of enemy columns on the south-east of the general line Agii Saranda-Tepeleni-Pogradetz and the enemy ships in the harbours of Agii Saranda, Avlonas and Dyrrahion.

-Covering, in the following sequence of priority: the friendly Airforce (aircraft- installations), the naval convoys, the road junctions of Ioannina, Larissa and Thessaloniki as well as the most important road and railway works.

*Configuration of the Albanian Theatre of Operations -Transportation*
(Sketch-map no. 4)

**45.** The Greek-Albanian borders extend over approximately 240 kms, of which nearly 80 are in a highly mountainous area. On the whole, the ground is highly mountainous on both sides of the borders and especially so within Greece, where the mountains are higher, their slopes steeper and the valleys narrower.

Lying close to the coastal zone of the Ionian sea, the mountain ranges of Kourvelesi and Tsamandas stand tall and inaccessible even for the mountain units, on account of their steep descent towards the narrow valleys of the rivers Aoos, Drinos and Kalamas. On the east of the narrow valley of Drinos rise the mountain ranges of Nemertska, Tymphi (Gamila) and Mitsikeli. North of Gamila, lies the mountain range of Pindos, with Smolikas to the south and Grammos to the north. The Northern extension of Pindos, Morovas, enters into Albanian territory. On the Northeast of Northern Pindos stands the mountain range of Vernon (Vitsi).

**46.** The road network of the Albanian Theatre of Operations was poor. There were four carriage roads which entered the Greek territory from Albania: the coastal road Avlonas-Konispoli-Filiates, two inland roads, the Argyrokastro-Kakavia-Elea (Kalpaki) road and the Premeti-Mertzani-Elea road (which were connected in Elea en route to Ioannina), and one from Koritsa to Kapestitsa which led from there either to Vatohori-Florina, or to Ieropigi-Kastoria.

There were two roads leading from Ioannina inland. The first led to Thessaly by way of Metsovo and the second to Preveza and Arta-Etoloakarnania by way of Philippiada.

In the area of Grammos there were also two roads, coming from the east. In the north, a carriage road in bad condition, from Kastoria to Nestori, and in the south another one in similar condition from Neapolis to Morphi. Nestori is approximately twenty-five kilometres away from the main ridgeline of mount Grammos. The village of Morphi is about fifty kilometres on a straight line from the nearest point on the frontier.

From the town of Kastoria, there was another carriage road, from the south towards eastern Vitsi and met the Florina-Koritsa road by the village of Vatohori. The mountainous area of Grammos and Smolikas, known as Northern Pindos, was traversed by mule paths that were difficult to cross. The carriage road Koritsa-Erseka-Leskoviki extended parallel, close to the border, within the Albanian territory.

It is obvious from the above description of the road network, that, the two furthermost areas of the Theatre of operations, that is to say the territorial regions of Western Macedonian and Epirus, did not communicate directly by means of carriage road because of the mountain bulk of Grammos. Communication between them could only take place by means of the carriage road Florina-Kozani-Kalambaka-Ioannina, that ran along a considerable distance of approximately 450 kms.

**47.** As regards the railway network, the stations of Florina and Amyndaeo, were the two furthermost stations for the northern approach. In the south, there were the railway stations of Larissa, which had a standard gauge line of the Greek Railway, and Kalambaka, which had a narrow gauge line of the Thessaly Railways.

The Theatre of Operations presented considerable difficulties, on the whole, not only as regards the strategic concentration of the field army and the conduct of operations, but also as regards its resupply and evacuation.

*The Outbreak of the Greek - Italian War and the First Greek Measures*

**48.** The war against Greece, so persistently sought by Italy, was essentially declared at around 0300 hours, on October 28, 1940, by virtue of the visit that Grazzi, the Italian Ambassador to Athens, paid to the Greek Prime Minister Ioannis Metaxas at his home in Kifissia, in order to present him with the following ultimatum:

*'The Italian Government has had to take notice from time to time, during the present conflict, of the way in which the Greek Government has adopted and maintained an attitude which is at odds not only with the normal relations of peace and good neighbourliness between two nations, but with the duties incumbent upon the Government of a neutral State.*

*'From time to time the Italian Government has found it necessary to recall the Greek Government to the fulfilment of its duties and to protest against their systematic violation, a violation particularly grave inasmuch as the Greek Government has allowed its territorial waters, its coasts and its harbours to be used by the English fleet in the course of warlike operations, has facilitated the refuelling of British airplanes, and has permitted the organization of a military intelligence service in the Greek Archipelago, all against Italy. The Greek Government is perfectly aware of these facts which have been the subject of diplomatic démarches by Italy to which the Greek Government - and it should have taken into account the grave concequences of such an attitude - has not responded by any measures to protect its neutrality, but, on the contrary, has increased its*

*assistance to the British armed forces and its collaboration with the enemies of Italy.*

'The Italian Government possesses proof that this collaboration has been foreseen and arranged by the Greek Government itself through military, naval, and aerial understandings. The Italian Government is not referring only to the British guarantee accepted by Greece as a part of action directed against the security of Italy, but to express and precise engagements entered into by the Greek Government for the purpose of placing at the disposition of the Powers at war with Italy important strategic points in Greek territory, by which is understood air bases in Thessaly and Macedonia, designed for an attack on Albanian territory.

'The Italian Government must remind the Greek Government of the provocative action carried on with regard to the Albanian Nation, by the terrorist policy which it has adopted with regard to the population of Tsamouria and by the persistent efforts to create disorders along its frontiers. On that account the Italian Government was compelled - but uselessly - to remind the Greek Government of the inevitable consequences which such a policy would entail where Italy was concerned.

'All this can no longer be tolerated by Italy. The neutrality of Greece has become more and more a pure and simple pretence.

'The responsibility for this situation falls primarily on England and on her intention to involve more and more countries in the war.

'The Italian Government considers it obvious that the policy of the Greek Government has been and is directed toward transforming Greek territory, or at least to allow Greek territory to be transformed, into a base for warlike operations against Italy. This would only lead to armed conflict between Italy and Greece, a conflict which the Italian Government has every intention to avoid. Consequently the Italian Government has decided to demand from the Greek Government - as a guarantee of Greece's neutrality and as a guarantee of Italy's security - facilities to occupy with its armed forces, for the duration of the present conflict with England, certain strategic points of Greek territory. The Italian Government demands that the Greek Government shall not oppose this occupation and shall not obstruct the free passage of the troops intended to effect it. These troops do not come as enemies of the Greek people, and the Italian Government has not the slightest intention by this temporary occupation of certain strategic points, dictated by necessity as it arises and having a purely defensive character, to prejudice in any way the sovereignty and the independence of Greece.

'The Italian Government demands that the Greek Government shall immediately give their military authorities the necessary orders to ensure that this occupation can be effected in a peaceful manner. If the Italian troops should meet with resistance, such resistance will be broken by arms, *and the Greek Government would have to assume the responsibility for whatever consequences might follow from it.'*

According to a verbal statement of the Italian Ambassador, this ultimatum expired at six in the morning, whereupon the Italian troops would commence the invasion of the Greek territory. The contents of the ultimatum together with the three-hour deadline, that was imposed according to the statement of Grazzi, left the Prime Minister with no choice but to reply 'No' to the Italian challenge, without any hesitation and by echoing the will and sentiments of the entire Greek people. Thus, the war between Italy and Greece, which the latter had taken such pains to avoid, became a reality.

**49.** Immediately after the departure of the Italian Ambassador, the Greek Prime Minister notified the King, the Commander-in-chief of the Army General Staff, Lieutenant General Papagos, the Commander in chief of the Navy General Staff, Vice Admiral Sakellariou and the British Ambassador to Athens by phone, and summoned the Cabinet in the Ministry of Foreign Affairs at 0530 hrs. King Georgios and Crown Prince Pavlos were present at the meeting. After the briefing by the Prime Minister about the Italian ultimatum and the unanimous agreement about the proud Greek answer that had been delivered, the Cabinet signed the decrees for the mobilisation of the Armed Forces and the declaration of a state of siege throughout the country. The King assumed General Command of the Armed Forces, according to the Constitution. Lieutenant General Alexandros Papagos was appointed Commander in chief of the land forces and established his General Headquarters (GH) in the hotel 'Grand Bretagne' in Athens. The General Headquarters remained there until the end of the war.

A circular was issued next, addressed to all Greek embassies, in order to inform the Greek diplomatic authorities abroad of the relevant facts. Moreover, the following proclamations were addressed to the Greek people by the Prime Minister, the King and the Archbishop.

### Proclamation issued by the Prime Minister

*'The moment has come for us to fight for the independence, for the integrity, and for the honour of Greece. Although we have observed the strictest neutrality, with absolute impartiality towards all, Italy, denying to us the right to live the life of free Hellenes, demanded from me at 3 o'clock this morning the surrender of portions of the national territory, to be chosen by herself, and informed me that her troops would move forward at 6 A.M. in order to take possession. I replied to the Italian Minister that I considered both the demand itself and the manner of its delivery as a declaration of war on the part of Italy against Greece.*

*'It is now for us to show whether we are indeed worthy of our ancestors and of the freedom won for us by our forefathers. Let the entire nation rise as one man. Fight for your country, for your wives, for your children, and for our sacred traditions.*

*'Now the struggle is for very existence.*

*Ioannis Metaxas '*

## Proclamation issued by the King

*'The Prime Minister announced to you a short while ago the circumstances which have compelled us to go to war in reply to Italy's threat to suppress the independence of Greece. At this solemn moment I am confident that every Greek man and woman will do their duty to the last and will show themselves worthy of our glorious past.*

*'With our faith in God and in the destiny of the Race, the Nation, united and disciplined as one man, will fight in defence of hearth and home until final victory.*

*'Given at the Palace of Athens, October 28th, 1940.*

*George II'*

## Proclamation issued by the Archbishop

*'Beloved children of God*

*His Majesty the King and the President of our National Government have called us all to take part in a Holy defensive struggle for Faith and Country.*

*The Church blesses the sacred arms and is convinced that, the children of the Country, obedient to Its call and to the call of God, will rush to fight as but a single heart and soul for altars and hearths and Freedom and honour, and will continue, thus, the centuries-old and unbroken line of honourable and glorious struggles and will choose a noble death over the ignoble life of slavery. And, let us fear not the ones who may kill our bodies but cannot destroy our souls, but rather let us fear the one who can lose both his body and his soul.*

*Let us relinquish our care to the hands of the Lord and He shall be our helper and protector against the unjustified attack of our enemies. Come as they may with chariots and horses, we shall be glorified by our courage and bravery in the name of God our Lord.*

*May the Grace of our Lord Jesus Christ and the love of God and Father always be with us.*

*The Archbishop of Athens and all of Greece*

*Chrysanthos'*

The Greek Commander-in-chief of the Army Papagos, also issued the following order:

'*In assuming the command of the Army, I call upon the officers and soldiers of the Greek Army to perform the highest duty towards the Country in the highest degree of self-denial and steadfastness. No one must fall short. The cause of the struggle, that was imposed upon us by the unbridled Imperialism of a Great Power, which never had anything to fear on our account, is the most just cause to be defended by an Army. This is a struggle for survival. We shall fight with persistence, indomitable perseverance and undiminished energy to our last breath.*

*I am firmly convinced that the Greek Army will write more glorious pages in the celebrated history of the Nation.*

*Be certain that we shall finally win, with the help and the blessing of God and the prayers of the Nation. Greek Officers and soldiers, prove yourselves to be heroes'.*

**50.**    In the meantime, the Commander-in-chief of the AGS, directly after the phone call of the Prime Minister, who had briefed him on the Italian ultimatum, issued, by phone, the following order to the Commanders of the VIII Division the WMFAS and the B', C', D', E' Army Corps: 'As of 0600 am this morning we are at war with Italy. Defence of National territory will be conducted according to the orders that you have received. Apply mobilisation plan. Papagos'.

The laconic briefings of this first command, comprising thirty words, demonstrates the impeccable staff preparation of the war plans for the country. Thus, without any hesitation, the Greek Military High Command decided to implement Plan IBa, which provided for the defence of the entire national territory on the defensive localities that had been organised along the borders, except for the area of Epirus, where the initiative was left to the Commander of the VIII Division.

The Army General Inspector, Lieutenant General Markos Drakos, was appointed Commander of the Kavala Field Army Section, that was stationed at Kavala, and Lieutenant General Panaghiotis Dedes was appointed Commander of the Division Group, that was stationed at Siderokastro.

The Western Macedonia Field Army Section, under the command of Lieutenant-General Ioannis Pitsikas, immediately began to implement the directives issued by the AGS since September 16, 1940, with view to securing the defensive position IBa from lake Prespa to mount Smolikas (not included).

The I Division was placed as a reserve, under the direct command of the Commander-in-chief of the Army and was ordered to concentrate its forces in the Kalambaka area.

The Greek forces that were oriented towards Bulgaria, also began to be mobilised and advance to the waiting areas of the strategic concentration, according to Plan IBa.

**51.** At 0530 hrs, half an hour before the prescribed deadline had expired, the Italian attack broke out on the entire Albanian front. Twelve Italian columns began to move against the light screening forces. A simultaneous vigorous attack of the Italian Airforce began, both against military targets along the front, as well as, against mobilisation Centres, road junctions, construction works and air bases in the mainland. Such were the harbour of Piraeus, the airfield of Tatoi, the town of Patra, the Korinthos canal, the Naval Base of Preveza, the waterworks at Fasideri in Kifissia, the Megara area, the Istiaea area etc.

In the meantime, according to information that had reached the AGS during the course of the day, the situation appeared to be developing more or less smoothly both in Epirus, where the cover forces were withdrawing according to Plan IBa, and in North-western Macedonia, where minor skirmishes had been confined to the borderline areas. On the contrary, in the Pindos Sector, the situation appeared rather alarming. The Greek forces there, having been unable to contain the attacking forces in front of the main line of defence, were forced to withdraw from its greatest part and occupy a new area behind it.

In order to deal with the situation that had arisen, the AGS placed the I Division at the disposal of the WMFAS along with a number of infantry and artillery battalions, to secure the liaison with the VIII Division.

The first war communiqué was circulated on October 28, at midday and merely referred to the commencement of war, as follows:

*'Since 0530 hrs this morning, the Italian forces have been attacking our covering forces in the Greek - Albanian borderline area. Our forces are defending our Native land.'*

The second communiqué of the General Headquarters, issued that evening, was the following:

'*During the day, Italian units of varying strength, have continued to attack our forces, which resist steadily. The fight has been limited to the border area. The enemy Air Force has hit some of our military targets, causing no damages. The bombs directed against the city of Patra resulted in casualties among the civilian population.*'

The Greek Prime Minister addressed the following message to the Army, the Navy and the Airforce, thus terminating the anguish of all who were waiting for some preliminary information.

'*At the end of the first day, during the course of which you have defended the sacred soil and honour of the Country with a strength of steel, I give you my warmest salute.*

*The entire Nation, from the King to the last citizen, the men, the women and the children, hold you in their thoughts with pride and tenderness and their prayers will follow you with God's blessing.*

*Think how you have been gloriously chosen to write your names in the golden volumes of the Greek history, beside the names of those who fought in the battle of Marathon, our medieval frontier-fighters, the heroes of the 1821 War of Independence and all the other victorious struggles. Yours are the hands that will make Greece even more beautiful and glorious than it is today, that will once again dazzle the whole world. The entire civilised world will look up at you and, I am in a position to assure you that, Greece will not be alone in this struggle.*

*Carry on, Greek soldiers, with the same courage and indomitable determination and crush the enemy, that dared insult the honour of our country.*

*Victory is for you, and glory awaits you.* '


### The Repercussions Abroad


52.    The rejection of the Italian ultimatum and the courageous decision of Greece to resist the unprovoked and unjustified Italian attack, aroused the admiration of all countries that had preserved their freedom until then. Telegrams by Heads of states addressed to the Greek Leadership, statements and speeches delivered by political leaders, enthusiastic articles written in the most serious newspapers, all stressed the significance of the Greek example during that period and offered the assurance that Greece would receive the unqualified support and assistance of all free peoples in its struggle against fascist Italy.

The British Prime Minister Winston Churchill, when he addressed the Greek Prime Minister refered to the fact that Italian intimidation proved useless in the face of his "calm courage". He then opined that Italy resorted to an unprovoked attack against Greece seeking justification for its attack in unfounded accusations. Churchill congratulated the Greek Prime Minister for the way in which Greek People, under his leadership, faced the dangers and provocation. He expressed the admiration of the British People for Greece and said that these virtues will make the Greek People stronger, even more so during this period of trial. Finally he promised to provide all possible assistance in fighting against a common enemy.

The Canadian Prime Minister MacKenzie King, in his telegram, alluded to Greece's historical past as "the cradle of the noblest civilisation that mankind has known" and promised assistance which he thought was the duty of all men, while the country was subject to such an attack.

**53.** At 1400 hrs, on October 28, the British Government issued a semi-official announcement, where it was stressed that, the British offer of assistance to Greece was an obligation arising from the corresponding British guarantee of April 13, 1939.

Twenty four hours later, at 1500 hrs, on October 29, the London radio station broadcasted an official announcement of the British Government referring to the rendering of every possible assistance towards Greece.

The most valuable military aid that Great Britain decided to offer Greece during that period were the four squadrons of 'Blenheim' and 'Gladiator' fighter and bomber aircraft along with the required personnel and equipment. This began to arrive in Greece after November 3 and the first operation of the British airforce detachment took place on November 5, with three 'Blenheim' aircraft for the support of Greek Army troops. A 'Wellington' squadron was also provided, which would be operating from the airfields of Egypt and would be using the airfield in Elefsina as an alternative airfield.

**54.** The rest of the material aid that Britain offered Greece during the war period 1940 - 1941, mainly in terms of small weapons and artillery, consisted of 89 combat guns, 34 antiaircraft guns, 30 antitank guns, 115 antitank rifles, 1,300 machine-guns, 1,290 light machine-guns, 351 mortars (old make), 8,000 rifles, a quantity of ammunition and a number of towed guns and reconnaissance vehicles.

A considerable percentage of the above material was part of the spoils of war sequestered by the British during the operations in Libya, and required servicing. Thus, the contribution of these supplies to the struggle of the army was relatively small and the fighting forces of Greece were obliged to depend primarily on their own resources.

*The Italian Invasion in Epirus*
(Sketch-map no. 5)

**55.** The only Greek forces in Epirus in the morning of October 28 were the troops of the VIII Division, which was directly subordinate to the General Headquarters and was deployed in the area from the Ionian sea to mount Smolikas.

Its mission was to block off the routes leading from Epirus to Etoloakarnania (main effort) and to provide powerful cover for the left flank of the Western Macedonia Theatre of Operations Section from the direction of Ioannina - Metsovo. According to the latest instructions issued to the Division by the AGS on September 16, 1940, the advance of the enemy had to be contained on the line of Elea-Kalamas river (line IBa), or the line of Arachthos river (line IB), or on a line south-east of Arachthos in Akarnania or even on an intermediate line between the above limits.

The above mentioned mission was flexible insofar as the manoeuvers were concerned and gave the VIII Division the initiative to select the defensive area. The Commander of the Division finally decided to resist with all his forces in the forward area of Elea-Kalamas, for, in addition to other advantages, it had been satisfactorily organised.

Based on that decision, the VIII Division had deployed its forces, as follows:

-Along the Greek-Albanian border area 5 Infantry battalions, 2 pack batteries and 3 escort platoons, constituted the screening echelon of the Division. This echelon, with the exception of one battalion (Infantry Battalion of Konitsa) would become the reserve of the Division, after its withdrawal. At the beginning of operations, the Battalion of Konitsa, minus one company and a Machine-gun platoon that had been allocated to the Pindos Detachment, would come directly under the orders of the VIII Division and would be assigned to cover its right flank and secure the liaison with the Pindos Detachment.

-At the defensive area, along the general direction: east bank of Kalamas river - Elea (Kalpaki) - Grambala - Kleftis height on mount

Smolilkas, the main bulk of the forces had been deployed comprising 9 Infantry battalions, 13 batteries (2 of which heavy), 2 self-propelled Machine-gun battalions (minus company), 1 heavy machine-gun company and one divisional Reconnaissance unit. These forces had been deployed in three sectors, the Sectors of Thesprotia, Kalamas and Negrades.

-In order to safeguard the coastal areas and the entrance of Amvrakikos bay, an additional sector had been established, the Preveza-Philippiada Sector, comprising 1 Infantry battalion, 1 field battery, 1 machine-gun company and 2 Escort platoons with antitank missions.

**56.** Opposite the above mentioned Greek forces in Epirus, was the Italian XXV Army Corps of Tsamouria, which had begun to advance its forces towards the frontier since the last ten-day period of August, 1940. On October 27, it had already completed its offensive disposition, that was the following:

-In the coastal area, the Cavalry Division, reinforced with certain infantry and artillery battalions. Its mission was to operate in the direction Konispolis-Igoumenitsa-Preveza and to cover the main effort towards Ioannina mainly from the west.

-In the centre, the 51st 'Sienna' Division, assigned to cross Kalamas river, at the position between Varfani and its confluence with the Langavitsa torrent, and then to turn east and advance to Ioannina in collaboration with the 'Ferrara' Division.

-Opposite the right flank of the Greek forces, the 23rd 'Ferrara' Division, reinforced with a battalion from the 131st 'Centaurs' Armoured Division. Its mission was to operate rapidly in the directions of Kakavia-Elea and Leskoviki-Elea, to seize the junction of Kalpaki and then advance to Ioannina.

-In the Tepeleni area, the 131st 'Centaurs' Armoured Division (minus), was employed as a reserve force.

**57.** Even though the deadline of the Italian ultimatum ended at 0600 hrs on October 28th, the Italian troops, aiming to secure the surprise, began, at 0530 hrs to advance towards the entire Epirus front. After crossing the border in the directions Mertzani-Hani-Bourazani, Drymades-Delvinaki, Kakavia-Hani Delvinaki and Konispolis-Parapotamos, they began to attack the Greek safe-guards, with the support of the Italian artillery and airforce.

The screening forces, having sufficiently resisted this initial attack, began to withdraw towards their predetermined positions, delaying the enemy in accordance with the plan and the instructions of the VIII Division. The withdrawal on the first day of the Italian invasion, despite the initial pressure of the enemy, was conducted in an orderly way and it was only in the Elea sector that some troops were forced to withdraw somewhat hurriedly. The demolition detachment of the Division, also accomplished its mission and blew up the bridges across the river Aoos, except for the Hani Bourazani bridge, which was not destroyed because of the improper firing of demolition. After the unexpected resistance of the screening forces, the Italians moved hesitantly and it was only on the evening of October 28th that they managed to occupy the line Kerasovo heights-Hani Delvinaki-Meropi heights-Bourazani bridge-Kavasila village with the 'Ferrara' Division and the village of Agii Pandes and the heights directly north of Philiates with the 'Sienna' Division.

**58.**   During the second day, the Italian troops continued to move with the same degree of hesitation. Although they had lost contact with the withdrawing Greek troops since the previous evening, small columns began to move at 1000hrs, in the areas of Hani Delvinaki, Vissani and Geroplatanos before the Elea area. At 1600hrs, a motorised column, moving from Hani Tzeravini, was hit by the Greek artillery and sought cover towards Hani Delvinaki. Small sections of the Italian infantry and cavalry, that had managed to cross Kalamas river near its mouth in the afternoon, were forced to withdraw once more to the north of the river, after a Greek counter attack.

On the Greek side, during the same day, the VIII Division considering that the keeping of the screening forces in front of the area of resistance and their possible casualties might be in vain, decided to withdraw them within that area, to their predetermined positions in the night of 29/30 October. At the same time, the Army General Staff ordered the 39th Regiment, which was stationed in Agrinio, to accelerate its advance towards Arta, so that its forces would also be placed at the disposal of the VIII Division as soon as possible.

The casualties suffered by the Greek troops, during their two-day withdrawal, were very few, except for the Delvinaki Border Battalion that had seventy soldiers missing and lost a large part of its supplies.

**59.**   From October 30 until November 1st, the Italians focused their efforts in Epirus on rehabilitating the appropriate routes, in order to advance the bulk of their forces closer to the area of Elea (Kalpaki)-Kalamas river, to conduct reconnaissance operations and generally to prepare the attack, without however gaining close contact with the defence area.

Meanwhile, the VIII Division withdrew its troops from Preveza and advanced them to the Sector of Thesprotia, in order to reinforce the latter. The Division decided this course of action after an intelligence estimate from the AGS that there was very little probability of enemy action in that coastal area. Parallel to this, due to the adverse development of the situation in the area of mount Smolikas, the VIII Division deployed a small number of troops on mount Gamila, so as to cover the crossings of Papingo and Astrakas. Furthermore, it withdrew the Konitsa Border Battalion, which had not been under any serious enemy pressure until then and had retained its positions on the Kleftis height-Peklari pass in the Vrysochori area, so as to block off the crossings on the south of Aoos river and cover the right flank of the Division.

In the meantime, the Army General Staff, because of the unfavourable development of the struggle for the Greek troops in Pindos, reminded the VIII Division of its principal mission, which was to block off the axis Ioannina-Metsovo-Kalambaka. Nevertheless, the latter stood by its original decision of retaining the position of Elea-Kalamas river.

### The Battle of Elea-Kalamas
( Sketch-map no. 5 )

**60.** In the morning of November 2, the Italians had completed their preparations for the decisive attack and, as of 0900hrs, consecutive waves of Italian aircraft flights began to bomb the Negrades Sector and in particular Grambala , Kalpaki, Velas Monastery, the Ioannina airfield and Mazaraki bridge, without any grave consequences. The town of Ioannina was also bombed, and suffered considerable damages and many victims among the civilians. The airforce withdrew at noon and a severe shelling of the entire defensive area by the Italian artillery began, mainly against the area Elea-Grambala with inconsiderable results.

Meanwhile, troops from the 'Ferrara' Division, which had been reinforced with tanks from the 'Centaurs' Division, began to move against the Negrades Sector and launched their first attack simultaneously, from many directions at 1500hrs, with particular severity against the heights of Grambala and Psilorrahi. Despite the preparation and preceding bombings, the attack was repulsed with considerable casualties for the Italians. Thus, the second day of November went by without the Italians being able to break through the Elea area.

The Greek artillery had contributed to decisively repulsing the Italian attack. By shelling the attacking enemy troops, with a barrage of sustained and accurate fire, it disorganised them and forced them to either slow down their pace or halt their advance because of the casualties.

During the course of the night, Italian infantry elite units, reinforced with Albanians, succeeded in surprising and overpowering the Greek company occupying Grambala height, and they seized it. However, this occupation was not destined to last long, for in the early hours of November 3, the Greek troops launched a counter-attack and succeeded in recapturing Grambala by force of bayonet. There, the enemy abandoned 20 dead, 6 prisoners and a lot of weapons and ammunition.

Moreover, the 47th Italian Infantry Regiment that was concentrated near Grambala -assigned to climb the height, seize it and continue to the heights of Psilorrahi and Assonissa- was detected in time. Thus, before it had any opportunity to move, it was hit by the fire of four Greek batteries and was forced to disperse.

61.   The morning of November 3 passed with the exchange of artillery fire from both sides, in the Sectors of Negrades and Kalamas river. As of l000hrs, the Italian airforce joined the battle and concentrated its attack mainly on the Negrades Sector. At 1600hrs, the enemy launched a new attack against the height of Kalpaki, using 50 - 60 tanks, accompanied by about 80 motorcyclists. This attack was also contained by the antitank ditches and the accurate fire of the artillery. Most of the tanks and the motorcycles were destroyed, while the rest were forced to withdraw, with great damages. The Italian infantry also suffered many casualties and was not able to launch its attack, having been hit by Greek fire in its area of concentration.

The failure of the enemy, at this point, greatly revived the spirit of the Greek fighters who confronted tanks for the first time, and it served to intensify their conviction about the effectiveness of the anti-tank defence.

62.   On November 4, the Italians had planned to spread the attack to the entire front, however, they decided to postpone it for the following day, evidently desiring to complete its preparation. Thus, the fourth day of November went by, with the bombing of the entire area with artillery fire and in certain cases with the added support of the airforce.

In the meantime, during the night of November 3 to 4, the VIII Division, in order to reinforce its defence positions in the area of Elea, withdrew its troops that were in the positions of Siastis, Sossinos Monastery and Repetista west of Kalamas river, and moved them to a new position east of the river, which was thought to be less vulnerable to the enemy tanks. The withdrawal was conducted in silence, during the night, without being noticed by the Italians.

63.   From the morning of November 5, the Italians began a heavy bombardment of the areas Grambala and Vrondismeni in the sector of Negrades, the positions that had already been abandoned by the Greek troops west of the river Kalamas and the area of Parapotamos (Varfani) in the sector of Thesprotia.

rfi

In the sector of Negrades, following the abovementioned preparation of the artillery and the air force, the Italians launched a new general assault at 1430hrs, against the whole area of the front, employing a large number of infantry troops and tanks. However, this attack failed as well, despite the strong support by artillery and airforce. The Italian forces were immobilised by the Greek fire before the defensive area, and suffered grave casualties. The tanks which had been employed in the area of Parakalamos were hit by the concentrated and accurate fire of the Greek artillery and were forced to disperse and remain immobilised in the marshlands of Kalamas river.

The Italian attack against that Sector continued during the two days that followed and focused mainly against the area of Elea, again to no avail. Greek forces launched a local counter-attack against the elite Italian troops that had managed to seize Psilorrahi height, a southern ridge of Grambala, on the evening of November 7. After a close combat, the Italians were forced to withdraw, abandoning on site 45 dead, 7 prisoners, 5 mortars, 3 machine-guns and 4 light machine-guns. The Greek casualties were one officer and 11 soldiers killed in action and one officer and 33 soldiers wounded.

This was the last Italian effort against the area of Elea. Grambala, which was the key to that area as well as to the broader area of the Ioannina highland, remained in the possession of the VIII Division.

In the sector of Kalamas, the Italians did not attempt any significant moves, apart from the occupation of the advanced positions to the west of Kalamas river, which had been abandoned by the Greek troops.

In the Sector of Thesprotia, the Italians, backed by airforce and artillery, succeeded in bridging Kalamas in the area of Tsifliki and the village of Vrissela and in crossing over to the south of the river and creating a small bridgehead. The following day, after widening the bridgehead, the Italian troops moved southwards, occupied Igoumenitsa and forced the limited Greek forces of that area to withdraw further south.

The VIII Division, due to the lack of sufficient reserves for the conduct of delaying action in that area, ordered its troops to break off contact with the enemy and withdraw to new positions in the area of mount Souli-Acherondas river, assigning them to block off the passages towards Preveza and Ioannina. In order to reinforce the above new position, the 39th Evzones Regiment (minus) of the III Division advanced to Philippias.

Nevertheless, the Italian forces did not harass the withdrawing Greek forces, neither did they seek to take advantage of their success. Their only move was to advance one Cavalry unit as far as the village of Margariti. This attitude of the Italians can only be explained by their fear of getting cut off from their stations, if they attempted to continue their advance in the Sector of Thesprotia, while the position of Elea was still intact.

**64.** As of November 8, the offensive operations of the Italians were suspended. As it was later revealed, during that day, the Commander-in-chief of the Italian forces in Albania, General Visconti Prasca, was ordered to suspend his offensive operations. At the same time, he was replaced by General Soddu.

As of November 9, the conditions of the adversaries in the Epirus front were reversed. In the Sector of Negrades, the Italians adopted a defensive attitude, while in the Sector of Thesprotia they began to withdraw, maintaining only one bridgehead of limited size, south of Kalamas river, which constituted the only achievement of their surprise attack in the Epirus Front.

Thus, after a twelve-day defensive struggle, it was made possible to contain the Italian forces before the Elea area. These forces consisted of two divisions and they had low moral due to the development of the struggle and lots of material damages, to such an extent that, their Supreme Command decided to suspend the offensive operations until the arrival of reinforcements.

**65.** On November 10, the VIII Division Headquarters, which had been stationed until then in the Fortress of Ioannina, moved to the village of Veltista (Klimatia).

During the three following days, the Division conducted reconnaissance in force, the most significant being the one that began in the Sector of Thesprotia and continued towards Igoumenitsa, resulting in the occupation of the heights Agia Marina-Neochori by November 13, and nearly in the total destruction of the Italian bridgehead in that area.

Meanwhile, by order of the Army General Staff, as of November 12, the VIII Division was no longer directly subordinate to the AGS and was placed under the command of the A' Army Corps. On the same day, the Headquarters of the A' Army Corps moved from Athens to Votonosi village, via Kalambaka, on the 43rd kilometre of the road Ioannina-Metsovo.

The Commander-in-chief, issued the following order, to the VIII Division, expressing his satisfaction about the successes recorded, until then.

*'We express our full satisfaction with the successful handling of the situation at the end of your activity as an independend division. This concerns the division commander and his colleagues'.*

The casualties suffered by the VIII Division during its defensive operations from November 1 to 5, amounted to 3 officers and 57 soldiers killed in action and 5 officers and 203 soldiers wounded. Most of these casualties were due to the bombardment of the artillery positions by the

Italian Airforce, as well as to the local counter-attacks that had been conducted to recapture the ground taken by the enemy.

According to the estimate of General Prasca, the casualties suffered by the Italian forces from the beginning of war operations until November 5, were 17 officers and 354 soldiers killed in action and 65 officers and, 1,134 soldiers wounded. Ten officers and 648 soldiers were reported missing in action.

## The Italian Invasion in Pindos
### (Sketch-map no. 6 )

**66.**   On the morning of October 28, the only Greek forces present in the mountain area of Pindos were those of the Pindos Detachment. The total strength of this Detachment was approximately 2,000 men and comprised the 5lst Infantry Regiment, a screening company, a pack battery of 75mm, a Cavalry platoon, an Escort Artillery platoon of 65mm. Furthermore, the detachment possessed two mortar barrels, a Signals platoon and a Muleteers company.

The 51st Infantry Regiment was a mobilizable unit, and its two battalions, the I/51 and the II/51, had been pre-mobilised in Trikala, on August 29 and had advanced to Eptachori from September 1 to 10. The III/51 Battalion was mobilised on October 15 and was moving from Pendalofo to Eptachori on October 27.

The zone of responsibility of the Pindos Detachment extended from mount Smolikas to Northern Grammos mountain, about 35 kilometres on a straight line.

The main line of resistance of the Detachment ran, from north to south, along the general line: Tsombanis height on mount Smolikas-Molista village-Kastaniani heights- Oxya village-Kiafa height-Katafyki height.

The Pindos Detachment was under the tactical command of the WMFAS and included the following three sub-sectors:

-The left sub-sector, which had its command post in the village of Kantziko and one Infantry battalion (minus company and Machine-gun platoon) at its disposal.

-The central sub-sector, which had its command post in the village of Oxya and one Infantry battalion (minus a Machine-gun platoon) together with the screening company of the Konitsa Screening Battalion at its disposal.

-The right sub-sector, that had its command post in the village of Palcochori and comprised one Infantry company, two Machine-gun platoons, a scout squad, an Escort Artillery platoon of 65mm and an Infantry platoon, which had been assigned by the IX Division, so as to secure the liaison and guard its left flank.

The III/51 Battalion, that began to arrive in the village of Eptachori on the morning of October 28, constituted the reserve force of the Pindos Detachment.

The pack battery was deployed south of Theotokos village, its firing capacity ranging from Gorgopotamos river to Sarandaporos river, while the Cavalry platoon was at the village of Stratsani and was instructed to engage in delaying action towards Pyrsoyianni.

The Pindos Detachment had been assigned to secure the IBa area on Pindos mountain, maintaining the liaison between the VIII and IX Divisions and blocking off the mountain passes of Pindos that led from west to east.

**67.** Opposite the Pindos Detachment, was the 3rd Alpine 'Giulia' Division, which was deployed in the area of Erseka and Leskoviki.

The Alpine Division was an elite Large Unit consisting of two Alpine regiments, one Cavalry company and six pack batteries, amounting to a total strength of approximately 10,800 men. This division had been in Albania since April 1939, and was totally familiar with the terrain and the conditions of the Pindos front. Moreover, it had been well organised, established and trained.

Its mission was to move from the Erseka and Leskoviki area, through the mountain lines of Stavros-Fourka-Samarina-Vovousa-Metsovon and Golion-west of mount Smolikas-Distrato-Vovousa-Metsovo, reach Metsovo and cut off the escape routes to the east, which might be used by the Greek forces of Epirus. The left flank of the Division would be covered by a platoon, which would conduct offensive operations between the heights of Kiafa and Katafyki.

**68.** The Italian offensive in Pindos was launched at 0500hrs on October 28, with five powerful columns and a few other smaller ones, of Infantry company or platoon strength. The Greek screening forces, that had been notified in the meantime, were expecting the Italian move and were not taken by surprise.

The Italians attacked the right sub-sector of the Pindos Detachment, using a force of about two company strength, without artillery or mortar support. These troops, which kept slowing down their pace, were finally held in position in front of the main line of resistance, during the course of the afternoon.

The main effort of the Italians was directed against the central sub-sector of the Detachment. The attacking forces were greatly superior to the resisting Greek ones and had strong artillery and heavy mortar support.

The defending Greek troops, after a persisted resistance, were forced to withdraw by the afternoon, to the heights of Patoma, Mouka and Upper Arena, were defence was then stationed.

The Italians attacked the left sub-sector at 1700hrs, with a strength of two Infantry Battalions. Despite the strong Italian pressure, the resisting Greek troops held their ground steadily.

Thus in the night of October 28/29, the Pindos Detachment occupied the general line: Molista village, Kastaniani village, Patoma height, Mouka height, Upper Arena height, Kiafa height and Katafyki height.

Meanwhile, the Commander of the Pindos Detachment, Colonel Konstantinos Davakis, in order to reinforce the fighting troops, ordered the companies of the III/51st Battalion, which had begun to arrive in Eptachori since the morning of October 28, to advance to the front-line. Furthermore, he issued instructions that all means of transport belonging to the villagers of Pindos should be concentrated in the village of Morphi, in order to be used for transportation of ammunition and other supplies to the troops in combat. His request addressed to the villages of Pindos was met with great enthusiasm and willingness. Elderly men, women and children worked hard and heroically for many days, under a spirit of self-sacrifice, carrying ammunition and supplies right up to the front-line and transporting the wounded under extremely adverse weather conditions.

**69.** In attempting to deal with the situation that had arisen in the sector of Pindos, in the meantime, the WMFAS took the following measures:

-It forwarded the following units towards this sector:

•     One Infantry battalion from Smixi towards Myrovliti, to cover the right flank of the Pindos Sector and secure the liaison with the V Infantry Brigade, under the command of which it would come.

•     One Infantry battalion from Servia towards Morphi, at the disposal of the Pindos Detachment.

•     One Infantry battalion and one battery from Eleftherochori towards Doutsiko, at the disposal of the Pindos Detachment.

•     One Cavalry company and one Machine-gun platoon from Karpero towards Neapolis.

•     The Metsovo Detachment, comprising one Infantry battalion, one Pack Artillery platoon and a Mortar platoon, from Metsovon towards Kerasovo.

-It ordered two battalions of the XI Infantry Division (which were in the area of the IV Infantry Brigade) to advance towards Argos Orestikon and the Headquarters of the V Infantry Brigade to Nestori, as soon as possible.

-It ordered the I Infantry Division, which, as of October 28, had been placed at the disposal of the Pindos Sector by order the Army General Staff, to advance, within the day of October 29, to Eptachori. The Division would assume the command of the Pindos Sector and had been assigned to defend it.

**70.** Since the morning of October 29, the Italians resumed their offensive against the Sector of Pindos, with particular intensity against the central and left sub-sectors.

In the central sub-sector, the Italians attacked against the heights of Mouka and Patoma. In the afternoon, after a fierce struggle, they managed to seize the height of Mouka, but were immediately subjected to a Greek counterattack which forced them to abandon it. And while the Greek troops on the height of Mouka held on to their positions, the ones on the height of Patoma were beginning to withdraw. After that, the Pindos Detachment ordered the withdrawal of the troops, that were fighting at those heights, to the line Kato Arena-Gousteritsa.

However, due to the continuous and tough two-day struggle and the inclement weather conditions (continuous rain and bitter cold), by midnight of October 29/30, the above troops along with those that had been sent to reinforce them, withdrew in haste towards Eptachori, despite the efforts of their officers and the personal intervention of the Detachment Commander.

The height of Kiafa and the right sub-sector were not subjected to any heavy pressure and retained their positions. However, the continuous snow and the bitter cold that prevailed, placed them at a grave disadvantage.

In the morning of October 29, a fierce attack began against the left sub-sector, which had been lightly reinforced in the meantime. The main objective of the attack was to seize the heights of Gyftissa, Tambouri and Kantziko, in order to open the way to Samarina, bypassing Molista. The fight continued until the afternoon, when the Italians managed to effect a slight breakthrough in the centre of the sub-sector and also to outflank Molista from the south.

Towards the end of the day, after this turn of events, the Commander of the Pindos Detachment ordered the commander of the left sub-sector to withdraw his forces to the line Gyftissa-Langada-Leivadia and to join the troops of the central sub-sector, that were stationed in the area of Sioumoulazari. Due to the break in communications, however, and the hardships suffered by the troops after the two-day fight, some of them did not conduct an orderly withdrawal and fled to the rear.

Thus, on the evening of October 29, the right flank of the Pindos Detachment was holding its ground firmly at the heights of Kiafa and Skala, while in the rest of the area and specifically at the heights of Upper Arena, Mouka, Patoma, Sioumoulazari, Tambouri and Molista, the situation was unclear.

71.   In the morning of October 30, the Italians resumed their offensive against the central and left sub-sector of the Pindos Detachment, while the commanders of the sub-sectors strove to re-organise their troops and contain the enemy for as long as possible.

The Commander of the Pindos Detachment, who had witnessed the situation of his troops after their two-day fight, decided to withdraw them behind the line Samarina- Koutsouro-Tsouka, that had been manned by the reinforcements already provided for the Pindos Sector.

At 1600hrs, on October 30th, the Commander of the I Division, Major General Vassilios Vrachnos, arrived at Eptachori accompanied by a section of his Staff and assumed the command of the forces belonging to the Pindos Sector.

The Pindos Detachment, that had suffered the might of the entire Giulia Division, conducted a two-day hard and unequal fight, under extremely adverse weather conditions and performed all that was humanly possible. Thereafter, control of the situation was assumed by the higher echelons.

72.   The I Division devoted the rest of 30 and the whole of 31 October, to the reorganisation of the Sector troops, the conduct of reconnaissance and the reinforcement of the troops on heights Vouzio-Koutsouro-Upper Arena. The purpose of the effort was to secure both the passages leading to Distrato and Eptachori and the liaison with the VIII Division.

A counter-attack was also decided to be launched on the morning of November 1, with a force comprising three Infantry units of two company strength each and one Cavalry company, in the directions of Priaspos-Lykorrahi-Oxya and Koutsouro-Fourka-Tambouri-Gyftissa in order to occupy the line Oxya-Gyftissa and to attack the left flank of the Italians, who were moving towards Samarina.

Meanwhile, the Italians continued their offensive and, by the evening of October 31, had fully occupied the general line Molista-Fourka-Tambouri-Kantziko-Lykorrahi-Aetomilitsa-Grammos. Thus, they managed to create a pocket that posed a threat for the entire Greek defensive disposition in the area between mount Smolikas and Grammos and at the boundary between the VIII Infantry Division and the IX Division.

**73.** The above mentioned unfavourable development of the situation in the Sector of Pindos alarmed the Greek Army General Staff that decided to block off, at first, the main passes in Pindos towards Neapolis, Grevena and Metsovo and then to launch a counter-offensive for the repulsion of the invader.

With view to the implementation of this decision, the Army General Staff proceeded as follows:

-Since October 31, the operational command of the Pindos Sector was assigned to the B' Army Corps, whose mission was to deploy its forces into the Sector of Pindos, to secure the stability of the front, to restore the liaison with the VIII Infantry Division and to hinder any further widening of the enemy pocket, and afterwards, to prepare and conduct offensive operations, to threaten both the enemy transport network in the valley of Sarandaporos river as well as the rear of the enemy forces operating towards the valley of river Aoos. With view to the accomplishment of its mission, the B' Army Corps was also reinforced with the Cavalry Brigade, which concentrated its forces in the area of Grevena, under the command of Colonel (Cav) Sokratis Dimaratos.

-The Cavalry Division was ordered to advance hastily to the area of Metsovo and secure the cover of the axis Ioannina-Kalambaka from the directions of the upper valley of the Aoos river and the valley of Zagoritikos river, linking up with the VIII Infantry Division and the B' Army Corps. As soon as the Division arrived in Kalambaka, it would be reinforced with an Infantry regiment and a battery of 155mm to accomplish its mission.

According to the above mission, the B' Army Corps decided the following:

-To occupy the passage of Arena with the V Infantry Brigade in order to cover the left flank of the IX Division.

-To concentrate all available forces in the area of Eptachori, under the I Division, so as to block off all passes towards Neapolis.

-To block off all routes from Samarina to Grevena with the Cavalry Brigade, which would also threaten, from the rear, the enemy forces that were directed towards Distrato.

-To undertake offensive operations in the direction of Eptachori-Kerasovo, after stabilising the front and securing the above passes, so as to cut off the movement of Italian forces towards Samarina and then crush them or repulse them west of Pindos.

## The Greek Counter-Attack in Pindos
### (Sketch-map no. 6)

**74.** The counter-attack that had been decided and planned by the I Division the previous day, was launched at 0730 hrs on November 1st, aiming at occupying the line Gyftissa-Oxya, so as to hit the left flank of the Italian forces operating in the direction of Samarina. The counter-attack was launched with troops of the Pindos Detachment that were both limited in number and extremely worn down. By that evening, after a fierce struggle, they managed to occupy the villages of Kantziko and Lykorrahi and take 222 prisoners, including three officers. Moreover, 140 pack animals and many supplies came into the hands of the Greek troops.

During this phase of the Pindos struggle, the first Greek officer of the Army in the Greek -Italian war was killed in action. This was, the heroic First Lieutenant Alexandros Diakos from the Dodecanese, who had led his company in successive attacks to occupy the height of Tsouka, east of Fourka, where the Italians were strongly organised and had resisted steadily.

On the same day, the V Brigade, (which had entered the action on October 30 and had assumed the right sub-sector of the Pindos Detachment), occupied the pass of Arena. Meanwhile, the first group of the Cavalry Brigade forces began to arrive at Doutsiko and seized the height of Skourtza, southeast of it.

The offensive operation of the I Division, though limited, improved the overall picture of the critical situation that had arisen in the Sector of Pindos and revived the spirit of the men. In parallel, with the arrival of new troops, the front was relatively stabilised, thus facilitating the movement and concentration behind the front-line, of the forces that were, in the meantime, forwarded by the Army General Staff.

**75.** The Alpine Division, after repulsing the light Greek troops on mount Vouzio, continued its rapid advance southwards regardless of the fact that its left flank was insufficiently covered. In the morning of November 2, it occupied the village of Samarina and during that evening, the village of Distrato, where the division's Headquarters moved. On November 3rd, forward troops of the division arrived at the village of Vovousa, in contact with the Greek company that was withdrawing in that direction.

However, after a while, these actions brought the Alpine Division to a very dangerous situation. Indeed, on November 2 and 3, the I Division, continuing its offensive effort, succeeded in seizing Tambouri height and Fourka village after a hard fight, thus cutting off the Italian troops that had advanced to the south of those two areas.

On the evening of November 2, Colonel Konstantinos Davakis was gravely wounded in the chest and was evacuated to Eptachori. The incident occurred, while he was in charge of a force conducting reconnaissance for the continuation of the attack, that would be launched from the height of Prophitis Elias of Fourka towards the height of Tambouri.

Since November 3, with the gradual entrance of the Cavalry Division into action, the enemy pocket that had been formed in the southern section of the Pindos Sector began to be constricted from all directions. Thus, the forces that had infiltrated into the areas Samarina-Distrato and Vovoussa, ran the risk to be captured.

During the evening of November 3rd, the Cavalry Brigade occupied Samarina and, on the following day, the Cavalry Division occupied Vovoussa.

On November 5 and 6, the Greek attack continued vigorously in all directions. The Alpine Division, that had occupied the area of Distrato village (where its command had been posted) and the south-western foot of Smolikas mountain with two regiments, abandoned its offensive effort and its forward foothold and began to withdraw.

**76.** In order to reinforce the Alpine Division and avert its captivity, one Infantry regiment of the 47th 'Bari' Division moved hastily to cover the valley of Sarandaporos river at the position of Pournia village and to secure the passes on Smolikas mountain. However, the fate of the Giulia Division had already been sealed.

By November 6, without hope for any effective reinforcement and lacking supplies, with the exception of the few that were dropped by aeroplanes, the Division began to withdraw its forces through the valley of Aoos river, its only way of retreat.

On the night of November 6 to 7, the Italian troops in the area of Distrato village withdrew towards the village of Armata, while the Division Command withdrew towards the village of Eleuthero.

**77.** On November 8, the Cavalry Division seized Distrato and the Field Surgery of the Alpine Division in that area with 200 wounded. One hour later, the troops of the Cavalry Division, that were moving from Vovousa, 'also entered the village.

The I Division seized the heights of Kleftis and Daliapolis as well as the village of Pournia, and forced the Italians to confine themselves to the summit of Smolikas mountain.

On the same day, the V Brigade seized the height of Stavros on mount Grammos and continued to move towards the border without encountering any resistance.

**78.** On November 9, the Greek troops continued to apply pressure against the Italians, who had become desperate by then. The Italians, seeking to secure their escape towards Konitsa, were only focusing their efforts on finding ways to loosen the pincer that tightened round them. On the night of November 9 to 10, Italian units repeatedly attacked Greek troops at the heights of Kleftis and Daliapolis. These attacks were repulsed and the Italian troops broke up, abandoning many dead on the battlefield as well as two artillery pieces, mortars, radios, and the war flag of the III/9 Alpine Battalion. On the following day, and during the course of the evening, a large number of men from the above unit surrendered to the Greek Cavalry Division troops that were operating in the direction of villages Pades and Elefthero.

On the following day, November 10, Greek troops from the I Infantry Division and the Cavalry Division, that were engaged in the seizure of Sousnitsa pass (west of Elefthero village), encountered a column of the 8th Alpine Regiment and managed to break it up after a fierce seven-hour fight. Fifteen officers and 700 soldiers were taken prisoners and war supplies of all kinds captured, including 100 mules and 5 mortars.

**79.** Since November 11, the Greek forces of Pindos (except for the Cavalry Brigade which was concentrated in Samarina and Distrato for re-grouping purposes) continued their advance. By the evening of November 13, they had occupied the main frontier crossings along the entire zone of the Pindos Sector.

The area of Konitsa-where the Italian forces had also been reinforced with the greater part of the 47th 'Bari' Division-was an exception, since the Italians were able to retain it until November 16, thus covering the passage of the rest of the Alpine Division.

By November 13, the mountain areas of Smolikas and Grammos had been fully recaptured. Thus, the passes of Pindos were secured and the Greek troops in Epirus and Western Macedonia were no longer facing the risk of separation.

The Battle of Pindos had ended with the crushing of the Alpine Division and the victory of the Greeks.

The local inhabitants contributed greatly to the Greek victory. During the Battle of Pindos, men and women offered their assistance to the fighting troops, carrying ammunition, food and other supplies to the front-line and evacuating the wounded to the rear, with great self-sacrifice and self denial. Their contribution was both grand and touching and constitutes a characteristic proof of Greek patriotism.

The causalties of the Greek forces, during the battle of Pindos, were considerable regarding the killed in action and wounded officers and soldiers. However, the Italian casualties were also extremely numerous.

According to the most modest estimates, there were well over five hundred killed in action and wounded, and over one thousand two-hundred prisoners.

## The Operations in North-western Macedonia

**80.** The WMFAS, according to the Plan of Operations, was responsible for the defence of the North-western Macedonia front. The WMFAS, with its Headquarters at Kozani, comprised the B' Army Corps, which had its Headquarters at Larissa and the C' Army Corps, with its Headquarters at Thessaloniki.

The forces, that had been pre-mobilised and had advanced to the above front by the evening of October 27, were the IX Division and the IV Brigade, which were under the command of the B' and C' Army Corps, respectively.

The IX Division occupied the section of defensive area IBa from the Skala height of the Grammos mountain to Ieropigi.

The IV Brigade occupied the section of the defensive area IBa from Ieropigi to lake Prespa Major.

The above forces had been assigned to defend IBa area, which lay in the direction south to north, along the general line Skala height - Yiannochori - Komninades - Ieropigi - Krystallopigi - Karyes - lake Prespa Major.

The fortification of this area had progressed considerably and included concrete or makeshift pill boxes, trenches, barbed wiring, antitank ditches etc.

**81.** On the evening of October 27, opposite the front of North-western Macedonia, were the deployed forces of the XXVI Italian Army Corps.

In particular, against the sectors of the IX Division and the IV Infantry Brigade, were the deployed forces of the 49th 'Parma' Division, comprising 10 Infantry battalions, 10 tanks, 16 batteries (5 heavy artillery), 1 Mortar battalion, 1 Cavalry company and 1 Machine-gun battalion.

West of Koritsa were the concentrated forces of the 29th 'Piedmonte' Division, comprising 7 Infantry battalions, 8 batteries and 1 Mortar battalion.

Between Elbasan and lake Achris, there were the concentrated forces of the 19th 'Venezzia' Division, comprising 7 Infantry battalions, 12 batteries, 1 Cavalry regiment and 1 Mortar battalion, ready to move southwards in order to reinforce the sector of Koritsa.

The abovementioned Italian forces had been assigned to provide the forces operating in Epirus, during the first days of the war, with cover from the north. After the occupation of Epirus, these forces would initiate offensive action along the axis of Koritsa-valley of the river Aliakmon-Thessaloniki.

**82.** In the areas of Epirus and Pindos, strong Italian Army troops crossed the borders by early morning on October 28 and initiated offensive action, whereas in the area between Grammos and lake Prespa their position was defensive. Activity was confined to artillery fire against various points of the Greek defence position and to few probing attacks against the outguards of the screening forces.

This attitude, on the part of the Italians, enabled the IX Division and the IV Brigade to move their troops (many of which were engaged in fortification construction) with relative ease. Thus, by the evening, on October 29, both had managed to occupy their positions at the defensive area IBa.

Meanwhile, during the evening of October 29, the Headquarters of the V Infantry Brigade arrived at Nestori, its troops having already advanced towards the front. On the night of October 29 to 30, this Brigade, by order of the WMFAS and after being reinforced by the IX Division, undertook to close the gap, between Lower Arena and Souflika, as well as to restore the line of Lower Arena-Upper Arena-Tsouka-Souflikas[1] .

**83.** According to the AGS instructions of September 16, 1940, in the event of an Italian attack, the B' and C' Army Corps, apart from securing IBa area, would have to conduct offensive operations on a limited scale. The objective of this action was to hold the enemy forces in position in that area and to occupy specific vital positions, within the enemy territory, in order to assist future operations towards mount Morovas and Koritsa.

During the first three days, despite the abovementioned instructions of the AGS, the B' and C' Army Corps displayed a hesitant attitude and did not conduct the planned offensive actions. Afterwards, the Army General Staff was forced to intervene and, on October 30th, ordered the Commands of the above Army Corps that had remained at their positions and were overseeing the mobilisation and advance of their troops, to move to Kozani and Florina respectively, and to conduct operations at their respective zones of action. This move was conducted immediately and by 2400hrs, on October 31, the B' and C' Army Corps Headquarters were operating from their new positions.

---

[1]  Sketch-map no. 6

The Army General Staff began to direct strong forces towards the area northwest of Koritsa, the objective being to create a strong foothold in that area because it was served by a good road network suitable for the transport and the supply requirements of significant forces throughout the year. The intension was to use the above forces to attack and overpower the Italian forces that had been concentrated in the mountain range Morova-Ivan, and then to occupy the junction of Koritsa. This success, apart from its strategic significance, would raise morale of the army and the people.

The town of Koritsa had been through the centuries the cultural and commercial centre in the region of Northern Epirus and the inhabitants were predominantly Greek. Thus, its occupation by the Greek army would be an event of great importance.

The initial actions taken by Army General Staff in this direction were: firstly, the placement of the XI Division, as of November 1, at the disposal of the WMFAS, under the binding condition that its use required the approval of the Commander in chief; secondly, the X Division remaining under the command of the C' Army Corps; thirdly, the advance of the XVII Division under the command of Major General Panaghiotis Bassakidis, -which had been allocated to the Bulgarian Theatre of Operations, by Plan IBa, - to the area of Veria, in order to use it in the Albanian Theatre of Operations.

**84.** The WMFAS, according to the intentions and instructions of the Commander in chief, ordered the IX Division to prepare the offensive for the occupation of the heights Pontsara, Trestenik and Kreda, which was to take place within the following days. The IV Infantry Brigade was also ordered to plan a similar operation against heights Talik and Vernik, on the defile that led to Biglista, as well as against heights Golina and Lokvat in the Pyxou peninsula.

The IX Division launched the offensive in the morning of November 1. By the evening of November 7, it had completed the occupation of the border line and had reached the line Deska height-Kiafa height-mount Grammos-Koromilies height-Pontsara village-Trestenik height-Kapestitsa village.

During the same period, the Italian reaction in the sector of the IX Division was mainly confined to the heavy bombing of various strategic positions and inhabited areas, and had no significant results.

The IV Infantry Brigade also launched its offensive at 0700 hrs, on November 1. Despite the adverse weather conditions, the rough terrain and the persistent resistance by the Italians, by that afternoon the Division had managed to seize the heights Talik-Vernik-Gremnia-Golina and Lokvat and to cause the enemy grave casualties. The Italian attempts to recapture the heights, during the two following days, came to no avail.

On November 4, by proposal of the C' Army Corps, the IV Infantry Brigade was reorganised into a division, under the name XV Infantry Division.

On the following day, November 5, after a fierce struggle, the XV Division managed to seize the heights directly east of the villages Biglista-Bitinska and it aligned its forces with the troops of the IX Division by the eastern bank of Devolis river. The strong support and the accurate fire of its artillery were largely instrumental in the success of this effort.

The Italians resisted with extreme vigour. All officers and soldiers of the escort artillery were killed beside their guns. Thirteen men including 2 officers were taken prisoners, and 6 mortars, 4 escort guns, 7 heavy and 25 light machine guns were captured.

After this crushing defeat, the Italians withdrew to the west of Devolis river, leaving behind only a few light screening forces east of the river. After that, the IX and XV Divisions suspended their offensive operations, in order to prepare the offensive against Morova mountain, in accordance with the intentions and instructions of the Army General Staff.

The IX Division had very few casualties in the above mentioned operations. The verified casualties of the XV Division were 1 officer and 20 soldiers killed in action, 8 officers and 128 soldiers wounded and 6 soldiers missing in action.

The Italians had a very high percentage of dead and wounded, but the exact figures are unknown. The prisoners were 10 officers and 107 soldiers, including 2 Albanians.


## *A General Review of the Events until 13 November 1940*


**85.**    The first part of this epitome refers to the political-military events that preceded the outbreak of the Greek - Italian War and, also, to the operations in Epirus and North-western Macedonia from 28 October to 13 November 1940.

The Spring of 1939 constituted the starting point for the above events. It was the time, during which, the Italian troops seized Albania and the expansionist aspirations of Mussolini were brought to light.

From that time onwards, the political and military balance in the Balkans was disturbed and the existing Balkan Pact was gradually invalidated.

**86.** Greece, situated in the area which had been the target of the Italian expansionist policy and strongly determined to remain neutral and free, did not hesitate to oppose Italy. Throughout the eighteen month period of threats, provocation and acts of violence committed by fascist Italy against it, Greece, wishing to avoid war strove hard towards that end, under the guise of apparent composure. At the same time, it took all the necessary military measures and continued to develop the national spirit.

Thus, Greece succeeded in its attempt to balance the situation during the first period, despite the surprise of the Italian assault as regards the timing, and was able to take the initiative in the events to come.

There were three factors, which mainly contributed to the success of the Greek arms.

Firstly, the high morale of the Greek Army and the entire Greek People, who defended themselves in the face of unjustified and unprovoked attack.

Secondly, the impeccable staff preparation, clarity and simplicity demonstrated by the war plans of the country. This had become obvious since the beginning of the war, when the whole war mechanism was automatically put into action, in the early hours of 28 October 1940, by means of a simple and laconic message of the Army General Staff.

Thirdly, the fact that the Italian leadership had underestimated the degree of preparation and readiness for war and the high morale of the Greek armed forces as well as their officers' professionalism.

**87.** During their offensive against Greece, the Italians had applied strong pressure against the Greek forces in Epirus and Pindos and had maintained a defensive stand in the area of North-western Macedonia.

In the Epirus front, the VIII Division succeeded in its effort to hold back the enemy and was able to crush the repeated forceful attacks. The Sector of Thesprotia was the only exception. In the face of the unquestionable superiority of the Italians, the Greek troops in that area were forced to withdraw as far back as the river Acheron. However, after receiving reinforcements, they were able to regain control of the area of Kalamas river as far as Igoumenitsa.

In the Pindos Sector, the Greek forces were also forced to withdraw far back, due to the overpowering superiority of the enemy. Thus, the Italians managed to infiltrate the area at great speed, reaching as far as Vovousa, threatening to envelop the Greek forces in Epirus from the east. However, the hasty concentration of all available forces near Pindos, served to close the gap and safeguard the area of Elea-Kalamas from the Northeast. Furthermore, after their successful defensive action in Epirus, the Greek forces managed to assume offensive action in order to destroy the Italian pocket.

To Thessalon

To Lariss

CES AT T
1940

3⁵  km
ber 1940

ber 1940

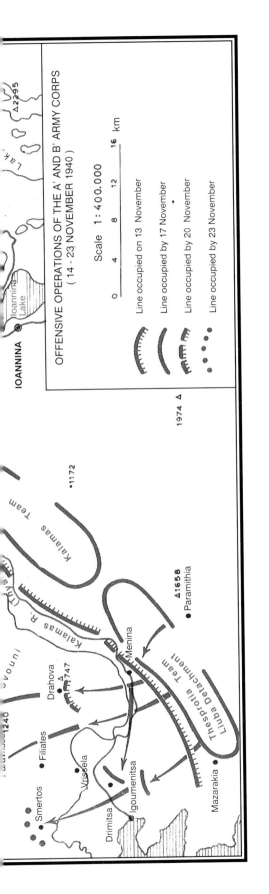

OFFENSIVE OPERATIONS OF THE A' AND B' ARMY CORPS
( 14 - 23 NOVEMBER 1940 )

Scale 1 : 400.000

0     4     8     12     16   km

Line occupied on 13 November

Line occupied by 17 November

Line occupied by 20 November

Line occupied by 23 November

IOANNINA

Ioannina
Lake

Δ2295

Lak

1974 Δ

•1172

Kalamas Team

Δ1658
• Paramithia

Kalamas R.

Menina

Drahova
Δ747

Thesprotia Team

Liuba Detachment

1240

Svouni

• Filiates

Smertos

• Vrissela

Drimitsa

Igoumenitsa

Mazarakia

By November 13, the Greek forces in Epirus and Pindos had regained possession of the greatest part of the national territory. In North-western Macedonia, they had occupied significant territorial points beyond the borders and were ready to launch an attack and occupy the mountain range of Morova and the road junction of Koritsa.

The Italian plan of operations had already been frustrated. Since the beginning of the operations the Italian infiltration of Pindos had not been supported with sufficient forces, even after the first successes. Thus, the threat to envelop and cut off the Greek forces of Pindos was halted and finally cancelled. The Italian Army had turned to the defensive on the whole.

The fighting spirit of all Greek forces, including both those who were fighting against the agressors as well as those who were on the move towards the front, soared, while the morale of the Italians collapsed.

**88.** The struggle in this period, is marked by the following essential facts concerning the Greek Fighters:

-It was the first time that the Greek Army, with its limited means for defence, confronted an Army of a great European power which was armed with all the up-to-date means and in particular tanks and a powerful airforce.

-The troops taking part in the fighting, except for the few Greek Army units that had been mobilised before the beginning of war, consisted of a large number of other units which were mobilised after the declaration of war. These were hastily transferred to the front, following co-ordinated night marches that covered distances ranging from 250 to 400 kms. On the contrary, the Italian divisions had been mobilised and completed, regarding the manpower and supplies, long before the declaration of war.

-During their struggle in the Sector of Pindos, the Greek troops encountered great difficulties, regarding the resupply of food and ammunition. The units that had been hastily advanced to the area immediately after their mobilisation, lacked the necessary number of pack animals or any other means of transport.

Motor vehicles for the resupply of the troops could only advance as far as Nestori, Morphi, Doutsiko and Metsovo. Immediately after the first rains in November, the roads to Nestori and Doutsikon were rendered uncarriageable. Furthermore, the mountain region of Pindos, already poor in resources, had suffered such looting by the Italians that, after it was retaken by the Greek forces, the provisioning for its inhabitants became a necessity.

Among the steps taken, in the attempt to resolve the resupply difficulties of the troops, was the decision to use groups of the local inhabitants including women and children to that end. They all volunteered spontaneously and carried the loads on their shoulders, crossing through areas that were inaccessible, under extremely adverse weather conditions. Thus, the people of Pindos presented the fighters with a brilliant example of patriotism and strong sense of duty. The rationing of the food for the Greek troops in that area, had almost become the norm, while on many occasions even this was not possible.

**89.** During the same period, the concentration of the mobilised Greek troops was conducted and was orderly and uninterrupted, despite the intense effort of the Italian Airforce to impede it.

In total, the forces oriented towards the Albanian Theatre of Operations on November 13, comprised 11 Infantry divisions, 1 Cavalry division, 2 Infantry brigades and 1 Cavalry brigade, the strength of which, including the non-divisional units, amounted to approximately 232,000 men, 556 guns and about 100,000 pack animals.

During the same period, the concentration of forces in the Bulgarian Theatre of Operations was conducted. These forces comprised the VI, VII, XII and XIV Divisions and the VII Infantry Brigade, with a total strength of 57,000 men and about 20,000 pack animals.

The V Division (Crete), that comprised 13,000 men and approximately 4,500 pack animals, was ordered to transfer its forces by sea and to disembark at Thessaloniki, as an additional reserve of the Commander-in-chief.

In total, the above Greek forces amounted to approximately 300,000 men and 125,000 pack animals.

**90.** The Italian forces in Albania were reinforced, during the same period, with the following units:

-The 47th 'Bari' Division, under the command of General Giacone, that landed in Avlonas during the period of 1 to 3 November and immediately began to transfer its forces to the area of Koritsa, by motorised vehicles.

-The 37th 'Modena' Division, under the command of General Giovanni Mali, that had landed in Avlonas, by November 11, and concentrated its forces in the area of Premeti.

-The 2nd Alpine Division, under the command of General Hugo Santovito, that landed in Avlonas on November 8 and moved immediately to the area of Darza-Koritsa.

-The 1st Bersaglieri Regiment, that landed in Avlonas on November 2 and was transferred to the Pindos Sector.

-The 2nd Bersaglieri Regiment, that landed in Avlonas in the beginning of November and transferred its forces to the area of Elea, by the beginning of November.

-The 4th Bersaglieri Regiment, that was transferred to Koritsa in the beginning of November.

-The 8th Alpine Regiment, that was transferred by air, on November 12 (the two battalions) and advanced to the area of Koritsa.

In total, the Italian forces in Albania on November 13, comprised a Group of Armies, under the command of General Soddu, comprising:

-The 9th Field army (General Nassi), that was deployed opposite the front of Pindos and North-western Macedonia and included 5 Infantry divisions, 2 divisions and 1 Alpine regiment, and 2 Bersaglieri regiments.

-The 11th Field army, (General Gelozzo), that was deployed opposite the front of Epirus and included 3 Infantry divisions, 1 armoured division, 1 Cavalry division and 1 Bersaglieri regiment.

The total strength of the above Italian Group of Armies amounted to approximately 240 - 250,000 men.

# PART TWO

# THE SECOND AND THIRD PERIODS OF THE GREEK - ITALIAN WAR

(November 14 - March 26, 1941)

## CHAPTER III

# THE GREEK COUNTER-ATTACK AND THE ADVANCE OF THE ARMY ON THE NORTHERN EPIRUS TERRITORY

## (November 14, 1940 until January 6, 1941)

*Intentions of the General Headquarters regarding Future Operations*
(Sketch-map no. 8)

**91.** During the first period of war and after the containment of the Italian offensive and the favourable outcome of the operations conducted by the Greek Army, the General Headquarters began to examine the question of the line which would have to be occupied and secured before the advent of winter, whereupon serious resupply difficulties were bound to occur. Various solutions were considered to that effect. In the end, the decision taken was to move all Greek forces west of the Pindos mountain bulk and to secure their resupply by using the carriage road of Koritsa-Erseka-Mertzani-Ioannina.

This solution was selected, because it would greatly facilitate the resupply of the forces allocated to the mountainous areas. Moreover, it presented an additional advantage, i.e. the capacity to transport troops from one part of the Theatre of Operations to the other rapidly, as compared to the long stretch of road, used up until then, that travelled through Koritsa-Kastoria-Grevena-Kalambaka-Metsovo-Ioannina-Elea.

**92.** In order to implement the above intensions of the High Command, by November 13, 1940, the Greek forces successfully accomblished the advancement and the strategic concentration so as to take on, as of November 14, large scale offensive operations. The objective of these operations was to repulse the intruder beyond the borders and to occupy the mountain bulk of Morova and the road junction of Koritsa.

The general deployment of the Greek forces in the Albanian Theatre of Operations on November 13, the eve of the Greek counter-attack, was the following:

In the area of Epirus: The A' Army Corps, with the VIII Division and the Cavalry Division, in contact with the enemy and the II Division, moving towards the zone of operations, via Metsovo.

In the area of Pindos: The B' Army Corps with the I Division, the V Infantry Brigade and the Cavalry Brigade.

In North-western Macedonia: The C' Army Corps, with the IX, X and XV Infantry Divisions.

The forces of Pindos and North-western Macedonia were under the command of the Western Macedonia Field Army Section (WMFAS). In addition, the latter had, as reserves, close to the area of the front, the XI Infantry Division, which, as of November 14, had been placed under the command of Major General of the Reserve Nikolaos Tsipouras, and the XIII Infantry Division which, as of November 3, had began to move from Alexandroupolis towards the Albanian Theatre of Operations.

The General Reserves of the Commander in Chief: The III Division which, as of November 7, had been placed under the command of Major General Georgios Bakos and was moving towards the area of Arta-Philippiada, the IV Division and the XVI Infantry Brigade, that were concentrating their forces in the area Trikala-Kalambaka-Koutsoufliani, the XVII Division, that was concentrating its forces in the area of Kozani and the V Division in the area of Thessaloniki.

**93.** The above manoeuvre and the general disposition of the Greek forces in the Albanian Theatre of Operations provided the basis for the final orders of the Commander in chief. The orders were issued to the A' Army Corps and the WMFAS, on November 12, 1940. They defined the objective of the operations that were to follow, which was to secure the free use of the road artery Koritsa-Erseka-Mertzani or at least to prevent the free passage of the enemy forces. The abovementioned two strategic formations were assigned the following missions:

-The A' Army Corps was assigned to act in the general direction Ioannina-Tepeleni and to provide wide coverage to the area of Mertzani. If unable to accomplish the above, it was to confine its activity to the task of consolidating the free use of the Hani Bourazani- Konitsa road.

-The WMFAS (B' and C' Army Corps), after the occupation of the mountain bulk of Morova and if according to its estimate, the conditions were favourable, following orders of the General Headquarters was to advance further, as deep as possible, in order to block off, the northern and western routes towards the plain of Koritsa, at least as far as lake Maliki. Further to the south, the WMFAS had been assigned to reach the carriage road that led towards Erseka or at least to place that road under its control by power of fire. Further advance of the forces to the west would be ordered once conditions were assessed as favourable.

-The left flank of the B' Army Corps, would assist the A' Army Corps from the right, by operating in the direction of Leskoviki.

### The A' Army Corps Operations in Epirus
### (14 to 23 November 1940)
(Sketch-map no. 9)

**94.**   On the evening of November 13, the A' Army Corps comprised the VIII and II Infantry Divisions as well as the Cavalry Division. As mentioned previously, the VIII Division and the Cavalry Division were in contact with the enemy, while the II Division was moving towards the zone of operations and it was estimated that its units would be able to enter into action within 3 to 4 days.

In order to accomplish its mission, the A' Army Corps ordered:

-Offensive action by the VIII Division, which would direct the bulk of its forces towards Kakavia and concurrently secure the occupied area. In parallel, the advance of the division's left flank towards the coastal sector, was also ordered so as to restore the integrity of the national territory.

-Converging action by the Cavalry Division in conjunction with the right flank of the VIII Division towards the road junction of Mertzani, in anticipation that the II Division would take over the action of the VIII Division within a short period of time.

**95.**   The VIII Division which, until November 12, had been operating as an independent large unit, was reinforced with the 39th Evzones Regiment of the II Division, and the 40th Evzones Regiment of the III Division and had formed three teams: the Team of Thesprotia, (7 Infantry battalions, 3 Cavalry companies and 4 batteries), under the command of Major General Nikolaos Liubas, the Team of Kalamas, (6 Infantry battalions, 1 Machine-gun battalion and 3 and 1/2 batteries), under the command of Colonel Dimitrios Yiatzis and the Team of Negrades, (8 Infantry battalions and 10 batteries) under the command of Colonel Georgios Dres.

The Italian forces deployed opposite the Divisional front, were the following:

-Opposite the team of Thesprotia, in the area between the sea and Keramitsa (not included) were the 'Siena' Division (except for one regiment and an artillery battalion), the 3rd Grenadieri Regiment, the 6th Cavalry Regiment and 2 Albanian irregulars corps (approximately 600 men).

-Opposite the rest of the Divisional front were the 'Ferrara' Division, that was additionally reinforced with the 2nd Bersaglieri Regiment, the 'Centaurs' Armoured Division and one regiment from the 'Siena' Division.

The VIII Division commenced the assault in the morning of November 14. By the evening of November 16, following a hard three-day fight, it managed, using the teams of Kalamas and Negrades, to seize the line that lay beside the villages of Ano Lavdani -Doliana-Mavrovouni and to take a large number of prisoners. An enemy counter-attack with tanks, in the area of Mavrovouni, was contained by the accurate fire of the Greek artillery.

In the coastal sector there was no significant progress to be recorded. An attempt on the part of the Thesprotia Team to break through the area at the lower flow of Kalamas river failed, mainly due to the severe bombardment by the enemy airforce.

**96.** On November 13, the Cavalry Division that had been reinforced with the 4th Infantry Regiment of the I Division, was in contact with the enemy at Prophitis Elias of Konitsa-Itia-Lithari, which was occupied by the 9th Alpine Regiment and the 139th Regiment of the 'Bari' Division. On November 14 and 15, reconnaissance operations of the area were conducted and an exchange of heavy artillery and mortar fire took place with heavy casualties on the Greek side. In the night of November 15 /16, a regiment of the Cavalry Division operated in the direction of Itia, so as to reinforce the effort of the I Division of the B' Army Corps which was operating on the right flank of the Cavalry Division.

On November 16, reconnaissance operations of the Cavalry Division revealed that the town of Konitsa had been deserted and that most of it had been set on fire. Division sections (3rd Cavalry Regiment and 4th Infantry Regiment) entered the town without delay and advanced westwards for about 3 kilometres. At that point they interrupted their advance, because of the continuous and vigorous bombardment by the enemy artillery and airforce.

**97.** In the meantime, on November 15, the General Headquarters ordered the A' Army Corps to accelerate the pace of the attack and to secure, as soon as possible, the passage of Kakavia and the junction of Mertzani. On the following day, with another order, the General Headquarters once again stressed that the Corps ought to increase its activitiy and ordered the advance of the III Division from the area of Arta to the south of Ioannina.

Then, as of the night of November 16/17, the A' Army Corps placed the 39th Regiment of the Negrades Team under the II Division and it ordered the Division to begin operations in the morning of November 17, in order to continue the offensive, that had been commenced by the VIII

Division towards the junction of Merdzani. At the same time, it placed the Team of Thesprotia (hereon referred to as the Liuba Detachment) under its command and ordered it to cross the river Kalamas and continue its offensive action, with the bulk of its forces towards Kotsika-Aghii Saranda and, with a group of two battalions and the necessary artillery, in the direction of Menina-Keramitsa-Tsamandas, so as to secure the liaison with the VIII Division.

The VIII Division was to continue its offensive effort, with the Team of Kalamas, in the direction of Kakavia-Bourato and, with the remaining forces of the Negrades Team, in the direction of Doliana-Vissani-Drymades.

On the basis of the above missions, as of November 17, the offensive operations óf the A' Army Corps continued throughout the entire front.

**98.** In the sector of Thesprotia, in the evening of November 18, the Liuba Detachment, with courage and determination, forced the enemy to withdraw to the north of Kalamas river. During their withdrawal, the Italians set fire to the town of Igoumenitsa and killed three notables.

On November 19, Detachment troops constructed an improvised bridge across the river Kalamas in the area of Menina and in the following morning began to move towards the height of Megali Rahi (height 861) which they seized on November 23, in the evening.

At the lower flow of Kalamas (north of Igoumenitsa), there was a delay in the advancement of bridge construction equipment, because of the lack of wheeled vehicles and the adverse weather conditions. Consequently, the bridging of the river Kalamas, in the area, was carried out on the night of November 22 to 23. As of the next day, the Detachment troops resumed their offensive effort in the area north of the river and, by that evening, had managed to occupy the line fixed by the villages of Smerto and Paravryso, forcing the Italians to withdraw to the frontierline.

**99.** In the sector of the VIII Division, on the outbreak of the offensive of the Greek troops in the morning of November 17, the enemy reacted with a severe bombardment of long duration, against the entire area of the Divisional front. The enemy resisted with vigour and thus, the attack of the VIII Division recorded but little success during that day.

On the following day, the offensive was resumed with greater intensity. Despite the resistance of the enemy and incessant and fierce counter-attacks, with infantry troops and tanks, on November 20 after close combat, the VIII Division managed to occupy the town of Vissani and its westerly heights. During the struggle, the Commander of the Delvinaki Battalion, Major Tzanis Alevizatos, was killed on the battlefield, while fighting at the front line.

On November 21, the height 597 south-west of the Hani Delvinaki defile was seized and many Italians were taken prisoners. Successive Italian counter-attacks to recover the height 597, during that day as well as on the next, were destined to fail with many losses for the Italians.

After these events, the Italians withdrew from the Hani Delvinaki defile on the night of November 21 to 22, moving towards Kakavia so as to occupy and organise a new line near the borders. The VIII Division troops continued their offensive efforts during the next two days and, in the evening of November 23, managed to fully occupy the western exit of Hani Bourazani defile. During this struggle, the Commander of the 'Ferrara' Division came close to being captured and was forced to abandon his vehicle and retreat on foot.

**100.** In the evening of November 16, the II Division concentrated its forces in the area of the villages Kipoi-Elati, east of Kalpaki. The Division troops along with the pack animals arrived there from the area of Kalambaka-Volos, after a continuous march under adverse weather and road conditions, all extremely worn out, to such an extent that the pack animals were no longer able to support their loads. Nevertheless, the morale of the troops remained high. Thus, on November 17, only the 39th Regiment of the Negrades Team, that had been placed under the II Division since that date, was operating whereas in the night of November 17 to 18, the 3rd Infantry Regiment of the above Division also entered into the action.

The Division, continuing its offensive, crossed the river Gormos, moved rapidly towards the Northwest and on November 19, after a severe fight, managed to seize the village of Agios Kosmas and the area around it. On the following day, despite the stubborn resistance of the enemy and the bombardment of its airforce, Division troops managed to break through the area and advance towards Aidonochori, forcing the Italians to retreat in disarray, abandoning a multitude of war supplies on site. At the same time, other sections of the Division seized the village of Drymades, without any resistance.

The Division exploited this success at once and by November 23, it had reached the frontier line and deployed its forces there.

**101.** The Cavalry Division also continued its offensive. On November 20, it arrived at the bridge of Bourazani, and discovered that it had been destroyed by the Italians

On the next day, continuing its offensive, it seized the village of Melissopetra and the vicinity after engaging in close combat, and forwarded its troops towards the bridge of Mertzani, in order to cut off the Italian defenders.

In the night of November 21 to 22, Division troops forded the river Sarandaporos (the enemy had already destroyed the Mertzani bridge at Sarandaporos and the Mesogefyra at Aoos river) moved towards the Northwest and on 23 November seized the village Tsarsova and the area of Randachova west of Leskoviki. On the same day, the bridge of Bourazani was restored and thus the motor vehicle communication between Ioannina and Konitsa was restored.

102. Following the above successes of the Greek forces, the enemy withdrew about 10 kilometres to the east of Premeti, to a new line of defence that extended from the snow-covered northern slopes of Nemertska mountain, along the western bang of the river Legatitsa to Frasseri, just before it.

Thus, after a fierce ten-day struggle, the A' Army Corps managed to repulse the invaders beyond the borders and succeeded in restoring the integrity of the national territory, due to the unequalled bravery and sacrifice on the part of its worthy combatants.

The losses were extremely numerous on both sides. On the Greek side, the casualties amounted to more than 600 dead and wounded. Most of them from the VIII Division. On the Italian side, the exact number of casualties, as regards the dead and wounded, is unknown, more than 950 officers and soldiers were taken prisoners.

### The B' Army Corps Operations in the area of Pindos
### (14 to 23 November 1940)
### (Sketch-map no. 9)

103. The B' Army Corps regarded the assumption of a general offensive by the Greek forces throughout the entire area of the front, as a sequel to its own counter-attack, which had been conducted in the area of Pindos, in order to repulse the Italian forces.

In the evening of November 13, the B' Army Corps, comprised within its zone of operations, the I Infantry Division, the V Infantry Brigade, the Cavalry Brigade and the IX, X and B' Reconnaissance Groups. The continuation of the counter-attack was assigned to the I Division which the B' Army Corps had provided with the V Infantry Brigade, as well as the IX, X and B' Reconnaissance Groups. The Cavalry Brigade retired from action and concentrated its forces in the area of Doutsiko-Samarina, as a reserve for the Army Corps.

**104.** After their defeat in the valley of the river Aoos, the Italians presented a powerful front, on November 14, at the western ridges of the Peklari-Itia-Tzournsko-Lithari pass, that covered the direction towards Konitsa.

In order to break through the position of the front, the I Division had organised two combat teams which were the following:

-The Southern team, that was under the command of Colonel Panaghiotis Spiliotopoulos and was assigned to cover the right flank of the A' Army Corps units, which had been instructed to act towards Mertzani. Furthermore, it was assigned to advance its Cavalry troops towards the Bourazani bridge, so as to cut off the carriage road of Ioannina-Konitsa.

-The Northern Team, that was under the command of Colonel Anastasios Kalis, Commander of the V Infantry Brigade, and was assigned to complete and secure the border line, and, furthermore, to block off, with fire, the transverse road Mertzani-Erseka-Koritsa.

**105.** In the morning of November 14, the I Division commenced its attack and occupied the Batra pass on the Greek Albanian borderline and, further to the south, the frontier line as far as the Ptetsio height. In the southern sector, its troops recorded but little success, due to the vigorous resistance of the enemy.

On the following day, November 15, the Division continued its offensive and, after a fierce battle, seized the Tzournsko height in the southern sector as well as the eastern ridges of the Maria height. In the northern sector, it seized the heights Ptetsio-Batra-Rosdol, on the border line, thus placing the carriage road Mertzani-Erseka-Koritsa under the control of the Division's artillery fire.

In the night of November 15 to 16, the Italians withdrew from the heights of Itia and Lithari and, on the following day, November 16, the Division seized the Kamenik height. There were no other essential changes within its sector.

After the turn of events until November 16, the Commander of the I Division proposed to the B' Army Corps that the bulk of the Division forces be directed westwards, in order to occupy Leskoviki and provide cover to the right flank of the Cavalry Division. The latter had been operating within the zone of responsibility of the A' Army Corps, in the direction of Mertzani. Initially, the B' Army Corps approved the Division. With a new order, however, the Corps informed the Division that the enemy appeared to be withdrawing from the entire area of the front and ordered it to advance its troops towards Leskoviki, Randani and Erseka, as soon as possible.

**106.** Meanwhile, incoming intelligence reported that the enemy was reinforcing its troops in the defile of Tsagoni and in the southern passes of Morova, in the area of Kiafe Kiarit, hence, the WMFAS ordered the B' Army Corps to secure, as of November 18, the area that was under its occupation. Furthermore, to orient all available Corps Forces towards the northern section of its zone of action and to keep them at a state of readiness to move north of Grammos. The blocking off of the road Leskoviki - Koritsa would be secured with fire.

Following the above mentioned, the B' Army Corps suspended its operations towards Leskoviki and issued an order that the saddles and passes along the border line should only be held with light troops, in order to secure the largest possible number of troops towards the northern section of its zone. Thus, the I Division troops, that occupied Erseka on the evening of November 17 and the villages Kiouteza and Borova in the morning of November 18, also withdrew to the border line. However, on November 19, the General Headquarters decided to assign the B' Army Corps with the mission of providing wide covering to the area of Leskoviki from the Northwest and instructed the Corps to co-ordinate its operations with those of the C' Army Corps in the direction of Koritsa. Following that the B' Army Corps notified the I Division that the reasons for the suspension of operations had ceased to exist and ordered the resumption of the Division westwards.

**107.** The offensive of the I Division commenced in the morning of November 21. By that evening, the Division had managed to regain control of the line Kiouteza-Borova-Erseka and, on November 22, it recaptured Leskoviki. Thus, the cross carriage road Leskoviki-Erseka-Koritsa was fully controlled by the Greek forces. During the following day the Division troops mainly dealt with the conduct of reconnaissance and the improvement of their positions.

The repulsion of the Italians beyond the borders into the zone of the B' Army Corps, from Grammos to the junction of the rivers Aoos and Sarandaporos, constituted the epilogue to the battle of Pindos and raised the morale of the struggling Greek troops.

The losses of the enemy were relatively small. The verified casualties on the Greek side amounted to 1 officer killed in action and 3 wounded, and 24 soldiers killed in action and 118 wounded. About 100 Italians were taken prisoners.

**108.** Meanwhile, after the favourable development of the A' and B' Army Corps operations, the General Headquarters issued a set of general guidelines on November 20, defining their future assignments. The A' Army Corps, that had been additionally provided with the III Division, was assigned to occupy the harbour of Agii Saranda and to fully secure the cross road road Kakavia-Agii Saranda. The B' Army Corps was assigned to fully secure the area of Leskoviki.

The accomplishment of the above objectives and the use of the harbour of Agii Saranda would serve to shorten the resupply route Preveza-Frontiers and would facilitate any further operations within the territory of Northern Epirus.

### The Battle of Morova-Ivan and the Occupation of Koritsa by the C' Army Corps (14-23 November 1940)
### (Sketch-map no. 10)

**109.** On the basis of the intentions of the General Headquarters, regarding the assumption of offensive operations for the occupation of the mountain bulk of Morova-Ivan and the junction of Koritsa, the C' Army Corps conducted a series of offensive operations within its zone of responsibility. These were conducted from November 1 to 6, and aimed at securing a suitable base for further operations.

These offensive operations, conducted by the C' Army Corps, were completely successful and enabled its units to improve their positions, by advancing their deployment into the northern-Epirus territory, as far as the eastern ridges of the upper valley of Devolis river.

Meanwhile, on November 5, the General Headquarters ordered the WMFAS to apply, together with the C' Army Corps, as soon as possible, the strongest possible pressure, so as to attain the final objective, the occupation of Koritsa. Subsequently, on November 6, the WMFAS assigned the C' Army Corps its new mission and pointed out the need to assume operations in haste, in order to complete the occupation of the Pyxos peninsula and Morova mountain. The precise moment whereupon the C' Army Corps would commence its offensive was to be determined after the WMFAS had received the relevant proposal of the Corps.

**110.** The naturally strong area of Morova-Ivan covered the road junction of Koritsa and, as of 1939, the entire area had been organised, with particular attention paid to the passes of Tsagoni and Darza. The C' Army Corps, seeking to break through the above area, decided to attack it from the flanks, with the main effort on the left, in the direction of Nestori-Darza-Koritsa. It was seeking thus to avoid any serious involvement in the Tsagoni defile, which, owing to its flat terrain, was suitable for the passage of enemy tanks along the road Koritsa-Tsagoni-Biglista.

manos

To Florina

△ 1386

ria

C'

CORPS

m

The offensive action of the Army Corps had been planned to commence on November 11, with the forces that were already on site, the IX, X and XV Divisions. The idea was, on one hand, to afford the enemy with no time to reinforce its troops and, on the other, to hold the enemy troops in position within their zone, so as to prevent their employment against the fronts of the A' and B' Army Corps in Epirus and Pindos.

The Italian forces that were deployed opposite the C' Army Corps during that period comprised the 49th 'Parma' Division, the 19th 'Venezzia' Division and the 29th 'Piedmonte' Division.

**111.** The WMFAS did not agree with the proposal submitted by the C' Army Corps, by which the date for the commencement of operations had been set on 11 November since it considered that the Army Corps did not have sufficient forces. Thus, it submitted its own proposal to the General Headquarters, requesting the suspension of operations and the timely advance of two additional divisions.

Finally, after a series of repeated contacts with the WMFAS and the C' Army Corps, the General Headquarters fixed November 14 as the date of the attack. Furthermore, it placed the XIII Division, that was concentrating its forces in the area of Andartiko-Vatochori, at the disposal of the WMFAS.

The C' Army Corps, in accordance with its own manoeuvre and in order to secure the surprise, ordered the attack, without any artillery preparation, in the following directions:

-Nestori-Darza-Koritsa, which was the main effort, with the X Division.

-Vratsa-height 1700 (Sveti Atanas)-Koritsa with the IX Division that was obliged to retain a constant liaison between its left flank and the X Division, so as to assist in the occupation of the height 1259 east of Sinitsa-Propa.

-Pyxos-Ivan-Koritsa, along with the XV Division.

**112.** The attack was launched, as authorised, on November 14, at 0630hrs, in the entire area of the C' Army Corps front, which extended from the height of Goubel up to the shores of lake Megali Prespa.

In the southern sector, the X Division sallied forth, as authorised, without artillery preparation and was engaged in action during the whole of that day. By that evening, despite the vigorous enemy resistance, the Division succeeded in penetrating to a depth ranging from 1 to 3 kilometres and seized Bataros height as well as the villages Nikolitse and Vozigrad.

The IX Division, in the middle of the offensive deployment, after a fierce struggle due to the stubborn enemy resistance, advanced to a depth ranging from 2 to 5 kilometres and occupied the west bank of Devolis river by the same evening. On the night of November 14 to 15, the Regiment of the X Division, that was assisting the left flank of the IX Division, was placed under the command of the latter.

In the northern sector, the XV Division also attacked without artillery preparation and, despite the fierce enemy resistance, managed to advance to a depth of approximately four kilometres and occupied the line Bitinska village-Tsernik height-height 1285. In many cases the battle was extremely ferocious and was conducted by bayonet and hand grenade. Many casualties were suffered by the XV Division, amounting to 42 dead and 161 wounded.

The results of the first day of action were regarded as satisfactory by the C' Army Corps, taking into consideration the considerable breadth of the attack front, and the vigorous resistance of the enemy that had been supported by the artillery, mortars and airforce. The WMFAS reported that it had committed its entire strength to the action, and that it was lacking in reserves. Furthermore, it supported the view that in the course of the following day the enemy would be employing motorised vehicles. The WMFAS ordered its forces to continue the attack, by shock action along a narrow front and to support it with all available means of fire.

After the favourable outcome of that first day and upon receiving the WMFAS order, the C' Army Corps, having no time to alter its plans, ordered the continuation of the attack, starting on the morning of November 15, in order to accomplish the set objectives.

**113.** The X Division launched its attack at daybreak on November 15. Despite the fact that it encountered great resistance, it succeeded in completing the occupation of the Bataros height and in seizing the Stavroeides height (two and a half kilometres west of Nikolitse village), which constituted a strong foothold to the south of the Darza pass.

The IX Division, in the centre, began the attack at 0700 hrs and by that evening, after a difficult struggle, succeeded in its effort to seize the heights 1259 and 1271, despite the vigorous resistance and the counter-attacks of the enemy. Furthermore, 11 officers and 250 soldiers were taken prisoners and an abundance of enemy supplies were seized, including 18 guns, 40 machine-guns, 200 pack animals etc.

In the northern sector, the XV Division continued its offensive effort, in order to improve the occupied positions and it managed to repulse local enemy counterattacks.

On the following day, November 16, the C' Army Corps had ordered Divisions X and XV, to increase their activity, in order to accomplish their objectives. The IX Division was ordered to act in the direction of Propa height-Darza pass-height 1878 (Nikolitse pass), so as to support the efforts of the X Division.

**114.** The offensive continued and, the X Division completed on the left flank the occupation of Stavroeides height and occupied height 1827 and Arza village, along with its northern heights.

The IX Division managed to occupy the range of Hepets, after a fierce struggle, and advanced its troops towards the heights 1779 and 1700 (Sveti Atanas).

The XV Division, despite its forceful assault, did not succeed in advancing significantly, because of the vigorous resistance of the enemy forces and the dense barrage of fire by their machine-guns, mortars and artillery.

Thus, on November 16, before nightfall, in the sector of the X and IX Divisions, significant heights, situated at the principal defensive area of the enemy in the Darza pass, had been taken and a serious break was achieved through the enemy's area.

During the course of that same day, prisoner interrogations revealed that a new Italian division, the 53rd 'Arezzo' Infantry Division had entered into action. Thus, the enemy divisions increased in number within the zone of the C' Army Corps, amounting to four.

**115.** After the above mentioned successes and the break through of the hostile position, the WMFAS, on the evening of November 16, ordered the active and daring advance of its units, that would occur mainly from the left, so as to complete the occupation of mount Morova and it placed the XIII Division at the disposal of the C' Army Corps.

The C' Army Corps then, assigned the missions for the next day, as follows:

-The X Division to attack and seize the height 1878.

-The IX Division to conduct its attack in the direction of the Darza-Lotto pass and at the same time, to take action northwards along the ridgeline of mount Morova, in order to threaten the rear area of the enemy and immobilise the enemy forces in that area.

-The XV Division to attack and seize Ivan mountain.

**116.** On the following day, November 17, after a hard fight, the X Division managed to occupy the southern feet of height 1878 and repulsed successive enemy counter-attacks against the heights of Stavroeides and 1827.

The IX Division completed the occupation of the ridgeline of Propa-Sveti Atanas (height 1700), in spite of the repeated counter-attacks of the enemy.

In the north, the XV Division seized villages Motsoritse and Goloberda, after a tough fight, without however managing to advance any further, owing to the natural strong terrain, the existing organised positions and the vigorous resistance of the enemy. There were grave casualties on both sides. The XV Division had 4 officers killed in action and 5 wounded during that day, as well as 79 soldiers killed in action and 280 wounded. The Italian prisoners, that were taken by the Division that same day, were 7 officers and 120 soldiers.

For the operations of the following day, November 18, the C' Army Corps was reinforced by the WMFAS with an Infantry regiment of the IX Division. The C' Army Corps assigned later this regiment to the X Division. In parallel, the Corps ordered the XIII Division to attack with an Infantry regiment detachment in the direction of Kapestitsa-Zeblac, between the IX and XV Divisions.

**117.** On November 18, the IX Division assumed action with an Infantry regiment detachment (the Beyetti Detachment) in the direction of Darza, in order to facilitate the offensive efforts of the X Division, and advanced strong forces towards Drenovo village and further to the north. In parallel, it managed to place the road Erseka-Koritsa, as well as the barracks and the base camp of Koritsa under its artillery fire.

During the same day, in the sectors of Divisions X and XV, there was no significant progress to be recorded, due to the vigorous enemy resistance.

At 0200 hrs, during a torrential rainstorm, the XIII Division Detachment concentrated its forces at its jump off base, south of Kapestitsa village. At 0230 hrs, the Division received an Army Corps order that altered the direction in which the Detachment was to attack and dictated that the latter should move towards the Hotsiste height. This decision was taken by the C' Army Corps, after the intelligence reported an impending retirement of the enemy forces from the line Hotsiste-Tsagoni.

This alteration imposed specific movements, that were conducted during the night under heavy rain, which, weakened the link between the various sections and created a state of disorder and confusion. Only two of the first echelon battalions that belonged to the Detachment were able to gain contact with the enemy. Eventually, however, these were held in position before Hotsiste height and lost all means of contact with the command of both the Detachment and Division. As for the second echelon of the Detachment, in spite of the fact that it was only forced to confront airborne bombing attacks, its troops were overcome with panic and withdrew in a state of total disarray.

Because of this unfortunate event, which, nevertheless, escaped the attention of the enemy, the commander of the XIII Division Detachment was replaced along with the Division commander. The command of the Division was entrusted to Major General Sotirios Moutousis, who had been Artillery Commander of the C' Army Corps up to that point, while the command of the Detachment was assumed by its Deputy commander, Lieutenant Colonel Georgios Kyvelos. After co-ordinating their efforts, the new commands were quick to restore the order and managed to raise the combat effectiveness of the Division troops to a satisfactory level.

118. The prolongation of the operations against the mountain range of Morova-Ivan and the gradual reinforcement of the enemy, forced the WMFAS to successively commit into action the XIII Division between IX and XV Divisions and the XI Division further to the south, between IX and X Divisions.

Meanwhile, since November 11, the General Headquarters had assigned the Commander of the D' Army Corps, Lieutenant General Georgios Kosmas, to the WMFAS. He was provided with the staff required in order to assume command of the left flank of the C' Army Crops, where X and XI Divisions were operating. This new command was named Division Group 'K' (DivGr'K'). The C' Army Corps would be confined to the north of the line Vozigrad-Darza-Bobostitsa (all to the C' AC), with the IX, XIII, and XV Divisions under its command. The resupply of Division Group 'K' would be conducted care of the C' Army Corps.

At the same time, the General Headquarters decided to organise a mobile reserve force for any case of exploitation. On November 14, as the Cavalry Division had been transferred to Epirus, the GH ordered four Reconnaissance groups to concentrate their forces in Plati and to advance in haste to the area of Florina. These comprised the VI, VII, XII and Division groups, that belonged to the Eastern Macedonia Field Army Section (EMFAS) and, as of November 18, were placed at the disposal of the WMFAS.

Finally, the GH gradually advanced part of its reserve forces towards the northern front of the Albanian Theatre of Operations. Thus, the EMFAS was ordered to provide an entire Infantry regiment for the area of Amyndaeo, while the XVII Division advanced to the area of Nestori-Argos Orestiko. On November 20, the division advanced to the area of Ieropigi-Komninades-Mesopotamia, where it was placed at the disposal of the WMFAS, under the binding condition that its use would be subject to GH approval. The V Division had concentrated its forces in the area of

Philotas-Ptolemaida and the XVI Brigade was in the area of Grevena-Kivotos, so that it could be committed to action in the Pindos Sector.

**119.** At 0700 hrs on November 17, Lieutenant General Georgios Kosmas arrived in Kozani, accompanied by a number of staff officers from the Headquarters of the D' Army Corps and two Signal companies. There, he was briefed by the commander of the WMFAS in regard to the tactical situation and the mission of Division Group 'K'. Directly afterwards, he advanced to Kastoria, where he assumed the command of Division Group 'K' (X-XI Divisions).

The Commander of WMFAS arrived in Kastoria almost simultaneously and issued his own orders to the Commanders of the C' Army Corps and Division Group 'K'. Both formations were instructed to continue operations within their respective zones of action, which had been redefined after the formation of Division Group 'K'. Furthermore, he underlined that after the occupation of Morova, any further advance in the plain of Koritsa was conditional on the issue of a WMFAS order.

Division Group 'K' then, ordered the continuation of operations in the general direction Nikolitse-Kamenitsa with the XI Division on the left and the X Division on the right (the main effort), aiming at the occupation of the line Moutke village -1508 height- Sepotista height (1570). Furthermore, in an attempt to keep contact with the enemy, reconnaissance troops were ordered to advance, at least as far as the Erseka-Koritsa road.

Since November 19, Reserve Major General Georgios Dromazos assumed the command of the X Division.

**120.** On November 19 and 20, the Division Group 'K' divisions mainly dealt with improving their positions and advancing some of their troops, in order to prepare for the attack that would be launched on the following day. Patrol units, sent by a detachment of the XI Division, advanced to the left flank of the disposition, as far as the road Erseka-Koritsa, without encountering any resistance on the part of the enemy. In the sector of the C' Army Corps, during the two-day period of November 19 and 20, the IX Division continued its offensive effort under adverse weather conditions and snowfall, in the direction of Darza and the height 1805 (the summit of mount Morova). By evening of November 19, the height 1805 was taken, being indispensable in the effort to complete the occupation of mount Morova. The following day, November 20, because of the adverse weather conditions, the Division did not undertake any important offensive action. However, it succeeded in placing the Bobotista-Darza road under the control of its fire.

The XIII Division seized the Hotsiste height and applied its efforts to the task of reinforcing the antitank protection of the Devolis river valley.

The XV Division improved its occupied positions and kept close contact with the enemy.

**121.** On November 21, the divisions of Division Group 'K' continued their offensive. The XI Division occupied Moutke village and assisted in the occupation of the height 1878. The X Division seized the height 1878 after a hard and stubborn fight. Due to the strong resistance of superior enemy forces, the division failed to occupy the Loto height.

On the same day, the offensive effort of the C' Army Corps continued mainly in the sector of the IX Division, where the western ridges of the heights 1805 and Hotsiste were seized. After being defeated, the enemy withdrew towards the plain of Koritsa. The left flank of the Division continued the pressing towards the Darza pass.

On November 21, the WMFAS issued an order for the continuation of the offensive operations, instructing the C' Army Corps and Division Group 'K' to continue their offensive, in order to complete the occupation of mount Morova and Tsagoni defile.

**122.** After the abovementioned successes of the Greek troops at the front of Morova, the Italians began to withdraw towards the valley of Devolis river on the night of November 21 to 22, so as to avoid encirclement within the plain of Koritsa.

At daybreak on November 22, the divisions of the C' Army Corps resumed their offensive action.

The IX Division occupied the remaining southern shoulders of Tsagoni pass and linked up with the XV Division at Zemlac. Further to the south, the Detachment of Colonel Beyetis, of the same Division, seized the village of Drenovo south-east of Koritsa. At 1745 hrs, detachment troops (the 1st Battalion of the 33rd Regiment and a company from the 1st Battalion of the 27th Regiment) entered the town of Koritsa without encountering any enemy resistance, and the native Greek population expressed to them their enthusiasm with displays of delirium.

By that evening, the Division advanced its outposts west of Koritsa and established its defence on the western feet of mount Morova, on the same level as the XV Division.

The XV Division occupied the pass of Tsagoni and the summit of mount Ivan, where it established its defence.

The XIII Division concentrated its forces in the area south-east of the Tsagoni pass.

Division Group 'K' continued its offensive action westwards on November 22. By nightfall on the same day, it succeeded in occupying the line Moutke village-Kiafe Kiarit height, with the XI Division and the line Kamenitsa-Bobostitsa, with the X Division.

The WMFAS suffered considerable losses in the course of the Morova-Ivan battle. The casualties have been estimated to 34 officers and 590 soldiers killed in action and 82 officers and 2,226 soldiers wounded, even though these numbers are thought to be far lower than the actual ones.

### The New Objectives of the General Headquarters
### (Sketch-map no. 8)

**123.** Since it became evident that the offensive action of the Greek troops was developing favourably in Epirus as well as in the sector of Koritsa, the General Headquarters began to consider the issue of the further continuation of the operations. This consideration was directed towards the two general axes of Ioannina-Avlona and Florina-Koritsa-Elvasan. The development of the operations would be decisively affected by the transportation for their support and by the advent of winter, the mountainous terrain as well as by the adverse weather conditions prevailing in the northern and central sectors, that is to say in the high plateau of Koritsa and the mountain bulks surrounding the valley of Aoos river.

Until then, the A' Army Corps had procured its supplies via the harbour of Preveza, while the B' Army Corps had used the central railway terminals of Kalambaka-Kozani and the C' Army Corps, the towns of Florina and Amyndaeo. From there on, the transportation of supplies to the front-line was conducted by motor vehicles and pack animals. The harbour of Agii Saranda and the cross road Agii Saranda-Kakavia-Merdjani-Leskoviki were critical locations for the support of any future operations due to the fact that the transportation route was bound to be shortened, if use was made of the above locations after managing to have them both secured. This fact assumed even greater importance, given that the motor vehicles of the Greek Army were numerically inadequate, of many different types, and in a bad state of repair. Most of these vehicles had been requisitioned and therefore could not be replaced with new ones from foreign sources and, what is more, there was no reserve stock of spare parts, so as to repair the damages. If used to their full capacity the vehicles were only expected to last as far as the area of the borders.

On the basis of the abovementioned facts, the General Headquarters decided to focus its main effort along the axis Ioannina-Avlonas, without ruling out the additional possibility of exploitation deep inside the northern sector of Koritsa. To that end, the A' and B' Army Corps were reinforced with the III and XI Divisions respectively.

**124.** In general, the manoeuvre of the General Headquarters aimed at:

-Securing the free use of the carriage roads Leskoviki-Koritsa and Kakavia-Agii Saranda, with the mountain bulks of Mali Ger (west of Argyrokastro)-Korie (Northeast of Argyrokastro)-Mali Kokoika (north of Premeti) as the desired objectives.

-Advancing the left flank of the A' AC northwards using the right flank of the entire disposition (C' AC-DivGr 'K') as a strong and secure pivot. The centre (B' AC) was assigned to follow and assist this advance, and also to provide a stable link between the two flanks.

The missions assigned to the Large units of the front were as follows:

-The A' Army Corps would operate in the general direction of Elea-Argyrokastro-Tepeleni-Avlonas, co-ordinating its move with the B' Army Corps on the right.

-The B' Army Corps would operate in the general direction Mertzani-Verati, through the valleys of river Aoos and Apsou (Ouzoun), co-ordinating its action on the right with the A' Army Corps and linking up with the two other flanks of the front (A' AC-WMFAS).

-The WMFAS (C' AC-DivGr'K') would secure the highland of Koritsa from the northern and western directions and apply strong pressure against the enemy forces, in order to engross their attention and detain them, to the advantage of the other Large Units of the front (A'-B' AC). The carriage roads, west of Koritsa, towards Moschopolis - Devolis - Pogradetz sould be the starting points for the respective directions of attack, in order to achieve the deepest possible infiltration. The aim of the promotion north of Pogradetz was to block off that direction and hinder the enemy from moving westwards.

The forces, that remained as general reserves of the Commander in chief of the Army, were the V and XIII Division, the XVI Brigade in North-western Macedonia and the IV Divisions in Epirus.

In the letters of instruction of the Commander in chief, there was no final definition of the objectives so that the commands may display their initiative, in order to take advantage of their successes until the time limit imposed by the onset of winter, when operations would essentially come to a halt.

### The Advance of the A' Army Corps towards the valley of Drinos river
### (November 24-30, 1940)
### (Sketch-map no. 11)

**125.** Since November 24, the A' Army Corps resumed its pursuit of the enemy within the northern Epirus territory. In parallel, it began to orient its units in the general direction of Ioannina-Avlonas, so as to prepare for any further operations, in accordance with the General Headquarters instructions.

In the coastal sector, the Liubas Detachment continued its offensive inside the northern Epirus territory, after having occupied the boundary line north of the village Sayada, on November 25, at the end of a fierce fight. By the evening, on November 26, it had managed to gain contact with the enemy position south of the river Pavla, despite the vigorous counter-action of the Italian Airforce. The latter succeeded in destroying the bridges of Vrysela and Menina on Kalamas river, an action which created considerable difficulties in the resupply of the Detachment troops.

Meanwhile, in order to assist the offensive of the Liubas Detachment, the Military Command of Kerkira had organised, by order of the General Headquarters, a detachment comprising 5 officers and 190 elite troops. This was transported by motor boats and landed at the area of Kato Aetos on November 23, at 0630 hrs. Its mission was to move towards Vangalati, in order to attack the rear area of the enemy. However, instead of acting as instructed, it moved southwards and along the coastline during the day, arriving at Konispolis, where it spent the night. On the following day, it continued to move southwards, in order to link up with the Greek troops that were acting towards the north. However, the Italian troops became aware of its presence and attacked it. The detachment disbanded and the majority of its troops were taken prisoners. Eventually, only 2 officers and 45 soldiers were able to link up forces with the Liubas Detachment.

On November 27, the Liubas Detachment resumed its offensive, continuously pressing the enemy positions and forcing the Italians to withdraw towards the valley of Bistritsa river, in the night of November 27 to 28. The pursuit of the enemy commenced on the following day. By the evening on November 30, the Detachment troops had reached the east bank of Bistritsa river and had established their forces there, in contact with the Italians who were occupying the west bank of the river.

**126.** In the sector of the VIII Division, the Greek troops continued their effort to occupy the defile of Kakavia, which had been organised by the enemy and was strongly occupied by the troops of the Alpine Division.

On November 24, the VIII Division launched an attack, in order to break through the abovementioned pass, but was contained, having encountered the vigorous resistance of the enemy. On November 27, after a fierce fight, in which the scales were constantly wavering between the two sides, the Division managed to occupy the mountain range of the heights 669 and Bourato. Nevertheless, it was not able to hold them, due to the strong resistance of the Italians in conjunction with the severe blizzard that had broken out in the meantime. By November 30, continuing its effort, the Division managed to occupy the line Kakavia village-Bouna forest-height 1672 (Makrykambos), where it consolidated its position.

**127.** As of November 25, the II Division began to act in the direction Drymades-Politsani. On the following day, after occupying the village of Politsani, it proceeded towards a defile of great tactical significance, the Sucha defile, extending over a distance of eight kilometres with a breadth of 200-600 meters and steep slopes on both sides.

In the evening of November 29, the Division managed to occupy the south-western exit of the defile and to establish its forces on the northern heights of Soucha village.

On the night of November 29 to 30, the Italians launched a powerful counter-attack which, nevertheless, was successfully repulsed. The next day, the Italians continued their counter-attacks, supported by their airforce. The struggle was fierce and lasted until the evening hours, whereupon the combat troops of the Division that were on site withdrew towards the entrance of the defile.

The Italian Airforce, with the exception of the units engaged in action, bombed all populated areas of the region, causing the death of more than 30 civilians.

**128.** As of November 21, the III Division, which had been moving towards the zone of operations, was placed at the disposal of the A' Army Corps. On November 23, it had reached the area south of Ioannina, having covered a distance of 350 kilometres with its troops marching under adverse weather conditions. On November 24, the Division was ordered to advance to the area of Doliana in order to commence operations by November 28 in the area south of the Delvinaki-Kakavia-Argyrokastro road.

During the two days November 26 and 27, the Division units continued their advance, in order to seize the positions from which their attack was to be launched, in the area of the villages Pepeli and Boularat. Nevertheless, the troops were not able to reach them in time and thus the attack was launched in the morning of November 30. By that evening, at the end of a fierce struggle, the Division managed to seize the eastern ridges of height 1297 (Kazania) and the southern outskirts of Boularat village.

## *The Advance of the B' Army Corps towards Frasseri*
## *(24-30 November 1940)*
## (Sketch-map no. 12)

**129.** In parallel to the advance of the A' Army Corps towards the valley of river Drinos, the B' Army Corps conducted new efforts, aiming at repulsing the Italians even further inside the northern Epirus territory and to fully secure the road of Mertzani-Leskoviki-Erseka-Koritsa within its zone.

On November 23, the B' Army Corps reinforced the Cavalry Brigade with Reconnaissance Groups B', D' and a pack battery and proceeded to order the speedy concentration of the Brigade in the area of Borova village. The Brigade was assigned to act in the direction of Premeti, in order to assist the operations conducted in the valley of the river Aoos.

The XI Infantry Division and the Cavalry Division, that by order of the General Headquarters had been placed at the disposal of the B' Army Corps, were incorporated in the latter as of November 27 and 28 respectively.

**130.** By November 27, after having seized the eastern ridges of the height 1500 (Mali Piscalit) on November 24 and having improved the positions it was occupying, the I Division resumed its action in the general direction of Mali Piscalit-Mali Kokoika. By the evening of the following day, the Division had completed the occupation of Mali Piscalit height, while some of its troops, that had advanced, entered the village of Gostivisti where they took 48 prisoners and seized 8 guns, 8 machine-guns, hundreds of rifles and other war supplies.

On November 29 and 30 the Division continued its offensive action, but was forced to slow down, owing to the vigorous enemy resistance. The occupation of a height range at the south-east of the Mali Kokoika height constituted its sole achievement during that time.

**131.** The Cavalry Brigade began to move in the direction of Borova-Navosela-Frasseri since the morning of November 25, without waiting to complete the concentration of its forces. By the same evening, it was able to gain contact with the enemy at the south-eastern ridges of the height 1305. However, due to the lateness of the hour it did not take any further action.

On November 26, Brigade troops occupied the height 1305 and the village of Zavalani. During the following days and up until November 30, the Brigade efforted to advance towards Frasseri, but its effort was not successful due to the strong resistance and successive counter-attacks of the enemy against the vulnerable troops of the Cavalry Brigade.

**132.** The V Infantry Brigade operated in parallel with the Cavalry Brigade, further to the north, in the direction of the heights Mali Kelkes-Mali Lires.

On November 27, after a close combat , it managed to occupy the height Mali Kelkes and advanced towards the south-west, as far as the height Kiafe Lires.

On the following day, November 28, it managed to mop up the area of the Mali Kelkes height and advanced as far as Apsos river. At the same time, it also directed its action towards the village of Frasseri, but the effort did not succeed due to the counter-action of the enemy forces that held their ground strongly at the occupied heights around the village.

The Brigade troops, that occupied the height of Kiafe Lires, remained at their positions awaiting their relief by the XI Division which, in the meantime, had been incorporated in the B' army Corps and had been assigned to pass through the lines of the V Brigade and act in the direction of the Kiafe Lires height. However, due to the favourable development of the operations within the zone of the V Brigade, the B' Army Corps issued a new order, by which the V Brigade was to continue to occupy its sector, while the XI Division was to remain as a reserve in the area of the Mali Randomit height. The Division was instructed to place a single Infantry regiment at the disposal of the Cavalry Brigade, in order to enable the latter to continue its action towards Frasseri.

**133.** The Cavalry Division had remained under the command of the A' Army Corps until November 27 and was operating in its right flank, closely liaising with the B' Army Corps. During this period, it managed to advance as far as Legatitsa river, where it ascertained that the enemy was firmly holding its ground with strong forces in the area of the west bank. On the following day, it managed to cross the river and moved towards Premeti.

By November 30, at the end of a stubborn struggle, the Division troops reached the eastern bank of Aoos river. Their attempt to move towards the western bank failed, due to the strong counter-action of the enemy, but they were able to ascertain that the Italians had begun to abandon Premeti and were in the process of withdrawing towards Klissoura.

*The  WMFAS (C'AC-DivGr'K') Operations,*
*for the complete  securing of the Highplateau of Koritsa*
(24-30 November, 1940)
(Sketch-map no. 12)

**134.** By order no. 13342 of the General Headquarters, issued to the WMFAS on November 22, the following was decided:

'Following my order No. 13174/1-11-40, continue your effort with intensity according to your judgement, aiming at blocking off the routes towards Koritsa highplateau and the carriage road Koritsa-Leskoviki, from the West and the North, and as far deeper as you can reach, in order to achieve safe and free use of the said road.'

The WMFAS, in order to relieve its troops that had been overcome with fatigue, decided to suspend its operations temporarily and raised objections to that effect against the order of the General Headquarters. Subsequently, the General Headquarters issued the following supplementary order:

'The continuation of the operations for the accomplishment of the order 13342/22/11 is to be sought after in haste. We acknowledge the fatigue of our troops, however, the enemy's condition is worse. It is not to our advantage to allow the enemy to reorganise and redeploy its forces. Each and every day that goes by actually serves to aggravate rather than facilitate your efforts. You must stress the above to the commanders of your units and demand positive results'.

**135.** On November 23, the WMFAS issued its own operation instructions, which comprised the following main points:

- During the first phase:  The C' Army Corps was to secure the mountain bulk of Ivan, the defile of Tsagoni and the section of Morova that was included within its zone. Simultaneously, it would keep contact with the enemy towards the arterial roads that ran along the lakes Maliki and Prespa Major. Division Group 'K' was assigned to occupy Kiafe Kiarit defile, hold its ground firmly at that position and cover the left flank of the C' Army Corps. Furthermore, it was to keep contact with the enemy in the directions of Moschopolis and Ostravitsa. The B' Army Corps was assigned to cover Leskoviki from the northwest, in close cooperation with the Cavalry Division, and was to link up with Division Group 'K'.

- During the second phase:  The C' Army Corps was to advance its deployment between lakes Megali Prespa and Maliki, as far as the northern exits of the defiles, and was ordered to hold its ground firmly inside the defile of Devolis river, as far as Prespa (Tsagoni). Division Group 'K' and the B' Army Corps were to continue and consolidate the efforts of the first phase.

- During the third phase: The C' Army Corps was to advance its disposition between lakes Achris and Maliki, as far as the defile of Devolis river as far as Tresova, with a strong bridgehead in the area of Pogradetz. Division Group 'K' was to cover the left flank of the C' Army Corps, while the B' Army Corps would provide full covering to the arterial road Melissopetra-Erseka-Koritsa within its zone.

**136.** The C' Army Corps assigned the IX and XIII Divisions with the offensive operations, in order to widely secure the highplateau of Koritsa from the Northwest. The XV Division was assigned to secure the Tsagoni defile and the mountain bulk of Ivan.

The IX Division commenced its action on November 24, in order to occupy the heights that lay to the Northwest of lake Maliki. By November 26 its troops had reached the line of the villages Tresova and Tseresniko without encountering any serious resistance of the enemy.

On the following day the Division resumed its offensive effort. After having successively seized the heights 1434 and 1652, it launched an attack against the height 1548 and managed to seize the latter on November 29, despite the stubborn resistance of the enemy. The enemy abandoned on the battlefield 55 killed in action and 120 wounded, including 10 officers.

On November 30, the Division had planned to operate towards the height 1532, but due to heavy snowfalls, this operation was not carried out.

The XIII Division commenced its offensive action on November 25. By that evening, the saddle of Grambotitsa was occupied. On the following day Division troops shifted their action to the west of the saddle, in order to link up with the IX Division and seized the height 1210. On November 27 and 28, the Division focused its activity on the effort to improve its positions and prepare its troops for the attack against the height 1292 which towered over the area as far as Pogradetz and had been powerfully organised.

The attack against the height 1292 commenced in the morning of November 29, without the required coordination between the artillery fire and the movement of the attacking infantry, mainly due to the inactivity of the latter. This had as a result the slow down of the entire operation and the seizure of the height in the morning of the following day. The fall of the height 1292 had a decisive effect on the Italians defending at Pogradetz who began to evacuate their defensive area as far as lake Achris and were in the process of withdrawing towards Elvasan. Reconnaissance troops of the C' Army Corps entered Pogradetz at 1000 hrs and occupied the town.

**137.** The advance of Division Group 'K' westwards, began in parallel with the advance of the C' Army Corps to the area Northwest of Koritsa.

On November 24, the X Division occupied Moschopolis and, in the course of the following day, it proceeded to advance towards the North-western heights, where it established its defence by order of Division Group 'K' . On November 26 and 27, the necessary rearrangements were conducted on the left flank of the Division, in order to facilitate the extension of its zone of action towards the left, that would occur after the assignment of the IX Division to the B' Army Corps. As of November 28, the offensive was resumed, and, by November 30, the line Maskoulori height-Pounemira village- Krousiva height had been occupied.

By November 25, while operating on the left flank of the X Division, the XI Division had managed to occupy the line Treska village-height 1843-Kourora height, having encountered no resistance on the part of the enemy, where it established its defence, having been assigned to cover the directions from Ostravitsa and Apsos valley to Belavonda and Koritsa. As of November 27, it was placed under the command of the B' Army Corps.

**138.** The operations conducted by the C' Army Corps and Division Group 'K' up until November 30, were entirely successful and as a result the Greek forces advanced as far as the eastern slopes of mount Kamia. Thus, the area of Koritsa was fully secured.

Following a request of the C' Army Corps, the XVII Division was assigned to it as of November 27. The XVII Division, which had just arrived at the area of Mesopotamia, was ordered by the C' Army Corps to gradually relieve the XIII Division, that after been relieved would act as a reserve of the General Headquarters.

The relief of the XIII Division was considered necessary, in order to allow its units sufficient time to rest and re-group, due to the weaknesses they had displayed during the most recent operations. These weaknesses being mainly the result of lack of professionlly competent senior and regular junior officers, did not fail to affect the cohesion of the Division, despite the active and continuous presence of its Commander on the field of action and notwithstanding the success of the Division during the battle of height 1292-Pogradetz.

## The Occupation of Agii Saranda and Argyrokastro
## (1-12 December 1940)
### (Sketch-map no. 11)

**139.** At the end of November 1940 and after a series of fierce battles, the A' Army Corps, that had been advancing in the direction of the Ioannina-Avlonas axis, deployed its forces along an almost 65 Km long front. This front extended from the shores of the Adriatic sea right up to the river Aoos.

In the coastal sector, the Lioubas Detachment operated in two directions. The left flank (Team of Colonel Konstantinos Papadopoulos) was able to reach Bistritsas river right before the town of Agii Saranda, while the right flank (Team of Colonel Panaghiotis Raftopoulos) managed to occupy the inaccessible bulk of the Tsamandas mountains.

The III Division, that had been committed to the action as of November 28, took over the sector that lay south of the carriage road Delvinaki-Kakavia and as far as the mountains of Tsamandas.

The VIII Division conducted a series of fierce battles, which lasted ten days, against the enemy forces occupying the area of Kakavia pass-Bourato, but eventually failed to break down their resistance.

The II Division operated on the right flank of the Army Corps and on either side of the rocky, steep and inaccessible mountain range of Nemertska, having placed the bulk of its forces on the north-eastern side of the Soucha defile.

**140.** As of December 1, the A' Army Corps resumed its advance within the territory of Northern Epirus, according to the instructions of the General Headquarters.

From December 1 to 4, the left flank (Papadopoulos Team) of the Liubas Detachment dealt with the reinforcement of its occupied positions located south-east of river Bistritsas. Furthermore, it directed its efforts towards the re-organisation of its troops. As of December 1, the right flank (Raftopoulos Team) was placed under the command of the III Division, which acted on the east of the Detachment. By the morning of December 4, the latter Team had managed to cross the upper valley of Bistritsas river and had succeeded in enveloping the enemy area facing the Detachment. Subsequently, the Italians withdrew to the Northwest on the night of December 4 to 5, after having destroyed the bridge in that area. The withdrawal was perceived on the morning of December 5, whereupon a new improvised bridge was constructed with the abandoned inflatable boat material and with the additional assistance of the local inhabitants. After the completion of the bridge, light troops belonging to the Liubas Detachment used it to cross the Bistritsas river. Further to the south, they forded the river at Mesopotamia village and proceeded to seize the heights which secured the control of the cross road Agii Saranda-Delvino.

By the morning of December 6, the rest of the Detachment troops had crossed over to the other side of the river, having had to endure the severe cold and facing grave hazards due to the dark and the high level of the frozen waters of the river. The troops continued their forward movement and, at 0900 hrs, entered and occupied the town of Agii Saranda, without encountering any serious enemy resistance. The Italians withdrew, setting fire to stores and warehouses and abandoning large quantities of war supplies, especially engineers equipment and fuel supplies.

The occupation of Agii Saranda created a great impression internationally. The repercussions were detrimental to the prestige of Mussolini, since the Italians had changed the name of Agii Saranda to Porto Enda, to honour Enda, the daughter of Mussolini and wife of the Italian Minister of Foreign Affairs, count Ciano.

However, the advance of the Detachment troops beyond Bistritsas river served to increase the difficulties of their already problematic resupply even further. For this reason and due to the general requirements of troop re-organisation and rest, instructions were issued ordering the hasty transportation of supplies from Sayada to Agii Saranda by motor boats. Furthermore, the sector of the Liubas Detachment was assigned to the II Division.

Nevertheless, the Detachment continued its advance and by December 8 it had occupied Pikerasi village and Tatezati pass where the Detachment linked up with the III Division which was acting on the east of Kalasas river. By December 11, the Detachment troops arrived before the village of Borsi and at the height of Koniak, where they awaited their replacement by the III Division.

**141.** During the third ten-day period of November, the III Division advanced from the area of Ioannina to the area of Kastaniani. Thereafter, in the end of November, it took over the left section of the VIII Division zone, where it deployed two·regiments, in order to conduct offensive action in the direction of Mouzina village.

On December 1, under extremely adverse weather conditions, it launched the attack and managed to seize the eastern ridges of Platyvouni height as well as the village of Boularat. On the following day, an assault launched by Division troops seeking to occupy the main core of the Platyvouni height ended in failure. The height, which covered the areas of

Delvino-Argyrokastro and had been strongly fortified, was protected by a barrage of fire, by guns of various calibres.

On December 3, the above height was taken after a fierce fight and the enemy withdrew towards Mouzina village. Further to the left, the Raftopoulos Team, assigned to the Division from the Liubas Detachment managed to occupy the southern bank of Bistritsas river on the same day, after a fierce battle. On the following day, it forded the river and deployed its forces on the opposite bank.

On December 5, continuing its movement it proceeded to occupy the village of Peza as well as the surrounding heights. Thus, the road of Mouzina-Agii Saranda was placed under the control of the Division. On the same day, the Reconnaissance Group of the Division crossed Bistritsas river and entered Delvino which had already been evacuated by the Italians who had left large quantities of food and other supplies behind.

On the following day, December 6, the Team Commander Colonel Raftopoulos entered Delvino, where the inhabitants welcomed him enthusiastically and their Mayor, in a symbolic gesture, offered him the keys to the town.

Meanwhile, the A' Army Corps ordered the successive relief of the III Division units by IV Division units. By order of the General Headquarters the latter Division was placed at the disposal of the A' Army Corps on the night of December 6 to 7. The III Division was to move further to the west and had been assigned to relieve the Liubas Detachment and to continue the offensive in the direction of Tatezati village-Koniak height-Mali Dzoret height.

However, the commencement of the relief was postponed for the night of December 7 to 8, because the IV Division troops did not arrive in time at their designated positions, due to the adverse terrain and weather conditions. Thus, the III Division continued its offensive action and, by December 7, had reached the line Makrykambos height (1537 height)-Souvliani village.

After its relief by the IV Division, the III Division concentrated its forces in the area of Delvino-Mouzina. The necessary administrative movements followed and by December 12 its units had replaced the Liubas Detachment troops and had gained contact with the enemy. The relief of the troops on the mountain bulk Koniak-Galitsi was conducted under a severe blizzard and encountered many adversities.

142. By the end of November, the VIII Division was in close contact with the strongly occupied position of the enemy on the heights of 669-Bourato. On December 1 and 2, under extremely bad weather, the Division failed in its successive efforts to seize the heights 669 and Bourato, suffering extremely heavy losses in the process.

On December 3, Division troops managed to occupy the Bourato height after another arduous offensive effort. Thereafter, they continued southwards, in order to envelop height 669, since a frontal attack against it had already been repulsed. The action south of Bourato also continued on December 4 but failed to seize the height 669.

In the evening of December 4, the Commander in chief arrived at the Headquarters of the A' Army Corps, in Kalpaki, accompanied by the Crown Prince where they had a briefing by the Commander of the VIII Division about the accomplishments up to that point. After congratulating the Division Commander on his work, the Commander in chief proceeded to demand the seizure of the height 669 by the following day, whereupon the Division would retire to become reserve of the Army Corps.

However, on the night of December 4 to 5, the Italians managed to withdraw from height 669 without being noticed by the Greek troops. The evacuation of the fought for height 669, was discovered in the morning of December 5. The enemy abandoned there about 100 unburied dead and more than 150 graves that attested the fierceness of the struggle and the perseverance of both parties for the control of the above height. During their withdrawal through the pass of Kakavia, the Italians abandoned large quantities of ammunitions, a fact which also revealed their hasty withdrawal.

The occupation of heights 669 and Bourato opened the way towards the valley of Drinos river. On December 6, a Combut Team of the VIII Division operated towards the village Libhova and seized it. Thereafter, it linked up with the II Division in the area east of Soucha. On the following day, the greatest part of the Division was relieved by the III Division and it remained as a reserve at the area north of Kakavia, for re-grouping.

Thus the forty-day continuous and uninterrupted struggle of the VIII Division ended on 7 December. During the operations it captured 46 officers and 1,490 soldiers of the enemy and seized approximately 30 tanks, of which 15 were in a good state, an entire 65mm battery, 3 Skoda guns, a large number of automatic weapons, rifles, radios etc. Most of these tanks were repaired and employed thereafter by the Greek troops.

The casualties suffered by the Division were heavy and amounted to 34 officers and 280 soldiers killed in action, 48 officers and 1,360 soldiers wounded and 84 soldiers missing in action.

**143.** On December lst, the II Division troops which held the north-eastern side of the Soucha defile repelled an attack by the enemy forces, while organising two combat teams, both of regimental strength, for the further continuation of operations, one to be employed south and the other north of the Loudzeritse mountain range. On December 2, the southern team launched an attack to seize the defile of Soucha. Despite the ferocious enemy counter-action in conjunction with the barrage of lethal machine-gun and artillery fire, the Team succeeded in reaching as far as the village of Seltska by the same evening. After a fierce and continuous struggle on 3 and 4 December it managed to force its way into the defile and to occupy the south-western exit.

This success surprised the enemy forces deployed at the area of Soucha village who were overcome with panic and fled, abandoning large quantities of weapons and supplies. The evacuation of the town of Argyrokastro commenced simultaneously, according to reports of the Italian prisoners.

On December 1, the team that acted in the northerly direction, between the mountain bulks of Loudzeritse and Nemertska-Debelit, managed to seize height 2145 of mount Nemertska. Nevertheless, because of the arctic cold and the resupply difficulties, the team retired to the western side of the height on December 3.

Since December 4, according to the order of the A' Army Corps, the Division resumed its offensive towards the saddle of Tsayioupi, in order to block the canalization of forces from the valey of Aoos river to and from the valey of Drinos river.

In the southern direction, the Division seized the village of Lambova Major, at the south of the Tsayoupi saddle as well as the heights to the east of Hormova village, both by December 10. In the northern direction, Topova village and its area had been seized by December 7, while the saddle of Tsayoupi was seized -without a combat- on the following day. The effort conducted by the Division in the direction of the Mouskes saddle was unsuccessful until December 12, mainly due to the adverse weather conditions and the numerous losses suffered by the Division in manpower and pack animals during the operations.

**144.** By November 19, the IV Division, which was mobilised in Nafplio and advanced to Kalambaka, had concentrated its forces in the area of Koutsoufliani. As of November 24 it began to move by night marches to the west of Ioannina, where it arrived on December 2. Thereafter, according to the order of the General Headquarters, it became subordinate to the A' Army Corps. By December 6, it had advanced to the area of the villages Kastaniani-Kerasovo-Baltsista, near the Greek -Albanian borders.

On the night of December 7 to 8, by order of the A' Army Corps, it replaced the III Division troops at the line Peza-Mouzina-Souvliani and on December 8 it began to advance to the Northwest of Argyrokastro. In the same evening, it managed to occupy the town of Dervitsani and the surrounding heights, despite the adverse weather conditions. At the entrance of Dervitsani, the troops were welcomed by about 700 young men and women, who were waving the Greek Flag and sang the National Anthem and the Easter hymn 'Christ is Risen'.

By the following day, the Division continued its advance 'and, on December 11, seized by a surprise attack the southern ridges of Mali Spat height as well as the Bouzae Sefer Agait saddle, continuing southwards towards the Skivovik height.

On December 12, following orders of the A' Army Corps, the IV Division directed its forces westwards, so as .to occupy the saddle on the east of Skivovik height and from there to have under its artillery fire the Koutsi village, as well as the saddle east of Mali Djoret height. The IV Division troops situated at the area of Bouzae Sefer Agait, were relieved by troops of the II Division.

**145.** Meanwhile, as of December 5, the A' Army Corps had organised a Combat Team in the area of Kakavia, comprising one Infantry battalion, two Field batteries and an Antitank Artillery battery. The Combat Team was principally assigned to provide antitank covering of the flanks of both divisions that were operating north and south of the Kakavia-Argyrokastro road.

On December 7, the above Combat Team advanced to Dervitsani, where on the following day, it was informed that the enemy had already evacuated Argyrokastro since the night of December 5 to 6, due to the advance of the Greek divisions. Following these reports, the Team proceeded in haste and occupied the town, establishing its forces on the heights situated approximately 4 kms north and Northeast of Argyrokastro. During their withdrawal, the Italians left the town intact and abandoned a multitude of war supplies. The entrance of the Greek troops into the town caused a storm of enthusiasm amongst the inhabitants, who welcomed them with flags and festivities. The same enthusiasm also prevailed throughout the Greek mainland.


*The Occupation of Premeti and Frasseri*
*(1-12 December 1940)*
(Sketch-map no. 12)

**146.** Towards the end of November, the B' Army Corps that was also advancing within the territory of Northern Epirus, had arrived in the area east of Premeti and Frasseri, while further to the north it had managed to occupy the Randomit heights.

As of November 30, the Army Corps ceased to be subordinate to the WMFAS and was placed under the direct command of the General

Headquarters. Meanwhile, on November 29, it had issued orders to its units by which they were instructed to continue operations and occupy the area of Premeti-Mali Kokoika-Frasseri, assigning them the following missions:

-The Cavalry Division were to attack in the direction of Delvina-Hotova, covering the left flank of the I Division.

-The I Division was to attack in the direction of Royanni-Selenitsa.

-The Cavalry Brigade, that had an additional XI Division Regiment under its command, was to operate in the direction of heights Mali Kelkes-Kiafe Lopouses and envelop the enemy position of Frasseri from the north.

-The V Brigade was to secure heights Mali Kelkes and 1305.

-The XI Division was to secure further north the area of Kiafe Lires and to cover the right flank of the Cavalry Brigade.

**147.** On December 2, the Cavalry Division, which was operating on the left of the B' Army Corps zone, had managed to place Premeti under its fire, and the bridge by Aoos river. That bridge was blown up by the Italians the following morning. On December 3, the Division resumed its offensive and, at around 1000 hrs, its troops (the Detachment of Lieutenant Colonel Dimokostoulas) occupied the town and took about 250 prisoners. The withdrawal of the Italians from Premeti was conducted under the covering of their tanks and a large number of aircraft. Further to the north, another section of the Division occupied the village of Gostivisti and the surrounding heights in the same day.

On December 4, the Division continued its offensive towards the north-west. Encountering no serious resistance during the occupation of the Mali Bodarid mountain range and Hotova village, it proceeded to advance beyond Loumnitsa river and by December 8, had taken possession of height 1150, on the Northwest of the village of Ali Postivani.

Since the following day, the Cavalry Division suspended the conduct of any further offensive operations. Following a B' Army Corps order, that was issued on December 3, the I Division was to gradually take over the zone of the Cavalry Division. The latter, after its replacement, was to concentrate its forces Northwest of Premeti, placing them at the disposal of the General Headquarters.

**148.** On December 3 and at the end of a fierce fight, the I Division had managed to occupy the southern ridges of Kokoika height, while acting on the right of the Cavalry Division. On the following day, it continued its offensive effort and, by the evening hours of December 6, its troops had reached the eastern ridges of height 1292, in close contact with the enemy.

From December 6 to 12, the Division mainly focused its efforts on the task of improving its occupied positions and relieving gradually the

Cavalry Division, a task that was completed by the evening of December 10.

**149.** On December 1st, the Cavalry Brigade occupied the Kiafe Kortses height and on December 2, the village of Seropouli west of Frasseri. This bold offensive action of the Cavalry Brigade was the decisive factor of the battle of Frasseri and forced the enemy to withdraw to a new position east of Klissoura.

On the following day, the Brigade continued its offensive and by December 5, it had arrived at the area of Malidi village, east of the Garonin mountain bulk. This action concluded the mission of the Cavalry Division, which remained, thereafter, as a reserve in the area of Frasseri. According to the orders of the B' Army Corps, further operations within the Brigade zone were assigned to the XI Division. The regiment of this Division, which had been temporarily assigned to the Cavalry Brigade since November 29, returned to its parent unit.

**150.** In December 3, after the required reconnaissance and preparation, the XI Division launched a strong attack against the entire front of its zone of responsibility and by the same evening, it had managed to seize the Mali Potomit height.

In December 5 the Division continued towards the height 1200 and seized it in the following day, after a fierce and wavering battle. Despite the adverse weather conditions and the ferocious counter-action of the enemy, the Division continued its offensive effort. Thus, by December 10, it had managed to take possession of the Galina height. The Italian troops withdrew westwards, abandoning 15 machine-guns, about 50 light machine-guns and over 200 rifles on the battlefield.

The Division casualties during the offensive against the Galina height were considerable, amounting to 9 officers and 24 soldiers killed in action, 8 officers and 122 soldiers wounded and 20 soldiers missing in action.

**151.** The incessant struggle of the B' Army Corps units as of November 14 and the adverse weather conditions wore out the men and created serious deficiencies. Thus, the Command of the Army Corps addressed the General Headquarters, requesting a rest period of 8 to 10 days for its troops after the occupation of Frasseri or, at the very least, the reinforcement of the Corps with an additional division before resuming operations.

In December 5, the Commander in chief and the Crown Prince arrived at the Headquarters of the B' Army Corps. After a briefing about the situation, the General Headquarters acknowledged the request of the B' Army Corps, regarding the urgency of its reinforcement, and decided to provide it with the XV Division in the place of the V Brigade and the Cavalry Brigade. These Brigades had already endured many hardships and were deficient in resupply equipment, a fact which further aggravated their efforts. After their relief they were to remain as reserves, at the disposal of the Commander in Chief.

The XV Division was relieved by the XIII Division , that was once again at the disposal of the WMFAS. The V Division was summoned to fill in for the XIII Division, as a reserve of the Commander in chief and had concentrated its forces at the area of villages Philotas-Perdika and was ordered to move to the area of Kastoria-Argos Orestiko.

On the night of December 5 to 6, the XV Division moved away from the area of Koritsa and by December 8, its forces had been placed at the disposal of the B' Army Corps. On December 12, in the course of the afternoon, the Division arrived at the area of Frasseri in full strength.

On December 12, the V Brigade was situated in the area of Seropouli, been under the command of Infantry Colonel Panaghiotis Kritikos since December 11. On the same day, the Cavalry Brigade was in the area of Frasseri.

During the evening of December 12, the I Division occupied the line Grambove village-1150 height, having been assigned to occupy the height.

Thus, after the occupation of Premeti and Frasseri, the B' Army Corps had completed the required administrative movements of its troops and held its ground firmly along the line Grambove village-height 1150-Tserevonda village.

### The Operations of the WMFAS in the Northern Sector of the Front (Koritsa) (December 1-12, 1940) (Sketch-map no. 12)

**152.** The WMFAS continued its operations in the northern sector of the front (Koritsa), while the A' and B' Army Corps were conducting their operations from December 1 to 12.

In the zone of the C' Army Corps the IX Division while holding its ground firmly at the heights 1652 and 1548, by the eastern feet of mount Kamia, continued on December 1 the frontal attack in order to occupy the height 1532 which towered over the area of Pogradetz and was of particular tactical importance. The progress recorded by that evening was minimal, because of the vigorous enemy resistance and the adverse weather conditions.

Meanwhile, as of December 1, the XVII Division took over the sector of the XIII Division and was ordered by the C' Army Corps to attack in the direction of Prenista village-height 1532-Tservenaka village. Subsequently, the action of the IX Division towards height 1532 was suspended, since the height was thereby included in the zone of the XVII Division.

On December 4, the IX Division attacked and seized the heights 1687 and 1642, without encountering any serious resistance by the enemy. With the occupation of the above heights the Division completed the occupation of the ridgeline of Kamia mountain. On December 6, it seized the height 1538, in an attempt to create a diversion in order to assist the XVII Division. However, it was unable to proceed towards the height of Koritsa, due to the enemy counter-action and a severe blizzard. On December 10, the Division repeated the offensive action against the Koritsa height, but once more the effort was not successful. Subsequently, the Division suspended its offensive operations and began the defensive organisation of its occupied positions.

**153.** On December 1 and 2 and under extremely difficult terrain and adverse weather conditions, the XVII Division undertook attack formations and advanced its units to the departure areas.

On December 3 the Division launched its attack, notwithstanding the prevailing weather conditions that had remained unchanged. After a hard and uncertain struggle, the Greek troops managed to occupy the height 1532. The contribution of Deputy Commander of the 31st Regiment, Lieutenant Colonel of the regular reserve Sotirios Basiakos, to this success was instrumental, for his action was one of unequalled courage and audacity. This officer, despite his age, took the initiative and placed himself in command of a force which surprised the enemy at its rear area, by virtue of a daring manoeuvre that was conducted from a precipitous slope using climbing ropes. Bayonet fighting ensued, at the end of which the height was finally occupied and 13 officers and 400 soldiers were taken prisoners. Furthermore, the casualties of the XVII Division were quite considerable, amounting to 6 officers and 50 soldiers killed in action, 17 officers and 350 soldiers wounded and 36 soldiers missing in action.

The bad weather and the limited visibility due to the fog and the heavy snowfalls, prevented the further exploitation of the above success. On December 6, the Division resumed the offensive and managed to occupy the northern ridges of the heights 1532 and 1211, despite the stubborn resistance of the enemy. On the following day, Division troops entered Pogradetz and proceeded to replace the reconnaissance troops of the XIII Division, that had already occupied the town since November 30 and had remained there.

The offensive effort of the Division continued during the following days as well. However, nothing significant was accomplished, because of the vigorous enemy resistance, the inaccessible terrain and the extremely adverse weather conditions that caused numerous cases of frostbite and deaths due to the extremely low temperatures.

Hence, the C' Army Corps temporarily suspended the offensive operations of the Division, ordering it to retain the areas it had occupied, that is, the line of height 1532-height 1211- Northwestern outskirts of Pogradetz.

The casualties suffered by the Division during the above operations were over 100 killed in action, 650 wounded and 80 missing in action. Furthermore, a large numbers of weapons were lost. The Italian losses were quite considerable, even though they were not confirmed. More than 500 Italians were taken prisoners.

**154.** The Division Group 'K' assigned its XI Division as a reserve to the B' Army Corps, after an order of the General Headquarters, and then advanced southwards along with the X Division, as far as Ostravitsa mountain.

On December 1, it was designated the 'K' Team, having as subordinate only the X Division and assigned to defend the occupied line, to cover the left flank of the C' Army Corps and to keep conduct with the B' Army Corps on the left.

On December 2, the 'K' Team repeated its offensive effort and by December 4, it had occupied the Marta saddle of Ostravitsa mountain, at the left of its zone, and the southern ridges of the Moglitsa height at the right of the zone, a venture that was carried out during a severe snowstorm.

On December 5 and 6 there was no significant activity to be recorded. On December 7, despite the continuing bad weather and the severe cold, the Division continued its offensive activity. Thus, by December 12 it had managed to occupy mount Ostravitsa and proceeded to advance as far as the heights Mnima Liamit and Skembi Bard with its left flank, while the right seized the Moglitsa height.

### Crisis within the Ranks of the Italian High Command

**155.** The repeated successes of the Greek Army alarmed the Italian High Command and created a crisis within its ranks.

On November 26, the Chief of the Army General Staff Marshal Badoglio submitted his resignation. On the same day, General Pricolo,

Chief of the Airforce Staff, returned to Rome from Albania, where he had been sent by order of Mussolini, and depicted the bleak situation at the front.

On November 30, Mussolini convoked a meeting, in order to brief his Cabinet Ministers, who were unaware of the situation. Furthermore, his move was an attempt to rid himself of the liabilities attributed to him by the whisper campaign of certain military circles and Badoglio's friends.

By December 3, this state of affairs that was both serious and dangerous for the Italians, turned into a panic. The occupation of the heights 1292 and 1532 by the Greek forces inflicted an additional blow to the already shaken morale of the Italian Commander in Chief in Albania. In his report to Mussolini, written on the night of December 3, he stressed the tragic situation of the two Italian Armies on the Albanian front. Flatly and without hesitation he expressed his opinion that 'any military action to reverse the situation that has been created, is no longer possible, and this can only be settled by political intervention'. In other words, he was aiming at concluding a truce.

On the following day General Kavallero was dispatched over to Albania to examine the situation and on December 6 he was assigned as Chief of the Army General Staff. In his report to Mussolini, dated December 5, he characterized the situation of the XI Italian Army, as very bad.

'The 'Bari' Division has lost everything. The 8th Alpine has lost 80% of its strength. The 9th Alpine suffered fewer losses. The 'Vincenza' and 'Aquila' battalions conducted themselves heroically. It is worth honouring the land upon which they fought. The 'Giulia' Division has been weakened but continues to fight. Three field battalions have not been completely damaged, however they have no pack transportation. The 41st and 42nd Infantry Regiments have suffered badly, especially the 41st, which was ill-treated by Colonel Manai, who was court-marshalled for unjustified withdrawal. The 139th Infantry withdrew due to lack of ammunition. The Army is provided with a day's supply of ammunition for rifles or automatic weapons, no hand-grenades and half a day's supply of artillery ammunition. Under these circumstances, the Army will be able to resist for eight days'.

Greece, isolated, according to Mussolini, and forced to fight alone, had crushed its powerful adversary to such an extent, that the enemy's leaders were calling this disastrous defeat 'the greatest military crisis of the entire Italian history, which could cover Italy with shame for centuries on end', and were seriously considering to be subjected to the indescribable humiliation of requesting a cease-fire from the Greek forces.

**156.** In order to avoid such humiliation and to deal with this critical situation, the Italian Leadership finally decided to turn to its great ally, Germany, for help.

Consequently, Ciano summoned Alfieri, the Italian Ambassador to Berlin, who was recuperating in Rome, and ordered him to depart for his post and to plead the Germans to hasten to Italy's aid, to make every effort possible in order to convince Hitler.

Alfieri indeed arrived in Berlin on December 7 and immediately had a meeting with the German Minister of Foreign Affairs, Von Ribbentrop. However, Ribbentrop was evasive in his reply to the urgent Italian plea for immediate help through the Romanian territory. He stressed the meteorological impediments and the military difficulties of such an intervention and cited the political and military situation in Europe as a major obstacle that did not allow such actions.

On the following day, the Italian Ambassador, who had naturally become totally pessimistic, was accepted by the 'Fuehrer'. In plain terms, laying aside the usual diplomatic conventions, Alfieri explained the situation in Albania. Hitler was shaken by this unvarnished presentation and, enraged by Mussolini's continuous inability to come up with solutions, made a few brief remarks concerning the Italian campaign and the fighting abilities of the Italian Army. After giving vent to his rage, he discussed the possible solutions.

Eventually, he promised to offer air transportation assistance to Italy. A few days later, the 3rd Team of the no.1 Airforce Squadron (49 'Younger 52' aircraft) would begin the operation of transporting Italian soldiers and supplies from Foggia in Italy to the airfields of the zone of operations, near Avlonas and Dyrrachio.

### The New Intentions of the General Headquarters regarding the Further Development of the Operations

**157.** The Commander in chief, seeking to be briefed on site and to form his own conclusions with regard to the situation, visited the zone of operations from December 2 to l0, accompanied by the Crown Prince Paul. During his trip, the Commander in chief conducted the following meetings with the commanders of the Large Units:

In Zitsa, with the Commander of the A' Army Corps. In Elea, with the Commander of the VIII Division, in the presence of the Commander of the A' Army Corps. In Konitsa with the Commander of the B' Army Corps and in Koritsa with the Commanders of the WMFAS, the C' Army Corps and 'K' Team.

During these meetings, the Commander in chief presented his new intentions and gave instructions with regard to the conduct of further operations. The instructions of the Commander in chief were formulated in a directive of the General Headquarters, on December 12, and assigned the following missions:

-The A' Army Corps was to operate, in order to seize and secure the junction of Tepeleni, seeking, furthermore, to break through the valley of the river Siousitsa.

-The B' Army Corps was to operate, in order to seize the junction of Klissoura-Tepeleni as well as the mountain bulks north of Klissoura-Tepeleni.

-The WMFAS was to operate on the basis of the above instructions. Furthermore, it was to consolidate the liaison with the B' Army Corps and to cover the left flank of the latter from the directions of the valleys of Devolis and Tomoritsa rivers.

**158.** For the most effective co-ordination of the future operations, an advanced General Headquarters echelon was organised and became operational on December 17, under the direct command of the Commander in chief, who held the overall command of operations along with his other duties.

On the basis of the above mentioned future operations and for the improvement of the organisation of the Command, Lieutenant Generals Kosmas and Demestihas were mutually transferred to the A' Army Corps and to the 'K' Team respectively. As of December 15, this particular Team was redesignated as the E' Army Corps and was additionally reinforced with certain non divisional units.

*The Operations of the A' Army Corps towards Tepeleni*
*and the Valley of the River Siousitsa*
*(December 13, 1940 - January 6, 1941)*
(Sketch-map no. 11)

**159.** On December 12, the A' Army Corps occupied the general line of Borsi village-Galisti height-south-eastern ridges of the heights Skivovik and Mali Spat-saddle of Bouzae Sefer Agait-Malesova village, with the III, IV and II Divisions deployed in contact with the enemy. The VIII Division and the Liubas Detachment remained inside its zone, in the areas of

Delvinaki and Delvino respectively, as a reserve of the Commander in chief.

On December 13 and 14, the Corps units dealt with the preparation of further offensive operations and with the additional task of improving their positions. Because of the continuing bad weather, the rough terrain and the vigorous resistance of the enemy forces, the II and III Divisions recorded but little progress. The IV Division, in spite of the above adversities, was able to occupy Pousi defile on south-east of Mali Spat, by employing a successful manoeuvre, and managed to gain contact with the strongly occupied line Gusmari-Progonati. More than 50 dead were found later on the battlefield, including the Commander of the 42nd Italian Regiment and his adjutant. Furthermore, 192 prisoners were taken, including a battalion commander.

**160.** On December 15, the A' Army Corps drew up its own plan of action, along the following guidelines:

-In order to seize the junction of Tepeleni:

Immediate attack with the IV Division, to seize the saddles of Verniko (4kms west of Kendersitsa height) and Salaria (3kms west of the Tersnitsa height). Thereafter, the same Division was to conduct offensive action towards Salaria-Aoos river, in order to cut off the carriage road of Tepeleni-Avlonas, with the main effort towards Nivitsa-Salaria. In the valleys of rivers Drinos and Zagoria, an attack with the II Division would be conducted in the general direction of the respective river flows. The objective of this attack was to engage and fix the enemy forces and in the event of a favourable outcome of operations, to conduct mopping up operations of the above valleys as far as Aoos river.

-In order to break through the valley of Siousitsa river:

Drastic offensive with the III Division, in order to seize the saddle of Koutsi, near the homonymous village and advance of the covering detachments towards the villages of Kalarati and Boliena, with a simultaneous action by the same Division in the coastal sector, so as to foothold the enemy forces that were present there.

On the same day, the A' Army Corps issued an operations order to its divisions, by which it assigned the conduct of the above missions and it stressed the fact that despite the efforts that had already been made and which had surpassed even the most optimistic expectations, the offensive operations would have to continue without any delay, in order to accomplish in full the objectives that had been set.

**161.** The IV Division, which·had the main effort, launched its attack finally on December 17, because of the repeated counter-attacks it had suffered on December 15 and of the severe frost. Despite the severe blizzard and the arctic cold, which caused a great number of frostbite cases among the men and numerous deaths of pack animals, the Division managed to take possession of the Mali Spat height, to capture an enemy battery and two field surgeries and was able to advance to the south of Progonati village.

The attack continued during the following days and by the evening of December 22, the line of eastern ridges of Kputs height-Gusmari village-Progonati village-Bouzae Sefer Agait had been seized.

From December 23 to 28, the units improved and consolidated their positions under dramatic weather conditions. On December 28, the village of Nivitsa was taken and the entire Italian battalion, of approximately 580 men, defending that area, was captured.

According to its mission and following the occupation of Nivitsa, the Division would conduct an offensive towards the village of Salaria. However, this operation was not carried out, due to the numerous frostbite cases that took a daily toll of approximately 200 men.

The total number of casualties suffered by the IV Division, since its entrance in the war on December 8, was 15 officers and 252 soldiers killed in action, 38 officers and 843 soldiers wounded and 9 soldiers missing in action. Furthermore, 51 officers and 2,650 soldiers were evacuated due to frostbite and approximately 2,800 pack animals perished. However, the Italian losses in manpower and pack animals were also numerous. Italian prisoners of war exceeded 1,300 , including many officers.

**162.** The II Division launched its attack on December 15 and seized the western side of the Mouskes saddle on mount Debelit on the same day.

During the following days, the arctic cold, the depth of the snow that had reached 75 centimetres, and the resupply difficulties, did not permit the conduct of any serious offensive actions.

On December 17, the Division troops operating in the centre of its zone of action seized the village of Hormova, where they captured 150 Italians and captured an abundance of war supplies belonging to the 'Ferrara' Division. Enemy counter-attacks conducted on December 19 and 20, in order to reoccupy the above village, were repulsed.

On December 19, a movement by the left flank of the Division towards the village of Leskoviki encountered a strong counter-action and was eventually blocked by the enemy. Due to the raging snowstorm and the extremely severe cold, this effort was repeated on December 26 and 28, but it was again unsuccessful. Subsequently, the Division temporarily suspended · the offensive operations and kept busy with the defensive organisation of the terrain and, furthermore, with the living conditions of the Division troops, and pack animals.

163. The III Division launched the attack on December 15. Despite the substantial support of the artillery, the attacking troops advanced very slowly, due to the enemy counter-action, the depth of the snow and the activity of the Italian Airforce, particularly in the coastal sector.

On December 19, the Division troops operating in the coastal zone seized the Giami height, after a hard fight that resulted in grave casualties on both sides. During the same day, other Division troops operating further to the north launched a surprise attack at daybreak, with no artillery preparation, against the powerfully organised Mali e Joret height. The surprise was successful and the enemy troops in the first pill boxes were caught off their guard. A fierce struggle ensued within the defensive area which lasted for three days and resulted in the occupation of the Mali e Joret height and the Koutsi saddle by the Greek troops. The successful outcome of this battle was of particular importance, since the occupation of the Koutsi saddle opened the road through the Siousitsa valley. On the Italian side, the casualties of this battle were approximately 400 killed in action and more than 950 prisoners.

Furthermore, they lost six guns, a mortar company and a multitude of war supplies. The Greek losses did not exceed 100 killed in action and wounded.

On December 21, the height of Tsipista, Northwest of Himara, was occupied by the Greeks. After that, the Italians abandoned Himara, into which the Greek troops entered, in the morning of December 22. The liberation of Himara from the Albanian occupation, for the third time, gave rise to intense emotions all over Greece and great enthusiasm.

The occupation of Koutsi saddle and Himara alarmed the Italian leadership to such a degree that on December 24th Mussolini addressed the following telegram to Cavallero:

'Whatever may befall you, I order you to resist to the very end in the sector of Progonati-Tepeleni-Klissoura, even if tomorrow should find yourself completely surrounded. I hereby appoint you personally responsible to carry out my order with full awareness as to its nature.'

By December 23, the Division troops continued their movement towards the villages Kalarati and Boliena and seized both on December 27. An action conducted by a Division tactical group on January 4, against the height of Skoutara in the coastal sector, was unsuccessful, because of the vigorous counter-action of the enemy.

164. In the meantime, the pace of the operations of the Army Corps kept decreasing on the entire front, due to the arctic cold and the extreme severity of winter. The difficulties of resupply became almost unsurpassable and the bread ration was often reduced to an eighth of the original portion. The frostbite casualties kept increasing and the pack

animals that perished due to exhaustion and low temperatures reached alarming numbers. In the Koutsi area alone, more than 1,200 pack animals perished.

Moreover, due to the discernible serious threat created by the opening of the valley of Sioustitsa, the enemy hastened to transport by sea and air substantial reinforcements and deployed them against the zone of the A' Army Corps. These reinforcements comprised two divisions and a number of independent battalions.

Meanwhile, the Army General Staff, which was constantly being kept informed of the losses and the terrible hardships endured due to the lack of supplies, placed the Liubas Detachment and the VIII Division, both of which had been reserves of the Commander in chief until then, at the disposal of the A' Army Corps. From January 1 to 6, the VIII Division gradually replaced the IV Division. After its relief, the IV Division concentrated its forces south of Argyrokastro as a reserve of the Commander in chief.

### *The Operations of the B' Army Corps towards Klissoura*
### *(December 13, 1940 - January 6, 1941)*
### (Sketch-map no. 12)

**165.** On December 12, the B' Army Corps occupied the line Grambove-height 1150-Tserevonda, with the I Division on the left along Aoos river, the V Infantry Brigade in the centre, the XI Division on the right to the north of river Apsos and the XV Division as a reserve in the area Frasseri-mount Randomit.

After completing the required reconnaissance and co-ordination, the Army Corps issued its operation order on December 18, which determined the following:

The Army Corps would attempt to break through the enemy position, by seizing the height 1292 at the Northeast of Fratari. Thereafter, the Army Corps would apply, its main effort along the ridgeline of mount Garonin (heights 1292-1237-1248) and at the same time would operate in the direction Ali Postivani-Toliari-carriage road towards Bouzi.

The final objective would be the line of Sendeli mountain-Voskopolia village-Dobrousia village, in order to secure the junctions of Klissoura and Tepeleni.

The I Division would operate on the left, in the direction of the carriage road Klissoura-Bouzi, having been assigned to occupy the area of Artza-Bouzi.

The XV Division would operate in the centre, in the direction of height 1292-height 1248, assigned to break through the enemy position and then to pursue to cut off the road to the north of Klissoura, in the area of Souka village.

The XI Division would operate on the right, in the direction of Tsepan-Dobrousia, assigned to occupy the area of Dobrousia village.

The operations were scheduled to commence on December 23.

**166.** In the meantime, according to various fragmentary orders of the Corps, the divisions conducted the following operations from December 12 to 22.

The I Division, continuing its offensive activity in the southern bank of Aoos river, advanced as far as the village of Brezdani. Further to the north, an effort of the Division, to seize the height 1292, did not record any progress and a further attempt was halted by an order of the B' Army Corps, which had planned to assign the seizure of the above height to the XV Division.

The XV Division, which had arrived at the area of Frasseri on December 12, was reinforced with the V Infantry Brigade as of December 13.

On December 15, the B' Army Corps notified the XV Division that it had been assigned to break through the enemy position at Garonin mountain, and ordered it to propose the appropriate time of attack after conducting the required reconnaissance. On December 19, the Division submitted a report by which it presented its situation as this had developed after the ten-day march under a severe and continuous snowstorm through nearly impassable paths and requested to postpone the attack.

The Army Corps, deeming that the launching of the attack was a matter of urgency, did not approve of the proposal of the Division and ordered that the attack should be carried out on December 23. In parallel, attributing irresolution to the Division Commander, the Corps initiated his replacement by the Chief of Infantry of the I Division, Colonel Panaghiotis Spiliotopoulos, who assumed command of the XV Division on December 22.

On December 13, the XI Division seized the height of Kresta (858) north of Apsos river, but failed to seize the bridge of Siarova. The continuation of its efforts became increasingly difficult because of the heavy snowfalls, the resupply difficulties and the constantly diminishing number of pack animals, which were eventually reduced by well over 60%.

On December 22, the command of the Division was assigned to Colonel Sokratis Dimaratos, who had been Commander of the Cavalry Brigade until that point. Major General Nikolaos Tsipouras was placed at the disposal of the General Headquarters.

**167.** On December 23, the attack that had been ordered by the B' Army Corps was launched by all three abovementioned Divisions.

The I Division, despite its efforts, managed to accomplish only a slight improvement of its occupied positions. On December 24, an action conducted by this division towards Koukiari, on the northern bank of Aoos river, came to no avail.

The XV Division having also under its command the V Brigade as well as a regiment of the XI Division, launched an attack under adverse weather conditions and dense cloudiness, directing its main effort towards the height 1292. However, its troops advanced at a slow pace due to the depth of the snow and the drastic fire of the enemy. Nevertheless, the fighting continued and, by a superhuman effort, the Division troops approached the summit. However, they were forced to withdraw to their departure base due to the combined effect of the severe enemy shelling and the extremely heavy casualties that amounted to 28 officers and 631 soldiers. On the following day, the Division did not have the chance to repeat the offensive due to the continuing adverse weather conditions and the inability to forward ammunition, especially of the artillery.

The XI Division, despite the snowfall, was also able to launch its attack westwards. After heroic efforts and close combat, its troops seized the saddle of Molasi and advanced westwards as far as the village of Dobrousia. On December 24 no significant operations took place in the Division zone, but efforts were made to improve the disposition and forward its artillery, a fact that was accomplished after many difficulties, due to the terrain, the weather and the significant reduction of its pack animals.

**168.** Meanwhile, the units began to face serious problems due to the continuous bad weather, the exhaustion of supplies and food and the great losses in pack animals. For, the ice and the slippery paths often caused the animals to fall down the ravines along with their load of supplies, without any hope of recovery. This situation of the units forced the B' Army Corps to temporarily suspend offensive operations, awaiting the improvement of weather conditions.

The suspension of the offensive operations lasted until December 29, whereupon the weather improved and the Army Corps ordered the renewal of operations, focusing its main effort on the task of seizing and securing the height 1292.

**169.** The XV Division troops (which had been assigned the main effort), launched their attack at 0645 hrs, on December 30, without any artillery preparation and under severe cold, managing to seize height 1292 and

1237 by surprise. The surprise was complete and the enemy abandoned many killed in action on the battlefield, about 600 prisoners and important war supplies, including 18 pack artillery pieces, 12 mortars and a number of automatic weapons and mortars of smaller caliber. Further to the south, the heights of Fratari saddle were seized.

On the following day, December 31, the offensive continued, yet the troops operating to the west of the height 1237 were contained before the organised position of Mali Topoyanit. Facing this situation, the Division requested the permission of the Army Corps to halt the offensive, in order to advance its artillery, supplies and ammunitions, which had lagged behind due to the snow depth, the rough terrain and the muddy surface of the mule paths because of the frequency of their use. On January 1 and 2, 1941, the Division troops retained their positions and repulsed enemy counterattacks.

The I Division, also continuing its offensive effort, seized the village of Koukiari on December 31 and proceeded to advance as far as the village of Riba, approximately 2 kms to the Northeast of Klissoura.

The XI Division seized Sirakoui saddle, west of Zalosgnia mountain, on December 30. Successive Italian counter-attacks to repossess the saddle came to no avail.

**170.** The conclusion of the two day fight, conducted by the B' Army Corps in order to break through the enemy position at the centre of its zone, was that the enemy, though surprised and utterly crushed at height 1292, was still holding its ground strongly at that highly organised position. Italian prisoners reported that the enemy divisions 'Aqui', 'Giulia' and 'Bari' were those units acting against the B' Army Corps, assisted by an Alpine regiment and a number of Blackshirts battalions.

Subsequently, the B' Army Corps issued an order, on January 3, for the continuation of the operations, from January 5, in order to break through the Mali Topoyanit area. The break through would be conducted by the I and XV Divisions, which thereafter would move their forces towards the south-west, in order to envelop the enemy forces, in the area of Klissoura.

The XI Division would operate in parallel with the central XV Division. However, by a new order of the B' Army Corps, the attack was postponed for January 8. The postponement was deemed necessary because of the problems that the units faced, regarding their resupply, due to the continuation of the adverse weather and to the bad condition of the roads.

*The Development of the Operations in the Northern Sector of the Front*
*(December 13, 1940 - January 6, 1941)*
(Sketch-map no. 12)

**171.** According to the General Headquarters instructions and after securing widely the high plateau of Koritsa, the WMFAS would become the powerful pivot around which the A' and B' Army Corps would conduct their manoeuvres in order to seize Avlonas. Thus, due to the extreme severity of that winter, as of December 13, the operations of the WMFAS were gradually limited to actions of local significance, which mainly sought to improve the occupied positions and to foothold the enemy forces.

In the zone of the C' Army Corps, the most noteworthy operations, after the above date, were the following:

The IX Division, which was in the area of mount Kamia, dealt with the organisation of the terrain and the problematic living conditions of its troops, and pack animals.

The XIII Division relieved the XVII Division from December 26 and undertook to block off the enemy routes from the valley of river Skoubi towards the highland of Koritsa.

The XVII Division, deployed at the Northeast of the Kamia mountain as far as Pogradetz, dealt with the problematic living conditions and the terrain organisation until December 26. On December 27 it was relieved by the XIII Division and concentrated its forces as a reserve in the area north of the Maliki lake.

**172.** In the zone of the 'K' Team, on December 14, the X Division crossed Tomoritsa river and seized the villages of Miliova and Rechova on the western bank. On the same day, the command of the Division was assumed by Major General Panaghiotis Gazis. Major General Dromazos, who had been the Commander of the X Division up to that point, was transferred due to health reasons.

On December 15, the 'K' Team was renamed to E' Army Corps and it received an order by phone to actively advance the X Division towards the valley of Tomoritsa river.

On December 17, the Division troops reached the village of Kovatsiani. Aiming to establish an additional liaison with the XI Division of the B' Army Corps, the E' Army Corps ordered the X Division to operate towards Devris saddle. However, due to the severe weather the operation was not carried out. On the following day, the height of Gouri Prer at the centre, between mountains Tomoros and Moglitsa, was seized.

In the afternoon of December 22, the troops of the right flank of the Division seized the height 1453. However, after successive enemy counter-attacks, which caused them extremely heavy casualties they were forced to withdraw to their base of departure.

From December 23 to 28 the situation remained unchanged. On December 29, the height 1732 was taken along with the village of Douska in the valley of Tomoritsa river, to the east of the Tomoros mountain. Any further action was not possible due to the continuing bad weather, the resupply difficulties and the hardships endured by the Division troops and its pack animals. Thus, the only Division of the E' Army Corps fell into a state of inactivity and was assigned thereafter to hold its ground and provide a liaison between the B' and C' Army Corps.

## Suspension of the Large Scale Offensive Operations

**173.** The Italian Leadership, facing the danger of an impending occupation of Avlonas, made every possible effort to halt the Greek advance. In parallel, it reinforced the Albanian front with new forces and abundant war supplies. From mid-December and until the beginning of January, five additional divisions arrived in Albania. These were the 'Aqui', 'Kouneense', 'Cuneo', 'Brennero' and the 'Wolves of Tuscany'.

Since December 29, the general command of the Italian forces in Albania was assumed by General Cavallero, who replaced General Soddu.

**174.** The Greek General Headquarters was facing very serious problems during the same period. The extremely severe winter together with the transportation problems that had arisen, had in many cases created unsurpassable difficulties in the resupply and evacuations. Furthermore, there was great need to supplement the shortages that had been created after the two-month expedition, in personnel, pack animals, armament and other war supplies.

Under those circumstances, the General Headquarters decided, at the end of December, to suspend the large scale offensive operations. However, it did not abandon the local offensive actions, in particular those of the B' Army Corps, in order to create favourable conditions for the future operations towards Avlonas.

The above decision of the General Headquarters was disseminated to the Large Units along with the instructions, issued on January 6, 1941.

# CHAPTER IV

## THE GREEK ARMY WINTER OPERATIONS AND THE ITALIAN GREAT "PRIMAVERA"(SPRING) ATTACK
### ( January 7 until March 26, 1941 )

*The General Military Situation in the beginning of 1941*
( Sketch-map no. 13 )

175. As previously mentioned in the development of operations until this point, on November 14, the Greek forces undertook to launch a general counter-attack throughout the entire Albanian Theatre of Operations. After a two-month hard struggle under extremely adverse weather conditions and despite the stubborn resistance and the continual reinforcement of the enemy with new units, they managed to repulse the Italians far beyond the Greek-Albanian borders, from 30 to 50 kilometres inland, and were able to reach the general line of Himara-Boliena-Tserevonda-Soukagora mountain-Kamia mountain-Pogradetz.

The general disposition of the Greek forces on the evening of January 6, 1941, was the following:

-In the Southern Sector, the A' Army Corps, with its HQ at Dervitsani, had been set up defensively in the zone from Himara to mount Debelit and had the III, VIII and II Divisions at its disposal in the direction west to east.

-In the Central Sector, the B' Army Corps, with its HQ at Premeti, continuing its offensive operations, occupied the zone from the valley of Aoos river (included) to Tomoros mountain and had the I, XV and XI Divisions at its disposal in the direction south to north.

-In the Northern Sector, the WMFAS, with its HQ at Koritsa, included the C' and E' Army Corps and occupied the zone from Tomoros mountain to Pogradetz.

The C' Army Corps, with its HQ at Koritsa, had the IX and XIII Divisions as first echelon and the XVII Division as the second echelon, from south-west to north-east.

The E' Army Corps further south, with its HQ at Bobotista, was provided with only the X Division, which had been defensively established as a first echelon. This Corps was also expected to be reinforced with the XVI Division, which had been formed in Florina from the XVI Brigade a few days earlier and was preparing to transfer to the area of the rivers Devolis and Tomoritsa north-west of Moschopolis.

-Reserves of the Commander in Chief, were the V Division in the area of Koritsa, the IV Division in the area Liebhova-Kakavia and the Cavalry Division in the area of Elea.

Thus, the Greek forces allocated to the Northern Epirus Theatre of Operations, on January 6, amounted to thirteen Infantry Divisions and a Cavalry division, with the prospect of the transfer of one additional Division, that of the VI from the Bulgarian Theatre of Operations.

**176.** Opposite the above Greek forces, in the evening of January 6, 1941, the Italians had the following units at their disposal:

-Fifteen Infantry Divisions, namely: 11th 'Brennero', 29th 'Piedmonte', 19th 'Venezzia', 23rd 'Ferrara', 33rd 'Aqui', 37th 'Modena', 48th 'Taro', 49th 'Parma', 51st 'Sienna', 53rd 'Arezzo', 56th 'Kazale', 2nd Alpine 'Tridentina', 3rd Alpine 'Giulia', 4th Alpine 'Kouneense' and 5th Alpine 'Pousteria'.

-The 131st Armoured Division 'Centaurs' reinforced with the 5th Bersaglieri Regiment.

-The 2nd Bersaglieri Regiment, the 3rd Grenadieri Regiment, two Cavalry regiments and a number of Blackshirts, Albanians and Machine-gun battalions.

-A section of the 'Cuneo' and 'Wolves of Tuscany' Divisions, which landed in Albania in the end of December and were gradually advancing towards the zone of operations.

**177.** The operations of the Large Units until January 6, 1941, were conducted, as already mentioned, in accordance with the General Headquarters instructions of December 12, 1940.

The operations were conducted under adverse conditions, such as severe winter, difficulties in the re-supply and evacuations and great losses due to frostbite which exceeded the casualties of battle. Furthermore, there was a necessity to supplement the shortages, that had arisen after the two-month expedition, in personnel, pack animals, automatic weapons and supplies - material of all kinds. The above conditions forced the High Command to suspend, as previously mentioned, the large scale offensive operations.

This decision, which was initially taken on December 28, was later implemented with the general instructions of the Commander-in-chief, which were issued on January 6, 1941. Through these instructions, it was determined that until the improvement of weather conditions, the large units would take measures to organise the defensive disposition of their forces in order to secure the occupied positions and would conduct local operations in order to improve their positions and preserve the aggressive spirit of their troops.

In general, the missions of the large units were the following:

-The A' Army Corps, in the valley of river Zagorias was to limit its activity in pushing the enemy north of Aoos river, in order to safeguard the junction of Klissoura. In the valley of the river Drinos, it was to limit its activity to small scale local operations in order to repulse the enemy towards Aoos and to safely block off the valley of Drinos from that direction.

-The B' Army Corps was to conduct offensive operations in order to seize the junction of Klissoura, to block off the defile of Klissoura from the west and seize the general line Podgorani-Souka-Mali Garonin[1].

-The WMFAS was to limit its activity to securing the high plateau of Koritsa. Furthermore, it was obliged to secure the liaison with the B' Army Corps in the valley of Tomoritsa river and to conduct limited, local operations as appropriate in order to improve its positions.

*The Offensive Operations of the B' Army Corps*
*towards Klissoura - Trebessina - Boubessi*
*(January 7-25, 1941)*
(Sketch-map no. 14)

**178.** The operations of the B' Army Corps for the occupation of the road junction of Klissoura had been prepared following prior instructions of the General Headquarters. On the basis of these instructions, the B' Army Corps issued its orders on January 3, which concerned the seizure of the mountain range Mali Topoyianit-Spi Varistolian and their safeguarding from all directions as far as Mali Hirotse and Mali Garonin. Afterwards, actions would be taken along the south western direction, in order to cut off the Klissoura-Verati road and to seize Klissoura.

The main attack would be conducted by the I Division to the left (south) and the XV Division to the right (north), while the XI Division was assigned to assist the effort of the XV Division.

**179.** The attack had been planned to commence in the morning of January 5. It was postponed, however, and was finally launched in the morning of January 8 so that in the meantime the XV Division could be reinforced with artillery.

---

[1] Sketch-map no. 14

The I Division commenced its attack at 1000 hrs while, in the meantime, the XV Division had seized the summit of the Mali Topoyianit height.

The attack was launched against the heights south and south-west of Mali Topoyianit in the direction of Klissoura and, by that evening, they were seized, by the Division, despite the stubborn resistance of the Italians. The enemy abandoned more than 300 dead and a large quantity of war supplies on the battlefield. On the following day, January 9, the Division seized the heights north of Togliari village and further south, the heights of Panariti village. This effort was supported with the fire of the Detachment headed by Lieutenant Colonel Dimokostoulas of the II Division (A' Army Corps), which operated at the same time south of Aoos river at the area of Bresdani village.

The XV Division commenced its attack at 0700 hrs and by 0900 hrs it had seized the summit of Mali Topoyianit by force of bayonet. In spite of the stubborn resistance and the successive counter-attacks of the enemy, it continued its offensive towards the Mali Hirotse height, which it managed to seize during the early hours of the evening, while further to the Northeast it took the height of Bregou Lipes. The morale of the troops engaged in the attack was excellent and the self-sacrifice of the officers and soldiers unequalled. The enemy abandoned more than 800 killed in action and wounded from the 'Giulia' Division units. The sight of the battlefield was indeed macabre. The prisoners included 14 officers and 341 soldiers on the Italian side. In addition, 4 pack artillery guns, 26 mortars of 81mm and an abundance of food and supplies were seized. The casualties of the XV Division during that day, were 7 officers and 199 soldiers killed in action and 9 officers and 286 soldiers wounded.

During the night of January 8 to 9, Division troops continued their offensive to the west of the Topoyianit height, in order to cut off the carriage road Klissoura-Verati. At 0200 hrs on January 9, they seized the Souka village, placed the abovementioned road under their fire and attacked the withdrawing enemy troops of the 'Aqui' Division, which had been sent to reinforce the 'Giulia' Division. By the morning of January 9, 17 Italian officers and 600 soldiers had been taken prisoners and abundant war supplies had been seized.

The XV Division attack continued on January 9 under adverse weather conditions and at around 1400 hrs the Mali Garonin height was occupied along with the area of the Tsepova village, to the south-west.

The XI Division, operating north of the XV Division, assisted the action of the latter with its fire on January 8 and 9, while preparing to cross Apsos river with part of its troops in order to seize the village of Slatina and to cut off the enemy that intended to escape in the direction of Verati.

**180.** The B' Army Corps, following this successful development of operations, issued a new operation order on January 9 according to which any further operations of the I and XI Divisions would be oriented towards the north-west, in order to seize the area lying on both sides of the deep line of river Desnitsa, along which the Klissoura-Verati road winds, with powerful cover from the direction of Tepeleni-Klissoura.

The I Division began its attack at 0730 hrs on January 10 and part of its troops seized Givanai village and the heights east of Podgorani village, while further to the north the Division seized the southern heights of Roden.

The 7th Regiment of the Division, which was operating in the direction of Klissoura and was supported by the fire of the Dimokostoulas Detachment, took possession of Klissoura at around 1030 hrs. By 1700 hrs it had advanced to the position of Kastelo ridge at the eastern slopes of the Trebessina mountain, which terminate in the river Aoos, directly west of Klissoura.

An Italian counter-attack with tanks, that was launched from the defile of Klissoura-Tepeleni, was contained by the fire of the artillery. In the course of their withdrawal, the Italians set fire to Klissoura and destroyed the stone bridge of the river Desnitsa towards Tepeleni as well as the wooden bridge of the Klissoura-Premeti road.

The XV Division operated Northwest of the Garonin mountain and, after a hard struggle, advanced as far as the steep slopes of Mali Tabayian, north-east of Roden.

In the sector of the XI Division, the situation remained unchanged. The seizure of Klissoura constituted an important success for the fighting troops of the B' Army Corps and a serious blow for the Italians. The latter attached great significance to this important road junction and had striven hard to retain it with the 'Giulia' Division. Since January 3, in particular, they began to reinforce the latter with the 'Wolves of Tuscany' Division, which had been transferred to Avlonas from Italy at that time.

The following dramatic plea by Cavallero, Commander in chief of the Italian forces in Albania, that was addressed by phone to the Commander of the 'Giulia' Division is characteristic of the significance attached to that location by the Italians. This has been recorded in the diary kept by Cavallero, in the entry of January 11, 1941:

'The 'Giulia' Division has fulfilled its duty. We are satisfied despite its withdrawal. Today, new forces are pouring in, part of which are already in Verati. It is necessary to close the gap, be it with your own sacrifice. If the area is broken through, we will no longer hold our ground. The Fatherland demands it, even if we are about to die for that cause, and I will come to die with you. I am asking you to make this last effort, in the name of Italy. I am certain that you too will be satisfied in the next few days, for then we will reach victory. The reinforcements are arriving and you will go and rest. We shall re-organise and create a glorious 'Giulia', but for now you must hold on'.

Moreover, the Prime Minister of Greece, in recognition of the importance of the seizure of Klissoura, addressed the following telegram to the B' Army Corps on January 13.

*'Officers and men, I congratulate you for your latest exploits in the area of Klissoura'.*

On the following day, January 11, the units of the B' Army Corps mainly had the task of securing the area of Klissoura from the direction of Tepeleni and the Northwest and they attempted to improve their positions. Concurrently, they repulsed enemy counter-attacks.

**181.** On January 12, the B' Army Corps communicated a plan of action concerning both the seizure of the Artza-Bregou Sialesi-Mali Spandarit line and the effort to secure the area of Klissoura from the direction of Tepeleni and the Northwest. The Corps would be operating in three phases with its main effort along the ridgeline of Mali Garonin-Bregou Memoulazit-Bosquetto and, by employing the IX Division, would simultaneously seek to establish bridgeheads south of Apsos river, up to the villages of Verziezia and Istrora. The attack was planned to commence in the morning of January 16, while the crossing of Apsos river by the XI Division would be conducted after orders of the Army Corps.

In order to secure Klissoura and mop up the area south of Aoos river as far as the Klissoura defile, since January 13 the General Headquarters provided the B' Army Corps with the Dimokostoulas Detachment along with the rest of the II Division that were operating east of the Zagoria Stream. After the order of the B' Army Corps, these troops formed the "Klissoura Team", a unified group, that was under the command of Lieutenant Colonel Dimokostoulas and was subordinate to the Army Corps.

During the period until the commencement of the attack, the units mainly dealt with the improvement of their disposition and their positions of departure, despite the adverse weather and the snow depth which had reached one meter in the area of Trebessina. Due to the weather conditions and the shortages in forage, 60% of the pack animals have perished .

**182.** Since the morning of January 16, the B' Army Corps resumed its offensive operations.

On January 18 the I Division, after having repelled enemy counter-attacks for two consecutive days and despite the adverse weather conditions, sent troops in order to conduct reconnaisance in force towards the Psari height of Trebessina mountain and also towards the height Tsouka Fesit. On January 19, it seized Pavari village, east of Hani Balaban.

The "Klissoura Team" repulsed an enemy counterattack that was launched from the direction of Tepeleni and seized the height 1620 on Trebessina mountain.

The XV Division, engaged in action since 0900 hrs on January 16, seized the heights Tsouka Fesit and Mali Tabayian under adverse weather conditions and after a fierce battle. On the following day, it seized the height Dras-e-Kais and continued its advance towards the Mali Korap and Bregou Memoulazit heights, where it took about 700 Italian prisoners including the Commander of the 77th Regiment of the 'Wolves of Tuscany' Division.

During the night and the following day, January 18, the snowfall and the severe frost continued, visibility fell below 10 meters and deaths due to frost were recorded in the battle positions. Thus, no important activity took place.

The Division resumed the offence during the next day, January 19, with its men displaying an excellent morale, in spite of the hardships and the severe frost. At 1600 hrs the height Kiafe Sofiout was seized, but any further advance was halted in the early evening hours.

The XI Division, awaiting the order of the Corps, in order to cross river Apsos, did not display any noteworthy activity within its sector during the same period.

**183.** Since January 19, the General Headquarters assigned the V Division (minus) to the B' Army Corps. The V Division had been a general reserve of the Commander in Chief within the zone of the C' Army Corps until then.

Subsequently, the B' Army Corps ordered the V Division to move from the Koritsa high plateau as of the evening of January 21 and to concentrate its forces in the area of Leskoviki by January 26. The Corps ordered the I Division to seize the ridgeline 1308-1060 at the northern section of Trebessina mountain and to retain the necessary reserve west of Desnitsa river, so as to cover the left flank of the Army Corps. The XV Division was assigned to mop up the area north of the Kiafe Sofout height, as far as the river Apsos.

**184.** The I Division, continuing its operations on January 20, managed to seize the height Bregou Psari under bad weather conditions and severe cold. At the same time, Division troops ascended the northern section of Trebessina mountain and seized the height 1308, east of Psari village. Furthermore, other Division troops seized the heights east of Hani Boubessi and the northern heights of Balaban. On the following day the weather improved and the enemy airforce mercilessly strafed not only the rear area but also the front line troops. Nevertheless, the Division continued the struggle and despite the enemy counter-action it managed to seize the eastern ridges of Kiafe Louzit, while Division troops crossed Desnitsa in the south of Hani Boubessi, in the night of January 21 to 22.

On the same day (January 21) in the sector of Klissoura, the enemy succeeded in overthrowing the troops on the height 1620 by counter-attack and these troops withdrew towards Gropa on the south-eastern slopes of Trebessina mountain, near the river Aoos. After this, the B' Army Corps reinforced the "Klissoura Team" with two battalions of the reserve.

The I Division continued its offensive effort and on January 22, after a tough fight that lasted the whole day, it managed to seize the height of Kiafe Louzit. Further to the north it seized the height of Spi Kamarate, where it took about 500 Italian prisoners and seized supplies of all kinds.

On January 23, the height 1620 in the sector of Klissoura was recaptured, while in the northern sector of the Division, in the area of the Hani Boubessi, the Bregou Rapit (717) height was taken as well as the 731 height. Two consecutive counterattacks of the enemy against the Bregou Rapit height failed. About 350 Italians were taken prisoners including many officers.

During the two-day period of January 24 and 25, the enemy launched powerful counter-attacks throughout· the entire front of the Division, concentrating its main effort in the sector of Klissoura against the height 1620 and in the northern section of Trebessina against the heights 1308-1060. Both counterattacks were repulsed with many losses for the enemy in personnel and equipment.

On January 20 and 21, the XV Division repulsed strong enemy counter-attacks against the saddles of Kiafe Sofiout and Kiafe Mourit respectively. From January 22 to 24, no important activity was recorded, because of the unfavourable weather conditions and the Division troops dealt with the re-organisation and the preparation of the attack.

On January 25, the Division resumed the offencive and in spite of the adverse weather conditions and the stubborn resistance of the enemy, it seized the Vinan village, the Bregou Lioulei height and by 1530 hrs and after a hard struggle, the height of Mali Spandarit. Ten officers and approximately 100 Italian soldiers were taken prisoners.

The XI Division, which was operating north of Apsos river, according to the Army Corps instructions, would assist the operations of the XV Division towards Mali Spandarit and to transport a combat team of regiment strength across Apsos to the west of this river.

Thus, on January 20, the Division seized the Kala height by surprise, with a small section of its troops that had crossed over to the west of Apsos river, while two days later, on January 22, it captured the ridge to the east of Mali Spandarit. Subsequently, on January 24 and 25, the Division transported one of its regiments to the west of Apsos and advanced it to the area of villages Zaberzani and Belezeska. The river crossing took place via the bridge of Lapani village and through the fords in the area of Zogas village.

**185.** With the above operations, by January 10, 1941, the B' Army Corps had managed to occupy the line Podgorani-Garonin and the road juction of Klissoura, and by January 25, it had occupied the north-eastern and south-western ridges of Trebessina mountain, the saddle of Boubessi and Mali Spandarit mountain.

Thus, on January 25, it had almost reached the end of its efforts and was likely to revert to a defensive disposition, since the bad weather, the terrain and the time of year hindered the continuation of large scale offensive operations.

The enemy divisions which it confronted within its zone were originally the 3rd Alpine 'Giulia' Division, the 47th Infantry 'Bari' Division, the 5th Alpine 'Pousteria' Division, as well as units from the 6th Infantry 'Cuneo' Division and the 7th Infantry 'Wolves of Tuscany' Division. Furthermore, around the end of the above period, the following divisions appeared within the zone of the Army Corps: The 24th Infantry 'Pinerolo' Division, the 22nd Infantry 'Alpine Hunters' Division and units from the 37th Infantry 'Modena' Division and the 51st Infantry 'Sienna' Division.

It is evident from the above that the I, XV and XI Divisions of the B' Army Corps encountered at least 7 Italian Divisions during this period. To this disparity of forces one must also add the numerical superiority of the Italian Airforce and the superiority of the Italian units in curved trajectory weapons that were appropriate for mountain fighting, as well as the re-supply difficulties of the Greek forces, which pulled them away from their supply bases, in contrast to the enemy forces which in withdrawing approached their own bases.

Furthermore, the continuous bad weather and the severe snowstorms subjected the men to harsh trials since the increasing number of frostbite cases incapacitated a greater number of men than the casualties of battle.

At the same time the situation of the pack animals kept worsening and the losses exceeded a third of their original strength, due to insufficient food, hardships and their intense use, a fact that hindered transportation and re-supply.

ON OF
1941)

m

ali

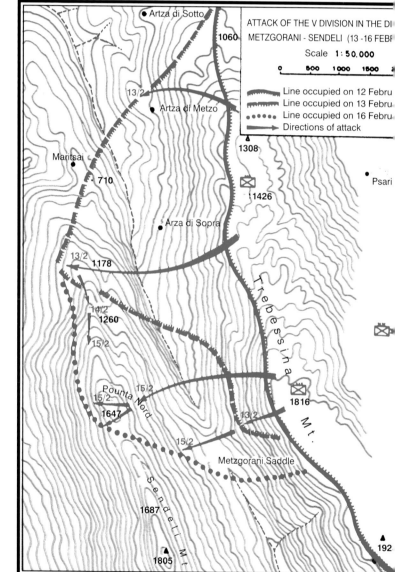

ATTACK OF THE V DIVISION IN THE DI
METZGORANI - SENDELI (13 -16 FEBR

Scale 1:50.000

Line occupied on 12 Februa
Line occupied on 13 Februa
Line occupied on 16 Februa
Directions of attack

*Operations in the Northern and Southern Sectors*
*(of the High Plateau of Koritsa and Epirus)*
*(January 7-25, 1941)*

**186.** In the Northern Sector, on the basis of the mission assigned to the WMFAS by the General Headquarters - concerning the securing of the Koritsa high plateau, the liaison with and the cover of the right flank of the B' Army Corps and, also, the conduct of limited local operations - there were no important operations carried out during this time.

Thus, as of the first ten-day period of January the WFMAS (C'-E' Army Corps) essentially reverted to a defensive disposition. The activity of the units was confined to the repulsion of local Italian attacks, the improvement of the occupied positions and the defensive organisation.

**187.** In the Southern Sector (Epirus), the same situation prevailed. The A' Army Corps, having reverted to a defensive disposition and due to the bad weather, suspended its offensive operations and its activity was confined to observing the situation, improving the occupied positions and organising and strengthening the front-line.

The General Headquarters, supplementing its general instructions of January 6, which outlined that on the part of the A' Army Corps, action was to be taken in the eastern areas of Drinos river, authorised the Corps, on January 10, to apply pressure, towards the west of Drinos as well, against Tepeleni. Besides, having planned to assume powerful offensive operations in the future as soon as the weather conditions and the re-organisation of the forces would allow it, the General Headquarters was regarding the reinforcement of the A' Army Corps with an additional division as definite possibility.

Nevertheless, it is a fact that the bad state of the lines of communication and the insufficient transportation means for the re-supply, constituted a fundamental obstacle. When this situation was partially improved - given that the IV Division had already retired from the A' Army Corps front, being in need of a long rest -the General Headquarters ordered the V Division, which was situated in the area of the Koritsa high plateau, to advance towards the front of Epirus.

On January 9, the General Headquarters informed the A' Army Corps that there was a disagreement between General Cavallero, the Italian Chief of the Army General Staff and Soddu, the Italian Chief of the Italian forces in Albania, because General Cavallero supported the assumption of a general attack against the Greeks, while General Soddu insisted that the only hope left for the Italian Army was the conduct of strategic withdrawal as far as the Skoubi river. The fact that on December 29 Soddu was relieved of his duties and Cavallero assumed the command of the Italian forces in Albania, proved that Cavallero's opinion had prevailed and, consequently, an Italian attack was to be expected.

On January 18, the A' Army Corps submitted its proposals to the General Headquarters, regarding the continuation of the operations towards Avlonas without the support of the V Division, provided that the B' Army Corps would first seize and hold the area of Glava as far as the river Aoos. The General Headquarters deemed that the assumption of offensive operations by the A' Army Corps was not possible in the immediate future and placed, as mentioned, the V Division at the disposal of the B' Army Corps.

### The Italian attack against Klissoura
### (January 26-31, 1941)
### (Sketch-map no. 14)

**188.** On January 25, the Greek Commander in Chief visited the Headquarters of the B' Army Corps in Bandiloyia and was briefed on the situation. Subsequently, on the same date, he issued an oral order which defined all that was relevant to the further continuation of operations.

On the basis of this order, the B' Army Corps was to operate in the general direction of Garonin-Glava with view to the occupation of the line Bouzi-Glava. At the same time it would operate in the south-west direction of Bouzi-Aoos-Deplan (14 km west of Tepeleni) in order to threaten and place the Tepeleni-Avlonas road under its fire.

Thereafter, and provided that conditions were favourable, it would advance northwards towards Verati and westwards, though not at the expense of its action towards Deplan. During a second stage, it would assist the operations of the A' Army Corps towards Avlonas.

During the same period, and depending on the extent of its operating abilities, the WMFAS (C' and E' Army Corps) would undertake operations in the sector of Pogradetz and in the valley of Tomoritsa.

However, the adverse weather conditions and the concentration of Italian forces opposite the B' Army Corps as a warning of the "Primavera" (Spring) attack, did not allow to conduct any of the abovementioned operations, with the exception of a few limited local ones in the valley of Tomoritsa.

**189.** The Italians, having lost the road junction of Klissoura and the eastern exit of the homonymous defile and despite the desperate pleas of Cavallero for 'defence to the end' in the area, finally managed to contain the advance of the Greek attack, holding their ground steadily in the area east of Tepeleni mountain that blocks off the western exit of the defile.

The Italians considered of great importance the retaining of these positions and thus they concentrated strong forces in order to create a 'wall' , according to the characteristic expression of General Cavallero. Against the- forces of the II Division that comprised 12 battalions defensively established south of Aoos river, the Italians had deployed 14 battalions on the east of Drinos and 12 battalions on the west of the river and the 'Centaurs' Armoured Division in the area of Tepeleni.

Thus, after consolidating their new positions, they sought to reoccupy Klissoura, in order to unlock the defile and break through the valley of river Desnitsa, whereupon a serious threat would be set up against the left flank of the Greek B' Army Corps. Taking advantage of a slight improvement of weather conditions, that occurred after January 20, they concentrated the forces of the 'Leniano' Division in the area of Tepeleni. This division was assigned to conduct the operation, with the assistance of troops from the 'Centaurs' Armoured Division and an Alpine battalion.

**190.** The Italian attack commenced in the morning of January 26, north of Aoos river in the direction along the ridgeline Trebessina-height 1923-1620- Gropa-Klissoura and south of Aoos river, in the direction of Pestani-Brezdani. The attack against the height 1620 was initially repulsed. However, it was repeated later and at approximately 1400 hrs, the enemy seized the height 1620 and spread further towards the south-east as far as Moutsin, Mertsoura and Frastani, threatening seriously Klissoura.

At this critical moment, the III Battalion of the 4th Regiment of the I Division launched an attack from the area of Podgorani towards the height 1923 at the centre of Trebessina mountain and struck the flank of the Italians, thus containing their move towards Klissoura.

The Italian counter-attack towards the south of Aoos from Pestani and Brezdani (height 1285) was repulsed after a heroic struggle at close combat during which the commander of the defending battalion and the battery commander were both wounded. After the repulsion of the counter-attack, the II Division reinforced the troops positioned on the height with one additional battalion.

The Italian attack against Klissoura alarmed the B' Army Corps. The pocket that had been created constituted a serious threat against its left flank. Furthermore, the possible seizure of Klissoura would serve to cut off the Army Corps troops that were engaged in action west of Desnitsa river.

In order to cope with the situation, the Army Corps considered necessary to seize the entire ridgeline of Trebessina mountain so as to prevent the Italians from using it either as an observation post or as a base of attack.

For the implementation of this decision, the Corps made the necessary predisposition of forces and, having reinforced the I Division with two battalions from the XV Division, it ordered the former to operate in the direction Podgorani-Givanoi, towards the heights 1923 and 1620, to repulse the enemy and to seize the height 1923.

Furthermore, it ordered the V Division to move towards and deploy its forces in the area of Klissoura, with the prospect of assuming an active sector in the zone of the Corps.

After taking the above measures, the B' Army Corps contained the further advance of the Italians in the area of Klissoura and established a continuous and stable front along its left flank, with the prospect of repulsing the enemy beyond the ridgeline of Trebessina.

**191.** The A' Army Corps, due to the situation that had arisen and the information provided by prisoners, concerning the importance attached by the Italians to the attack against Klissoura, requested and received the approval of the General Headquarters to extend its right boundary as far as the river Aoos, in order to include the "Klissoura Team" under its command.

January 27 went by with no important activity recorded in the sector of the "Klissoura Team". About twenty enemy tanks, that attempted to break through the defile, were hit by the anti-tank guns of the Team and retired after three had been destroyed. Moreover, in the southern leg of the Klissoura defile the Italians also made persistent efforts to seize the height 1285 (Brezdani). The attack was confronted successfully, after a fight during which the scales were constantly wavering between the two sides, both of which suffered heavy losses. On the following day, January 28, in the northern section of the defile, the height 1620 was recaptured by the "Klissoura Team".

On January 29, in the southern sector and after the ferocious shelling of the artillery, the attack against the height 1285 and the villages Limari and Malesova was repeated and repulsed. Furthermore, five probing attacks of the enemy, which took place during the night of January 29 to 30 were also repulsed with success. On January 30, there were two further counter-attacks of the enemy against the height 1285, which were again repulsed and with heavy losses for the enemy.

The final effort of the Italians against the height 1285 was made at 2100 hrs on January 31 and was successfully repulsed. Thus, due to the Greek resistance, their effort to break through the defile of Klissoura ended without any territorial gain. However, they succeeded in engaging and holding the Greek forces in position, whereas in a different case these would be operating in the direction of Verati.

Despite the failure of the Italians to seize Klissoura, the General Headquarters considered that the threat in that direction continued to exist. It was therefore necessary not only to resolve the situation and block off the defile to a great depth, but also to improve the front by reducing its deployment. Furthermore and regarding the creation of a general diversionary action, the General Headquarters issued an operation order on January 29, by which it authorised the conduct of offensive operations within the zone of the WMFAS towards Pogradetz and the valley of river Tomoritsa.


*The mopping up of the Ridgeline of Trebessina Mountain*
(Sketch-map no. 14)

**192.** Following the measures taken in order to resolve the situation, the B' Army Corps issued specific orders defining the missions assigned to the I and V Divisions.

Thus, the V Division was to seize and hold the ridgeline of mount Trebessina and then advance and secure the saddle of Medzgorani, Mali Sendeli and the village of Medzgorani and to mop up the defile of Klissoura as far as the village of Dragoti.

The I Division would conduct an attack from the height 1816 along the ridgeline of Trebessina mountain.

**193.** Meanwhile, on the evening of January 28, the V Division terminated its concentration and reconnaissance, with its regiments in the area of Klissoura-Koukiari and Kosina.

At 0700 hrs on January 29, Division troops sallied forth to complete the seizure of Trebessina ridgeline from the area of Gropa height. After a tough, alternating fight, that carried on for the entire day, the attacking troops managed to seize the height 1923 in the late afternoon hours, taking at the same time 173 Italian prisoners and seizing important war supplies.

The following morning, the Italians launched a vigorous counter-attack, supported by the concentrated fire of their artillery and airforce, in order to recapture the height 1923. Their attempt failed due to the self-denial and self-sacrifice of the defending Greek troops that launched a counter-attack and forced the attackers to withdraw in disarray, abandoning their dead, wounded and numerous war supplies on the battlefield.

On the following day, January 31, a severe blizzard did not permit the continuation of the operations beyond the height 1923, neither an action against the height 1816 in the northern section of Trebessina to consolidate the liaison with the I Division, nor towards the Medzgorani saddle at its southern section.

The situation in the other sectors of the B' Army Corps during this period did not present any essential changes.

Enemy counter-attacks against the front of the XI Division, which had extended its boundary south of Apsos river and had included Mali Spandarit within its zone, were successfully repulsed. The counter-attacks against the front of the XV Division were also repulsed with success in the area of Hani Boubessi as well as those against the I Division in the area of Bregou Rapit and the height 731, against which the enemy had launched successive counter-attacks.

The involvement of the V Division in the operations forced the General Headquarters to organise a reserve in the zone of the B' Army Corps. Hence, it assigned to the Corps the XVII Division, which had been a reserve of the WMFAS until then. In its place it assigned to the WMFAS the VI Division that was to withdraw from the Bulgarian Theatre of Operations. The movement of the XVII Division to its destination, the area of Borova-Leskoviki, was scheduled to commence on February 2.

**194.** Within the zone of the WMFAS in the northern sector (Koritsa), no important operations took place during this period. The units dealt with the reorganisation, the improvement of their positions and also with the improvement of the living conditions of the troops, and pack animals, that had suffered a lot due to the weather. Regarding the disposition of forces, as of January 26, the XVI Division was placed under the command of the E' Army Corps and its forces were deployed in the area of Liozani-Poptsisti-Tresova-Boritsa.

In the Southern Sector (Epirus), within the zone of the A' Army Corps, small-scale local operations took place for the improvement of the positions, without effecting any essential changes in the front-line.

In the zone of the II Division, repeated counterattacks by the Italians against the area of Boliena that constricted the pocket of Tepeleni, were repulsed after a hard fight. During the two-day period of January 25-26, the Italians bombed the area with more than eight thousand artillery shells, while on January 27, they bombed the town of Argyrokastro, using 250 and 300 Kg bombs, causing 180 dead and about 400 wounded of the inhabitants and soldiers.

While this was taking place on the front, in the mainland the Prime Minister Ioannis Metaxas died suddenly, on January 29. On the same day, Alexandros Koryzis, economist and politician, who had been Minister of Social services from 1936 to 1939 and head of the National Bank since 1939, was appointed as Prime Minister.

## Local Operations from February 1 to 12, 1941

**195.** During the period from February 1 to 12, despite the adverse weather conditions and the fact that the troops, the pack animals and weapons had been worn down, the operations continued, though on a limited scale, in all three sectors of the front, in accordance with the General Headquarters instructions, issued on January 29.

The principal factor that dictated the limitation of the operations were the bad weather conditions with the continuous snowfalls. In many mountainous areas the snow depth exceeded the two meters. Consequently, the cases of frostbite surpassed the casualties of battle and the deaths of pack animals, due to the low temperatures and exhaustion amounted to one third of their total strength. This fact seriously affected the transportation and re-supply units.

**196.** Under such adverse conditions and having opened a passage in the snow of one and a half meter wide and two to three meters deep, on February 9 and 10, IX Division troops seized within the zone of the C' Army Corps, in the Northern sector, the Mnima Greas height and part of Gouri Topit in the mountain range of Sara Gravpova. After this operation, the Division managed to secure the minimum depth required for the better support of its left flank.

In the Central Sector, XV Division troops seized the village of Boubessi on February 4, as well as the height 802, by close combat and despite the vigorous resistance of the enemy which abandoned 27 officers and 300 soldiers killed in action, more than 180 prisoners and all kinds of war supplies.

Actions of the B' Army Corps against Sendeli and the saddle of Medzgorani failed to have the desired results, due to the enemy counter-actions and the adverse weather conditions. To the south of the river Aoos, continuous enemy counter-actions against the height 1285 and Hormova were repulsed.

Local actions of the A' Army Corps units during the same time sought to improve the occupied positions and create favourable conditions for the conduct of further operations towards Tepeleni and Avlonas.

In the meantime, from February 1 to 4, the Commander in chief visited the Headquarters of the WMFAS, the C' and E' Army Corps and, also, the XIII, XVI and XVII Divisions, where he had a briefing on the situation and issued the necessary instructions.

## The Organization of the Epirus Field Army Section (EFAS)

**197.** Until the beginning of February, the A' and B' Army Corps were directly under the orders of the Commander in Chief, whose advanced Headquarters had been in Ioannina since December 16, 1940, in order to ensure better co-ordination of the operations in Albania.

However, in the event of a confrontation of forces in the direction of the Bulgarian Theatre of Operations, whereupon the Commander in chief would be forced to move from the Theatre of Epirus, it was necessary to organise, from then on, a Headquarters to co-ordinate the actions of the A' and B' Army Corps. To that end, the General Headquarters, by its orders on February 6 and 7, authorised the organisation of the Epirus Field Army Section (EFAS), which would have its HQ at Ioannina under the commands of Lieutenant General Markos Drakos, who had been Commander of the Eastern Macedonia Field Army Section (EMFAS) until then.

The Command of the EFAS was assumed at 0400 hrs on February 14. The EFAS comprised the A' Army Corps with the II, III, IV and VIII Divisions and the B' Army Corps with the I, V, XI, XV and XVII Divisions. The boundaries of its zone of responbility were the Ionian sea to the west and the Apsos river to the east, in liaison with the WMFAS.

The General Headquarters, by its orders of February 12, assigned the EFAS with the co-ordination of the operations of the A' and B' Army Corps for the seizure of Avlonas. The missions of the Army Corps were generally outlined as follows:

-The A' Army Corps would operate along the valley of the Siousitsa river and the carriage road Tepeleni-Avlonas, in order to seize the harbour of Avlonas.

-The B' Army Corps would operate to seize the heights of Glava. Then, it would advance towards Aoos river and it would operate with its left flank towards Avlonas in conjuction with the action of the A' Army Corps.

*New Attempts towards Tepeleni*
*(February 13 - 28, 1941)*
(Sketch-map no. 15 and 16)

**198.** According to the order issued by the B' Army Corps on February 9 for the assumption of operations towards Trebessina-Sendeli, in the morning of February 13, troops of the V Division, which had taken their positions of attack on Trebessina during the night of February 12 to 13 under a heavy blizzard, launched their attack and by 1400 hrs seized one after the other the village of Artza di Sopra, the height 1178, the Artza di Mezzo and the height 710. Further to the south, other troops of the Division seized the height 1816 on Trebessina mountain but, because of continuous snowstorm, they were unable to advance towards the saddle of Medzgorani.

On the following day, February 14, the attack to seize the Punta Nord height continued in the northern section of Sendeli mountain, but without any success. Furthermore, fierce enemy counter-attacks to recapture the height 1178 were repulsed with the attacking troops suffering heavy losses. Despite their hard struggle, by the evening hours, the Division units had only slightly improved the positions which they had occupied on the previous day.

The attack went on the next day and after a tough fight at close quarters, the eastern section of the Punta Nord height was seized, but its occupation was not completed. In the direction of Medzgorani, the saddle of Medzgorani between Trebessina and Sendeli was taken at 1400 hrs.

The enemy launched ferocious counter-attacks, to recapture the Punta Nord and Medzgorani during the daytime and in the night of February 15 to 16, which were unsuccessful. The Italians abandoned about 200 killed in action and 500 prisoners.

The occupation of the Punta Nord was completed on February 16. The repeated enemy counter-attacks to recapture that height as well as the heights 1260 and 1178 were repulsed with many casualties on both sides. In the direction of Medzgorani, no success was recorded due to the snowstorm, the high depth of the snow and the rough terrain. New Italian counter-attacks, that launched in the night of February 16 to 17, in order to recapture the heights 1260 and Punta Nord, were successfully repulsed. From February 18 to 25, no changes were recorded in the occupied positions of the V Division, because of the severely bad weather that had occurred and did not permit the continuation of operations towards Sendeli mountain.

Since its entry into combat, on January 29, the V Division had endured severe hardships and its casualties, including the killed in action, wounded and frostbite cases exceeded 3,350 men. During the same period, the number of its pack animals was reduced by. 758.

The I and XV Divisions had also endured hardships, fighting continuously on the front-line since the beginning of war. This is why, the EFAS authorised their gradual relief, when conditions would permit it.

**199.** In conjuction with the action of the V Division of the B' Army Corps towards Sendeli-Medzgorani, an offensive of the II Division (A' Army Corps) had been planned to take place towards Lekli and Pestani.

This operation was not carried out on February 13, because the units of the B' army Corps which would operate towards Medzgorani were unable to advance in that direction. The Commander of the EFAS, after assuming his duties on February 14, ordered the A' Army Corps to conduct the offensive against Lekli and Pestani, as prepared. Thus, the attack of the II Division was launched on February 15, between Aoos river and mount Nemertska, despite the heavy Italian bombing against the positions of the attacking troops since 0200 hrs.

The attack was launched at 0730 hrs against the height 1285, yet its occupation was not completed during the day. After a night probing attack the seizure of the height 1285 was achieved with the exception of its north-western part. The action towards the village of Pestani was unsuccessful.

On February 16, the attack was continued from the direction of the height 1285 and the bridge of Zagorias river was placed under control. During this two day struggle, more than 400 Italians were captured, including two senior officers. The attack also continued during the following day, however without any noteworthy results, mainly on account of the enemy flanking fire from the dominating Goliko height, in the south.

On February 18, the height 1723 in the range of Goliko was seized and the entire force engaged in its defence and comprising three officers and eighty five soldiers were captured. Furthermore, the north-eastern outskirts of the Pestani village were taken, but many losses were suffered by the attacking regiment of the Division.

In the direction of Lekli, no progress was recorded, due to the strong organisation of the terrain and the counter-action of the enemy with an incessant barrage of fire.

After the limited successes in the direction of Lekli and Pestani, the Division decided to focus its main effort towards Goliko, assisting thus the moves towards Lekli on the left and Pestani on the right.

Thus, on February 19, the attack continued and the village of Pestani was seized, where over 300 prisoners were taken and war supplies of all kinds were captured. However, further advance was contained by the flanking fire of the tanks, that were firing from the northern bank of Aoos along the road Tepeleni-Klissoura. An effort against the height 739, to the west of Pestani failed due to the artillery barrage that spread to the village of Pestani and caused many losses to the attacking troops as well as to the inhabitants.

On February 20, an action towards Lekli did not have any progress, while the advance on Goliko towards the height 1615 continued and the eastern part of that height wàs seized.

During the period from February 21 to 28, the offensive operations were suspended, on account of the extremely adverse weather that prevailed in the area in conjunction with the continuously increasing number of casualties due to the ceaseless pounding of the enemy artillery and frostbite cases that had arisen to alarming proportions. The attack against the height 739 was repeated on February 28, despite the unfavourable weather conditions, but with no success; neither did the Italian counter-attack against the height of Goliko.

The casualties of the II Division during the month of February amounted to 13 officers and 268 soldiers killed in action and 26 officers and 720 soldiers wounded, not including the frostbite cases, which amounted to 60-80 per day, only in the area of Goliko.

**200.** During the same period, in the other sectors of the front, there were no large-scale operations taking place, apart from local engagements for the improvement of positions within the occupied front-line. The activities of the commands and units were focused on the organisation of the terrain, the protection of the personnel and animals from the bad weather conditions, the maintenance of weapons and equipment, the reorganisation and resupply of the units and, in general, the preparation of future operations.

## On the Eve of the Italian "Primavera" (Spring) Attack

**201.** The repeated Greek successes and the continuing advance of the ·Greek Army into the Northern Epirus territory, greatly alarmed the Italian high Command, as mentioned previously. Thus, on December 29, 1940, Mussolini was forced to order the replacement of the Commander in chief for the Albanian Theatre of Operations, General Soddu, by the Chief of the Army General Staff, General Cavallero. Furthermore, he requested Hitler to reinforce the Italian forces in Albania , with the strength of a German Army Corps. A series of meetings ensued, on the study of the transportation and use of German forces in Albania in order to strengthen the front.

Mussolini took to heart the defeat of his forces in Albania, which constituted for him the main theatre of operations. Thus, he was seeking for a victory, even with the German aid, over the Greeks, who were, at that moment, threatening Avlonas and Verati.

Hitler, on his part, being in a hurry to begin the campaign against Russia, was disheartened by the Italian inability to overpower the Greek forces, despite the reassurances of Mussolini, and therefore ordered the planning of a German attack against Greece.

On January 19 and 20, 1941, a great conference took place in Salzburg, and apart from Hitler and Mussolini, the Ministers of Foreign Affairs Von Ribbentrop and Ciano took part, as well as the German Generals Jodle, Halder, Von Brauhitz and Von Ridelen along with the Italian Generals Guzzoni and Maras, who was the liaison in the German Headquarters.

In the conference, the Italians stated that their intention was to halt the Greek advance and to hold the front, which was supported by twenty-one Italian divisions, while there was an intention to send another three. In the near future they would reinforce it with ten additional divisions, in order to launch a counter-attack within the next two and a half months from the direction of Koritsa towards Erseka.

In the minutes kept during the conference, which were later found by the Americans, the Germans state their reservations as to whether the Italians would be able to concentrate the required forces in the appropriate time, which meant that Germany should not expect any help from Italy, in the event of a German attack from Bulgaria against Greece. On the contrary, the German attack would greatly relieve the Italian front in Albania.

**202.** After the definite and final decisions of the Germans to attack Greece, Mussolini, in order to save his fallen prestige, renounced the German reinforcement and, as early as the next day, began to reinforce the Albanian front aiming at a victory against the Greeks before the outbreak of the German attack, that would put an end to the campaign against Greece and would secure the German Army flank during the campaign against Russia.

Thus, by the end of February, ten new Italian divisions were transferred to Albania, while tens of ships were daily transporting thousands of tons of supplies, ammunitions, motor vehicles and weapons. At the same time, in order to heal the moral crisis and restore the fighting spirit of the Italian Army, he issued, immediately upon his return from Salzburg, an order of the day through the Ministry of Armed Forces, encouraging all the fascist factors, even ministers, to enlist and join the Italian Armed forces at the Albanian front.

Responding to the above call, by the end of February those that volunteered to enlist and join the Italian forces as officers in order to inspire the Italian Army were the Ministers Bartai, Pavolini, Richardi, Rizzi, Gorla, the loudest of the senior officials of fascism, Marinazzi and Gianetti, as well as the son-in-law of Mussolini Galeatso Ciano.

**203.** At the end of February everything was ready for the new attack against the Greek forces, codenamed 'PRIMAVERA' (SPRING) by the Italians and was organised and prepared to the last detail by Mussolini, who had placed himself in charge of it. Indeed, when the Duce was convinced that he had completed all preparations, he departed in the morning of March 2, with his personal aeroplane which he piloted himself, for the airfield of Tirana, where he was received by the Commander in chief Cavallero, the Governor appointed by the Italian Crown Giacomonti and General Ranza.

Cavallero assured him that the situation in Albania had improved and that everything was ready for the attack.

From the speech delivered by Mussolini, on June 11, 1941, it can be concluded that the forces provided for this purpose comprised twenty five full divisions and three Cavalry regiments, four Bersaglieri regiments, one Grenadieri regiment and a number of Blackshirt battalions, which were equivalent to five additional divisions. As he added himself this was 'an assembly of forces which were truly imposing'.

As soon as he arrived in Albania, Mussolini visited and inspected all forces of the front, even the battalions of the Albanian volunteers, he delivered speeches and dined with officers, stressing the importance for Italy of this new attack.

In the event that this great effort, with which Mussolini had associated his personal prestige and the honour of Italy, would be successful and his legions, as he had hoped and promised Hitler, managed to break through the Greek front and flood Greece, the Balkan Peninsula would belong to the Axis by the end of March 1941. Thus, Germany would not be forced to send the enormous strength of 24 divisions against Greece and Yugoslavia. On the contrary, it would be able to orient its forces towards the eastern front and to commence the attack against Russia by mid May, thus gaining time, of about 40 days.

The development of the situation according to those predictions would have influenced the outcome of the Russian resistance, the duration of the war as well as the final victory, as is accepted by military experts all over the world, including the Russians.

## Warnings of the Italian Attack and the Decisions of the Greek High Command

**204.** The concentrations of the enemy forces in the Central Sector, against the B' Army Corps, had been noticed since February 10, by both ground and air reconnaissance. Simultaneously, intelligence reports, provided by prisoners and other sources refered to an impending serious operation in the direction of Glava-Boubessi-Klissoura. Thus, the General Headquarters, as of February 18, drew the attention of the EFAS to a possible Italian attack in the zone of the B' Army Corps and placed the IV and VI Divisions at the disposal of the EFAS by the end of February.

During a meeting, in Athens on February 25, with the attendance of the King, the Prime Minister, the Minister of the Military and the Commander in Chief, the Commander of the EFAS delivered a detailed account of the situation of his units. Furthermore, he expressed his personal opinion about a large-scale operation, to gain possession over the area of mount Tepeleni, which held the particular interest of the Government. His belief was that it could not be undertaken with great chances of success, unless there was a relief of the I, XI and XV Divisions of the B' Army Corps or of their greatest part and only following the replacement of their casualties and a rest period of 20 to 25 days. Moreover, he added that local operations, with the forces that were already deployed in the front, were not considered to be advantageous, since they would only serve to wear out the personnel, and exhaust supplies and ammunitions, producing no worthwhile results. Instead, he proposed a short period of waiting in order to reinforce, re-organise and redeploy the units 'and create favourable conditions for the assumption of large scale operations, as these were defined in the principal mission of the EFAS.

The Commander of the EFAS returned to Ioannina on March 1 and, on the following day, a meeting was held in the Army Headquarters and was attended by the Commander of the EFAS, the Commanders of the A' and B' Army Corps and Crown Prince Paul. During the meeting it was decided that the operation would be conducted in order to complete the occupation of the Medzgorani-Sendeli area, north of Aoos river and the area of Lekli in the valley of Drinos south of Aoos. Particular attention was given to the co-ordination of the actions of the A' and B' Army Corps.

Based on the conclusions of the meeting, the EFAS issued an order to the A' Army Corps on the same day, instructing it to assist the action of the B' Army Corps, that was to commence on March 7 aiming at the completion of the seizure of the area Medzgorani-Sendeli. The assistance would include artillery fire and a co-ordinated offensive effort from the area of Goliko towards Kondra, in order to seize the valley of Aoos and to cut off the Italian forces at Lekli.

The EFAS estimated that, with the occupation of the Lekli-Kondra area favourable conditions would be created in order to block off the sector of Mouzati and to complete the seizure of the ridgeline of Sefer Agait towards Tepeleni.

**205.** While the above events took place in the Theatre of Epirus, other serious events of greater overall importance for Greece were happening in the neighbouring countries and within Bulgaria in particular. The latter had already joined the Tripartite Pact and German troops began to enter into its territory on March 2 and were advancing towards the Greek-Bulgarian borders.

The discernible immediate threat against Greece from that direction and the expected repercussions on the troops fighting in the Northern Epirus territory, forced the General Headquarters to issue an order on March 1, by which it decreed that, whatever the development of the situation in the Balkans, the mission of the fighting forces in the Northern Epirus front was clear and definite and sought to:

-Secure the occupied territory and conduct active defence.

-Conduct the necessary operations with view to the improvement of defence conditions, whenever the weather conditions and the available forces would allow it.

-Protect and maintain the high morale of the Army from being possibly affected by any causes or threats regardless of their source.

At the same time, the General Headquarters, in order to prevent the potential encirclement and cut off that threatened the forces of the Northern Epirus front in the occasion of a German invasion from Bulgaria, ordered on March 7, the EFAS and the WMFAS to consider the possible withdrawal of their forces to the line of Pieria-Aliakmonas river-Venetikos river-Smolikas mountain-Merdzani and from there on to the Greek-Albanian borders or even further to the south as far as the line of Pieria-Aliakmonas-Venetikos-Zygos Metsovou-Arachthos river.

Furthermore, on account of the difference of opinions that arose regarding the further continuation of the operations, on March 6, the High Command proceeded to replace the Commanders of the EFAS and the A' and B' Army Corps. Thus, the Commander of the EFAS, Lieutenant General Markos Drakos, was replaced by Lieutenant General Ioannis Pitsikas, who had been Commander of the WMFAS until then and whose Headquarters were abolished. The C' Army Corps was renamed and was thereby known as WMFAS, under the command of the Corps Commander Lieutenant General Georgios Tsolakoglou. The Commander of the A' Army Corps, Lieutenant General Georgios Kosmas was replaced by

Lieutenant General Panaghiotis Demestihas, who had been Commander of the E' Army Corps until then and whose Headquarters was abolished and his units had come under the command of the WMFAS. The Commander of the B' Army Corps Lieutenant General Dimitrios Papadopoulos was replaced by the Commander of the III Division, Major General Georgios Bakos.

*Offensive Operations towards Sendeli and Tepeleni*
*(March 7 - 8, 1941)*
(Sketch-map no. 17)

**206.** Since February 26, the B' Army Corps had defined that the mission of the XVII Division would be the completion of the seizure of Medzgorani area and the seizure of the area Damsi-Katsisti on the western borders of mount Sendeli. The operation would take place in two phases. During the first phase, the rocky ridgeline to the west of Medzgorani village would be taken along with heights 1232-Besisti, while in the second phase the area Katsisti-Damsi would be seized.

A proposal of the Commander of the XVII Division to free, by preliminary action, the carriage road Klissoura-Dragoti was accepted by the Army Corps, in spite of its own reservations regarding the outcome, because of the action of the Italian tanks along that road.

The terrain was rough, precipitous and with deep ravines, presenting enormous difficulties. The only approach to the Sendeli mountain was possible through the saddle of Medzgorani, which connects the Trebessina mountain to the Sendeli mountain. Despite these difficulties, in the night of March 2 to 3, the Division acted with a battalion group, reinforced with an Engineers company, from the north towards the village of Medzgorani, in order to create footholds and a base of attack. The Group managed, by raiding action, to infiltrate deep into the defile, establish its forces on the height 730 and cut off the carriage road, by digging a ditch 7 meters wide and 2.80 meters deep. Thus, it managed to cut off and then capture the entire company, the tanks, the anti-tank and the anti-aircraft guns that covered the defile, extending the control of the Division by nine kilometres west of Senegol.

After the success of this probing attack, the Division launched its attack, on March 7, in the direction of Medzgorani-Sendeli. Despite the adverse weather conditions and the snow depth which in many places had risen to one meter, by 1400 hrs, benefiting from the fog and the excellent co-ordination of the artillery fire, the Division managed to pass through the village of Medzgorani, seize the rocky foot to the west of the village and to

halt the retreat of the Italians. During the same period, the stone bridge on the carriage road was taken and destroyed in order to block off the movement of the enemy tanks eastwards.

Thus, as the area north of the village of Medzgorani was being tightly constricted, by 1700 hrs, the enemy resistance gave in and the enemy forces began to surrender in large groups. By dusk, the village of Medzgorani with the entire area around it had been seized. More than 1,000 prisoners were taken (including 20 officers) along with their armament, and 4 field guns, 3 anti-tank guns and many automatic weapons and mortars were captured along with depots filled with war supplies and food.

During the night of March 7 to 8, the advance westwards continued and the height 1437 on the eastern slopes of Sendeli was seized.

On the following day, March 8, the effort to occupy the ridgeline of Sendeli continued, but the adverse weather conditions, the precipitous terrain and the drastic fire of the defending troops, which were continuously reinforced, did not permit an advance beyond the eastern ridges of the Sendeli ridgeline, whereon the line of defence was finally consolidated.

**207.** During the same period, in the zone of the A' Army Corps, the II Division, in co-ordination with the XVII Division operations towards Medzgorani-Sendeli, launched an attack against the area of Goliko (between Drinos and Aoos, east of Tepeleni), at 0615hrs, on March 7 and, in the area of Bouzae Sefer Agait (west of Drinos), it adopted a defensive attitude , in order to cover its left flank as well as the right flank of the VIII Division. The attacking troops managed to repulse the enemy by close combat west of the Goliko height and to seize the height 1615, taking about 200 prisoners. An effort towards the height 556, in order to envelop Lekli village and place Louzati bridge of river Drinos under control, failed, because in the meantime, the enemy had created a strong wall of forces and equipment, east and south of Tepeleni.

A parallel action towards the height 739, to place the Dragoti bridge of Aoos river under control, recorded no progress. It was finally seized on the following day, March 8, after a fierce close combat, during which 300 Italians were taken prisoners, including the commander of the defending battalion and his staff. Further advance was halted, due to the enemy resistance.

In the other sectors of the front, during the same period, no noteworthy events took place, except for the usual artillery and patrol activity and the action of the enemy's airforce. The units dealt with the organisation of the terrain, the improvement of the road network, their **regrouping and the resupply.** Meanwhile, administrative movements of units took place, in order to make relieves on the front-line or return to their parent formations.

### The Great "Primavera" (Spring) Attack of the Italians
### ( March 9-15, 1941 )
### ( Sketch-map no. 18 and 19 )

**208.** So far, the feverish preparations of the Italians in order to inflict a decisive blow against the Greeks have been referred. The Italian Army in Albania, after a three month desperate resistance, had been considerably reinforced in personnel and means and was already in a position to launch a general attack. An impressive victory was expedient, in order to save its prestige, before the Germans launched their own attack against Greece.

However, contrary to the hopes and aspirations of the Italian Leadership and of Mussolini himself for an impressive victory, the plan that had been worked out by Cavallero had limited goals, since its final objective was Ioannina. The entire operation was assigned to the Eleventh Army, under the command of General Gelozzo, while the Ninth Army, that was deployed further to the north, was not even notified that the Italian Army would be engaged in its greatest effort since the beginning of the war.

According to the plan of Cavallero, the Italian attack would be launched on March 9 and along a limited front between the rivers Aoos and Apsos, in the general direction Glava-Boubessi, so as to create a gap and break through the valley of Desnitsa river. The main effort, along a front of six kilometres, was assigned to the VIII Army Corps, under the command of General Gabara, with the 'Cagliari', 'Puglia', 'Pinerolo' and 'Bari' Divisions as well as two Blackshirt Battalions. The VIII Army Corps would operate between the 'Sforzeska' Division of the XXV Army Corps on the right (south) and the 'Alpine Hunters' Division of the IV Army Corps on the left (north).

More specifically, the plan provided for an attack in three directions. The main effort would be directed to the sector of the Greek I Division. The first objective would be the line Podgorani-Souka, and the second the line Klissoura-Fratari-Mali Kressova. Thereafter an advance towards Leskoviki-Ioannina would be anticipated. The final result would be pursued by frontal attack in conjuction with local enveloping actions, immediately after the creation of the gap.

From the abovementioned and also from other evidence, it turns out that the Italians were planning to advance, after breaking through the front in the sector of the I Division, between Trebessina and Boubessi, towards the road junction of Klissoura. Thus, having cut off the V and XVII Greek Divisions in Trebessina and Sendeli and having repulsed the XV and XI Divisions towards Garonin, they would break through the valley of Desnitsa. Afterwards, they would advance through the valley of Aoos, towards Premeti-Leskoviki-Merdzani and the area of Erseka, in order to separate the north front from the south front and would then proceed in the direction of Ioannina.

**209.** The B' Army corps, in the zone of which the final attack would be launched, had the XVII, V, I, XV and XI Divisions at its disposal, from Aoos to Apsos. Behind the front-line on a second echelon, as reserves of the EFAS, there were three regiments, one from each of the XV, XVII front-line Divisions and one from the VI Division, which was in the area north of Klissoura. Furthermore, in the area of Liebhova village (SE of Argyrokastro), the IV Division was ready for a possible move within the zone of the B' Army Corps.

Against the forces of the B' Army Corps, the Italians were provided with a first echelon which comprised, from north to south, the 22nd 'Alpine Hunters' Division, the 59th 'Cagliari' Division, the 38th 'Puglia' Division, the 152 and 155 Blackshirt Battalions (on the saddle Sisiput and astride the carriageable road), the 24th 'Pinerolo' Division and the 2nd 'Sforzeska' Division. On a second echelon they had the 47th 'Bari' Division and, later on, the 51st 'Sienna' Division and the 7th 'Wolves of Tuscany' Division. Lastly, their reserves in the area of Tepeleni were the 29th 'Piedmonte' Division and the 131st 'Centaurs' Armoured Division. Apart from the abovementioned forces, between Apsos and Aoos they had various Bersaglieri regiments as well as Alpine and Blackshirts battalions at their disposal, the total strength of which amounted to about fifteen Infantry battalions and two Machine-gun battalions.

**210.** The Greek forces, however, did not lack in preparation for the confrontation of an impending Italian attack. The preparations of the Italians had attracted their attention, as previously mentioned, as of the first ten-day period of February and, on February 9, the B' Army Corps, in accordance with the General Headquarters instructions, while still continuing its local offensive operations, had issued an order of defensive organisation. Thus, time was given to the necessary preparation for the confrontation of the Italian attack. This period was decisive in order to complete the defence and to create the high morale of the troops, who had got used to the idea of the impending enemy assault and its repulsion.

During the last few days before the outbreak of the attack, the Italian airforce escalated its activity with bombardments along the front-line and the rear area. On March 8 in particular, it bombed reserves, concentrations, artillery positions, command stations and observation posts.

**211.** The expected great Italian attack was launched at 0630 hrs, on March 9, with artillery preparation that lasted on for two and a half hours along the entire front of the B' Army Corps. In the sector of the I Division, along a six kilometre zone, the density of fire corresponded to that of 300 guns, -which fired about 100,000 shells- not to include the shells of the 60 mortars of 8lmm calibre of each Italian division engaged in the attack. The heights 717 (Bregou Rapit) and 731 were dug up and everything was destroyed. The telephone communications were cut off and the smoke, dust and flames did not allow the function of visual signals' equipment. The Italian Airforce also supported the attack, by bombing the area.

The attack was launched along the entire front of the I Division, from height 1308 on the northern slopes of Trebessina mountain and as far as the village of Boubessi, where the enemy also directed its main effort in order to create a gap. The enemy attacked with similar intensity against the height 731 as well, but the defenders of the height decimated the attackers by close combat and forced them to fall back. A new effort of the Italians, with another unit, managed to seize the height 717 (500m west of 731), an advanced outpost which was outside the defensive area. The height was soon recaptured by counter-attack. At approximately 1200 hrs, the Italians launched a new attack against the heights 1060, Kiafe Louzit, 731 and 717, only managing to recapture height 717 that was off the defensive disposition.

At 1400 hrs and 1650 hrs, two new attacks against the heights Kiafe Louzit-731 and Bregou Rapit failed as well, with the enemy suffering considerable losses. Thus, during the first day, the enemy attack against the sector of the I Division, where the main effort was directed, was a flat failure, despite the successive attempts and the overwhelming support of the abundant means of fire and the 190 aircraft, of which 70 were bombers. The Italian losses were extremely heavy.

**212.** The B' Army Corps, after ascertaining during the course of the battle that the enemy was directing its main effort in the zone of the I Division, proceeded to reinforce the division with a new regiment from the VI Division and with two additional battalions from its own reserves.

In the zone of the XV Division that was engaged in defence further to the north of the I Division, the enemy met with a similar fate and its successive attacks were repulsed with heavy casualties. At the right flank of the Army Corps that was occupied by the XI Division, the enemy sought to gain possession of the Bregou Lioulei and the Mali Spandarit heights with fierce attacks that were, however, repulsed by the defending troops. The same fate befell the attack in the zone of the V Division, which was engaged in defence further to the south of the I Division in Trebessina.

The XVII Division -which, as mentioned, was conducting offensive operations since March 7, to the north of Aoos river as far as the saddle of Medzgorani- also succeeded in confronting the Italian attack within its zone that was directed with greater intensity against the height 1437 and the saddle of Medzgorani.

In the sector of the II Division, south of Aoos, the Italian activity was confined to severe shelling with artillery and mortars. Thus, the first day of the great 'Spring' attack of the Italians ended with entirely insignificant territorial gains on their part, despite their enormous effort and to the great disappointment of Mussolini, who had been watching its development during the whole day from his observatory on the Komarit height (Glava). The B' Army Corps kept the main defensive area intact, and its troops that had suffered the attack fought back with exceptional courage and high morale.

**213.** By 0645 hrs in the following morning, March 10, the Italians renewed their offensive effort by attacking the area of the I Division with the sustained fire of the artillery and infantry, the intensity of which were similar to the shelling of Verden during the First World War. Everything was dug up again, but the heroic fighters remained unshaken. Successive attacks ensued against the heights 731, Bregou Rapit and Trebessina, that lasted the entire day, failing, however, to produce any result and causing heavy casualties on the Italian side. The fight was hard and, in many cases, the Greek troops were forced to confront the enemy by force of bayonet.

A Regiment of the 'Puglia' Division moving as of 1115hrs along the carriage road, which attempted to envelop the height 731 from the south, was hit by the sustained fire of all Arms from the occupied heights Trebessina-Kiafe Louzit and 731, and was thus overthrown and forced to disband. Another enveloping action of the Italians through the ravine of Proi Math was similarly halted before the height 731.

The B' Army Corps, acknowledging the outstanding action of the I Division during the two-day fight, issued the following order on March 10.

' *Fighters of the I Division*

*Before your indefatigable heroism since yesterday all desperate enemy attempts have been shattered. Before your lines of steel, three new Divisions were crushed during the two day period. I am proud of being in command of such heroes. The Fatherland is also proud of you. This order should be communicated down to the last soldier of the Division.*

*Major General G. Bakos* '

As of 0700hrs, in the sector of the XV Division, the heavy shelling of the artillery and mortars that was mainly directed against the Boubessi (height 710) and the height 869 centre of resistance, was followed by successive attacks which were repulsed with serious losses on the enemy's side.

In the sector of the XI Division, the sustained fire of the artillery and mortars lasted from 0650 hrs to 0800 hrs with particular intensity against the height Mali Spandarit, against which a powerful Italian attack was launched at 0930 hrs. The close combat that ensued, under thick fog and pouring rain, ended in a Greek victory. Enemy troops that had managed to infiltrate through to the south of Mali Spandarit, hidden in the fog, were destroyed by the counter-attacks of a battalion that advanced in time to regain control of the area.

The XVII Division, according to a previous plan, launched an attack to seize the height 1623 of Trebessina west of the height 1437, but the extremely adverse conditions and the barrage of fire forced it to halt its attack.

In the sectors of the II and V Divisions, the enemy attacked with its artillery and mortars, pounding mainly against the height of Punta Nord.

**214.** The third day of the offensive effort to break through the area commenced at 0430hrs, with the same momentum as on the previous days and with the main effort once again directed against the height 731. The defenders were on the alert and counter-acted with a barrage of fire and an immediate counter-attack, thus causing the attackers against both the height 731 and the Bregou Rapit to break up.

The enemy, together with the frontal attack, proceeded in the direction of Hani Vinokazit, continuing the enveloping action that had been launched through the ravine of Proi Math and which had been halted temporarily. Despite the thick fog that prevailed, the anti-tank artillery troops positioned in the ravine were able to perceive the Italian infiltration in time and directed their sustained fire against it from the sides and the rear. Pandemonium followed. The Italians frantically rushed to their safety, but as they were fired against from all directions, they were eventually decimated. The fire finally ceased at noon, when the Italians raised white kerchiefs all along the Proi Math ravine and surrendered unarmed with their hands in the air. The mop up of the ravine delivered 521 prisoners, including three senior officers. There were 250 dead counted and all kind of war supplies were seized.

Meanwhile, there was an escalation of the bombings of the Greek positions in Trebessina-Kiafe Louzit and 731, against which the enemy launched a new powerful attack. The fight continued with obstinacy on the entire front of the I Division until 1300hrs, whereupon the attack was finally confronted with terrible losses for the enemy. A new attack following strong bombarding against the height Bregou Rapit faced a similar fate.

In the sector of the XV Division, after heavy shelling by the artillery, the Italians launched two attacks (at 0800 hrs and at 1600 hrs), which were repulsed with heavy losses.

In the sector of the XVII Division, after an equally heavy shelling, the enemy attacked the heights Medzgorani and 1437, but here too, its forces were repulsed with great losses. Two new successive attacks at 1700 hrs and at 1930 hrs were once again repulsed.

In the sectors of the V and XI Divisions, the pounding of the area with sustained artillery and mortar fire was continued, while small-scale enemy attacks were successfully repulsed.

In the sector of the II Division too, the activity of the enemy artillery did not display the intensity of the two previous days.

Thus, the third day of the attack ended, without the Italians being able to 'set foot' on the main defensive area of the B' Army Corps. The losses of the Italian 'Puglia' Division that was fighting against the I Division and those of the Blackshirts battalions were enormous, forcing the Italian command to advance the reserve 'Bari' Division to the above area on March 11 and on the night of 11 to 12.

**215.** At 0045 hrs on March 12, a new Italian attack was launched in the sector of the I Division, against the heights 731 and Bregou Rapit, with the support of artillery. The attack also spread on the height Kiafe Louzit was extremely vigorous and was conducted by intact units of the newly-committed to action 'Bari' Division. The enemy had velied on the surprise, but the Greek troops, that had stepped up the alert, confronted the attackers with a dense barrage of fire and repulsed them by close combat.

At 0530 hrs, the attack was repeated without any preparation -it was the eleventh in a row- in the sector from the height 1060 of Trebessina to the height Bregou Rapit. The counter-action of the defending Greek troops was immediate and decisive, forcing the Italians that were engaged in the attack against the heights 1060 and Kiafe Louzit to be held in position by the barrage of defence fire. Meanwhile, on the height 731, the fight continued until 0645 hrs, whereupon the attackers were finally repulsed by hand-grenades and bayonet.

At 0930 hrs enemy troops attempted to infiltrate through to Kiafe Louzit, but were hit by the heavy fire of the artillery and fell back. As of 1100 hrs, the enemy activity was confined to artillery shelling throughout the entire area of the I Division front.

In the sector of the XV Division, the Italians conducted two attacks against Boubessi, which were repulsed.

In the sectors of the II, V, and XI Divisions, the artillery fire continued during the entire 24-hour period.

In the sector of the XVII Division, a raid towards the south-west of Medzgorani, conducted by two squads headed by a First Lieutenant, resulted in capturing 12 Italian officers and 223 soldiers at their base of attack. The glorious success of this small detachment came as a surprise even to the Italian prisoners, as soon as they realised its actual strength.

The fourth day ended, like the previous one, with a flat failure of the Italians. This situation greatly alarmed Mussolini, who had been watching the development of the attack from the day of its commencement. On the morning of March 12, the fourth day of the Italian attack, Mussolini received a report of General Gelozzo, Commander of the II Army, by which he claimed that the whole operation was to be regarded as a failure. After this, on the evening of the same day, Mussolini convoked a meeting of all the Large Unit commanders, in order to assess the situation, as it had developed and which was turning into a flat failure for the attackers.

During the meeting, Mussolini stressed the need to continue the offensive with all available forces, in order to achieve the objectives before the Germans launched their own attack against Greece in the beginning of April, as was expected, and concluded as follows:

'I have always done my utmost to keep the name and prestige of the Italian Army high but it is now expedient to alter the situation. I have told his Excellency Guzzoni to send all existing supplies in Italy here, because the Italian Army is here, the war is here, and it is here that we must win'.

On the basis of this decision of his to provide all the means of support required for the success of the offence, at 2115 hrs, he summoned General Priccolo, Chief of the Airforce General Staff and ordered him to place the entire Airforce at the disposal of the offensive operations.

**216.** On the following day, by noon, the front of the I Division displayed the usual shelling action of the artillery and mortars. As of 1330 hrs, a vigorous bombardment started throughout the entire front of the Division, covering the entire depth of its zone.

At 1530 hrs an extremely powerful attack was launched against the heights 731 and Bregou Rapit, while simultaneously, 31 fighter aircraft, which escorted 20-25 bombers, which were bombing in groups of 5, were continuously flying over the Division sector and bombing the artillery and reserve positions, while incessantly strafing the front-line troops.

The fight was conducted with unprecedented obstinacy. Wherever the attackers managed to approach the trenches, their brave defenders would spring from them with fixed bayonets and would overrun them by a hand to hand fight. The fight lasted until the evening, whereupon the attackers were finally overrun. The losses were great on both sides. At

1800 hrs, the Italians launched a new attack without artillery preparation against the height 731, the thirteenth in a row, which was also repulsed.

In the sectors of the V, XI, XV and XVII Divisions, there was only artillery action taking place, with particular intensity against the Centre of resistance of height 710 (Boubessi) and south, as far as Kiafe Louzit. The Italian Airforce, with 200 sorties in consecutive waves, bombarded the entire zone of the B' Army Corps and, in particular, heights 1308, Kiafe Louzit and Mali Spandarit.

Thus the fifth day of continuous fighting ended, with a complete failure for the Italians, in spite of the exhortations, admonitions and agonised pleas of Mussolini, the massive use of the Airforce and the terrible barrage of their Artillery. The brave defenders of the heights 731 and Bregou Rapit retained their positions unshaken and overran the successive attacks against them.

**217.** The night of March 13 to 14 displayed the usual artillery and mortar activity. Within the sector of the I Division, the Italians, as of 0030 hrs, began to advance small sections to the Proi Veles ravine, north of Bregou Rapit, which were, nevertheless, perceived at dawn and were thereafter held in position. A Greek counter-attack was launched and the Italian troops were forced to retreat in disarray, abandoning, apart from the war supplies, about 25 prisoners as well.

In the morning, heavy shelling by the artillery recommenced against the right flank of the Division without interruption until 1000 hrs, whereupon the Italians once again launched an extremely vigorous counter-attack against the heights 731 and Bregou Rapit with a regiment of the 'Bari' Division and a regiment of the 'Cagliari' Division respectively. The fight lasted until 1230 hrs and the attackers were repulsed with extremely grave losses. The shelling of the artillery and the bombing of the airforce against the front of the Division continued and at 1500 hrs a new attack, the fifteenth, was launched against the heights 731 and Bregou Rapit.

The fight was relentless with alternating phases until 1700 hrs. During this period, the Italians succeeded in 'setting foot' on the west of the height 717 and for the first time on the front-lines of the height 731, but only for a very short while. With a strong counter-attack, their heroic defenders overran the attackers, who abandoned on site a considerable number of automatic weapons, mortars and prisoners.

An attempt of the enemy to concentrate its forces in the Proi Veles ravine and to reorganise them for a new attack against the height 717, was impeded by the fire of the artillery.

At 1800 hrs, the Italians launched a new surprise attack against the height 731, the sixteenth in a row, with no artillery preparation, yet with a vigorous bombardment of the remainder of the Division zone. The attack was repulsed at 1930 hrs. The same fate befell the attack that was launched against the height 1060, on the left flank of the Division.

The fight was marked by such violence from the very first day of the attack, that the forest covering the heights 731 and 717 (Bregou Rapit) disappeared as if full-scale timberfelling had been conducted beforehand.

In the sectors of the XI, XV and XVII Divisions , only limited artillery action was recorded.

In the sector of the V Division, two attacks were launched against the height Punta Nord, at 0700 hrs and at 1200 hrs, and were repulsed. During the sixth day of the attack the Italians also failed completely.

The successive attacks and the continuous bombings of the Italian Airforce, that came in waves and which had exceeded 300 sorties during that day, could not shake the heroic fighters of the I Division.

**218.** On the following day, until 1300 hrs, calmness prevailed, though a little later, the enemy artillery again began to fire effectively against the heights 731 and Bregou Rapit and, from time to time, against the heights Kiafe Louzit and Maziani.

The shelling continued until 1830 hrs and at 2000 hrs the Italians launched a surprise attack against the height 731, without any artillery preparation. With the commencement of the attack, however, the artillery support was immediate and almost covered the entire front of the Division simultaneously. The fight was stubborn, but, in the end, the attack was repulsed at approximately 2100 hrs, by hand-grenades and direct counter-attacks. The losses were considerable on both sides.

In the sectors of the II, V, XI, XV and XVII Divisions, only artillery action was recorded, without any offensive moves.

The seventh day of the Italian attack March 15, was decisive, since its final flat failure, convinced the Italian Leadership that the 'Spring Attack', on which it had placed so many hopes and which had been prepared in every detail, supported by numerous troops, was an unmitigated disaster.

On the previous day, March 14, in a discussion between Mussolini and Marshal Cavallero, the latter had supported that if the attack of the next day was to fail, the action would have to be suspended and strength would have to be saved so as to resume action at a later date.

Thus, after the failure of the attack on March 15, the Italian Leadership decided the gradual suspension of operations, awaiting more advantageous conditions, yet with the fixed perspective of Mussolini, to secure even a small success before the German attack against Greece.

**219.** The Greek Commander in chief, in appreciation of the glorious feat of the B' Army Corps units and, above all, the self-sacrifice and heroism of the men of the I Division, that had taken on the weight of the Italian attack and had repulsed it successfully, communicated his following Order of the Day, on the night of March 15:

*'The seven-day effort that the enemy is making against you, has not shaken you, it has given you a new occasion to prove yet once again your glorious virtues and above all your faith as to the righteousness of your struggle.*

*The struggle of over four months which you are victoriously conducting has covered you with laurels of unsurpassable glory. The effort of the enemy is crushed, your will remains unbowed and your conviction as to the victory undiminished.*

*Our Entire Army that You of the Central Front so gloriously represent and to the history of which you have added new glorious pages, is watching you and admiring you. I address the warmest of congratulations.*

*Long Live the Greek Army*
*Al. Papagos.*
*Commander in chief'*


*Gradual Slackening off and Suspension of the Italian Offensive*
*( March 16-26, 1941 )*
*( Sketch-map no. 19 )*

**220.** From the morning of March 16 and until March 18, the front of the B' Army Corps presented the usual picture before the attack, i.e. the exchange of artillery fire, patrol activity and limited action of the Italian Airforce.

The Greek Command, estimating that the Italians had exhausted the possibilities of repeating their offensive actions on a large scale, decided to redeploy the forces in the Central Sector, in order to relieve those units which had been sorely tried. Thus, on March 16, the EFAS, by approval of the General Headquarters, ordered the following redistribution of the divisions within the sector of the B' Army Corps: On the first echelon, Divisions IV, V, VI and XVII, were placed, the VI between the rivers Apsos and Desnitsa, the XVII between Desnitsa and the eastern slopes of Trebessina, the V from the village of Artza di Mezzo and as far as Punta Nord-saddle of Medzgorani and the IV (moving from the area of Argyrokastro) astride Aoos, from the saddle of Medzgorani to Goliko.

On the second echelon, the I and XV Divisions east of Klissoura would remain as reserves of the EFAS, and the XI Division in the area Roden-Psari as a reserve of the General Headquarters. The replacement of the I Division by the XVII Division would take place by March 23, while the re-arrangements of the other divisions would have to be completed by the end of March.

221. After a three day respite, on March 19, the Italians launched a new attack, the eighteenth in succession, against the height 731, that stood like an impregnable rock, on which all raging attacks of the enemy were shattered.

The attack was launched at 0630 hrs, after intense shelling of the 731-Kiafe Louzit heights and Trebessina, by elite troops of the 'Sienna' Division, that had been specially trained for this operation and were supported by light combat tanks. The infantry troops, taking advantage of the sustained shelling, managed to approach the southern shoulders of the height 731. However, there they were encircled by the counter-attacking Greek troops and after being depleted, they were pushed back at approximately 0740 hrs, abandoning more than 100 killed in action. As for the tanks, two of them fell into the Proi Math ravine, one was destroyed before height 731 and the others retreated to their base of departure.

The repulsion of the attack was followed by an extremely heavy shelling by the Italian artillery, due to which most of the field defences at 731 height were swept away. In the remaining sectors of the B' Army Corps, no noteworthy activity was recorded.

222. In the area of the XVII Division, at 2200 hrs, on March 20, the Italians launched a powerful attack from Aoos to the height 1437, west of Medzgorani. Even though the attack was supported by a volume of artillery and mortars, it was repulsed at approximately 2400 hrs. As of the evening of March 21, the XVII Division troops at Sendeli began to be replaced by troops from the IV Division. The XVII Division, concentrated in the area Panariti, Riba, Goritsa. There, it attended to the re-organisation and repose of its units until the evening of March 24, whereupon it commenced, with delay, the gradual replacement of the I Division troops and parts of the XV Division, terminating its task on April 2. The delay in the commencement of this replacement was due to the abovementioned Italian attack against the XVII Division.

In the sector of the V Division there was no important activity recorded from March 20 to 28.

In the sector of the I Division, March 21 went by without any noteworthy events. At 0930 hrs on March 22, a group of Italian messengers, comprising three army priests and a number of litter bearers, appeared before the Greek lines on the height 731. Representing the Italian Command, they proposed a cease-fire of 4 to 6 hours, to bury the dead. The Greek Command, after a communication between the I Division and the B' Army Corps, accepted the Italian proposal. In parallel, it set terms of which the most basic one was that, the cease-fire had been requested by the Italians, and that, the burial of the dead from the height 717 and further east as far as the Proi Math ravine southwards, would be conducted by Greek troops in the presence of unarmed Italians from their medical corps.

The proposals of the Greeks were not accepted by the Italians and the fight re-commenced. Nevertheless, the representative of the Greek Command, Commander of the 1/67 battalion of the XVII Division, had the opportunity to traverse the terrain in front of the Greek lines and ascertain the terrible massacre suffered by the Italians in their attacks against the height 731. The same officer, in a report with regard to the situation, related that, even though he had witnessed pictures of massacre in the battlefields of Macedonia and Asia Minor, the macabre and horrifying spectacle that he was faced with, in the area between the heights 731 and 717, went beyond all bounds of his imagination. The entire visible zone (approximately 150 meters wide) of the ridgeline between the two heights was covered with corpses strewn in heaps, amongst which mutilated members of the slaughtered fighters protruded. The macabre picture was heightened by the view of the deadly embrace of adversaries, many of which were Greek. A similar sight was also bound to be encountered on the slopes towards the Proi Math and Proi Veles ravines.

The terrible losses suffered by the Italians before the height 731, justify their decision to build the monument to honor their men who fell fighting in Albania, on that height, which they named 'the Sacred Ground'.

**223.** On the night of March 22 to 23, the Italians shelled the zone of the I Division with intensity, in retaliation for the Greek refusal to accept the cease-fire to bury their dead on their own terms. The shelling continued during the entire day and was particularly heavy against the height 731. At 0020 hrs on March 24, they launched another surprise attack against the height 731, where they we repulsed once again at 0120 hrs by its brave defenders. The attack was repeated at 0330 hrs, but it was also repulsed with heavy losses for the attacking side.

March 25 and 26 went by with limited activity and the Division troops dealt with the terrain organisation and strove to increase the strength of their position.

In the sector of the XV Division, no noteworthy events took place from March 20 to 26, except for artillery and patrol activity, terrain organisation and the preparation for the relief that would occur at the end of the month.

In the sector of the XI Division, there were no noteworthy actions during the same period. From the evening of March 26, its relief by the VI Division commenced. The XI Division was to complete its concentration in the area Roden-Bali-Psari, by the night of April 3 to 4, as a reserve of the General Headquarters, leaving one detachment ( Colonel Yiannakopoulos) north of Apsos under the command of the WMFAS.

**224.** The casualties of the Greek units that had participated in the fight to repulse the Italian 'Spring' attack, were 47 officers and 1,196 soldiers killed in action, 144 officers and 3,872 soldiers wounded and 42 soldiers missing in action. The I Division, which had taken on the principal load of the Italian attack, suffered the heaviest casualties.

The casualties of the Italians during the same period, according to the records of official Italian sources, exceeded 11,800 killed in action and wounded. Furthermore, the number of the Italian prisoners, from January 7 to the end of March 1941, were 189 officers and 7,645 soldiers.

**225.** The Italian 'Spring' attack did not have any serious effect on the other sectors of the front, nor did it negatively affect the morale of the forces. In fact, in reply to a relevant sounding by the General Headquarters with regard to the assumption of diversionary offensive operations in the sector of Kamia-Pogradetz, the WMFAS reported that it was ready and fully convinced of the success of its actions. In the end, the General Headquarters did not undertake to implement the abovementioned action, in order to economise mainly on artillery ammunitions.

Thus, its activity in both the Southern and Northern Sectors was limited to artillery and patrol action. Attacks were launched only against troops of the II Division in the Southern Sector and troops of the XVI in the Northern sector, that were adjoining the area of the B' Army Corps. However, all these attacks were repulsed successfully and with great losses for the Italians.

### The Inglorious End of the Italian Attack

**226.** All the above is a detailed account of the development of the Italian 'Spring' attack, which constituted the most serious effort of the Italians since the beginning of the war. The momentum of the attackers began to gradually slacken off since March 14. One last effort made by the Italians in order to seize the fought-for 731 height, with the use of tanks, was an unmitigated disaster and convinced Mussolini of the inability of the Italian army to resolve the situation, despite the great sacrifices and the heroic attitude of its troops.

In the morning of March 21, Mussoli humiliated and disheartened, departed from the airport of Tirana to Rome.

In his report submitted to King Umberto, an attitude of resentment approaching hostility towards the military leadership is prevalent, as underlined by General Cavallero and confirmed by the Chief of the Airforce General Staff and trusted colleague of Mussolini, General Priccolo, to whom he stated on the eve of his departure for Rome: 'I have summoned you, for I have decided to return to Rome within the following day. I have been disgusted by this environment. We have not moved one step forward. So far I have been deceived. I have deep contempt for all these people'. He refered to his military leaders.

On his return to Italy, Mussolini was still nourishing a small hope that, the repetition of the attack against the Greeks, prepared for the end of March, would give him at least a small success in order to be able to face his German allies without shame. He was once again disillusioned, however, for in the meantime, a coup d' etat in Berlgrade, overthrew the pro-axis Government of Cvetkovitch which, on March 25, had aligned Yugoslavia with the Tripartite Pact.

The coup d' etat brought the Government of Simovich into power, which sided with the western allies. Thus, the new situation created in Yugoslavia forced the Italians to take measures in the direction of the Yugoslavian borders on Albania, and to cancel the new attack planned against the Greek front, awaiting the German assault against Greece that would relieve them from the dead-end situation to which they had been led by the heroic resistance of the Greek Army and the national solidarity of the Greeks.

*A General Review of the Operations during the 2nd and 3rd*
*Period of the Greek - Italian War*
*( November 14, 1940 to March 26, 1941 )*

**227.** The operations conducted from November 14, 1940 until March 26, 1941, constitute the second and third periods of the Greek-Italian war.

During the second period, from November 14, 1940 to January 6, 1941, the Greek Army, after having contained the advance of the intruders, assumed a general counter-attack, in order to restore in full the integrity of the national territory. Confronted with adverse conditions, due to the superiority of the adversary in armament and airforce, the roughness of the terrain, the great difficulties in the re-supply and the severity of the untimely winter, the Army made superhuman efforts, that bore results beyond any expectation.

In the Southern Sector, the A' Army Corps, after occupying the harbour of Agii Saranda on December 6 and the town of Argyrokastro on December 8, continued its offensive operations and by January 6 had taken the line Himara-Vranitsa-Boliena, thus creating favourable conditions for the full-scale breakthrough of the Siousitsa river valley and the continuation of the advance towards Avlonas.

In the Central Sector , the B' Army Corps, after occupying Premeti on December 5 and securing in full the free use of the carriage road Leskoviki-Koritsa, managed to reach, by the end of December and despite the stubborn resistance of the enemy, approximately 15 kilometres east of the road Klissoura-Hani Balaban and was ready to seize the junction of Klissoura.

In the Northern Sector, the WMFAS (C' and E' Army Corps), after occupying the mountain bulk of Morova-Ivan on November 21 and the junction of Koritsa on the following day, advanced west of the junction to a depth of approximately 40 kilometres along the line Ouyianikou-mount Soukagora-Grambova-mount Kamia-Pogradetz, securing the high plateau of Koritsa from the west and north-west.

During the operations of the second period, the Italian Command committed eight new Infantry Divisions to the action, the 2nd Alpine 'Tridentina', the 4th Alpine 'Kouneense', the 11th 'Brennero', the 33rd 'Aqui', the 37th 'Modena', the 48th 'Taro', the 50th Alpine 'Pousteria', the 53rd 'Arezzo', as well as a large number of various other units, of regiment or battalion strength.

During the same period, the Greek Command committed seven new Infantry Divisions, to the action, namely the II, III, IV, X, XI, XIII, and XVII Divisions.

In total, the Italian forces in the Albanian Theatre of Operations amounted to 15 Infantry Divisions and one Armoured Division, against 11 Infantry Divisions, one Infantry Brigade and one Cavalry Division of the Greek forces. Furthermore, what must be taken into consideration is that the Italian Airforce had total numerical supremacy and that the Greek Army was completely lacking tanks.

Nevertheless, the offensive operations of the Greek forces were crowned with success. The Greek Army, however, lacked in armoured and

motorised vehicles, thus there was no possibility to take advantage of the offensive actions, even if there had been opportunities which could have borne important results. This weakness compelled the Greek forces to avoid the zones of the plains and to conduct their moves and manoeuvres from mountainous directions mainly. This resulted in the extension of the columns, added to the fatigue of troops, and pack animals and created difficulties in the re-supply.

On the contrary, by virtue of the means available to the enemy forces, in the zones of the plains, with the use of motor vehicles, the adversary was able to withdraw in haste and establish its troops elsewhere at relative ease. In the mountainous areas, the enemy was able to delay the Greek advance with a relatively small number of forces. Moreover, the Italian units that were newly committed to the action, were quickly transferred to the front with motor vehicles, whereas the Greek ones lacked such means of transportation and arrived at the front after long night marches unable to join the action.

The Greek troops, preserving a high morale and emanating a spirit of self-sacrifice defying the hardships and their disadvantageous position against the adversary, had managed, within, a month and a half not only to chase away the intruder but also to repulse him into the Northern Epirus territory, to a depth ranging from 30 to 80 kms, adding new pages of glory to the age-long Greek History.

**228.** The third period, from January 7 to March 26, 1941, covers the offensive operations of the B' Army Corps towards Klissoura-Verati, the local Italian attack to recapture Klissoura and the great 'Spring' attack of the Italians.

The B' Army Corps, seeking to take possession of the road junction of Klissoura and to advance its forces in the direction of Verati, seized Klissoura on January 10, after a series of hard struggles, and by January 25, had advanced to the general line of the height 1308 (of Trebessina)-Boubessi- Mali Spandarit. There, it suspended its further operations, on account of adverse weather conditions and difficulties in the re-supply of its troops.

On January 26, after stabilising their positions to a certain degree, the Italians attempted to recapture the road junction of Klissoura, to which they attached great importance. The Italian attack was launched by the 'Leniano' Division, which was reinforced with an Alpine battalion along with troops from the semi-armoured 'Centaurs' Division and was supported by a strong air force. During its first day, the attack recorded only small local successes.

The B' Army Corps, realising the danger that a possible loss of Klissoura would entail, hastened to advance strong forces in that direction and to repulse the Italians with relentless fights, that lasted until January 30. Thereafter, the Italians terminated their effort, which had caused them heavy losses in both manpower and supplies.

**229.** However, the most important event of that period of the Greek-Italian war, was the third phase, the great 'Spring' attack of the Italian Army. The Italian High Command, after the stabilisation and the actual suspension of the operations due to the extremely severe winter, was seeking to inflict a serious blow against the Greeks, in order to propitiate the Italian people and its German allies and to atone for its failures up to that point.

Mussolini, aware of the fact that the Germans were ready to invade Greece but uninformed as to the actual time of the attack, was agonising over the possibility that his ally would forestall him and that Italy would thus find itself in the extremely humiliating position to owe the Germans its relief from the dead-end situation to which it had been driven by its deplorable failure in the Albanian front.

The expected Italian attack was launched in the morning of March 9. In total and only on a frontage of approximately six kilometres, five divisions and one Blackshirt battalion had been deployed on a first echelon and five divisions operating as reserves.

Mussolini, full of hope, had positioned himself on the Komarit height (Glava) as of that morning, and from there he observed the development of the attack together with the Commander-in-Chief and the Leaders of the attacking forces. The attack continued with undiminished momentum until March 14, yet failed to record any success, due to the indomitable courage and self-sacrifice of the Greek soldiers, who did not surrender not even one inch of their land to the attacking Italians.

By March 15, the Italian effort had begun to lose momentum and it was abandoned completely after the 25th of the same month. Mussolini disappointed, departed from Tirana on March 21, to Italy, planning to repeat the attack at the end of the month. However, the siding of Yugoslavia with the Allies, which had occurred in the meantime, did not permit for this new attempt to be carried out. The German attack against Greece that followed, finally shattered the hope of the Italians for any success.

# PART THREE

# THE GERMAN ATTACK AGAINST GREECE AND THE FINAL PERIOD OF THE GREEK - ITALIAN WAR

# CHAPTER V

# THE GERMAN ATTACK AGAINST GREECE AND THE FIGHTING IN EASTERN MACEDONIA AND THRACE
## (April 6 to 9, 1941)

*The German Threat*

**230.** Once Hitler decided to turn against Russia, in the summer of 1940, the Balkan Peninsula became of special strategic importance for the Germans. The occupation of the Balkan peninsula constituted a necessary condition for the assumption of this campaign, in order to safeguard the German Armies that would be operating eastwards, from the south.

The occupation of the Balkan Peninsula was also supported by the argument that, the presence of strong German forces would force Turkey to join the Axis or at least to reinforce its neutrality. Furthermore, it would secure the oil-wells of Romania, which were very important for the conduct and spreading of the war, from possible British air raids which would make use of the airfields in Greece for that purpose. What is more, the descent of the Germans to the Balkan peninsula was bound to prevent the unfortunate consequences of a possible failure of the Italian attack against Greece, according to the estimate of the German General Staff.

Thus, Hitler decided to attack Greece, having secured, from the beginning of November 1940, the silent consent of Russia and while all the German officials continued to offer reassurance as to their peaceful and friendly intentions. On November 12, he issued his first confidential instructions to the General Staff to prepare the said operation.

**231.** A month later, on December 13, Hitler issued his no. 20 confidential directive, in which the operation against Greece is referred to, for the first time, by its code name 'MARITA'.

The objective of the operation was the seizure of the northern shores of the Aegean and the bay of Thessaloniki, in readiness to proceed southwards for the occupation of the whole of Greece. Twenty-four German divisions were assigned in the operation, for the accomplishment of this objective.

Operation 'MAPITA' was decided to begin and end during March 1941, so that the above German forces would be disengaged as soon as possible in order to be used in the assault planned against Russia. The main concern of the German Chancellor was to begin the attack as early as possible, in order to complete it before the advent of the Russian winter.

Indeed, five days later, on December 18, 1940, Hitler issued his no. 21 directive for the operation 'BARBAROSSA', which was the code name for the assault against Russia, the commencement of which he had made dependent on the termination of the campaign against Greece.

**232.** Meanwhile, on November 23, 1940, Romania joined the Axis of Germany-Italy-Japan. In December, after its consent, the 12th German Army of Marshal Von List, that was assigned to operate against Greece, began to concentrate within its territory.

On March 1, Bulgaria joined the Axis as well, after the tempting promise that it would be offered the whole of Eastern Macedonia and Western Thrace. Thus, on March 2, the German troops began to enter into the Bulgarian territory, where they were enthusiastically received by the population. On March 9, the advance guards of the forward German divisions reached the Greek - Bulgarian borders.

The war correspondents described the move as 'a river of steel, which runs long and endless, through plains and valleys, mountain passes and towns'. At the same time, air forces also began to arrive at the Bulgarian airfields.

On March 17, a meeting took place at the Chancellery, in which the occupation of the whole of the mainland and of the most important Greek islands was decided on. In the course of that meeting, the Chief of the land forces Von Brauhtitz reported to Hitler that, the 12th Army would be ready to attack Greece on April 1.

**233.** In parallel with the military preparations, the soundings on the issue of a peaceful subjection of Greece to Germany continued.

It is characteristic that, shortly before December 17, 1940, the Military attache of Germany to Athens let it be understood, during the course of a conversation with Major Skylitsis of the General Headquarters, that it would be possible to call a truce in Albania under the condition that the Greek Army would remain in the occupied territories until the end of the war, whereupon the Greek - Italian dispute would be resolved by settlement. German troops would be interposed between the adversary forces.

A similar and more concrete proposal was also put forward, at the time, to Argyropoulos, the Greek Ambassador to Madrid, through the Hungarian Ambassador, after the prompting of the German Admiral Von

Kanaris. The Greek Ambassador recommended the acceptance of the proposal to the Government. The answer, however, was negative.

Similar proposals were also repeated after the death of I. Metaxas (January 29, 1941), only to receive the laconic reply of the Prime Minister Alexandros Koryzis: '*we are fighting*'.

## British Aid to the Defence of Greece

**234.** Greece, a 'de facto' Ally of Great Britain, after involvement in the war against Italy, was forced to confront the abovementioned German threat as well.

The Albanian Theatre of Operations had absorbed part of the forces intended for the Bulgarian Theatre, because there was solid evidence to prove that Bulgaria did not wish to interfere in the Greek - Italian conflict, Yugoslavia would remain strictly neutral, and Turkey had declared that it would turn against Bulgaria, in the event that the latter was to operate against Greece. Thus, in Eastern Macedonia and Western Thrace, only four divisions were left, which had inadequate war manning level and did not suffice to confront the new threat, that had already been discernible since January 1941.

This military situation, that was unfavourable for Greece, could only be altered by a timely and serious British assistance, in conjunction with a decision by Yugoslavia to side with the allies.

**235.** After the Italian attack, the British government sought to assist Greece with army and air forces, both for the sake of prestige, since it had previously guaranteed the territorial integrity of Greece, and also in order to serve the overall British interests in the Middle East. On its part, the Greek Government, given that the extent of the assistance would have been inadequate, did not wish to have British troops landing in Greece, in order to avoid offering a pretext for German intervention. Thus, the British aid was confined, at the beginnings of the war, to the naval defence and the protection of Greece against the actions of the Italian Fleet and to the provision of a light air support.

Since the beginning of 1941, when the danger of a German attack had started to become discernible, the Commander-in-Chief, General Papagos, in a report to the Prime Minister estimated that the required reinforcement would have to comprise eight to nine divisions, powerful means of active anti-tank and anti-aircraft defence and appropriate air strength.

**236.** At the meetings that took place in Athens on January 15 and 16, 1941, the Commander-in-Chief of the British Forces in the Middle East, General Wavell, announced that, after two months, he would be able to provide two or three divisions of the imperial troops, of the nine divisions requested by the Greek Commander-in-Chief General Alexandros Papagos. Direct assistance available comprised few artillery and tank support units, but it was turned down by the Greek Prime Minister, since this immediate yet totally inadequate aid, would provide a pretext for the German intervention and would also have an adverse effect on the position of Turkey and Yugoslavia.

The decision of the Greek Government forwarded to the British Government and communicated to the Yugoslavian one, was that it would summon the British to land in Greece in case that the German troops were to enter Bulgaria, whereupon the German intentions would be finally revealed.

## The Problem of Selecting the Defensive Area
### (Sketch-map no. 20 and 21)

**237.** After the abovementioned statement of the Greek Government, which was repeated on February 8 by the Prime Minister Alexandros Koryzis, as to when, that is, the British forces would arrive, it became necessary to study how the British-Greek forces would be employed.

The reinforcements of the British, in conjunction with the Greek forces which were deployed in Macedonia and Thrace, did not suffice for the defence of Eastern Macedonia, let alone Western Thrace.

The weak point of the fortified position in Eastern Macedonia, where the fortification had not been completed, was the section of Beles, starting from the boundary point of the three nations and ending at Popotlivitsa Fort. The field defences, that had been hastily constructed in that area, were of a limited extent. A hostile offensive action from Stroumnitsa valley towards Thessaloniki, within the section of Beles, would result in the envelopment of the entire fortified position and would serve to cut off all forces present in Eastern Macedonia and Western Thrace from the rest of Greece.

From a military point of view, it was advisable to evacuate the fortified position in time and to move the defence to the more economical and 'naturally fortified' position of Kaimaktsalan-Vermio-Aliakmonas river.

Nevertheless, the desertion of Thrace and of the greatest part of Macedonia with Thessaloniki, beyond the psychological aspect and the moral repercussions upon the Greek population, was also connected with the position of Yugoslavia. The latter not only did directly influence the defence of Greece but also kept 'a sphinx-like silence' and made no effort to clarify its foreign policy.

**238.** Thus the strategic plans for the defence of the Greek territory were inevitably founded on assumptions, with regard to the position of Yugoslavia, and were the following:

-If Yugoslavia were an ally of Great Britain and Greece, the fight had to be conducted at the fortified area from Beles to Nestos, which was known as the 'Metaxas Line'.

-If Yugoslavia remained neutral and did not allow the passage of German troops through its territory, then the area of Kaimaktsalan-Vermio-Aliakmonas, west of Axios river, would have to be occupied, with the exception of the fort garrisons which would remain at their positions as a gesture of national sovereignty and in order to delay the German advance.

-If Yugoslavia allowed the passage of German troops through its territory or became an ally of the Germans, then the above mentioned area would be unsuitable for the defence, since a German move along the axis of Monastiri-Florina would then threaten the rear area not only of the forces present there but also of the Greek troops fighting in Albania.

This last alternative demanded the timely clarification of the Yugoslavian attitude, in order to provide the entire Greek Army with the time needed for its withdrawal to the more appropriate line of defence: Greek-Albanian frontier-Smolikas mountain-Orliakas mountain-Aliakmonas river-Olympus mountain.

**239.** On the basis of the developments that were likely to occur, a joint effort was made with the British officers, to study the possible use of the area Kaimaktsalan - Vermio -Aliakmonas (Vermio area). This 'L' shaped region covers approximately 110 kilometres, between the sea and the mountain bulk of Kaimaktsalan (Voras), and constitutes an anti-tank area throughout, with few exceptions in the coastal sector.

On February 22, the British Foreign Minister, Anthony Eden, the Chief of the British Staff, Marshal Deal, the Airforce Marshal, Longmore and a representative of Admiral Cunningham arrived in Athens, in secret. During a meeting, chaired by the King, the Commander in chief Alexandros Papagos agreed to evacuate the entire Greek region east of Axios river and to transfer the forces to the area of Vermio, where the British reinforcements would also be deployed, on the condition that every hope for Yugoslavia entering the war by the side of the Allies would be lost.

**240.** The evacuation of the above region was considered untimely and unprofitable, after the Germans had entered Bulgaria on March 2, and also due to the yet unclarified attitude of Yugoslavia.

**241.** Thus, during the successive meetings which took place from March 2 to 4 in order to consider the situation, while the German troops were passing through Bulgaria, the Greek General Staff proposed the deployment of all Greek - British forces at the fortified area of Beles-Nestos. Nevertheless, faced with the insistence of the British, who supported the abandonment of the Beles-Nestos area and proposed the occupation of the Vermio area instead, the Greek Commander-in-Chief submitted the following compromise proposal, which was accepted by the British:

-Western Thrace would be evacuated and only the forces of the Echinos and Nymphaea Forts, as well as certain screening companies would remain in the area.

-The Greek forces that would be thus conserved, with the addition of those in Eastern Macedonia, would be allocated to two echelons, which would be engaged in defence at the following two areas:

• On the fortified 'Metaxas Line', with three divisions, one brigade and the troops of the forts.

• At the Vermio area with the XII and the 20th Infantry Divisions, the XIX Mechanised Division and the British forces that would arrive in Piraeus and would then advance to the above area.

The abovementioned decision of the High Command to set up the defensive Vermio area together with the British Expeditionary Force, created the need to form a General Headquarters, which would have all the Greek forces of the above area under its command. Thus, as of March 6, the organisation of the Central Macedonia Field Army Section (CMFAS) began in Kozani and its Headquarters constituted the Thrace Field Army Section (TFAS) which was under the command of Lieutenant General Ioannis Kotoulas[1].

The above Field Army Section (CMFAS) comprised the XII and 20th Divisions, one Field Artillery battalion, one Skoda howitzer battalion of 150 mm, one battery of 85mm, one Antiaircraft Artillery battalion and a limited number of non divisional units from the T'FAS. The XIX

---

[1] The Thrace Field Army Section had originated from the E' Army corps, which ceased to exist as of December 15, 1940. Furthermore, as of February 8, the D' Army corps (of Kavala) was also abolished and its units were placed under the command of the EMFAS.

Mechanised Division had also been placed under the command of the CMFAS and was deployed in the area of Katerini. However, as of March 27, it was re-located to the area of Kilkis and was placed under the command of the EMFAS.

**242.** The British were faced with the dilemma either to withdraw their offer to reinforce Greece or to co-operate with the meagre Greek forces to occupy an area, where the terrain had not been organized defensively.

On March 6, Churchill, the British Prime Minister, in a telegram to Eden, stated the following, among others. ' *....We have done whatever was possible, in order to create a permanent front of the Balkan states against Germany. We must take care not to press Greece to undertake a desperate resistance despite its contrary opinion. The Greeks should not consider themselves obliged to reject the German ultimatum. If they themselves decide to fight, then we must share their trial up to a certain degree........'*

Eden replied that *'in the present situation all agree on the implementation of the solution that has become acceptable and that Greece must be assisted.........'*

General Wavell later wrote that, during that stage *'there were difficulties of a practical nature in a potential reversal of the plan. The troops were in motion and any change would create confusion '*.

**243.** Under these circumstances it was agreed that a British Expeditionary Force be sent to Greece, for the prestige of the British and with very little hope of a successful outcome of the operation.

This Force was formed out of various British units operating in the Middle East, and its commander was General Wilson.

The total of forces that landed in Greece, from March 7 until the day of the German invasion, amounted to 24,206 Englishmen, 17,125 Australians and 16,720 New Zealanders.

The Greek population had a warm welcome in store for the men of the British Expeditionary Force, showering them with flowers upon arrival and in the course of their movement through the Greek territory.

The Commander in Chief of the Middle East General Wavell in his inspired order to the troops that were being transported to Greece said: *'you shall fight until the last drop of your blood for Greece, exactly as you would have fought for England'*.

## Description of the Defensive Areas in Eastern Macedonia and on Vermio
### (Sketch-map no. 20 and 21)

**244.** The zone of operations of Eastern Macedonia, on the basis of the strategic situation at the time, extended between Axios and Nestos rivers. The Axios river flows into the Greek territory, between the mountain bulks of Voras from the west and Beles from the east. Its valley, within the Greek territory, widens continually from north to south and thus constitutes a worthwhile axis for invasion from the Yugoslavian territory towards Thessaloniki and vice versa.

Further to the east, Strimonas river crosses flowing the Rupel defile runs southwards through the plains of Serres and Nigrita and flows into the Aegean sea. This valley constitutes the main route from the plateau of Sofia to the Aegean and vice versa. However, its many defiles (Rupel, Kresna and Tzoumayia), the operations along this axis impede because they run against natural strong lines.

The river Nestos is constricted along its course from north to south, between mountain bulks with near vertical banks on both sides. Consequently, its valley is not suitable as an axis for a north to south advance and vice versa. On the contrary it constitutes a major defence obstacle for repulsing offensive sections against Eastern Macedonia from the south-east and the east.

The mountain range of Beles is a characteristic feature of the entire area, with a ridgeline that also serves as a boundary line. Defence is problematic on mount Beles, if not impossible, without the occupation and use of at least some parts of its northern slopes.

**245.** In the northern section of the area under consideration and all along the Greek - Bulgarian and part of the Greek - Yugoslavian borders lay the fortified area of the 'Metaxas Line', which had been constructed from 1936 to 1940. This was aligned with the permanent forts, which were built mainly in order to block off the passes upon and between the mountain bulks of Beles, Tsingeli, high plateau of Kato Nevrokopi and Boz Dag. From the beginning of 1939, the line had been extended eastwards, as far as the western bank of Nestos, from Paranesti to its estuary. From the beginning of 1941, when the German threat became apparent, it had been extended westwards between Axios river and Doirani lake.

Initially, the objective of the organisation of the above line was to cover the mobilisation and the strategic concentration in this area and, later on, to constitute the main defensive area of the Greek Army as well as the base of departure for offensive operations, in case favourable conditions arose. The defensive potential of this line was considerable and its value would have surely been multiplied, had it been manned as initially authorised, with sufficient field troops to cover the fort flanks and conduct counter-attacks. Nevertheless, there had been a considerable reduction in numbers of these troops to the benefit of the Albanian front.

The forts constructed in the above position were the following:

-At Beles: Popotlivitsa, Istibei, Kelkayia, Paleouriones, Arpalouki.

-In the area of Angistron: Rupel, Karatas, Kali.

-Between Ali Boutous and Mavro Vouno (Black Mountain): Fort Persek.

-At the high plateau of Kato Nevrokopi: Babazora, Maliaga, Perithori, Partalouska, Dasavli, Lisse, Pyramidoeides.

-In the area of Volakas: Kastilo, Agios Nikolaos, Bartiseva.

-In the area of Western Thrace: Echinos, Nymphaea.

Twenty one forts had been constructed in total, which were planned to be manned, in case of war, by approximately 10,000 men.

Each fort, constituted an enclosure work, comprising one or more self-contained strong points, and had a capacity for defence against any direction, including active shelters (emplacements, pill-boxes, observation posts, stations of visual communications) as well as exits for re-supply purposes and for the conduct of counter-attacks.

Various other constructions completed each fort compound, such as underground men's quarters, depots with sufficient supplies to cover 15 days of defence, command stations, dressing stations, sanitary installations, kitchens, water supply outlets etc.

The ventilation and lighting of the underground spaces were ensured with the aid of electrical installations in the large fort compounds, whereas in the smaller ones they were achieved by manually operated fans and oil lamps.

**246.** Between the borders and the fortified position, hasty field ·fortifications had been constructed in order to delay the enemy. Starting from the border and reaching fairly deep within the position, powerful passive anti-tank obstacles had also been constructed, as well as active anti-tank means, a full-scale demolition system, an excellent road network and multiple communication networks.

It is worth noting that, both the German as well as the Bulgarian Intelligence Service did not possess sufficient information regarding to the positions, the armament and the strength of the forts. They assumed, in general, that concrete shelters were strewn about and, therefore, the revelation of the shape of these forts came as a big surprise to them after the attack.

As the entire area of Beles-Nestos ran the risk of envelopment from the left (west), which bordered on the Axios river, where the terrain organisation had not reached a satisfactory level, a second defensive area, the 'Krousia Area', was organised, between the lakes of Doirani and Kerkini.

The organisation of the above second line was also dictated by the fact that the Beles area presented a relatively low defensive capacity, since the fortification had been built very close to the borders and thus the enemy could neutralise the frontal fire, by using flat trajectory weapons. Moreover, the area lacked the depth required to conduct defence manoeuvres, since the slopes of Beles descended steeply onto the Greek territory.

**247.** In the event that the Beles-Nestos area would be broken through, the Vermio area had been chosen for the defence of the Greek mainland.

In this area there were important artery roads, which ran across the mountain bulks of Kaimaktsalan, Vermio, Pieria and Olympus and permitted the operations of motorised enemy troops. Moreover, it would have been easy for the enemy forces to envelop the area, operating from the direction of Monastiri, through the field corridor of Monastiri-Florina.

Starting in mid-March, the area was manned in haste with Greek - British forces. These forces dealt intensively with the terrain organisation. However, in spite of the serious works that had been conducted, its defensive capacity could not be compared with that of the Beles-Nestos area.

*The Re-consideration of the Deployment of the Greek - British Forces and the Clarification of the Yugoslavian Attitude*

**248.** The deployment of the Greek-British forces in two areas constituted, naturally, a serious disadvantage. These forces, which were insufficient to confront the enemy at one area, were forced to be divided between two, because of a combination of political and military reasons. The position of the Eastern Macedonia Field Army Section (EMFAS) forces was particularly precarious, since they faced the danger of being cut-off, in the event of an enveloping action of the enemy from the west.

In the face of the impending German attack, the Commander of the EMFAS, Lieutenant General Bakopoulos submitted a report to the General Headquarters, requesting the provision of serious reinforcements for the defence of the Beles-Nestos area. After successive studies and exchanges between the General Headquarters and the EMFAS, a meeting was finally held in Thessaloniki on March 25, headed by the Commander of the EMFAS. During the course of this meeting, the latter supported the need to unite the forces of the two areas and indicated the Beles-Nestos area as the more appropriate choice. On the contrary, the British representative supported that the defence should be transferred to the Vermio area. The representative of the General Headquarters Lieutenant Colonel Dovas, stated that backward movement was impossible, for it required time and that consequently the EMFAS would have to conduct the defence at the Beles-Nestos area, where it had already been deployed anyway.

**249.** During a new meeting held in Athens on the following day, March 26, in the presence of the Commander-in-Chief General Papagos, the Commander of the Central Macedonia Field Army Section (CMFAS), Lieutenant General Kotoulas supported with great persistence the transfer of the EMFAS forces to the area of Vermio. This view was eventually accepted by Lieutenant General Bakopoulos, on account of the objections of the British and chiefly due to the fact that, on the previous day, Yugoslavia had joined the Axis, having been promised Thessaloniki in return. A discussion ensued, concerning the manner in which the transfer of forces to the new area would be conducted and the duration of this operation. In the meantime, however, information arrived concerning an impending coup d' etat in Yugoslavia in order to overthrow the Government of Tcvetkovitch, which had signed a treaty with Germany Subsequently, it was decided that the EMFAS would be reinforced in the area of Beles-Nestos.

Indeed, at midnight on March 26 to 27 and before Hitler was able to brag about the entry of Yugoslavia into the Axis, to which he attributed great political importance, a pro-ally coup d' etat broke out in Belgrade and the new Government of General Simovitch denounced the treaties with Germany.

The coup d' etat in Yugoslavia was well received by ally circles and created hopes for a favourable development of the situation.

**250.** On the other hand, the situation created in Yugoslavia, alarmed the Germans, who had been planning to commence the 'MARITA' operation on March 28. Without awaiting any display of faith on the part of the new Yugoslavia, Hitler decided, in parallel with the attack against Greece to invade Yugoslavia as well. A meeting was held on March 27, in Berlin, over which he presided, and during which the commencement of the operation 'MARITA' was decided on, after altering the initial plan as regards the objectives and the allocation of forces, since no plan against Yugoslavia, had been drawn.

## The Co-operation with the Yugoslavians and the Stands of Turkey

**251.** Although the impending threat against both Yugoslavia and Greece was clearly discernible, there was no immediate effort to co-ordinate the common defence against the Germans.

Following persistent Greek pressure on the British allies to take the initiative for co-operation, the Chief of the British General staff, Marshall Deal, met with the new Yugoslavian leaders in Belgrade and he ascertained that a state of true anarchy prevailed and that firm and final decisions could not be taken, due to the existence of many impediments.

He only managed to bring about a meeting between the officers of the Yugoslavian Staff and the Greek Commander-in-Chief. This meeting was held on April 3, at the railway station of Kenali (Kremenitsa). A new meeting ensued, attended, on the British side, by General Wilson, and as observers the Minister of Foreign Affairs, Eden and the Chief of the British Staff, Marshal Deal.

**252.** The view of Commander-in-Chief A. Papagos, was that the Yugoslavians ought to avoid deploying their troops to defend the endless northern borders of their country. The dispersion of the Yugoslavian forces and the weakened defence would produce fatal results, whereas the concentration of their bulk in Southern Serbia, would protect the Greek and Yugoslavian forces from being cut off in the area of Monastiri-Florina-Kozani.

He stressed the dangers that could arise for both armies, if the enemy managed to create a gap in the area at the Bulgarian-Yugoslavian borders and advanced towards the high plateau of Skopje and the mid valley of Axios river.

During the meeting, it was considered extremely urgent to liaise the Yugoslavian front with the fortified Greek area of the borders.

The Yugoslavians formally adopted the Greek plan and assigned 4 divisions to cover Southern Serbia. Nevertheless, the plan and the co-operation in general, were marked by laxity and inadequacy.

It was, however, decided that in the event of a German attack from the direction of Bulgaria, the valley of Stroumnitsa river, (tributary of Strymonas river), would be blocked off with Yugoslavian forces, in order to avoid the possibility of endangering the liaison with the Greek forces and to impede a German manoeuvre for the envelopment of the Beles-Nestos area.

Lastly, on the whole, common offensive actions were to be conducted, in order to drive the Italians out of Albania.

Thus ended the only meeting of the three Allies, about which General Wilson later wrote in his book that it was the most useless and the least satisfactory meeting he had ever attended.

**253.** Regarding the stands of Turkey during the same period, it was simultaneously inclined towards both sides. Being obligated by convention and having at first declared that it would maintain neutrality in favour of Greece, with the intention of remaining faithful to its alliance with Great Britain, on February 17 it signed a pact of friendship and non-offence with Bulgaria. The subsequent entry of Bulgaria into the Axis, (March 1, 1941 ) proved that, by this pact, Turkey had knowingly facilitated Germany in conducting a future unobstructed attack upon Greece.

During the negotiations with the British Foreign Minister, Anthony Eden, Turkey insisted on its neutrality, claiming that the combat effectiveness of its armed forces was unsatisfactory. According to Wavell, the British Commander-in-Chief and Longmore, the Airforce Marshal, with whom Eden apparently agreed, the entrance of Turkey into the war had nothing positive to offer from a military point of view. However, it was likely to restrain Yugoslavia from joining the Axis.

Subsequently, Eden's effort was directed, in those anguished and uncertain days, to the task of convincing the Turkish Government to adopt a decisive attitude in order to somehow encourage the Yugoslavians. Even a simple statement that Turkey would not remain indifferent to offensive acts by a foreign power in the Balkan peninsula, would have sufficed. In the end, however, not even this statement was offered by the Turkish Government.

### The Deployment and the Plan of Operations of the German Forces
( Sketch-map no. 20, 21 and 22 )

**254.** The new German plan of the parallel attack against Greece and Yugoslavia, as this was decided during the meeting of March 27 in Berlin, was drawn within 24 hours and provided for the application of the 'advance by bounds' method, because of the non-completion of the strategic concentration of those forces which would be operating against Yugoslavia. The dates and the forces for the commencement of operations were then defined as follows:

-The 12th Field Army of Marshal Von List, deployed along the Greek and the south-eastern Yugoslavian borders, would operate in the direction of Thessaloniki and Skopje on April 6.

# SKETCH - MAP  **No 22**

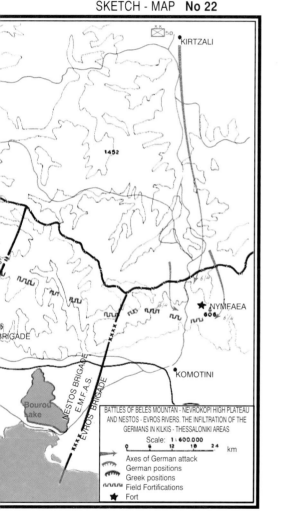

KIRTZALI

1452

NYMFAEA
606

RIGADE

Bourou
Lake

NESTOS BRIGADE
E.M.F.A.S.
EVROS BRIGADE

KOMOTINI

BATTLES OF BELES MOUNTAN - NEVROKOPI HIGH PLATEAU
AND NESTOS - EVROS RIVERS. THE INFILTRATION OF THE
GERMANS IN KILKIS - THESSALONIKI AREAS

Scale: 1 : 600.000

0      12    18    24    km

Axes of German attack
German positions
Greek positions
Field Fortifications
Fort

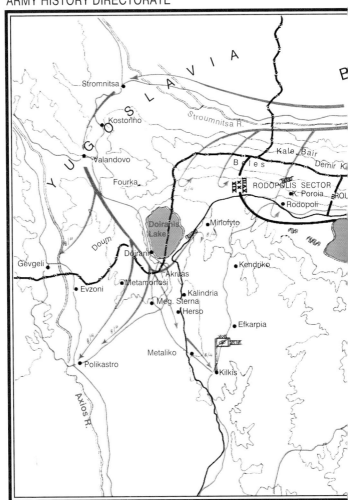

-The 1st Armoured Division Group of General Kleist, deployed in the area of Sofia and initially allocated for the attack against Greece, would launch a surprise offensive towards Nyssa-Belgrade on April 8, whereas the XLI Armoured Army Corps, that belonged to this Group, would operate towards Belgrade, from the direction of Romania, on April 10.

-The 2nd Field Army, organised by the German Staff for the invasion of Yugoslavia with 9 divisions at its disposal, would be operating, on April 10, from Austria and Hungary, towards Zagreb and Belgrade respectively. In the meantime, advanced Field Army elements would seize the bridges and tunnels at the borders of Austria-Yugoslavia in advance, so as to facilitate the further advance of the Field Army.

-The German Airforce would undertake to destroy the Yugoslavian air force installations and the town of Belgrade, with successive air raids.

255. The forces of the 12th German Field Army, that were available for the operations against Greece, were the following:

-The XVIII Mountain Army Corps, deployed from Petritsi to Nevrokopi comprising the 2nd Armoured Division, the 5th and 6th Mountain Divisions, the 125th Independent Infantry Regiment (Reinforced) and the 72nd Infantry Division.

-The XXX Army Corps, deployed in the Pasmakli and Kirdzali areas, comprising the 164th and 50th Infantry Divisions.

-The XL Armoured Army Corps, concentrated in the area of Doubnitsa, comprising the 9th Armoured Division, the 73rd Infantry Division and the SS Leibstandarte (Adolphe Hitler Bodyguards).. This Corps was initially employed against Yugoslavia, however, after the occupation of Skopje on April 8, it turned southwards in the direction of Monastiri-Florina-Amyndaeo and attacked the Greek - British forces. Later on, the 5th Armoured Division of the Kleist group reinforced the above forces, after having originally operated in the direction of Nyssa.

-One of the two Infantry Divisions of the Field Army, in the area of Philipoupolis, as a reserve.

The task of screening the entire front remained a responsibility of the Bulgarians, who employed three divisions to that effect.

256. Regarding the Airforce, the Germans allocated the following forces for the operations against Greece:

-The VIII Airforce Corps, under the command of Air Chief Marshal Richthoven, which had been assigned to the 12th Field Army from the beginning and comprised 650 aircraft (280 bombers, 150 vertical assault 'Stukas', 90 single-engine fighters, 90 double-engine fighters and bombers and 40 reconnaissance ).

-The 4th Airforce Fleet, which was organised after the political reform in Yugoslavia and included 744 aircraft of various types.

The total number of the German front-line aircraft amounted to approximately 1,000, including those of the close air support unit that had been assigned to the Large Units.

**257.** The outline plan of the 12th German Field Army which would operate against Greece, was in general, as follows:

-A westward attack for the occupation of Southern Yugoslavia with the XL Army Corps, which, after joining forces with the Italians in Albania and managing to separate the Yugoslavian and Greek forces, would turn southwards along the axis Monastiri-Florina-Kirli Derven-Grevena, so as to threaten the Greek forces of the Albanian front and the Greek -British forces at the Vermio area from the rear. Thus, conducting a broad envelopment of the fortified Beles-Nestos area as well as the Vermio area and it would continue its operations towards the mainland.

-Seizure of the 'Metaxas Line' with the bulk of the XVIII Army Corps forces at the valley of Strymonas river and breakthrough of the Rupel defile, with simultaneous envelopment of this fortified area with the 2nd Armoured Division from the west, through the valleys of Stroumnitsa and Axios, for the occupation of Thessaloniki and the isolation of the whole of Eastern Macedonia.

-Occupation of the Western Thrace coastline and the islands of Northern Aegean with the XXX Army Corps, which would then turn westwards and, crossing Nestos river, would operate towards Thessaloniki in order to assist the operations that were being conducted there.

The plan of operations of the Field Army in the direction of the main effort, where the XL Army Corps was operating, was based, in spite of the rough terrain, on the high mobility of the armoured and motorised units.

*The Disposition and the Missions of the Greek and British Forces*
( Sketch-map no. 20 )

**258.** The Greek and British forces, that were assigned to confront the German invasion, had been echeloned at the fortified area of the 'Metaxas Line' and the Vermio area , as follows:

In Eastern Macedonia, that is, at the fortified Beles-Nestos area, the EMFAS was deployed under the command of Lieutenant General Konstantinos Bakopoulos, comprising:

-The Division Group, under the command of Lieutenant General Panaghiotis Dedes, comprising the XVIII and XIV Infantry Divisions, that were deployed as follows:

The XVIII Division under Major General Leonidas Stergiopoulos, occupied the mountain bulk of Beles, from Triethnes to Strymonas river with 7 Infantry battalions and the troops of 5 Forts. In order to cover a front of about 40 kilometres, the Division had allocated, its forces in three sub-sectors:

• The Rodopolis Subsector: 70th Infantry Regiment (2 Infantry Battalions plus one company).

• The Roupesko Subsector: A battalion of the 70th Infantry Regiment plus one company and Fort Popotlivitsa.

• The Thylakas Subsector: 91st Infantry Regiment (2 Infantry Battalion plus one company) and Forts Istimbei, Kelkayia, Arpalouki and Paleoouriones.

The XIV Division, under the command of Major General Konstantinos Papakonstantinou, occupied the sector from the eastern bank of Strymonas to the western approaches of the Kato Nevrokopi high plateau with 6 Infantry battalions, 5 Screening companies and the troops of 8 Forts. In order to cover its front of about 80 kilometres, the Division had organised two sectors:

-The Siderokastro Sector: 41st Infantry Regiment (3 Infantry Battalions), Forts Rupel, Karatas, Kali and three Screening companies.

-The Karadag Sector: 73rd Infantry Regiment (3 Infantry Battalions) and Forts Persek, Babazora, Maliaga, Perithori and Partalouska.

As a reserve of the XIV Division, 2 Screening companies.

As a reserve of the Division Group, one battalion of the 81st Infantry Regiment minus a company.

- The VII Division, under the command of Major General Christos Zoiopoulos, that was deployed from the Libahovo crossing as far as mount Kouslar, comprising 10 Infantry battalions, 2 Screening companies and the troops of 6 Forts.

The width of the division zone was about 85 kilometres in total and had been divided into three sectors:

• The Sector of Falakro mountain: 26th Infantry Regiment (4 Infantry Battalions) and Forts Lisse, Pyramidoeides, Dasavli, Kastillo, Agios Nikolaos and Bartiseva.

• The Sector of Touloubar: 92nd Infantry Regiment (3 Infantry Battalions)

• The Sector of Paranesti: 71st Infantry Regiment (3 Infantry Battalions).

-The Nestos Brigade, under the command of Colonel Anastasios Kalis, which had been deployed on the western bank of river Nestos, from the village of Paschalia as far as the estuary of this river, and comprising 5 Infantry battalions, one Reconnaissance team and the Echinos Fort.

-The XIX Motorised Division, under the command of Major General Nikolaos Liubas, which was in the area of Kilkis, with the 191st Infantry Regiment in the area of Siderokastro (at the disposal of the Division Group), the 192nd Infantry Regiment in the area of Efkarpia-Kilkis and the 193rd Infantry Regiment in the area of Kalindria-Herso.

-The Krousia Detachment: Command of the 81st Infantry Regiment, a Cavalry Regiment, a Security battalion and a Screening company.

-A reinforced Infantry battalion in the area of Thessaloniki to defend against parachutist action.

In Thrace, the Evros Brigade was deployed under the command of Major General Ioannis Zissis, comprising 7 Screening Companies and the Nymphaea Fort.

**259.** In the Vermio area, the Greek-British 'W' Force, comprising the Central Macedonia Field Army Section and the British Expeditionary Force, was deployed under the command of General Wilson, who reported directly to the Greek Commander-in-Chief.

-The Field Army Section of Central Macedonia, under the command Lieutenant General of the Reserve Ioannis Kotoulas (on 8-4-41, he was replaced by Major General Christos Karassos) occupied, the left (northern) section of the area, comprising:

• The 20th Division, under the command of Major General Christos Karassos (on 8-4-41, he was replaced by Colonel Miltiades Papakonstantinou), with three Infantry Regiments and a Screening Company. Its mission was to secure the passes of Northern Vermio, the pass of Edessa-Kelli and the mountain passes of Vegoritida lake as far as the Greek -Yugoslavian borders on Kaimaktsalan mountain.

• The XII Division, under the command of Colonel Georgios Karambatos, which had four Infantry Regiments, each one comprising two battalions, and a Reconnaissance group, and was deployed south-east of the 20th Division as far as the Hadova defile.

• The X Frontier Sector was under the command of Colonel of the Reserve Aristotelis Sergios, with three screening Companies from Gevgeli to Kaimaktsalan mountain.

-The British Expeditionary Force, under the command of General Wilson, was deployed in the rest of the Vermio area and comprised:

• The 1st Australian Army Corps, which was under the command of Major General Blamey and included the 6th Australian Division, under the command of Major General Mackay, and the 2nd New Zealand Division, under the command of Major General Freyberg. The 6th Australian Division had the 16th and 19th Brigades at its disposal and occupied the defile of Hadova. The 2nd New Zealand division had the 4th, 5th and 6th Brigades and occupied the coastal sector of Katerini.

• The 1st Armoured British Brigade, under the command of Brigadier General Charrington, in the area of Edessa, with a Demolition squad, west of Axios river.

On the left of the area and behind the 20th Division was the Amyndaeo Detachment, which consisted of British forces.

The British Airforce in Greece comprised, 4 bomber and 4 fighter squadrons and 1 air ground liaison squadron. These forces were organised in two wings in order to support the Albanian Front and Macedonia respectively. In total there were 80 aircraft in good fighting condition, which, nevertheless, did not suffice to cover all of the support missions. The Greek Airforce was essentially insignificant.

**260.** The Greek and British forces had been assigned the following missions:

-The EMFAS would defend the fortified area of Beles-Nestos. In case of failure and after all efforts to secure the above position had been exhausted it would withdraw its forces, depending on the situation, either towards Thessaloniki and then west of Axios river or towards Kavala and Amphipolis, in order to transport its troops by sea and employ them in another area.

The Krousia Detachment had been assigned to occupy the protective Krousia area and to block off the advance of the enemy towards Thessaloniki in case there was a breakthrough of the Beles area.

-The Evros Brigade would seek to secure the bridgehead of Pythio. In case it was unable to retain it, it would withdraw into Turkey.

-The Greek - British 'W' Force was assigned to block off any attempt of the enemy to advance west and south of the general area of Kaimaktsalan-Vermio-Aliakmonas river.

## The Commencement of the German Attack

**261.** At 0515 hrs on April 6, without adhering to the usual diplomatic formalities of the ultimatum and deadline offer for the reply, the German troops simultaneously invaded the Greek territory and Southern Yugoslavia. At 0530 hrs on the same day, the German Ambassador to Athens presented the Greek Prime Minister with a note, which expressed unfounded allegations that the neutrality had been violated and announced the German invasion.

A modest and plain announcement informed the Greek people that morning: 'Since 0515 hrs, the German Army that was in Bulgaria all of a sudden attacked our troops on the Greek - Bulgarian frontier. Our troops are defending our fatherland'.

**262.** The main effort of the Germans was directed towards the left of the fortified area and mainly against Beles mountain and Fort Rupel, whereas further to the east, on the high plateau of Nevrokopi and in Western Thrace, the German attack was less intense.

Epic fighting ensued and scenes of splendid heroism took place in the area of the forts, arousing not only the admiration of the entire free world but also of the Germans themselves.

*The First Day of the German Attack*
*(April 6, 1941)*
(Sketch-map no. 20 and 22)

**263.** The German attack against the area of the XVIII Division (Beles) began at 0515 hrs and was supported by a great number of dive bombers and the vigorous fire of the artillery. The fight that followed was hard and evolved in each Subsector from west to east as follows:

In the Rodopolis Subsector, action was taken by the 6th Mountain Division, which conducted its attack against the heights Demir Kapou and Kale Bair and, by 0700 hrs, had seized the main line of resistance on the ridge-line of Beles mountain. Then, it seized the protective position left of the Subsector and, at approximately 1100 hrs, the villages Platanakia and Kalochori fell into the hands of its troops that had taken a large number of prisoners in the meantime. After delaying the German troops until the evening hours, the troops of the Subsector withdrew to the Krousia area during the night.

The 5th Mountain Division conducted operations further to the east, in the Roupesko and Thylakas Subsectors. Its attack was supported by 165 guns of various calibre and by a large number of aircraft.

Fort Popotlivitsa, despite the severe bombardment, resisted all day long and it was only during the night that the enemy managed to set foot on the surface of the fort. Two enemy aircraft were shot down by the anti-aircraft fire of the Fort.

The brunt of the German attack was borne by Forts Istimbei and Kelkayia, which were the key to the area. The attack against these two Forts was launched simultaneously, at 0700 hrs, following heavy bombardment by the infantry, artillery and airforce. At 0800 hrs, enemy troops managed to set foot on the surface of Fort Istimbei. Its Commander requested artillery fire on the surface of the Fort and a counter-attack by the reserve of the Subsector in order to clear it. The counter-attack was launched shortly before noon, but it was repulsed by the Germans who had been reinforced in the meantime and had seized other heights, further to the east, between Istimbei and Kelkayia.

At 1300 hrs, enemy troops set foot on the surface of Fort Kelkayia as well, and attempted to crush the resistance of its defenders, unsuccessfully. A counterattack by a section of the fort garrison successed temporarily.

Fort Arpalouki was only subjected to artillery and airforce bombardment, whereas at Fort Paliouriones many infiltrations were attempted, which were repulsed with heavy losses for the attackers.

**264.** In the zone of the XIV Division (Sectors of Siderokastro and Karadag), the German attack was also launched at 0515 hrs, with great momentum, especially on the left of the Siderokastro Team against Fort Rupel, whereas Forts Karatas and Kali were only subjected to artillery fire and Airforce bombardment.

The attack against Fort Rupel was conducted by the 125th Independent Infantry Regiment, which had been reinforced with a battalion from the 5th Mountain division. This regiment had also been used in France against the Mazineau line.

The attack began with strong artillery support and continued with a bombardment by vertical assault 'Stuka' dive bombers, which made use of special sirens during their dives intenting to break the morale of the defenders. At 0600 hrs motorised Infantry, assault guns and motorcyclists crossed the border en mass and moved towards the Fort, while flat trajectory weapons began to fire from suitable positions against the openings of its defensive works. Simultaneously, a flotilla of 18 assault boats appeared, moving downstream towards the bridge of Siderokastro. The escort, consisting of three boats, got entangled in a wire net installed underwater and was immobilised. The crews were annihilated by the fire of the forts and the boats were sunk.

At approximately 1100 hrs, after the withdrawal of the outposts, the attacking troops approached the forts, but their advance was halted by the defensive fire and only small elements were able to ascend momentarily to the surface of the 'Molon Lave' [Come and take it] Monument of Fort Rupel. However, while the frontal attacks of the Germans were repulsed, a battalion force managed to infiltrate the area between the Forts of Rupel and Karatas. From there, an assault unit, of company strength, taking advantage of the screen of smoke, by-passed six pill-boxes and moved towards the rear of the area where, at 1600 hrs, it seized the village of

Klidi. The remainder of the above Battalion suffered heavy losses and only few men were able to cross the barrage of fire and move in the direction of Klidi.

The Germans constantly supported their attack with their Airforce and artillery. During the day, 100-200 aircraft flew above Rupel. The one and only anti-aircraft gun of the Fort shot down three of them.

Thus ended the first day of the German attack against Rupel, marked by failure to achieve their objective.

Further to the east, in the Sector of the Karadag Team, the effort of the 72rd Division was mainly directed against Forts Perithori-Maliaga and Babazora, before which it was held in position, whereas Fort Partaloushka had only to deal with the activity of small patrols.

Here, the main effort was applied at Fort Perithori, where a tough battle took place, the Germans failing to capture it.

265. In the zone of the VII Division (Sectors of Falakro-Touloubar-Paranestio), the 72nd German Division commenced its attack at 0515 hrs, laying heavy pressure mainly on the Sector of Falakro, whereas in the other sectors its activity was confined to the repulsion of the screening forces.

At approximately 1100 hrs, after having overthrown the screening forces and the troops at the forward resistance area, directly north of Kato Nevrokopi, the enemy attempted to move between the Forts of Pyramidoeides and Lisse and to force its way through the defile of Granitis. However, the attempt was not successful because of the effective fire of the abovementioned Forts, especially of the latter. Thereafter, the German troops made another attempt to infiltrate into the space between Forts Perithori and Lisse, but once again they were repulsed. A simultaneous action of the Germans to envelop the defile of Granitis from the east, by seizing the Ousoyia height was also unsuccessful and their troops were held in position before that height, suffering heavy losses.

266. In the zone of the Nestos Brigade (in the area of Xanthi), the Germans commenced their attack at 0515 hrs with the 164th Division along the axis of Pasmakli-Melivoia-Echinos-Xanthi. After overthrowing the frontier posts, they gained contact, in the afternoon hours, with the main area of resistance and Fort Echinos, where they were held in position by the fire of the Fort.

267. In the zone of the Evros Brigade (Sector of Evros), the German attack commenced at 0505 hrs with the 50th Division along the axis Kirdzali-Nymphaea-Komotini. The screening forces of the Evros Brigade withdrew, delaying the enemy, in accordance with the existing plan. At

0700 hrs, Fort Nymphaea was subjected to the effective fire of the artillery at the openings and the exits from a distance of 600-1,500 meters and by 1100 hours it had become encircled. Attempts on the part of the Germans to ascend to the surface of the fort were contained by the effective fire. The pounding of the Fort, which was conducted by the greatest part of the XXX Army Corps artillery in conjunction with the Airforce, continued until eight o'clock that evening.

268. The occupation of the western section of the Beles ridgeline and the infiltration of German troops into the valley of Rodopolis, posed a threat for the entire Beles-Nestos area. The command of the EMFAS, in order to deal with the situation, issued an order at 1030 hrs to the XIX Motorised Division (minus the 191st Regiment), at the disposal of which it also placed the Krousia Detachment, aiming at the occupation of the area from Doirani lake to Kerkini lake.

During the evening hours, the German forces sallied forth into the valley of Rodopolis and took contact with the Krousia area, while the forts on Beles mountain continued their defence. East of Strymonas river and as far as Nestos river, the Germans kept contact with the main area of resistance, which remained intact. Further to the east, in the area of Xanthi and Komotini, the German troops, after bypassing the forts, proceeded to move southwards.

After this development, the EMFAS ordered the withdrawal of the XVIII Division to the area of Strymonas river - Kerkini lake, retaining the liaison with the Krousia area. The greatest part of the 41st Regiment, which was in Achladochori, was deployed on the eastern bank of Strymonas river, in the section between the bridge of Siderokastro and Fort Rupel, in order to secure the continuity of the front. At the same time, the forts were ordered to defend 'to the last man'.

## The Second Day of the German Attack
### (April 7, 1941)
### (Sketch-map no. 22)

**269.** In the Beles Sector, the XVIII Division began to withdraw, since the morning on April 7, to the area between the bridge of Siderokastro and Kerkini lake, whereas the forts continued their struggle, with no external support any longer.

At Fort Kelkayia, the Germans blocked off the openings during the night and piped choking gases and thick smoke into the galleries, an act which forced the garrison to surrender at 1130 hrs.

Fort Arpalouki, being no more under the protection of Kelkayia, was dangerously encircled. In the night of April 7 to 8, the garrison, which amounted to approximately 200 men, retired unimpeded and reached the bridges of Strymonas, which were found destroyed. There, it was attacked while attempting to cross the river by makeshift means and was overpowered at the end of a three-hour tough struggle, surrendering to the Germans, with the exception of a very small number of men who managed to escape.

The garrison of Fort Istimbei was forced to surrender at 1600 hrs, because of the choking gases and the flaming petrol used by the Germans.

Fort Popotlivitsa and the permanent pill-boxes in the Rupesko Subsector continued their resistance during the whole day of April 7.

**270.** In the XIV Division zone of operation, the German effort remained undiminished, in spite of the foggy and rainy weather.

In the Siderokastro Sector, the effort of the 125th German Regiment was once again directed against Fort Rupel, which continued its heroic resistance. However, the enemy troops that had infiltrated into its rear area (approximately 200 men), occupied the Goliama height where, after organising a perimeter defence, they managed apart from harassing the Fort and cutting off its communications to also pinpoint targets to their Airforce. An attempt by the XIV Division to neutralise the above troops failed.

In the Karadag Sector, the Germans launched a surprise attack and seized the Stavros height, only to lose it later after a counter-attack, which was supported by the fire of Fort Maliaga. At approximately 0900hrs, other German troops managed to set temporarily foot on the surface of Fort Perithori and enter into the underground galleries, were the fight was fierce and presented a picture of a virtual inferno. The Fort garrison fought for two hours with heroism and self-sacrifice and managed to annihilate all the Germans that had entered into it. At the same time, a counter-attack was launched by a small section against the Germans that had set foot on the surface of the Fort. After a hard fight, the Germans were forced to withdraw with heavy losses.

At 1630 hrs, a new vigorous attack by a force of about regiment strength also failed. The same fate awaited the attempts to destroy the Fort with assault guns and small infiltration groups.

271. Further to the east, in the VII Division zone of operation, the 72nd German Division continued its main effort against the Sector of Falakro mountain, whereas the screening forces of the Sectors of Paranesti and Touloubar withdrew in order towards the area of resistance. During the night of April 6 to 7, the Germans concentrated sufficient forces and, in the morning, began to fire with machine-guns against the openings of Fort Lisse. These forces, supported by assault guns and taking advantage of the fog, attacked Fort Dasavli at approximately 1000 hrs, without success.

Further to the east, a German force that had managed to infiltrate through the Yiannen valley, seized the Ousoyia height at approximately 1600 hrs. A Greek counter-attack, that was launched during the night of April 7 to 8, in order to re-capture the height, was unsuccessful.

Furthermore, in the field corridor between Forts Dasavli and Perithori, a strong German force, taking advantage of the fog and the bushes, approached and attacked the Kresti height (before Kalapotio pass), and seized it at approximately 1400 hrs. In order to deal with that threat, the VII Division organised a Detachment (Kalapotio Detachment), which was assigned to secure the saddle of Kalapotio and recapture the height of Kresti in the next morning.

272. In the area of Xanthi, (Nestos Brigade), the screening forces, after conducting the authorised demolitions and the blowing up of the Nestos bridge at Toxotes, withdrew in order to the area of resistance. Fort Echinos, in spite of the strong pressure and the successive bombings it had suffered, managed to contain the German attackers throughout the April 7.

273. In the Sector of Evros, the screening forces, (approximately 100 officers and 2,000 soldiers), after having withdrawn according to the existing plan, crossed over to the Turkish territory where they were disarmed, except for a small section that withdrew towards Makri and was afterwards transported inland by steamboat.

The Commander of the Brigade, Major General Ioannis Zissis, taking the disarmament of his Brigade to heart, committed suicide on April 9, at Ypsala of Eastern Thrace. Most officers and about 1,300 soldiers that had taken refuge in Turkey went to the Middle East in July, 1941, whereas the rest returned to Greece in February, 1942.

In the meantime, the German troops by-passed Fort Nymphaea and, during the night of April 6 to 7, reached Komotini.

Fort Nymphaea continued to resist, although it was isolated within an area which was totally controlled by the Germans, who were urgently seeking to break through the advance routes from Komotini to Alexandroupolis and Kavala. Despite the night attacks, the pounding of the artillery, the successive assaults of the infantry and the severe air bombardment, the Germans were unable to ascend to the surface of the Fort for the whole day (April 7). Late in the evening at approx 2100 hrs, after the effective fire of more than a hundred guns of all calibre against the openings of the Fort and the destruction of its weapons and exits, the Germans managed to set foot on its surface. Nevertheless, the Fort continued the defence until 2330 hrs, whereupon it was forced to surrender, since the atmosphere inside it had by then become suffocating, due to the smoke agents thrown by the Germans through the wrecked openings of the pill-boxes.

**274.** In the Sector of the XIX Motorised Division, there were no events worth recording; however, the unfavourable turn of events became apparent.

The Germans attempted to force their way through the defence in the area of the field corridor that lay east of Doirani lake and momentarily succeeded in creating a gap, which was nevertheless immediately closed after counter-attacks of a company and a tank platoon.

At approximately 1230 hrs, the Division took contact with the Yugoslavians at the outpost of Doirani during the course of which a common limiting point was defined together with the probable course of action at the point. Furthermore, the Division was informed that the 2nd German Armoured Division had already occupied Stromnitsa and was engaged in offensive action in the direction of Kostourino-Valadovo. The Yugoslavians requested the urgent dispatch of Greek troops or British motorised units and anti-tank weapons to Valadovo. They also requested the strike of the German columns in the valley of Stroumnitsa, by the British Airforce. This request was satisfied in the afternoon.

At 1700 hrs, the Yugoslavians communicated that they would be withdrawing west of Axios river.

Subsequently, the EMFAS ordered the XIX Motorised Division to extend its left flank as far as the eastern bank of Axios, having previously reinforced it with the XI Frontier Sector (2 Screening companies), a force of two companies from the Security Battalion of Thessaloniki and the XIX Motorised Reconnaissance Group. The latter had been situated in the area of Laina village and originally came from Drama. The mass of the Division forces, according to its new mission, was thereby transferred to the zone between Doirani lake and Axios river, where the Division deployed one of its two regiments and its Reconnaissance group.

In the meantime, a German motorised column had seized the villages of Valadovo and Fourka and was directed towards the field corridor between Doirani lake and the Doum height. Further to the west, the Germans seized Gevgeli.

**275.** On the whole, during the second day of the German attack, the Beles-Nestos defensive area, despite the loss of Forts Istimbei, Kelkayia and Arpalouki, remained essentially intact. However, the rapid breakdown of the Yugoslavian resistance -especially in the area of the valley of Axios- in conjunction with the absence of forces available to cover the left flank of the organised area, created a situation that was extremely serious for the entire area, which was in danger of being cut off from the mainland.

The EMFAS addressed a request to the General Headquarters that, the British Armoured Brigade should attack in the following morning in the direction of Doirani against the advancing German column and that the Airforce should hit the German columns. However, the General Headquarters replied that the implementation of this action was impossible. It was evident that the disposition of the XIX Division, in order to fill the gap created by the breakdown of the Yugoslavian resistance, did not bear any chances of success. The inadequate reinforcements could not reach the area in time to repulse the German advance. Thus, the sensitive area of the Axios river valley constituted the vulnerable spot of the entire defensive area.

*The Third Day of the German Attack*
*(April 8, 1941)*
(Sketch-map no. 22)

**276.** On April 8, the third day of the German attack, in the Sector of Beles, the Germans advanced and in the early hours made contact with the XVIII Division troops in the area of the Megalochori bridge, while the forts, that had not surrendered, continued to fight. Fort Popotlivitsa, following a hard and uneven struggle, was forced to surrender at 1900 hrs. On the contrary, the guard of three concrete pill-boxes at the southern feet of the Rupesko height, continued to resist, stubbornly. Fort Paliouriones, though subjected to a severe bombardment and the sustained fire of portable weapons against its openings, resisted and caused heavy losses to the Germans.

**277.** In the Sector of the XIV Division the fight continued with unflagging intensity. The Germans tried to break through the area of Forts Rupel and Karatas, but were repulsed and suffered heavy losses, while three German aircraft were also shot down. However, the troops of the 125th German Regiment -which had been positioned on the Goliama height- and the concurrent descent of the 5th Mountain Division to the valley of Rodopolis, began to seriously threaten the left flank of the XIV Division. In order to deal with the situation, the left flank of the Division, was reinforced from the Division Group with two Infantry battalions, one light tank company (Carriers) and a number of guns of various calibre.

**278.** Further to the east, the efforts of the Germans to capture Forts Maliaga and Perithori during the night were unsuccessful. A counter-attack against the troops that had set foot on the surface of Fort Perithori took on the form of a close combat and, in the end, the Germans retreated in disarray. As of 1245 hrs, the Fort and the heights lying beside it were subjected to an attack by nearly two Infantry regiments, which were held in position after a three-hour fight and suffered very significant loses.

**279.** In the Sector of the VII Division, the 72nd German Division attempted to capture Forts Pyramidoeides, Lisse and Dasavli, once again, but was unsuccessful. Further to the west, the Germans retained their positions on the Kresti height, despite the efforts of the VII Division to recapture the latter with the Kalapotio Detachment.

**280.** In the Sector of the Nestos Brigade, the 164th German Division took contact with the area of resistance on Nestos river at Stavroupolis, while Fort Echinos continued to resist, even though by that time it had been encircled and fired from all directions. At approximately 2100 hrs, the Germans managed to set foot on the surface of the Fort and piped in smoke and various choking gases to the galleries. This led the fort garrison, which consisted of 18 officers and 550 soldiers, to abandon the Fort and move towards the western bank of Nestos river. Upon arriving at Kentavros village at approximately 0300 hrs, on April 9, the garrison was informed that the Germans had already occupied Xanthi and Komotini. Subsequently, no longer possessing any way of escape, it surrendered to the Germans.

**281.** However, while the 'Metaxas Line' remained essentially intact, thanks to the heroic resistance of the fort defenders, during the third day of the German attack as well, in the sector of the XIX Motorised Division, where the left flank of the EMFAS was situated, a critical situation developed, due to the collapse of the Yugoslavian resistance in Southern

Serbia, from the first day. The bulk of the troops that were hastily assigned to block off the valley of Axios river, were unable, to reach and occupy the deffensive area in time, because of the enemy intervention.

At 0600 hrs on April 8, strong German motorised forces of the 2nd Armoured Division crossed the border by Doirani lake and invaded the Greek territory. They proceeded to overthrow the troops that were positioned in the area Akritas-Oveliskos and moved towards Herso-Kilkis and Megali Sterna-Polykastro, breaking up or by-passing the resistance they met on the way.

At the same time, other troops of the 6th Mountain Division, a five battalion force, attacked the Krousia area and managed to create a gap, west of the Dova Tepe height. At approximately 2300 hrs, a German column seized Metalliko village and continued its movement towards Kilkis, while the Headquarters of the XIX Division, that was taken by surprise by the speed of the German advance, moved to Kentriko village.

### The Capitulation of the Eastern Macedonia Field Army Section

**282.** The continuing deep infiltration of the Germans and the impending occupation of Thessaloniki on the following day, constituted an immediate danger for the EMFAS, which was bound to be captured if it remained at the defensive area. Therefore, the Commander of the EMFAS, Lieutenant General Bakopoulos, decided to withdraw his units, as of the evening of April 8, towards the harbours of Eastern Macedonia, since any attempt to withdraw them to the west of Axios was out of question, because of the German advance towards Kilkis-Thessaloniki and the impending demolition of the bridges across the Axios river. Yet the transportation of forces by sea also presented serious impediments, since the available vessels were insufficient.

At 1630 hrs, on April 8, the Commander of the EMFAS communicated by phone to the Commander in chief his decision to withdraw his forces, due to the situation that had arisen. Five minutes had merely elapsed after the telephone conversation, when the Commander of the EMFAS received a General Headquarters order, issued by phone, authorising him to enter into negotiations with the Commander of the German forces in order to seek capitulation and to request a cease-fire. The General Headquarters, assessing the situation and realising the futility in continuing the uneven struggle and aiming to avoid any pointless sacrifice, had already issued since noon a relevant written order for capitulation. Besides, the mission of the EMFAS, which was to delay the Germans in the direction of the Vermio area, had by then become impossible since there were already two directions of attack against that area, from the valley of Axios and from Monastiri, both of which had been broken through by that time.

**283.** After the above events, the Commander of the EMFAS sent a letter, at 2100 hrs on April 8, to Lieutenant General Feiel, the German Commander of the 2nd Armoured Division, proposing a cease-fire, on the condition that the soldiers be allowed to keep their weapons, or at least, if this was unacceptable, that these be returned to Greece after the end of the war. At the same time, he briefed his lower rank officers of the Large Units in confidence and stressed that they had to retain their positions until the capitulation was signed, both as a matter of military pride and because it was the only way to secure favourable and honourable conditions.

At around 2230 hrs, the Military Commander of Thessaloniki, Lieutenant General Rangavis, received a letter of the Commander of the German advance guard, demanding the unconditional surrender of the city by midnight.

The surrender of Thessaloniki was carried out at 0800 hrs on the following day, April 9, by a committee comprising the Metropolitan Bishop of Thessaloniki, the Mayor and the Chief of Police of the city.

**284.** Lieutenant General Feiel, placed the Greek terms before Marshal Von List, who agreed to the cease-fire, which was to commence at 1000 hrs on April 9. Regarding the issue of the return of war supplies he stated that this would be negotiated in the future.

At 1400 hrs, on April 9, a Protocol and Negotiations Supplement were signed at the German Consulate in Thessaloniki between the Commander of the EMFAS and the Commander of the 2nd German Armoured Division.

The Protocol included the term that the officers would get to keep their swords. As for the two other terms on which Lieutenant General Bakopoulos insisted that they be added to the Protocol, those being the return of the war materiel and the non-entrance of Bulgarian troops into the Greek territory, Lieutenant General Feiel declared that he lacked the appropriate authority.

With the Supplement the heroic fighting of the EMFAS was acknowledged and the intention to avoid sending officers or soldiers to a concentration camp was expressed. As for the civil authorities it was decided that they would remain at their positions.

Thus ended the struggle in Eastern Macedonia with highly honourable terms for the Greek troops that defended the area Beles-Nestos with extreme vigour.

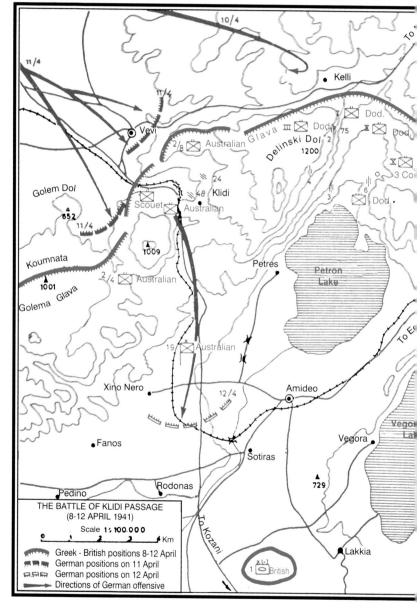

THE BATTLE OF KLIDI PASSAGE
(8-12 APRIL 1941)

Scale 1:100.000

0    1    2    3    4 Km

Greek - British positions 8-12 April
German positions on 11 April
German positions on 12 April
Directions of German offensive

At 1600 hrs, the Commander of the EMFAS notified his units of the terms of the capitulation and ordered a cease-fire. This order of the EMFAS caused great displeasure to those units which were still retaining their positions and were continuing to fight with success. The idea of a dishonourable conclusion in captivity was bound to create a justifiable reaction and the first thought of many unit leaders was to escape with their troops towards that part of Greece which was still free and fighting.

### The Fighting on April 9 and the End of the Battle of the Forts
( Sketch-map no. 22 )

**285.** While the Commander of the EMFAS was dealing with the negotiations for capitulation and the Germans had already entered into Thessaloniki since the morning of April 9, the fight continued within the entire fortified area.

In the Sector of the XVIII Division, the Germans conducted successive attacks against Fort Paliouriones, though without being able to capture it. At 1730 hrs, German messengers informed the Fort garrison of the capitulation. Subsequently, the cease-fire was decided to take place during the night. The surrender of the Fort to the Germans was carried out at 0900 hrs on April 10. A German battalion was arrayed in order to render honours, while the German Colonel who received the Fort addressed the Commander and congratulated the garrison men on their heroic resistance. Then he led the Commander of the Fort before the German battalion in order to inspect it. The German flag was hoisted at the Fort only after the withdrawal of its garrison.

Other such manifestations were also made in honour of the Commanders of Forts Rupel, Lisse, Pyramidoeides, Perithori, Echinos, Nymphaea, Istimbei and Kelkayia.

The garrison of the Rupesko defensive area, after having resisted during the day, managed to escape during the night of April 9 to 10, without attracting the attention of the Germans.

**286.** In the sector of the XIV Division, the fight continued vigorously, the Germans not being able to break through the defensive area.

In the Siderokastro Sector, the Fort Rupel did not surrender, despite the intense shelling, and refused the German call to capitulate.

In the Karadag Sector, an attempted infiltration during the night of April 8 to 9, by a German force of battalion strength, between Forts Maliaga and Perithori, was repulsed with heavy losses on their part. Another battalion force, that had managed to infiltrate during that same night into the area between Forts Perithori and Partalouska and attack the rear of the Sector, was pursued after a valiant counter-attack of a joint section of reserve platoons, that also took 102 German prisoners.

The Germans, benefiting from the occupation of the Kresti height, attempted a new infiltration during the same night of April 8 to 9 and succeeded in seizing the Agios Konstantinos height with a strength of two companies, at the rear of the Karadag Team. Nevertheless, after a Greek counterattack, the height was recaptured and 250 German prisoners were taken.

**287.** In the Sector of Falakro mountain, the German troops that had seized the Ousoyia height, did not attempt to advance any further, due to the intense fire from Fort Pyramidoeides and artillery. At 1010 hrs, the Kalapotio Detachment repeated the attack in order to recapture the Kresti height, an action which had been halted on the previous evening. After a hard fight, that lasted until 1300 hrs, the Detachment managed to drive the Germans away and to recapture the height.

Fort Pyramidoeides continued to resist as well. At approximately 1300 hrs, a German motor-vehicle with a white flag approached the Fort. The officer in charge informed the Fort commander that after a request of the EMFAS, negotiations for capitulation were being conducted and asked for a mutual cease-fire. The event was immediately reported to the Command of the VII Division, and at 1410 hrs a cease-fire was ordered.

**288.** In the Sector of the Nestos Brigade, an attempt by the Germans to cross the river Nestos in the area of Paradeisos village was unsuccessful. However, the Commander of that Sector, being aware of the imminent capitulation, withdrew his troops during the night of April 9 to 10, in the direction of Chrysoupolis-Keramoti, intenting to ferry them across to the isle of Thassos.

**289.** In the Sector of the XIX Motorised Division, the 193rd Regiment was attacked at 0230 hrs, on April 9, and surrendered at the end of a brief fighting. The remaining troops withdrew, in the early morning hours, to the area of Elliniko village, near Lahanas.

**290.** By the morning of April 10 all EMFAS troops had been informed of the capitulation signed and were awaiting the implementation of its terms.

The Greek casualties during the above four-day titanic struggle, were relatively few and did not exceed 1,000 killed in action and wounded. The German casualties, from April 6 to 10, were considerable and amounted, according to German sources, to 555 killed in action, 2,134 wounded and 170 missing in action. A report by the Commander of the Group of Forts

Rupel and Karatas, Lieutenant Colonel Plevrakis, which relates the German casualties, states that during his meeting with the Commander of the 125th German Regiment, after the truce, the latter said in tears: ' I do not mourn as a soldier, for the sacrifice was necessary, but I weep as a human being for only few of my men are left'.

**291.** Thus ended the Greek resistance in Eastern Macedonia and Thrace, after a four-day unequal struggle. Despite its brief duration, this struggle of the Greek Army can be characterised as an example of courage and self-sacrifice and as one of the most glorious pages of the Greek Military History. The Greek forces, in spite of the overwhelming superiority of the enemy, managed to repulse nearly all German attacks with success. They only capitulated after the rapid collapse of the Yugoslavian resistance, which led to the envelopment of the fortified area of Beles-Nestos and the speedy advance of the German armoured forces towards Thessaloniki.

Admiration for the valour and the fighting spirit of the Greek Army was also expressed by many Germans from all ranks of their military echelon of command. Such characteristic statements are listed below, bearing witness to the high esteem in which the Germans held the Greek fighters.

The Chief of Staff of the XXX German Army Corps, made the following statement to Lieutenant General Dedes, Commander of the Division Group. 'You have fought admirably, your artillery was superb, your flank guard extremely effective. Upon every move the battle group was successfully hit. If your shells did not suffer from misfires at a rate of 4 to 5[1] none of our troops engaged in the fight would have survived that hell of fire.'

The Commander of the 72nd German Division, that operated on the high plateau of Kato Nevrokopi, stated to the same Greek Lieutenant General: 'I have fought in Poland and in France, but nowhere have I encountered such an effective and destructive resistance as in Greece.'

The Commander of the XVIII German Army Corps which operated in the fortified Beles-Nestos area, told the EMFAS Chief of Staff: 'We had heard references made to the bravery and heroism of the Greek Army, yet we could never have imagined the bravery and heroism displayed by your soldiers. You have fought admirably! Superbly! I congratulate you once again, wholeheartedly.'

Marshal Von List, in his order of the day directly after the struggle, acknowledged that 'the Greeks defended their country valiantly' and advised the German soldiers to 'confront and treat the Greek prisoners as befits brave soldiers'.

---

[1]  This is an exaggeration although numerous misfires were indeed recorded.

Lastly, Hitler himself, in a speech on May 4, 1941, before the Reichstadt, reviewing his campaigns, said: 'Historic justice, however, forces me to - ascertain that among all the adversaries that we have confronted, it was the Greek soldier in particular who fought with the greatest heroism and self-sacrifice. Only when the continuation of the resistance was no longer possible and no longer had any meaning did he capitulate'.

Furthermore, there were equally laudatory judgements made by the Germans with regard to the value of the fortification of the Beles-Nestos area, which was considered much better than that of the Mazineau line and comparable to the Ziegfrid line. They stressed in particular the admirable selection of the positions of the defensive works, their perfect concealment and the excellent adaptation of the fire to the ground.

As assessed on the Greek side, it was proved how necessary the fortification of the above area was because it secured the smooth conduct of the mobilisation as well as the strategic concentration of the Greek Army and allowed the conservation of forces for the struggle in the Albanian Theatre of Operations. Moreover, it offered the opportunity of an initially successful repulsion of the German invasion, a fact which was internationally recognised.

# CHAPTER VI

## THE BATTLES IN CENTRAL AND WESTERN MACEDONIA-THE WITHDRAWAL AND THE CAPITULATION OF THE EPIRUS ARMY-THE WITHDRAWAL OF THE BRITISH AND THE COMPLETION OF THE OCCUPATION OF GREECE BY THE GERMANS

### (April 9 - May 8, 1941)

*Final Gleams of the Epirus Epopee*
(Sketch-map no. 20)

**292.** The Greek Army, in the Albanian Theatre of Operations, after its victorious struggles and its advance deep into the northern Epirus territory, was confined, during the months of January and February 1941, to static fighting, mainly due to the extreme severity of the winter. From March 9 to 26, it had confronted the 'Spring' attack of the Italians with success and retained the occupied territory.

Despite the fatigue and the hardships of war, the Greek Army preserved its high morale and aimed at new successes.

Since March 27 and until the German attack of April 6, the situation in the Theatre of Operations did not present any significant changes. The war activity was mainly confined to artillery and patrol action, in order to maintain contact. The conduct of a few local operations in the sector of the Western Macedonia Field Army Section (WMFAS) was an exception aiming mainly at the improvement of the occupied positions.

**293.** After the German attack had been launched on April 6, the General Headquarters, implementing what was agreed on during the conference of the Allies, held at the Kenali railway station on April 3, ordered the WMFAS to commence the offensive on April 7, on the general axis Koritsa-Elvasan-Dyrrahio, in co-operation with the Yugoslavian forces which were to operate from the area of Debar-Strouga towards Elvasan.

For the implementation of the above mission, the WMFAS sought to co-operate with the Yugoslavian forces and after many efforts, this was finally achieved through telephone communication with the Yugoslavian Army of Tetovo at 0230hrs, on April 7, and an operation was agreed to begin in the morning of the same day by both Armies, at the same time if possible. However, on the Yugoslavian side there was only artillery fire from 0700-0800 hrs in the direction of Lin, whereas the WMFAS launched an attack at 1330 hrs with the XIII Infantry Division.

The XIII Division, despite the vigorous Italian resistance, managed to seize the height 1116 and to capture almost an entire Italian battalion of 20 officers and 527 soldiers. Subsequently, the attacking troops were held in position before the height 1301, suffering heavy losses.

The Yugoslavians, who were asked at 1400 hrs about their failure to launch the attack which had been agreed assured that this would commence at 1730 hrs with only a single battalion of the Strouga Division, because the Division was in the process of mobilisation. Nevertheless, they were once more confined to some artillery fire and the minimal infantry fire of the screening forces.

Thus, the joint operation of the Greek and Yugoslavian forces against the Italian forces in Albania was not carried out, since the Yugoslavians did not conduct any serious offensive north of Achrida lake.

For the following day, April 8, the WMFAS had decided to launch an attack, starting at 0630 hrs with the IX and XIII Divisions. However, the attack was postponed, because of the untimely arrival of the artillery ammunitions and the adverse weather conditions. Nevertheless, IX Division troops, carried away by the enthusiasm and impetuosity of their officers, sallied forth before the new time of attack was set and infiltrated the Italian lines, where they took approximately 250 prisoners. These troops, however, were eventually forced to withdraw, suffering heavy losses.

**294.** Meanwhile, the incoming intelligence, at the WMFAS since the morning of April 8, presented the situation in southern Yugoslavia as chaotic and the Yugoslavian forces in that area in almost total disarray.

Subsequently, the WMFAS proposed the suspension of offensive operations to the General Headquarters. This proposal was approved and thus, as of 1000 hrs, on April 8, all further offensive activities were halted. The troops of the IX and XIII Divisions remained at the positions they had occupied through previous small-scale operations, until that evening and then returned to their bases. Only the troops occupying the height 1116 were ordered to remain at their positions.

## Changes in the Greek-British Disposition
(Sketch-map no. 20, 23, 24)

**295.** The rapid development of the situation in Yugoslavia posed new serious problems for the General Headquarters, since by that time a danger situation had arisen, threatening the front of Central Macedonia and the eastern flank of the Greek Army in Albania. The German advance southwards via Monastiri would outflank from the left the 'W' Force troops in the Vermio area and threaten the rear of the Greek forces in Albania.

Thus, the General Headquarters decided to transfer the defensive disposition further to the west, facing northwards, in order to block off the corridor from Prespa Major lake to Vevi. Thus, on April 8, it ordered the 'W' Team to evacuate hastily the northern sector of its area, from Kaimaktsalan to Vegoritis lake and to occupy the Stena Kirli Derven (Klidi) area, as far as Nymphaeo, advancing the 1st Armoured British Division towards Monastiri, in order to delay the enemy. Furthermore, it assigned the Cavalry Division again to the WMFAS, with mission to cover the Varnous-Verno mountain area from the east, as far as the area of Nymphaeo, where it was to join with the 'W' Team forces.

At the same time, since April 8, the Commander of the CMFAS, Lieutenant General of the Reserve Ioannis Kotoulas, was replaced by Major General Christos Karassos, who had been commander of the 20th Division until then. The command of the 20th Division was assigned to Colonel Miltiades Papakonstantinou, who had been its Infantry Commander until then.

**296.** The required re-disposition followed. The Cavalry Division, that was also reinforced with the 21st Infantry Brigade, was positioned in the Varnous-Verno area, chiefly assigned to cover the Pisoderio pass. This Brigade began its organisation on March 23, in Biglista and comprised the 88th Infantry Regiment, a Machine-gun battalion and two Artillery battalions. The Greek - British forces of the 'W' Force were positioned at the remainder of the area Klidi-Vegoritis lake-Vermio mountain-Olympus mountain, as follows:

The Klidi defile was assigned to a team under the command of Major General Mackay, Commander of the 6th Australian Division, which comprised:

-The command of the 19th Australian Brigade with 1st Australian Anti-tank Artillery Regiment, two Australian Infantry battalions, the Motorised Scout Battalion of the 1st Armoured British Brigade and a New Zealand Machine-gun battalion, astride the defile.

-The Dodecanese Regiment, Southwest of Kelli, organised in Athens on November 13, 1940, and relocated at the end of February to the area of Vevi-Klidi.

- The 1st British Armoured Brigade (Hussars Armoured Battalion, 3rd Tank Regiment), as a reserve in the area of Perdika village.

The 20th Division was ordered to secure its left flank at Vegoritis lake and to block off the routes from Edessa westwards. The troops, that withdrew from the Kaimaktsalan area occupied positions on the heights that lay west of Vegoritis lake.

The XII Division, which had been operationally under the command of the 1st Australian Army Corps, was ordered to block off the Hadova pass and the mountain routes of Vermio mountain.

Thus, the new disposition of the Greek - British forces in the area of Vermio, which was completed on April 10, was the following:

-On the left, the Cavalry Division (under the command of the WMFAS) along the pass of Pisoderi, further on, the Mackay Team along the Klidi defile and further to the east the 20th Greek Division (under the command of the CMFAS) as far as the Agra pass, Northwest of Edessa.

-On the right, the 1st Australian Army Corps with the 2nd New Zealand Division along the passes of Olympus mountain, the 16th Australian Brigade on southern Vermio mountain and the XII Division along the Hadova defile.

The width of this area was approximately 170 kilometres, and was therefore sparsely manned and unsuitable for prolonged defence. Further more, the extension of the front to the north of Amydeo absorbed all the reserves.

**297.** Meanwhile, the events developed at a rapid pace. The XL Army Corps, operating south of Nyssa in order to cut off the Yugoslavian forces that were present in the area of Leskovats, seized Skopje in the night of April 8 and Monastiri in the afternoon of the following day. Continuing its advance into the Greek territory, it seized the defenceless town of Florina at noon on April 10. Further to the north, on the same day, the German forces seized the area of Achris lake and gained contact with the Italians.

The Germans, following these successes in southern Serbia and the capitulation of the EMFAS, began to prepare the second phase of their operations against Central Greece. To that effect, the Commander of the 12th German Army Marshal Von List organised two attack teams:

- The Western team, under the command of General Stume, Commander of the XL Armoured Army Corps, that comprised the 5th and the 9th Armoured Divisions, the 73rd Infantry Division and the 'Adolph Hitler SS Bodyguard' and would be operating along the axis of Florina - Larissa.

-The Eastern team, under the command of General Boeme, Commander of the XVIII Mountain Army Corps, that comprised the 2nd Armoured Division, the 5th and 6th Mountain Divisions and the 72nd Infantry Division and would be operating along the axis of Thessaloniki-Litohoro.

**298.** After the rapid advance of the German forces, General Wilson, deeming that the defensive area of Klidi could not withstand the attacks of the Germans and would thus place the Vermio area at a risk, proposed the abandonment of the occupied position and the occupation of the Siniatsiko-Vourinos-Kamvounia-Pieria-Olympus area.

This proposal was approved of by telephone by the Commander-in-Chief, on April 10, and was officially confirmed at their meeting in Farsala on the following day, April 11.

The new defensive area was strong and more economical and could be held, provided that, the two Greek divisions that were at the Vermio area, would occupy positions in time to conduct an effective defence of the Siatista and Klissoura defiles.

The British forces would take over the zone from the coast of Platamonas to the river bend of Aliakmonas. The Greek XII and 20th Divisions would take over the zone Vourinos-Siniatsiko and the Cavalry Division with the 21st Infantry Brigade would remain at their positions on Varnous and Vernon mountains. The troops would have to settle in their new positions by April 13. The XII and 20th Divisions, after withdrawing to the new defensive area, would cease to be subordinate to the 'W' Team and would return to the CMFAS, which would come under the command of the WMFAS as of April 14.

The Mackay Team, after covering the withdrawal of the XII and the 20th Divisions from the direction of the Klidi defile, would then withdraw to the new defensive area, delaying the enemy with the 1st British Armoured Brigade. After the termination of the withdrawal, this Team, which had been especially organised to defend the Klidi defile, would cease to exist. The Australian units would return to the 1st Australian Army Corps, while the 1st British Armoured Brigade would concentrate in the area of Grevena as a reserve.

*The Seizure of the Klidi Area and the Withdrawal towards Siniatsiko*
(Sketch-map no. 23)

**299.** Following the occupation of Florina, the XL Armoured Army Corps focused its main effort on breaking through the defile of Klidi (Kirli Derven), employing the 'Adolph Hitler SS Bodyguards' for that purpose along with elements of the 9th Armoured Division. Concurrently, other troops moved along the road Florina-Pisoderi. East of Vermio, in the valley of Axios river, there was no activity worth recording.

In the night of April 10 to 11, forward German motorised troops took contact with the area of the Klidi defile. On the following day, April 11, the German activity was limited, due to the severe cold and the continuous drizzle. Two German battalions attacked the Australian positions astride the defile, at nearly the end of the day, but were repulsed. The German tanks were not used because they had been immobilised before the minefield on site.

An action towards Pisoderi saddle, in the sector of the Cavalry Division, during that same day, was repulsed with considerable losses on the German side.

**300.** On April 12, the Germans continued their attacks under the same adverse weather conditions. At 0830 hrs, the elite team of the German Army 'SS Adolph Hitler Bodyguard' launched a frontal attack, with artillery support, against the Klidi area, with its main effort towards the east of the road, at the limiting point between the British Motorised Scout battalion and the Australian Infantry battalion. At approximately 1100hrs, the German troops managed to infiltrate and envelop the Australian battalion. The British Motorised Scout Battalion suffered heavy pressure and was forced to withdraw towards the railway station of Klidi, under the impression that the Australians had retreated. The Australian battalion held its ground all afternoon, but after being attacked by German tanks at 1730 hrs, it was forced to retreat in disarray with serious losses, abandoning many weapons and other war supplies.

The other Australian Infantry battalion, that was defending the western section of the defile, was not notified about the withdrawal, because of the destruction of the telephone communications, but was able to retreat in small sections in the evening, when the Germans had nearly infiltrated its lines.

Further east of the defile, the Germans launched an attack upon the empty positions of the Dodecanese Regiment, at the time when the latter had already retired, after receiving an order to that effect. The German troops arrived at the village of Petra at 2015hrs, where they took 60 Australians and 40 Greeks prisoners. The Dodecanese Regiment, manned mainly by volunteers, after its withdrawal from the Klidi area ceased to exist as an organised unit, since part of its troops climbed British motor vehicles and were directed towards Ptolemaida, Kozani, Siatista and Grevena and part of them were attacked by German tanks near Amydeo and fled to the south in disarray.

Further to the west, in the sector of the 21st Greek Brigade, Battalion 1/88, which was situated at its right, confronted nearly two German battalions from 1530 hrs until 1800 hrs. The struggle was unequal and the Battalion suffered heavy losses. Those of its men who survived and were not taken prisoners, dispersed towards the woodland of Radosi.

The Commander of the 88th Regiment, Lieutenant Colonel of the Reserve Georgios Hondros, wanted to counter-attack with a small reserve force and sallying forth first, revolver in hand, was shot dead by the fire of an automatic weapon.

**301.** In the morning of April 13, the Germans continued their advance southwards and gained contact with the rear guard of the 1st Armoured British Brigade. The latter, assigned to cover the other Greek - British forces, was forced to conduct a tough fight in the area of Amydeo and to the south of Ptolemaida, where its forces had been echeloned. The conduct of the entire retrograde movement was orderly completed. In the area of Amydeo, there was the only incident of tank fighting that occurred during the German invasion, in the course of which the German tanks abandoned their effort to advance towards Kozani. The British troops, successfully supported by the artillery, managed to be disengaged in time and to retreat towards Kozani and from there on to Grevena, where they arrived in the morning of April 14.

It is worth noting that the Artillery units of the British Expeditionary Corps, though enveloped by the Germans, remained at their positions, firing effectively until nightfall. Furthermore, the Infantry and Tank units also displayed unequalled bravery, self-control and faced the attacks of the elite and far stronger German forces with self-sacrifice.

After the Klidi area had been abandoned, the Team of Major General Mackay ceased to exist and the Australian forces returned to the 1st Australian Army Corps, which as of April 12 was named 'ANZAC Corps' (Australian-New Zealander's Army Corps), in memory of the First World War.

**302.** Meanwhile, based on the decision taken on April 10, to retire from the Vermio area and settle in the area Siniatsiko-Vourinos-Kamvounia-Pieria-Olympus, the 2nd New Zealand Division, after having left delaying troops in the area of Katerini, began, on April 12, to move towards Olympus-Platamonas.

The Greek 20th and XII Divisions began to withdraw the bulk of their forces in the evening of April 11 and 12 respectively, towards their new positions at Siniatsiko and Vourino, after having left a third of their forces in the area.

The Cavalry Division, after coming to an agreement with the neighbouring 20th Division, altered its disposition and took up positions on mount Vernon, from the lake Prespa Major to the west of the Verbista height.

The withdrawal of the 20th and XII Divisions was conducted under adverse weather and psychological conditions and only part of their forces managed to reach their positions in the new area by the night of April 11 to 12. Many soldiers, particularly those who came from the areas that had already been occupied by the Germans began to slip away to their homes. Consequently, the forces of the above Divisions were no longer considered to be in good fighting condition, capable of confronting elite German units, such as the 'SS Adolph Hitler Bodyguard'.

**303.** The establishment of the Greek - British forces in the new area of Siniatsiko-Aliakmonas-Olympus was completed by the evening of April 13 and was, from east to west, the following:

-The 2nd New Zealand Division (comprising the 4th, 5th and 6th Brigades) was established with the 4th Brigade at the defile of Porta, as far as the Aliakmonas river, and with the 5th Brigade at the right flank, with three battalions at the defile of Petra and with one battalion at the coastal crossing of Platamonas. The 6th Brigade remained as a reserve in the area of Elassona.

-The 6th Australian Division (comprising the 16th, 19th Brigades) occupied the area south of Servia with the 16th Brigade, in order to cover the mountain passes between the defiles of Petra and Porta, and west of Servia with the 19th Brigade, on the western bank of Aliakmonas river. The liaison between the 19th Australian Brigade and the 4th New Zealand Brigade was assigned to a battalion of the latter Brigade which had advanced in the area of the village Rymnio.

-The XII and 20th Greek Divisions occupied the Vourino and Siniatsiko area in order to secure the passes of Klissoura, Vlasti and Siatista.

-The Cavalry Division, together with the 21st Infantry Brigade, occupied the Vernon area, assigned as before to secure the Pisoderi pass.

-The 1st British Armoured Brigade was at Grevena as a reserve and possibly as a flank guard.

**304.** In the evening on April 13, the total strength and disposition of the Greek - British forces that were expected to confront the two German Army Corps, (the XL Armoured Division, operating from the field corridor of Florina, and the XVIII Mountain Division, operating from the direction of Thessaloniki), the total strength of which was seven and a half divisions, of which three and a half were armoured. Furthermore, the Germans had indisputable air superiority and, with the improvement of the weather conditions, had commenced vigorous action throughout the entire front.

Under these circumstances, General Wilson began to perceive how dangerous the situation was, having also in mind the intelligence reports about the disorganisation of the Greek units to his left. That could result in an unopposed German invasion on either side of Pindos mountain towards Ioannina and Grevena. There were also reports about an impending capitulation of the Yugoslavian Army and because there was no possibility of reinforcement from Egypt, he finally decided on April 13, to withdraw the British forces to the Thermopilae area. For that, he sent the appropriate troops to make reconnaissance. At the same time he decided to send the 17th Australian Brigade, under the command of Brigadier General Savage, to Kalambaka, in order to block off the exit of German forces from Ioannina to the plain of Thessaly, via Metsovo, and from Kastoria, via Grevena. This Brigade, that had the 6th Australian Division as a parent unit, arrived in the area of operations on April 12.

This decision of General Wilson to retreat to Thermopilae, could be considered as premature, since the ANZAC Corps had not yet made contact with the Germans in any part of the Aliakmonas river area, and the Greek forces that were situated on the mountains, west of the Florina and Kozani high plateaux, also retained their positions.

### Battles in the Area of Siniatsiko-Olympus mountains
#### (Sketch-map no. 24, 25)

**305.** The Western Assault Team (XL Armoured Army Corps) after breaking through the defile of Klidi, which is the main gate of invasion from the north to the high plateau of Kozani, ordered the 'SS Adolph Hitler Bodyguard' to operate in the direction of Ioannina, via Grevena and Metsovo, in order to cover the right flank of the 12th Army and to gather concrete information about the situation of the Greek Army which was on the west of Pindos. The operation, if successful, would naturally cut off the withdrawal route of the Greek forces that were fighting in Albania. At the same time, it ordered the 9th Armoured Division to continue its advance towards Kozani and further to the south, in pursuit of the retreating British.

The 'SS Adolph Hitler Bodyguard' and elements of the 9th Armoured Division moved rapidly towards Klissoura and the passes of Vlasti and Siatista and by midday, on April 14, after a twenty-four hour fighting, forced their way through the Klissoura defile, which had not been manned in time by the 20th Division with sufficient forces.

The Greek troops that occupied the passes of Vlasti and Siatista were not pressured as heavily and retained their positions, without, however, possessing the means to confront a strong German attack.

**306.** The break through of the Klissoura defile permitted the Germans, by this point, to advance towards the Southwest and to cut off all the forces of the CMFAS east of Aliakmonas river, leading to their defeat and captivity.

Facing this situation, the Commander of the CMFAS decided to withdraw his forces west of the river, in the night of April 14 to 15. The withdrawal of the two CMFAS Divisions was conducted in order, via the bridges of Giagovo and Neapolis, but the morale of the troops had suffered irreparable damage and all efforts, on the part of the commands, to re-organise the units were unsuccessful. The notion of the futility of continuing the struggle had penetrated within all ranks and the common effort to avoid captivity was evident.

This led the units, after an attack by German aircraft and artillery fire on April 15, to disperse and break up almost completely. The CMFAS Headquarters began to move towards Kalambaka, but, at approximately 1000 hrs, on April 16, it received an order of the WMFAS, to move, with all available troops, to the area of Metsovo following mountain routes.

Thus, as of April 16, the co-operation between Greek and British forces was finally terminated.

**307.** The lst British Armoured Brigade -that had been deployed in the area of Grevena- also withdrew, during the night of April 14 to 15, to the southern bank of Venetikos river. The withdrawal of the British troops was conducted under adverse weather conditions and incessant air attacks.

In the following night, April 15 to 16, the Brigade was ordered to continue its withdrawal, without being involved in any fight, and to reach Kalambaka, where the 17th Australian Brigade had already arrived.

**308.** In the meantime, the 9th German Armoured Division arrived in Kozani in the morning of April 14, and part of its forces advanced further southwards, in pursuit of the British who were retreating. Nevertheless, it was unable to achieve a rapid crossing of Aliakmonas river, north of Servia, because the bridge had already been destroyed and thus halted its advance.

From the morning of April 15, the Germans attacked the 4th New Zealand Brigade and the 19th Australian Brigade, with troops that had crossed the river during the night using assault boats, in the area of Rymnio village, but were subjected to the sustained fire of the New Zealanders and were forced to surrender. Two more attacks were also repulsed with heavy losses during the day. The total number of casualties, on the German side, were 395 prisoners and approximately 200 killed in action and wounded, whereas the casualties of the British, who retained their positions, where exceedingly few, due to the good cover and terrain organisation.

After the failure of the German attack at Servia, General Stume decided, continuing the frontal engagement of the British forces on site, to by-pass the area of Aliakmonas river with the 5th Armoured Division, that had just been placed at the disposal of the XL Armoured Army Corps and to advance towards Lamia via Grevena-Kalambaka.

The 5th Armoured Division seized Grevena on April 16 and continued its movement towards Kalambaka, where it arrived in the afternoon of April 18, since the entire previous day had been taken up with the bridging of Venetikos river. Subsequently, Marshal List ordered General Stume to advance towards Lamia, sending at the same time a force towards the pass of Metsovo.

**309.** The Eastern Team (XVIII German Mountain Army Corps), that had occupied Thessaloniki since April 9, should operate against the Vermio area, with the 6th Mountain Division towards Edessa, (Agra defile) and with the 2nd Armoured and 5th Mountain Divisions towards Veria (Hadova pass). However, the rapid advance of the XL Armoured Army Corps in the corridor of Monastiri-Florina and the withdrawal of the 'W' Force, made this frontal attack against Vermio unnecessary.

After the occupation of Veria on April 11, the bulk of the XVIII Mountain Army Corps was directed southwards with the objective to seize the passes of Olympus (Petra defile-Platamonas-Tempi) and to invade the plain of Thessaly. At the same time, a flank guard, comprising a regiment of the 2nd Armoured Division and a Motorcyclist battalion of the 72nd Division was sent towards the defile of Servia (Porta defile) via the defile of Tripotamos.

On April 14, forces of the 2nd Armoured Division and the 6th Mountain Division after a two-day hard fighting with heavy losses crossed the Aliakmonas river in the area of the railway bridge south of Alexandria and continued their advance towards the northern slopes of Olympus.

On April 15, the German 5th, 6th Mountain Divisions, 2nd Armoured Division as well as a detachment from the 72nd Division, attacked the zone of the 2nd New Zealand Division and advanced towards the eastern passes of Olympus. The 2nd Armoured Division operated with two columns from the area of Katerini. One towards the defile of Petra, which forced the New Zealanders to withdraw towards Agios Dimitrios, without recording any further success and the other from Litohoro towards Platamonas, pressing strongly and creating a danger of envelopment of the area from the direction of Platamonas-Tempi-Larissa.

On the following day, April 16, the 6th Mountain Division began an enveloping movement from the southern slopes of Olympus and from the pass of Leptokarya-Kallipefki towards the village of Gonni, where a German battalion arrived on the following day. At the same time, the troops of the 2nd Armoured Division advanced as well, arriving in the afternoon on April 17 at the north-eastern entrance of the Tempi valley.

**310.** What could be concluded from the development of the battles that took place in the passes of Olympus and the area of Aliakmonas river, was that the situation of the ANZAC Corps was entering a new phase, starting in the morning of April 16. The principal threat against it was by then discernible at its eastern flank, in the crossing of Platamonas, and not in the western, where the situation was quite satisfactory.

The initial assessment was that the passes of Olympus could be held without great difficulty and for sufficient time to allow the unoposed disengagement of the ANZAC forces. However, the outcome of the battle of Platamonas on April 16, and the already discernible threat on the right (eastern), made it expedient that the situation should be dealt with immediately, in order to block off the German infiltration towards the plain of Thessaly via the Tempi valley.

### The Withdrawal of the Greek Army from Albania
(Sketch-map no. 24, 26)

**311.** The rapid development of events in Macedonia, which came as a natural consequence of the collapse of the Yugoslavian resistance, placed, as previously mentioned, the Greek High Command, before a series of problems demanding a quick solution.

The advance of the XL German Armoured Army Corps towards Monastiri and the rapid invasion to the Greek territory, in conjunction with the forces advancing through the valley of Axios, threatened to cut off the Greek - British forces at the Vermio area.

Furthermore, if the Germans would occupy Kastoria, they would be at the rear of the WMFAS and their subsequent advance towards Grevena-Ioannina would cut off the retreat route of the EFAS.

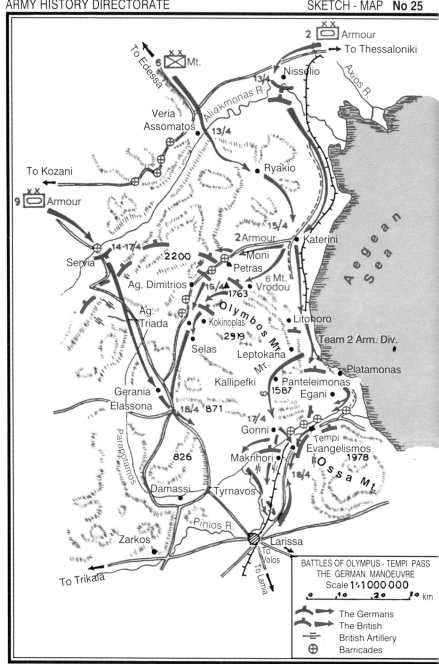

BATTLES OF OLYMPUS - TEMPI PASS
THE GERMAN MANOEUVRE
Scale 1:1 000 000

The Germans
The British
British Artillery
Barricades

R.

ıssa

ᴋos R.

So far, the measures taken to avert the first threat have already been mentioned as well as the manner in which the 'W' Force conducted its withdrawl from the Vermio area and was deployed in the area of Siniatsiko-Vourinos-Olympus. Nevertheless, the confrontation of the second threat demanded the abandonment of all or part of the occupied territories in Northern Epirus, which had been gained after glorious struggles and heavy sacrifices and on which Greece had indisputable historic and racial claims.

312. This withdrawal of the forces of the Albanian Theatre of Operations had always been considered, both from the political and the military point of view, by the Greek General Headquarters, ever since the problem of confronting the German threat had been posed in January 1941. Regarding the military point of view, the purpose of the withdrawal was always to bring the forces of the Albanian Theatre of Operations in good fighting condition onto a certain defensive line, that would allow the safe containment of the Italians and would save forces in order to use them against the Germans.

Such a line was either the Greek - Albanian borders, from the sea to Mertzani, or the internal line of Kalamas-Elea-Smolikas or the line further south, from Aoos river towards Orliaka mountain-Venetikos river-Aliakmonas river as far as its estuary, onto which the forces of the Bulgarian Theatre of Operations would also withdraw.

This deep withdrawal, even if regarded solely from the viewpoint of movement, presented a very serious danger of disorganisation for the units, which had already been worn down by the five-month winter campaign. In order to reduce this danger, the withdrawal would have to be conducted in successive phases. The time required to conduct the withdrawal in order, was estimated to be approximately one month.

313. However, after the collapse of the Yugoslavian resistance and the appresiable imminent German threat and in order to avert irreparable disaster, the Greek High Command was forced to cope with the immediate evacuation of Albania.

Thus, after the seizure of Monastiri by the Germans on April 9, the General Headquarters decided to gradually evacuate Northern Epirus and Western Macedonia as fast as possible and also to occupy and secure, with the Greek -British forces, the area Vouthrotos lake-Greek Albanian borders-Smolikas mountain-Aliakmonas river-Olympus mountain.

The British would occupy the territory between the coastal passage east of Olympus and the bend of Aliakmonas river, north of Deskati. The forces of CMFAS and WMFAS (under the command of the latter) would occupy the territory between the bend of Aliakmonas river and Smolikas mountain, while the forces of the EFAS would occupy the remaining territory as far as the Ionian Sea.

The evacuation of Albania was to begin since April 12 with the withdrawal of the WMFAS forces on the general direction of Koritsa-Kastoria-Grevena. The withdrawal would be covered from the directions of Monastiri and Thessaloniki by Greek and British-Greek forces, deployed initially in the area of Varnous-Verno-Kirli Derven pass (Klidi)-Vermio-Olympus and in the case of a German break through of the Klidi passage in the area of Megali Prespa lake-Verno-Siniatsiko-Aliakmonas-Olympus. The area Varnous-Verno as has already been mentioned, was assigned by the WMFAS to the Cavalry Division and the 21st Infantry Brigade.

In order to secure the transportation towards the rear areas, which could be threatened in the event of an unfavourable development of operations on the front of Central Macedonia, on April 10 the General Headquarters ordered the XI Division, which was a reserve at Leskoviki, to move through Mertzani to the pass of Zygos in the area of Metsovo, and to secure the communication with Kalambaka.

**314.** In the meantime, the Greek Army in Albania continued to hold on firmly to the territory it had gained until then and to stand as an immovable rock, before which the Italian "Primavera" (Spring) attack had been crushed with heavy casualties, for the enemy.

The general disposition of the Greek forces in Albania, during the period of the German invasion of Greece was, from south to north, the following:

- In the Southern and Central Sector, the Epirus Field Army Section (EFAS), with the A' and B' Army Corps under its command:

• The A' Army Corps occupied the Southern Sector of the front and had at its disposal the III Division, from Himara to the valley of Sousitsa river, the VIII Division, in the area of Argyrokastro, and the II Division, Southwest of Klissoura, on either side of Drinos river.

• The B' Army Corps, occupied the Central Sector and had at its disposal, in contact with the enemy, the IV Division on Sendeli mountain, the V Division on Trebessina mountain, the XVII Division from the northern slopes of Trebessina mountain to the saddle of Boubessi and the VI Division west of Apsos river. On a second echelon, it had the I Division north of Premeti, the XV Division in the area of Klissoura and the XI Division in the area of the villages Bali and Roden.

- In the Northern Sector, the Western Macedonia Field Army Section (WMFAS), with the XVI Division, from Tomoros mountain to Devolis river, the X Division, north of Devolis river, the IX Division in the area of Kamia-Mnima Greas, and the XIII Division, in the area of Pogradetz, under its command and in contact with the enemy. On second echelon, there was only the Cavalry Division Southwest of Koritsa.

315. The general situation of the units in the Albanian Theatre of Operations could not be considered satisfactory. The strength was 10-20% below the war establishment and there were great shortages in pack animals and ammunition. The weapons of the infantry battalions were reduced by approximately 50%.

The invasion of the Germans into the valley of Axios river, the occupation of Thessaloniki and the collapse of the Yugoslavian resistance in southern Yugoslavia, created an alarming atmosphere with serious repercussions on the morale of the Army.

This rapid and dramatic turn of events affected the higher ranks as well, within which the notion of the futility of resisting the Germans began to grow. A first manifestation of this damaging influence on the leaders' morale, was the letter sent on April 11, by the Commander of the A' Army Corps to the Commander of the EFAS, in which he proposed a capitulation with the Germans.

Similar notions prevailed within the B' Army Corps as well, the Commander and some of the division commanders of which believed that the withdrawal would signify the commencement of the disorganisation and communicated their views to the Commander of the EFAS.

The Commander of the EFAS, having forbidden any talk of capitulation, submitted the following report to the General Headquarters:

'Corps Commanders inform me: Recent events following the German invasion have affected troops. They believe that retrograde manoeuvres in great depth will not be devoid of the dangers of an inglorious disintegration of the Army. They request that a solution be found ensuring the salvation and the victorious prestige of our Army'.

On the contrary, in the WMFAS the events were initially confronted with greater composure and the situation regarding the morale was aggravated later on, even though, there too, there were discussions concerning the need for some quick decision-taking. Indicative of the spirit that prevailed, is that the Commander of the XVI Division expressed his impatience considering a decision as to what ought to be done and he threatened that, in the evening of the same day he would commence the withdrawal of his Division on his own initiative.

## The Retrograde Manoeuvre of the WMFAS
### (Sketch-map no. 24)

**316.** The WMFAS, being certain of the withdrawal, began preparations since April 11 and notified its divisions, so that they could plan the manoeuvres of their units. When the Commander-in-Chief requested the Chief of Staff of the WMFAS to submit specific proposals, the latter at once submitted the following report: 'The opportunity to assume the retrograde manoeuvre has gone by at the expense of the army, which though victorious was forced to stand as an onlooker, watching the enemy advance on its rear'.

With this answer, the WMFAS underlined the direct danger of getting cut off from the retreat routes and the need to start the retrograde movement the soonest possible, so as to avert the encirclement of forces in the Albanian Theatre of Operations.

Within this depressing atmosphere, the WMFAS received, at midday on April 12, the order of the General Headquarters to the WMFAS and the EFAS for a retrograde manoeuvre that was to commence in the evening on that same day, whereas the evacuation of Koritsa was to start immediately.

The first objective of the WMFAS withdrawal would be the occupation of the area of Apsos river-Kiafe Kiarit saddle-Grammos mountain-western branch of Aliakmonas river-Smixi-Klissoura pass, in four nights (April 12-15).

In order to avoid any unforeseen incidents, the WMFAS assigned two of its reserve battalions to the Tsangoni defile, one to Koritsa and one to the pass of Kiafe Kiarit. The Cavalry Division would retain its positions until the other WMFAS divisions arrived on the line of Dipotamia-Ieropigi-Vatochori and would then continue, delaying the enemy.

**317.** The WMFAS Headquarters was relocated since midnight, April 12 to 13, in Kastoria. The movement of divisions and non-divisional units and formations began in the evening on April 12, according to the plan.

The XIII Division, commencing its retrograde movement towards Tsangoni-Ieropigi-Smixi, would retain the Tsangoni defile until the units of the IX and X Divisions were conveyed east of Darza. The intention of the Division was to bring the bulk of its forces behind the Tsangoni defile at a bound and to move to the Greek - Albanian frontier at a second bound. Smixi had been designated as the third and final location (area of Vogatsiko). The withdrawal of the Division was conducted in order.

The break-up of contact, was a full tactical success because it did not attract the attention of the Italians, due to the full preparation and the high morale of the men of the Division. The Headquarters of the Division was relocated in Biglista as of midday, April 13.

The IX Division began to withdraw, along two mountain routes, as far as Maliki lake and then continued along the axis of Maliki-Koritsa-Darza. By midday, April 13, it had reached between Maliki and Koritsa. Starting that same afternoon, it continued its movement and by the morning of April 14 it had deployed east of Morova.

The X Division commenced its withdrawal along the axis Devolis river-Koritsa-Darza-Nestori. In general, the retrograde movement was conducted in order, except for the passage through the plain of Koritsa, where movement was difficult, because the Division troops met the withdrawing troops of the IX Division.

The XVI Division withdrew towards Erseka, along the axis Tomoritsas river-Moschopolis, in order to occupy the saddle of Kiafe Kiarit (Southwest of Koritsa) and to cover the withdrawal of the EFAS from the direction of Koritsa-Erseka-Leskoviki. For that, the I Division of the EFAS moved also to the same area. The two divisions comprised a Division Group after April 13, which was designated the 'Borova Division Group' as of April 17.

**318.** On April 13, the XIII, IX and X Divisions continued their orderly withdrawal, without being harassed by the Italians. The General Headquarters notified the WMFAS and the EFAS that the final general line onto which their forces would withdraw was that Vouthroto lake- Greek-Albanian borders-Smolikas mountain-Venetikos river. The WMFAS upon arriving with the bulk of its forces at the upper valley of Aliakmonas, would take the CMFAS (XII and 20th Divisions) under its command and would continue the withdrawal onto the axis Kastoria-Kalambaka, as far as the final line.

In the meantime, the Germans, advancing in the Florina corridor, had broken through the locality of Klidi on April 12 and were moving to occupy the defile of Klissoura. If their attempt was successful, they could turn in the direction of Argos Orestiko and threaten the only retreat route of the WMFAS units.

Subsequently, the XIII Division, which at midday on April 14, had the bulk of its forces in the area Tsangoni-Biglista, was ordered to hasten its movement and cover the withdrawal of the remaining of the WMFAS forces by the evening of April 15, securing the territory of Smixi in connection with the CMFAS in the area of Klissoura. At midnight, April 14 to 15, the XIII Division was reinforced with a battalion in the area of Maniaki village and was deployed with the XIII Reconnaissance Group on the heights that lay south of Kastoria lake, in order to cover the route of retreat of the Division towards Argos Orestiko-Grevena. The Division Commander intended to contain the Germans at all costs until the evening of April 15, so that the bulk of the Division could escape through the only route existing towards Grevena. The occupation of the Smixi area, according to the WMFAS plan, was by then pointless, since after breaking through the Klissoura defile, the Germans were moving unopposed towards Neapoli-Grevena and the CMFAS had been almost completely disintegrated.

The deployment of the above troops contained the Germans and secured the timely escape of the bulk of the XIII Division forces during the night of April 14 to 15.

The IX and X Divisions continued their retrograde manoeuvre towards the frontier, where they arrived in the morning on April 15. In the 30th Regiment of the Division, a serious incident of insubordination took place in the night of April 14 to 15. Two second lieutenants of the reserve took 280 soldiers with their armament and led them to Grevena, where they surrendered to the Germans.

The XVI Division arrived in the night of April 14 to 15 to the area of Kiafe Kiarit and began its deployment which continued during the following day.

The Cavalry Division and the 21st Infantry Brigade, which had been assigned to the area of Verno in order to cover the withdrawal of the WMFAS as well as that of the left flank of the 'W' Force from the area of Klidi, after the loss of the Klissura defile, send forces towards the area of Aposkepos village and blocked off the pass of Photini, north of Kastoria lake.

**319.** In the morning of April 15, the 'SS Adolph Hitler bodyguard' was contained while advancing after the break through of the Klissoura defile, by the XIII Division troops that had been positioned south of lake Kastoria and which had been reinforced in the meantime. The Cavalry troops on the pass of Photini kept their positions, despite the successive tank assaults and the airforce action. Motorised German troops that launched their main effort against Argos Orestiko and their secondary effort in the direction of the Photini pass, were repulsed.

As of midday, new German infantry and tanks began to move towards the villages Ambelokipi and Militsa. A Pack Artillery battalion, reinforced with four additional batteries and deployed west of Ambelokipi village, contained the German troops and impeded the approach of the reinforcements from Klissoura. The German artillery counteracted and, at 1330 hrs, managed to neutralise the above Artillery battalion. Its Commander, Major Paparodou was killed, his body falling on his guns.

At 1330 hrs, the Germans launched another serious effort, the third in succession, and at approximately 1400 hrs they seized Ambelokipi. The Commander of the Cavalry company on site, Captain Kleitos Hatzeliadis, fighting heroically, also fell on the line of duty. The troop resistance was bowed after a new serious German attempt, supported by approximately 40 aircraft. At approximately 1900 hrs, the Germans encircled and seized Argos Orestiko and at approximately 2000 hrs Kastoria from the south. Those of the troops that were able to escape captivity, moved towards Skalochori village, since the retreat route towards Grevena-Kalambaka had already been cut off.

The IX Division started moving in the afternoon of April 15 and continued during the night of 15 to 16, towards its final area east of Nestorio. The Division Headquarters was established at Anthiro village.

The X Division continued its withdrawal without any harassment by the Italians and passed Grammos mountain at the borders. Then it was forced, after the development of the situation in the area of Argos Orestiko-Kastoria, to turn to the southwest towards the mountainous area of Pindos.

**320.** Meanwhile, the WMFAS notified its divisions, by phone, that the retreat route had been cut off and defined that the troops would have to move towards Metsovo via the mountain passes of Pindos, their re-supply provided by local sources. A new Command Station was set up in Kalambaka.

As of 1700 hrs, on April 15, all telephone communications with the divisions were interrupted and were only restored after the concentration of the latter in the area of Metsovo.

Thus, the first phase of the retrograde manoeuvre of the WMFAS, i.e. the disengagement, had been conducted so skilfully that the Italians never regained contact with it.

Since April 17, the WMFAS was redesignated as C' Army Corps with the IX, X, XI, XIII and XVI Divisions, under the same Commander, Lieutenant General Tsolakoglou and was made subordinate to the EFAS. Its Headquarters was initially established at Metsovo as its Command Station and, later on, at Votonosi. The Mission of the C' Army Corps was to cover the areas of Epirus and Akarnania in the general line of Aoos-Mavrovouni-Katara-Tzoumerka.

### The Retrograde movement of the EFAS
### (Sketch-map no. 26)

**321.** The withdrawal of the EFAS units began under conditions of nervousness and within a defeatist mood. The aim was to initially occupy the defensive line southern bank of Aoos-Klissoura-Sevrani-Mali Kelkes-Kiafe Kiarit by the morning of April 16 and then to defend the final line, from the Vouthrotos lake to Venetikos. river. The EFAS had been authorised by the General Headquarters to order the direct withdrawal, as far as the final line, throughout its entire zone.

The withdrawal began on the night of April 13 to 14. The B' Army Corps, would begin first, whereas the A' Army Corps would begin to withdraw on April 16. Nemertska mountain was a barrier between the A' and B' Army Corps and thus the A' Army Crops would have to conduct its manoeuvre separately, having the possibility to use two main routes (Argyrokastro-Kakavia and Himara-Konispolis) within its sector. The B' Army Corps would have to cross mainly through the bridge of Mertzani and secondly through the nearby bridge of Skordilis (foot soldiers only) of Sarandaporos river, where the routes, from Klissoura and Kiafe Kiarit, converge.

322. The withdrawal of the B' Army Corps began with the V Cretans Division, which was in a state of real exhaustion, having remained on the front-line since the beginning of February and under adverse weather conditions.

The movement of its troops, that began at 2100 hrs, on April 13, soon became, in many cases, a true flight of panic-stricken soldiers. The Division's efforts to halt the flight failed and the leak continued. In the morning of April 15, after an order of the B' Army Corps, the command of the Division was assigned to its Infantry Commander, Colonel Dionysios Papadongonas. Its units continued to withdraw under the same conditions and in the morning of April 16 they arrived and stopped in the area of the villages Petrani-Fourka.

The IV Division was also disengaged in the night of April 13 to 14. The Italians noticed the withdrawal in the morning of April 14 and gained contact during the same evening. A leak, of soldiers, happened in some units of this Division as well, and in many cases the officers of those units were required to man automatic weapons by themselves. In the night of April 16 to 17, the Division withdrew west of Aoos river and came under the command of the A' Army Corps.

The XVII Division which occupied the sector of northern slopes of Trebessina-Boubessi, was subjected, at 0630 hrs on April 14, to an extremely powerful Italian attack, with the main effort directed against the centre of resistance of the fought for 731 height, which was very important for the entire defence of the Division. The Italians, despite their effort, were unable to climb the height and, at approximately 0830 hrs, were forced to temporarily suspend the attack due to the heavy losses, yet continuing to shell the area with artillery fire. The Italian attack was repeated at 1730 hrs, on the same day, but was once again repulsed.

The withdrawal of the Division commenced at 2030 hrs and was conducted orderly, without attracting the attention of the Italians. The withdrawal continued on the following day and in the morning of April 16, the Division had reached the area of Kossina village.

The VI Division, into which the Yiannakopoulos Detachment had been incorporated since April 3, began to withdraw its units, in the night of April 12 to 13, to Kapina village, whereas the bulk of the Division moved in the night of April 14 to 15. The Italians engaged in intense artillery activity and small-scale counter-attacks in various parts of the Division front, but were repulsed. In the morning of April 16, the Division had reached the area of Hairopouli village.

The XV Division, which was on a second echelon, seized and held positions at the height of the area of Tabayian village since April 13 and remained there until April 15. In the meantime, many men of the Division, who were affected by the disorderly withdrawal of the V Division troops, abandoned their positions and fled to the rear. The Division adopted hard measures to avert any further leak and to punish the fugitives. The court-marshal, that was immediately convoked in the village of Rabani, sentenced to death two soldiers of the 90th Regiment, who were executed on the same day. After this, any further leaks were terminated.

The I Division, which together with the XVI of the WMFAS comprised the Borova Division Group, arrived in the area of Kiafe Kiarit on the morning of April 14 and undertook to defend the pass in the north of the Bataros height. The morale of the troops was very low, especially in the 5th Regiment, where a great leak had been recorded, leaving a mere 40-50 men per company, despite the shooting of fugitives on the spot - as an exemplary punishment.

The XI Division, that was a reserve of the EFAS in the area of the villages Bali and Roden, had been ordered on April 12, to move to the area of Metsovo, in order to cover the EFAS from the direction of Katara. Due to the urgency of the situation, five battalions were transported by motor vehicles, whereas the remaining of the Division followed on foot. At 1730 hrs, on April 14, after the rapid turn of events in Western Macedonia, the Division was ordered to dispatch four of the preceding battalions, to the area of Eleftherochori (south of Grevena) at the disposal of the 'W' Team, in order to cover its left flank. Its fifth battalion was positioned on the saddle of Katara and undertook to carry out the entire initial mission of the Division. Thus, on the morning of April 15, one part of the Division was in Kalambaka, one in Metsovo and another one within the Albanian territory.

323. It was evident that the general situation of the EFAS in the morning on April 16 was extremely alarming, due to the development of the situation in Western Macedonia and the discernible threat from that

direction, while its retrograde manoeuvre was still at its first stage. The A' Army Corps, had not yet begun its retrograde manoeuvre, remaining at its positions, west of Aoos, until the first stage of the B' Army Corps manoeuvre had been completed.

Yet, the most alarming fact of the entire situation was that the troop morale continued to decline. The rate of insubordination and flight to the rear kept rising. On April 15, the situation was reported to the General Headquarters, which, by order of the Commander-in-Chief, made a plea, that every effort should be made to restore the discipline and to defend the fatherland. That was a matter of national interest.

The Commander of the EFAS, Lieutenant General Pitsikas called a meeting of the Commanders of the A', B' Army Corps and the WMFAS, after which the views were expressed in a written report that was conveyed to the Commander-in-Chief. Bearer of the report, was the Deputy chief of Staff of the EFAS, Colonel Grigoropoulos, who appeared before the Commander-in-Chief at approximately 1900 hrs, on April 16.

The report was as follows:

"(a) The situation of the Army from the aspect of morale and discipline is extremely crucial. It is getting worse every moment.

(b) The corps leaders painfully foresee that we shall not reach the final area in time. The Army would have been disintegrated.

(c) The causes of this situation are the fatigue, the occupation of Greek territories and the fear of being captured by the Italians.

(d) We believe that any further resistance is impossible. An eventual dispersion of the Army will create internal disorder and brigand bands with indescribable disasters for the country. The spectre of dispersion appears evident in those units which contain soldiers who come from territories that have been occupied by the enemy, such as the XV, the XVII, the VI Division..."

On April 16, the EFAS reported to the General Headquarters, in a cryptogram, that after the situation that had arisen, the need for political intervention was dire. The reply of Athens, after successive meetings with the officer sent by the EFAS, was that the Government could not accept the solution of capitulation, since the British troops were still remaining and fighting in the country. It was only by fulfilling its allied duties completely, that Greece would have the full support of Great Britain after the end of the war.

**324.** At 2200 hrs on the same day, during a new meeting -attended by the Army Deputy Minister, Papadimas, and the Minister of Public Security, Maniadakis - the Army Deputy Minister said that when the Government would depart, the solution of the capitulation requested by the Army could be implemented. This was accepted by the Minister of Public Security and the Commander-in-Chief.

Colonel Grigoropoulos directly reported, by phone, his impressions to the EFAS. In the evening of April 16, the latter issued an order to the A' and B' Army Corps and the Borova Division Group, regarding the orderly continuation of the retrograde manoeuvre and the need to maintain the cohesion of the Army.

**325.** The A' Army Corps began the withdrawal of its units in the night of April 16 to 17, along the axis of Argyrokastro-Kakavia-Zitsa, without attracting the attention of the Italians.

On April 20, the Corps was already established, without serious problems, at the designated final area on the Greek - Albanian borders.

**326.** The B' Army Corps continued the withdrawal without serious harassment by the Italians, but with increasing decline of morale and alarming escalation of insubordination incidents. By April 20, all Corps divisions had crossed south of Aoos, under the cover of the XV Division, which had undertaken to secure the bridge of Mertzani.

**327.** The Borova Division Group (I and XVI Divisions) had decided to withdraw by the morning of April 17, to the area of Borova, abandoning the Kiafe Kiarit area, because it was considered difficult to retain, due to the constant aggravation of the situation of its units. To that end, it organised a Detachment, comprising some of its units which were already at the new area, under the command of Colonel Spyridon Georgoulis, Infantry Commander of the XVI Division. The Detachment was assigned to secure the area of Borova and to cover the right flank of the B' Army Corps.

The enemy attached I Division in the morning of April 16. The attack lasted the entire day, but the enemy was unable to break through the Division's positions, despite the leak of a great number of its men towards the rear, which in many units exceeded 50% of their strength. On the night of April 16 to17, the Division withdrew to the area of Barbasi village, under the cover of the Georgoulis Detachment. On the following day, April 17, it was ordered by the Division Group to move towards Konitsa so as to regroup and rest temporarily. The movement of the Division troops was conducted during the night of April 18-19 and 19-20 without any particular problems.

The XVI Division, in accordance with the order of the Division Group, withdrew on the night of April 16 to 17, to the area of Borova and, since April 18, assumed the command of the fighting in its entire front. The

Georgoulis Detachment ceased to exist, since the same day, and its troops were placed under the command of the XVI Division.

On the following day, April l9, the enemy launched succesive attacks which the Division which it was nevertheless able to repulse, in spite of the heavy pressure it was subjected to and the continuous action of the Italian airforce. In the evening on April 20, by order of the Division Group, it too began to withdraw towards Konitsa.

*The Withdrawal of the British Expeditionary Force towards Thermopilae*

**328.** In the morning of April 16, the Commander-in-Chief Papagos met with General Wilson outside Lamia. During that meeting, they agreed that the British forces should withdraw, starting on the night of April 16 to 17, to the locality of Thermopilae. The retirement of the l9th Australian Brigade, from the area west of Servia, had already begun by the previous evening, which meant that the Greek Commander-in-Chief was placed before a 'fait accompli'.

At the end of the discussion, the Commander in chief declared: 'The time has come for the British troops to deal with their evacuation from Greece in order to avoid any further destruction of the country'.

**329.** The withdrawal of the British forces from the locality of Olympus to the new area of Thermopilae, according to General Wilson's plan, would be conducted as follows:

-The 6th Australian Division would initially withdraw, under the cover of the 2nd New Zealand Division, to the area of Pinios and would occupy positions between Zarko village and Larissa. A Division section would advance to Domokos, as a rear guard, assigned to block off the road of Lamia-Larissa. Then, after the withdrawal of the 2nd New Zealand Division, it would withdraw as well, along the axis of Larissa- Farsala-Domokos-Lamia, in order to deploy its troops on the pass of Brallos, on the left (west) of the Thermopilae area.

-The 2nd New Zealand Division, after having covered the withdrawal of the other forces by deploying part of its troops in the area of Elassona, would withdraw along the axis Larissa-Volos-Stylida-Lamia, so as to deploy its forces on the right (east) of the Thermopilae area.

-The lst British Armoured Brigade, which by April 16, was incorporated in the ANZAC Corps, would cover the withdrawal from the direction of Grevena and Kalambaka, and would then withdraw to the area of Atalanti as a reserve force.

- The 17th Australian Brigade, which was deployed in Kalambaka, after having covered the left flank of the withdrawing forces, would then withdraw along with the 6th Australian Division to the pass of Brallos.

The movement of all forces would be conducted by motor-vehicles and their deployment in the area of Thermopilae would have to be completed by the morning of April 20.

**330.** The 6th Australian Division, according to General Wilson's plan, was the first to begin the withdrawal under the cover of the 2nd New Zealand Division.

Its 19th Brigade that had begun to withdraw from the area west of Servia by April 15, crossed Aliakmonas river over a makeshift bridge, after having previously destroyed on site the trucks and the armoured vehicles that could not cross it. After crossing the river, the units moved, on foot towards the village Mikrovaltos, where they mounted other vehicles and moved in the direction of Domokos.

The other Brigade of the Division, the 16th, began its withdrawal on the night of April 16 to 17 from the area east of Servia, but the pace was very slow, due to the mountainous terrain. In the morning of April 17 and while the Brigade withdrawal continued, German troops began to move through the mountain passes of Lower Olympus, towards the western entrance of the Tempi valley, creating a threat on the right (east) flank of the British forces.

Subsequently, the Commander of the 1st Australian Corps (ANZAC), Lieutenant General Blamey formed a detachment under the command of Brigadier General Allen, Commander of the 16th Australian Brigade, comprising two battalions from the 16th Australian Brigade and one battalion from the 5th New Zealand Brigade, that was deployed, on April 17, on the southern bank of Pinios at the valley of Tempi. The detachment was assigned to delay the German forces until nightfall on April 18, securing Larissa from the east.

In the afternoon of the same day, April 17, German troops appeared on the ridgeline above Gonnoi village and entered the latter in the evening. The following morning a German battalion moved towards the village of Evangelismos and, by 1830 hrs, managed, after engaging in close combat with the Allen Detachment troops that were on site, to cross Pinios and break through the British defence. At that time, the village of Tempi was seized (25 km Northeast of Larissa) and the British were pressed at the railway station of Makrychori, while two other battalions also began to cross Pinios river. With the advent of darkness, the Germans suspended their advance.

The Allen Detachment, after having completed its mission to the full, withdrew in Larissa on the night of April 18 to 19. However, approximately five kilometres north of the town, it was attacked by German troops, which had been able to envelop it and had occupied the road at that point, thus surprising its men and causing them to disperse in various directions. Thus, as of that time, the Allen Detachment ceased to exist as an organised unit.

**331.** The withdrawal of the 2nd New Zealand Division commenced on April 17 under the cover of its 6th Brigade, which had timely occupied positions between Elassona and Tirnavos. The 5th Brigade was the first to withdraw, from the defile of Petra, and the 4th Brigade followed suite, from the defile of Porta. On the morning of April 18, the last British troops had crossed the lines of the 6th Brigade and were moving towards Thermopilae.

At approximately midday, the first German tanks appeared before the 6th Brigade front, but were nevertheless contained and almost completely destroyed by the effective artillery fire and the mine laying that had been carried out in the various tank approaches. The 6th Brigade troops repulsed another fresh German attack at midnight, on April 18 to 19, and then withdrew as well, since their mission had been successfully accomplished.

**332.** The lst British Armoured Brigade withdrew on the night of April 16 to 17, from Grevena towards Kalambaka, where it arrived in the morning on April 17. After leaving a small detachment, as a rear guard for the l7th Australian Division, it moved via Trikala towards Atalanti.

**333.** The l7th Australian Brigade began to withdraw, in successive sections, towards the area of Zakros village on the night of April 17 to 18 and to establish its defence on the eastern bank of Pinios river, in order to cover the withdrawal of the final sections of the British Expeditionary Force from the west. In the evening on April 18, the Brigade conducted the authorised demolition on the Kalambaka-Trikala road with the Pioneer company and during the night of April 18 to 19, continued its withdrawal towards the pass of Brallos.

The last troops of the Brigade passed through Larissa at 0400 hrs, on April 19. During the early morning of the same day, forward troops of the 2nd German Armoured Division entered the town without encountering any resistance.

### The Political Crisis and the Departure of the King and the Government to Crete

**334.** At 1000 hrs, on April 18, a meeting was held at the Palace, headed by the King and attended by Prime Minister Koryzis, the Ambassador of Great Britain Paleret, General Wilson, Commander in chief Papagos and others.

The Commander in chief, presenting the military situation, reported that the British forces, though still in good fighting condition, could not hold their ground at Thermopilae for a sufficient length of time. Furthermore, he referred to the serious difficulties faced by the Greek troops and to the decline of their morale.

The British declared that they were capable of holding their ground at Thermopilae until May 6, provided that the Greek troops would continue to fight in Epirus. The meeting came to an end without any decision being taken.

**335.** At 1400 hrs on the same day, the Cabinet held a meeting in the presence of the King. The Deputy Minister Papadimas, expressed the opinion that even if it were possible to extend the defence at Thermopilae, this would be to no avail as the situation in the Albanian Theatre of Operations was tragic from every aspect.

After many discussions, the prevailing opinion was that the Greek resistance should be extended for the sake of the retirement of the British Expeditionary Force. The Deputy Minister who regarded the aggravation of the situation as unavoidable, deemed that, the only way out was the immediate departure of the King and the Government.

Thus, a political issue arose, because the Government would be either obliged to retire to Crete and leave the Generals free to call a truce or to give the order for that.

The Prime Minister Koryzis was at a loss and at the end of the meeting, during which no decision had been reached, he proposed the formation of a Government comprising other more dynamic members. Koryzis, who was clearly suffering from a nervous breakdown, went back to his home, where he committed suicide.

**336.** At 1300 hrs, on April 19, a new meeting was held at the General Headquarters. This was also attended by General Wavell, who had arrived from the Middle East and Lieutenant General Mazarakis, who had been assigned by the King to form a new Government.

General Wavell declared that, the British Army would defend, provided that the Greek Army continued to resist, but because of the alarming information regarding its morale and added that his own troops were ready to retire, should the Greek Government wish so.

Afterwards, the British Ambassador read a telegram of British Prime Minister Churchill, who specified that the retirement of the British Expeditionary Force should take place with the full accord and approval of the King and the Greek Government.

Following a proposal of Lieutenant General Mazarakis, that retirement was the best solution, the King and the Government approved of the evacuation of Greece by the British Expeditionary Force. The Greek forces in Epirus would continue to fight until the retirement of the British was secured.

337. Meanwhile, due to the complaints of the British regarding the bad situation of the Greek side in Central Macedonia, the Commander of the B' Regulating Centre in Florina, Major General Panagakos, was summoned during the meeting and explained the way in which the operations were conducted. After this, General Wilson made the following statement: 'After the information and explanation provided by the General, the honour and the reputation of Greece are fully restored. Furthermore, I declare, in the name of England, that she has no complaint against Greece, which has accomplished its duty to the end, fully and honourably'. At the same time, the British Generals expressed their admiration for the Greek resistance against the Germans and the Italians.

During that same evening, Lieutenant General Mazarakis did not accept to form a Government, because the intelligence reports on the military situation had become extremely disheartening.

At 1715, a new government gave the constitutional oath, with Vice Admiral Sakellariou as vice-president, and the King was temporarily the Prime Minister. On April 21, Emmanuel Tsouderos gave the oath as the Prime Minister. The King and the Government departed for Crete, at 0400 hrs, on April 23. Before leaving, the King issued the following proclamation in which he declared the decision of the entire Nation to continue the fight until the final victory.

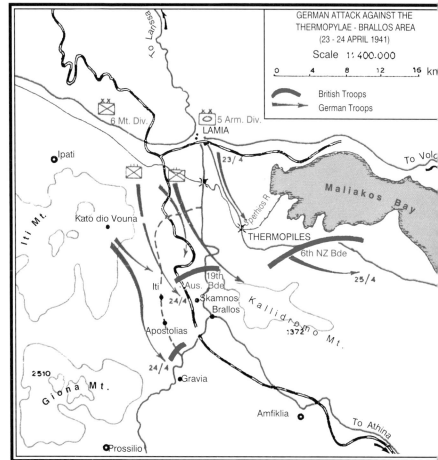

GERMAN ATTACK AGAINST THE
THERMOPYLAE - BRALLOS AREA
(23 - 24 APRIL 1941)

Scale 1:400.000

| 0 | 4 | 8 | 12 | 16 km |

British Troops

German Troops

## The King's proclamation of 23 April 1941

' *The cruel destinies of war compel Us today, to depart from Athens, along with the Crown Prince and the lawful Government of the Country, and to transfer the capital of the State to Crete, from where we shall be able to continue the struggle which, the will of the entire Nation and the duty of safeguarding the independence and integrity of the Country, have compelled us to undertake, after the aggression of two empires.*

*The will of Ours, of the Government and of the Greek People, which has manifested itself in various ways until today, has required resistance to the end from the Greek forces, which despite the uneven struggle, especially after the German invasion, fought stubbornly against the enemy, with the assistance of the British troops that came to help us and fought gloriously and are still fighting on the Greek soil for a just cause.*

*Our forces, exhausted by the rough and victorious war, that they have conducted for six months against a far more powerful enemy, having written the most glorious pages of our military history, continued the struggle against Germany with inconceivable heroism.*

*We are still unaware of the exact conditions under which the army of Epirus signed a truce with the enemy unbeknown to Us, the Commander-in-Chief and the Government. This truce does not essentially bind the free will of the Nation, the King and the Government, which is to continue the struggle, with all of our remaining forces in order to safeguard the highest national interests.*

*Been obliged to go to Crete for this purpose, we are only doing so in order to be able to continue, freely and from free Greek territory, the struggle against the invaders until the final victory, which shall fully reward the great sacrifices of the Nation.*

*Greeks, do not be discouraged, even at this painful moment of our history. I shall always be with you. God and the right of the cause will help us to achieve the final victory with all means, despite the trials, the sorrows, the dangers, which we have suffered in common and shall suffer in the meantime.*

*Be faithful to the idea of a united, undivided, free country. Have strong your will. Set your Greek pride against the violence and the temptation of the enemy. Be courageous, the good days are to come. Long live the Nation.*

*Georgios B'*

## The Capitulation of the Epirus Field Army

**338.** From the moment the withdrawal of the Greek Army began from Albania, threatened by the double danger of encirclement by the Italians and the Germans, in nearly all of the units there was alarm about the development of the situation, a factor which affected their fighting capacity to a considerable extent. Indeed, in many EFAS units, the notion that it was futile to continue the fight any further, began to prevail and serious cases of insubordination and dispersion were recorded. Men abandoned their troops on their own or in small groups, armed or unarmed, and hastened to their homes. As time went by, the decline of the morale began to affect a large number of higher rank members, who believed that the continuation of the fight was futile and would no longer serve any purpose.

The creation of the situation was also influenced by the following actions of the Ministry of the Army and the General Headquarters, which were of a more general nature. On April 15, the General Headquarters ordered the Regiment of Thessaloniki, that was stationed at Thiva, to grant 15-day regular leave to all soldiers who were natives of the occupied areas. At the same time, it requested the Ministry of the Army to apply the same measure to all officers of the Reserve and soldiers who were not indispensable. On the same day, the Deputy Minister ordered preparations to be made in order to transport to Crete all trained soldiers of classes 1940b, 1941, that were at the Peloponnese Training Centre as well as the army cadets of the Military academy. On April 16, he ordered a two-month regular leave to be granted to all untrained soldiers of the Reserve, who had been called until March 16, 1941, as well as a monthly leave to the officers of the Reserve of classes 1926 and prior to that date.

**339.** The Commander of the EFAS, after the development of the situation in his units and the information he had received from Colonel Grigoropoulos, who returned to his base in the meantime, submitted the following report to the General Headquarters and the Prime Minister, in the morning of April 18: 'The situation has reached its limit. The XVII [Division] troops are abandoning Legaritsa which covers the left flank of the Division Group. The A' Army Corps similarly reports a military leak of the VIII Division. The XI Division, which covers Metsovo is leaking away. In the name of God, save the Army from the Italians. PITSIKAS'. Furthermore, at approximately 1100 hrs, he communicated by phone with the Prime Minister, whom he requested to provide a solution to the matter within the same day, because it was impossible to restrain the men any longer. The Prime Minister assured the Commander of the EFAS of a favourable solution to the matter within the course of the day. However, this solution was not offered, due to his committing suicide on the same day and to the political crisis that ensued.

Meanwhile, the Commanders of the A', B', and C' Army Corps, as well as the Orthodox Metropolitan Bishop of Ioannina, Spyridon, pressed the Commander of the EFAS to take the initiative to call a truce with the enemy at once. After the decisive refusal of the latter to take such an initiative, the Commanders of the Army Corps with the active participation of Spyridon, decided to put him aside and offer the initiative to their senior Lieutenant General Tsolakoglou, Commander of the C' Army Corps.

**340.** The Commander of the C' Army Corps reviewed the situation that had arisen with the Commander of the EFAS and discussed the posibility of an immediate cessation of hostilities. The latter agreed but refused to take the initiative to that end, thus on April 18, he sent his Chief of Staff, Colonel Athanasios Chrysochoou, to Athens, in order to report to the Prime Minister and the Commander-in-Chief and to ask for immediate decisions.

Colonel Chrisohoou arrived in Athens at 1600 hrs, on the same day, and met at once with the Commander-in-Chief, whom he briefed accordingly. The latter replied that he was fully aware of the situation, but being also the Commander-in-Chief of the British forces in Greece, he was unable to proceed to negotiations for capitulation with the enemy, at least not before the departure of the British from the country, which was planned to be carried out by May 5.

From this meeting, as well as from other contacts that the C' Army Corps Chief of Staff had in Athens, he concluded that the situation had come to a dead end and that nobody wished to assume responsibility for the cease-fire. Thus, he send the following telegram to the Commander of the C' Army Corps in the morning of April 19: ' Confidential personal for the General. To authority of the Field Army. If you assume the responsibility, first you ought to get authorisation from the other Army Corps, to assign the action to you as having contact with the Germans. Chrisochoou from Garrison Station Theta'. 'Garrison Station Theta' was the code name for the General Headquarters.

The above telegram, regardless of the fact that it bore the sign of the General Headquarters was sent unbeknown to the Commander-in-Chief and expressed only the views of the C' Army Corps Chief of Staff.

**341.** Lieutenant General Tsolakoglou, though he believed in the necessity of immediate capitulation, hesitated, until the evening of April 19, to take the initiative. However, the above telegram of his Chief of Staff, which he received at 0200 hrs on April 20, cleared his doubts and urged him to decide to finally ignore General Pitsikas and take the initiative for capitulation.

At 0545 hrs, on April 20, Lieutenant General Tsolakoglou telephoned the Commander of the EFAS and announced that he had been authorised by the General Headquarters as well as by the Commanders of the A' and B' Army Corps to call a truce. At the same time, he read out to him the abovementioned telegram, as if coming from the Commander-in-Chief, though he was definitely aware that this, had been sent by his Chief of Staff. Soon, a three member committee of C' Army Corps officers departed to negotiate the terms of the truce with the Germans.

The military situation at that point was obviously serious but not yet desperate. Many threats were apparent but the main came from the direction of Kalambaka towards Metsovo, where the XI Division defended the passes of Katara and Zygos. The Germans had made reconnaissance as far as Koutsoufliani since the previous day. In the morning on April 20, a forward German column was shelled by the defenders but the fire was held after the fourth round, by order of the C' Army Corps, because the abovementioned committee has been sent to the Germans to negotiate the truce.

**342.** At 1800 hrs, on the same day, Major General Dietrich, Commander of the "Adolph Hitler SS Bodyguards" and Lieutenant General Tsolakogou signed a truce protocol at Votonosi village, in which it was decreed that, from 1800 hrs, the hostilities between Greece and Germany would cease. After a few hours, the hostilities between Greece and Italy would end as well, with the responsibility of the German Commander-in-Chief. By the morning of April 21, the Germans would be positioned between the Italian and the Greek forces in order to secure the cease-fire. The Greek forces were obliged to withdraw to the old Greek-Albanian borders within ten days and to demobilise after surrendering their armament, and then return home. The officers would keep their weapons and equipment in honour as they were not considered to be prisoners of war.

An hour after signing the capitulation, a Staff officer of the C' Army Corps notified the EFAS by phone that the truce had been signed. After that, the Commander of the EFAS, Lieutenant General Pitsikas considered himself 'resigned' and in the morning on April 21, he left for Athens. The command of the EFAS was assumed by Lieutenant General Tsolakoglou.

**343.** On April 21, the Chief of Staff of the 21st German Field Army and Major General Dietrich arrived in Ioannina with another protocol, different to the one that had already been signed. This change of attitude of the Germans was due to the Greek Government's announcement for 'defence to the last' and to the necessity of a similar agreement with the Italians. Lieutenant General Tsolakoglou protested, but was forced to sign it 'as a prisoner of war' and 'not of his own free will'.

The terms were worse than those of the initial protocol. The officers and soldiers were considered as prisoners of war, all supplies constituted spoils of war for the German Army, and part of those would be given to the Italians. Instead of the Greek-Albanian frontier, which was the withdrawal limit, it was stated that the separation zone for the cessation of hostilities would be defined in co-operation with the Italian Command. However, it was not mentioned clearly where this zone would be nor the time at which hostilities would end.

At midday, on April 21, the EFAS received an order of the General Headquarters, by radio, to relieve Lieutenant General Tsolakoglou, as Commander of the C' Army Corps, but it was already too late.

**344.** On the following day, April 22, the Germans violated the agreement again. They demanded that messengers should be sent to the Italians in order to facilitate the signature of a truce with them as well. The carriage road of Igoumenitsa-Bisdouni-Metsovo was designated as the line separating the Italians and the Germans and it was made clear that the Greek forces, north of that line, would be considered as prisoners of the Italians and those south of it, as prisoners of the Germans, without specifying the precise time after which the above limit would be in force.

Lieutenant General Tsolakoglou, protesting because the original terms of the capitulation were altered for the second time within 48 hours, replied that 'he is forced to comply under violence'.

Messengers sent to the Italians, signed a preliminary truce protocol, by which the hostilities would cease as of 2300 hrs, on April 23.

In the morning on April 23, Lieutenant General Tsolakoglou departed for Thessaloniki by German aircraft and there he signed the third and final capitulation protocol, with Marshal Jodle, Chief of Staff of the German Armed Forces High Command, and Italian General Ferrero, Supreme Commander of the Italian Forces in Albania. The protocol was as follows:

## CAPITULATION AGREEMENT

*Between the High Command of the German Army and the High Command of the Italian Army in Albania on the one side, and the Greek Field Army of Epirus-Macedonia on the other,*

*The High Command of the Royal Field Army of Epirus-Macedonia, represented by Lieutenant General Tsolakoglou, has delivered a demarcate to the High Command of the German Forces in Greece and the High*

Command of the Italian Army in Albania, requesting the acceptance of the unconditional capitulation of the Greek Field Army of Macedonia-Epirus.

Article 1. The German and Italian High Commands accept the said unconditional surrender of the Greek Field Army of Epirus-Macedonia.

Article 2. Those belonging to the Greek Field Army of Epirus-Macedonia are prisoners of war. Bearing in mind the bravery displayed by the Greek Troops, on the battlefield and the consequent preservation of their military honour the Greek Officers will keep their sword and equipment.

All Italian prisoners of war, who are located in the area of the Greek Field Army of Epirus-Macedonia must be delivered immediately to the Italian troops. The Greek prisoners of war will be concentrated, for the time being, into concentration camps.

After the end of hostilities on the Greek mainland and the Ionian isles, the liberation of all officers and soldiers has been authorised.

Article 3. The Greek High Command will make sure that the Greek troops will remain under the command of their officers and that all measures will be taken for the orderly implementation of the capitulation.

The re-supply and medical care of the troops in captivity is primarily a task for the Greek High Command.

Article 4. The weapons, the entire war material and the stock of this Field Army, including the airforce supplies, as well as the ground installations of the airforce are all considered as spoils of war.

Article 5. The Greek High Command will make sure using all possible means, that the hostilities will cease without delay, that all destruction or neutralisation of war material and supplies will end and that the roads located in the premises of the Field Army will be repaired at once.

Article 6. All departures from ports and all air communications in the area of the Epirus-Macedonia Field Army must be forbidden, and this condition comes in force immediately. The Greek High Command is responsible for the confiscation of ships present in the ports, including their cargoes, as well as the port installations and also that these remain under the supervision of the Greek troops, until a final decision has been taken about them.

Article 7. The High Command of the Greek Forces will appoint fully authorised staff liaisons, who will settle the details of implementing the capitulation with the German and Italian services, which will be fully named.

These staff liaisons will deliver, as soon as possible a complete list of the strength, equipment and army establishment of Epirus-Macedonia to this moment.

*Article 8. The cessation of hostilities between the German Forces and the Greek forces of the Epirus-Macedonia Field Army remains in force, as defined in the surrender protocol of April 21. The cessation of hostilities between Italian troops and the Field Army of Epirus-Macedonia is to come in force on April 23, at 1800 hrs, unless the Greek troops before the Italian front have surrendered their arms beforehand.*

*Article 9. The present agreement invalidates the surrender protocol of April 21, which was drawn between the High Command of the German Forces in Greece and the Commander in chief of the Greek Field Army of Epirus-Macedonia.*

|  |  |
|---|---|
| *On behalf of the Italian* | *On behalf of the German* |
| *High Command in Albania* | *Military High Command* |
| *Ferrero* | *Alfred Jodle* |

*The Commander in chief of the Greek Field Army of Epirus-Macedonia*

*Tsolakoglou*

In the meantime, during the night of April 22 to 23 and the next day of April 23, the Greek units continued to move towards Ioannina in order to be found south of the line Igoumenitsa-Bisdouni-Metsovo by the evening of April 23, in order to avoid being captured by the Italians.

The Germans eventually extended the time limit, so as to enable the remotest units to enter south of the dividing line, as well.

**345.** On April 23, Commander-in-Chief Papagos handed in his resignation, which was immediately accepted by the King, who had already arrived in Crete.

On April 24, the organisation and disposition of the Greek Large Units was as follows:

-The A' Army Corps (II, III, IV, V, VI, VIII, XV, XVII Divisions) in the area south of Ioannina, as far as Preveza.

-The B' Army Corps (I Division) in the area of Metsovo.

-The C' Army Corps (IX, X, XI, XII, XIII, 20th Infantry Divisions, Cavalry Division and 21st Infantry Brigade) east of Metsovo, as far as Kalambaka.

The Divisions were reduced to about one fourth of their original strength and remained at their above positions until their demobilisation.

On April 25, Lieutenant General Tsolakoglou, after assigning the command of the Epirus Army to Lieutenant General Demestichas, departed from Ioannina, headed to Athens, and on April 29 formed a Government of military and political personalities.

On May 2, Hitler granted complete freedom to the officers and soldiers who were, officially at least, regarded as prisoners of war until then.

The A' Army Corps units, which, by approval of the German Command of Ioannina, had begun to move towards Agrinio and Messolongi since the previous day, continued fheir movement and kept on sending officers and soldiers back to their homes, according to the instructions given by the Ministry of National Defence.

The units of B' and C' Army Corps that had been greatly reduced in strength, disbanded on the spot. The officers and soldiers moved to their native area, according to the orders of Greek Command present.

The last to depart was the EFAS echelon, on May 4, by motor-vehicles, and which arrived in Athens on May 7.

*The Departure of the British and the Completion of the Occupation of the Mainland of Greece*
*(Sketch-map no. 27)*

**346.** The British Expeditionary Force, after its successful disengagement from the area of Olympus, managed, by the evening of April 19, to withdraw the bulk of its forces onto the general line Brallos pass-south of Sperchios-Molos, as follows:

- The 6th Australian Division, in the evening of April 19 arrived, at the pass of Brallos, with the 19th Brigade astride the road and the 17th Brigade further to the west. The 16th Division remained as a reserve. During the night of April 23 to 24, the 16th and 17th Brigades moved towards Megara to board ships and depart.

- The 1st Armoured British Brigade in the evening on April 18 arrived in Atalanti and moved directly to Thiva, with the exception of its artillery units, which reinforced the 2nd New Zealand Division.

- The 2nd New Zealand Division seized and held the pass of Thermopilae, with the 6th Brigade on the right, from the coast to Molos, and the 5th Brigade directly on the left. On the night of April 22 to 23 the 5th Brigade arrived at the port of Portorafti from where it departed for Crete on the night of April 24 to 25. Thus, the cover of the entire Thermopilae front was assumed by the 6th Brigade. The 4th Brigade was assigned to survey the coast southwards, in order to repulse a possible landing attempt of the Germans from Evia. On the night of April 23 to 24, the Brigade moved to Erithres, south of Theves, where it established its defence in order to cover the withdrawal of the remaining forces towards the south.

**347.** Thus, in the morning on April 20, nearly all the troops of the British Expeditionary Force were in the area of Thermopilae, covering a front of about 50 kilometres, from the coast to the pass of Brallos. The two weakened ANZAC Divisions, should confront five German divisions (2 Armoured, 2 Mountain and one Infantry Division) , which continued their advance unrestrained.

In the evening of April 20, the bridge of Alamana was blown up, after a report, that was later proved to be inaccurate that German tanks had moved to the south of Lamia.

On the following day, however, German tanks actually moved to the plain of Lamia, but they were fired by the New Zealand artillery and temporarily halted their advance.

In the evening of April 22, a German motorised column of the 5th Armoured Division, that was operating in the sector of the 6th New Zealand Brigade, took contact with the troops that were deployed in Thermopilae, where it was contained by the effective fire of the artillery.

On the following day, April 23, the Germans continued their offensive with the 5th Armoured Division, against the sector of the 6th New Zealand Brigade at Thermopilae and with the 6th Mountain Division, against the sector of the 19th Australian Brigade at the pass of Brallos. A fierce fight ensued as well as intensive artillery duel. The British forces, in spite of the enemy superiority in force as well as its air supremacy, managed to retain their positions until the evening of April 24, containing, the German advance for a period of time necessary to facilitate their disengagement.

In the night on April 24 to 25, the British abandoned the area of Thermopilae-Brallos and withdrew southwards.

In the morning on April 25, the only troops left north of Athens (at Erithres) were the rear guard of the 4th New Zealand Brigade and part of the 1st British Armoured Division.

**348.** In the meantime, on April 24, Marshal Von List also reinforced the XL Armoured Army Corps with the XVIII Mountain Army Corps, and ordered it to advance in the direction of Athens-Korinthos and to establish a bridgehead on the Isthmos as soon as possible. There was a plan to seize the latter with parachutists, while, simultaneously, motorised units would conduct an enveloping action from Evia.

Elements from the 5th Armoured Division that had pursued the British, occupied Thebes, in the evening on April 25, while a motorcyclist battalion that landed in Evia, was ferried over to Viotia and continued to Athens which was occupied on April 27, without any resistance.

A committee had been appointed for the surrender of Athens, comprising the Head of the Athens Garrison, Major General Christos

Kavrakos, the Prefect, Vice Admiral Konstantinos Petzopoulos and the Mayor, Amvrosios Plytas. That committee waited the Germans at the suburb Ambelokipi and surrendered the city to them. During the entry of the Germans and the passage of German troops, through Athens the inhabitants remained shut inside their homes. Soon after, the swastika would be raised on the Sacred Rock of the Acropolis.

**349.** The defence of the Korinthos Isthmos from the attack of airborne troops was assigned to the Isthmos Detachment, under the command of Brigadier General Lee. Its mission was to keep the Megara road open and also to prepare the demolition of the railway and the road bridges at the Isthmos canal after the passage of the last British troops.

The Germans employed over four hundred tri-engine aircraft, with approximately 800 parachutists, in order to seize the Isthmos. The aircraft took off from Larissa at 0500 hrs on April 26. The parachutist dropping began after a severe bombardment of the British positions. Although many of the parachutists were killed in the air and others fell into the canal, the Germans eventually managed to seize the bridge intact, taking advantage of the confusion on the British side. Nevertheless they were unable to cut the firing wires and remove the demolition charge in time. The bridge was eventually blown up by two young British officers, who managed, by firing accurately with rifles and from a distance of 200 meters, to detonate the explosive charge.

By 0800 hrs, the activity around the bridge had ended, since the Germans had occupied both banks of the Canal.

**350.** At the same time, the Division "Adolph Hitler SS Bodyguards" moved from the area of Ioannina towards Agrinio and Messolongi and in the evening on April 26, arrived in the area of Patra. From there, one of its regiments moved by train towards Korinthos, where at 1730 hrs, on April 27, it was informed that the parachutists who had occupied the Isthmos had already been relieved by other Army units, that had arrived from Athens. Subsequently, the 'SS' units returned to Patra and continued towards Kalamata via Pyrgos, assigned to cut off the departure of the British from the area.

The 5th Armoured Division, after a makeshift repair of the Isthmos bridge, crossed over to the Peloponnese and moved in the direction of Argos-Tripolis-Gythio and Kalamata, where on April 29, it met the troops of the "Adolph Hitler SS Guard" that had arrived by train from Patra.

**351.** In the meantime, by order of the British Expeditionary Force, the command of all troops that were in the Peloponnese was assumed by Major

General Freyberg, as of the night of April 24 to 25, whereas General Wilson departed by sea plane, for Crete.

The departure of the British was to take place from the ports of the south-eastern coast of Attiki and the Peloponnese and in particular from Rafina, Portorafti, the area of Megara, Agii Theodoroi, Nafplio, Monemvasia and Kalamata. These ports were severely attacked by the German Airforce, with considerable losses to both the task and the merchant fleet of the British and the Greeks.

The 19th Australian Brigade embarked at Megara on the night of April 25 to 26.

The 16th and 17th Australian Brigades, in the evening hours, moved from Myli to Kalamata, where part of them managed to embark on the night of April 26 to 27, while approximately 7,000 men waited on the pier, because the night hours did not suffice to permit the completion of the embarkation.

The 4th New Zealand Brigade, that operated as a rear guard at Erythres, moved and occupied positions south of Markopoulo in the morning of April 27 and retained the last bridgehead there before Portorafti. In the evening, it embarked without any incidents and sailed for Crete, while the remaining personnel of the 1st British Armoured Brigade departed from Rafina.

The 6th New Zealand Brigade, that moved via Tripolis, arrived in the morning on April 28 at Monemvasia. In the night of April 28 to 29, its entire strength boarded the ships and sailed for Crete. Major General Freyberg departed with it as well.

352. A force of approximately 1,700 men, in the area of Nafplio primarily formed by units of the interior, were taken prisoners by the Germans on April 28. Only few men avoided captivity, managing to escape by small boats to the nearby islands.

The 7,000 men force that remained in Kalamata grew to 10,000 men on the same day, of which 8,000 were unarmed. Among them, there were approximately 2,000 Yugoslavian soldiers, Cypriot and Palestinian men from the Pioneer company, as well as Greek civilians. This force had been organised into four detachments that were in readiness to embark at 2100 hrs on cruisers and destroyers, that would sail into the harbour in the meantime.

In the early evening, the troops began to move towards the sea, but an advance guard of the 5th German Armoured Division entered the town and hastened towards the pier. Armed British troops counter-reacted effectively and the embarkation began by 2130 hrs. Shortly after, however, the ships sailed away in haste, in order to join the fleet, by order of the

British Commander-in-Chief, because the Italian Fleet had appeared. Thus, approximately 10,000 men were doomed to captivity for the entire war.

In the morning on April 29, the Germans took about 7,000 prisoners, while the rest fled. What was so tragic in this case was that, the information about the appearance of the Italian Fleet proved later to be inaccurate.

353. With this surrender, the British expedition in the mainland of Greece was terminated. On April 30, the last British troops had been captured or had escaped and the hostilities had ceased.

In total, 50,732 British men departed, that is, 80% of the forces that had been despatched to Greece and of these about 27,000 landed on Crete, while the rest were transferred to Egypt. Approximately 1,400 British men, who remained in Greece without being captured, later escaped to Crete, Chios and the Aegean islands as well as to the coast of Asia Minor.

The occupation of the mainland of Greece was gradually completed by German and Italian troops.

On May 3, a triumphant parade of the Germans and the Italians was conducted in Athens before Marshal List, with the complete abstention of the inhabitants, who remained shut inside their homes. The participation of the Italian troops in the parade was ordered by Hitler himself, in order not to hurt the pride of his allies.

The total number of casualties of the British Expeditionary Force were approximately 12,000 men. Moreover, 209 aircraft and 8,000 vehicles were either lost or abandoned. The German casualties were approximately 5,000 men. According to German sources, the Germans in Greece seized 54 heavy and 444 light guns, 431 mortars and infantry escort guns, 49 antitank guns, 151,050 rifles, 134 armoured vehicles, 2,710 motor vehicles and approximately 600 other wheeled vehicles as well as large quantities of supplies.

## The Occupation of the Greek Islands

354. At the same time with the occupation of mainland Greece, the most important islands were taken by the Germans and the Italians without any resistance, with the exception of Limnos and Crete. The battle of Crete constitutes a special operation and is thus examined in the last Part of this book.

Thassos was occupied on April 15 and Samothraki on April 19.

In Limnos, the Naval Commander, who was the head of the Garrison, of Infantry company strength, replied to the German ultimatum that he would resist. On April 24, the Germans after an air bombardment of the Garrison positions, landed a regiment on the coast of Bournia bay (on the northern part of the island) as well as on Moudros. The Garrison, after fighting and immobilising the Germans for a few hours withdrew towards the cape of Agia Irini, where those of the troops that were not captured, dispersed.

In Evia, after the German aircraft repeatedly had bombarded from April 10 to 24, Halkida, Limni, Orei and on the night of April 24 to 25 the naval station of Gouves, troops landed at Orei and moved towards Edipsos and Halkida, occupying the latter on April 25.

The Cyclades islands were occupied within the first fortnight of May.

Kerkyra. was occupied by the Italian troops, that had begun to land there since April 28.

The Italians also occupied the islands of Kephalonia, Ithaki and Zakynthos, from May 1 to 5.

Lesvos and Chios were occupied by German troops on May 4 and Samos, on May 8.

Greece was already writhing under the pressure of the conquerors, but the spirit was never subjugated and the hope for freedom warmed her existence so as to continue once more on the road leading towards the destiny of the Nation.

### A General Review of the German Attack against Greece and the End of the War

**355.** The decision of Germany to attack Greece was taken in the beginning of November 1940, in order to secure the flank of the German Army that would be operating against Russia.

The begining and the conduct of the 'MARITA' operation, which was the code name for the German attack against Greece, had been scheduled to take place in March 1941. Indeed, on March 2, 1941, the 12th German Field Army began to enter the Bulgarian territory and by March 9, its advanced guards reached the Greek - Bulgarian borders.

**356.** To face this new threat, successive meetings were held in Athens between the Greek and the British political and military Leadership, from the beginning of January until the beginning of March 1941. As a result of these meetings, it was finally decided on March 26, that the Greek forces should defend in the Beles-Nestos area and the Vermio area would be secured by the joint Greek -British forces.

This decision was largely influenced by the intelligence reports about an impending military coup d'etat in Yugoslavia, which since March 25 had entered the Tripartite Agreement (Germany-Italy-Japan).

Indeed, on the night of March 26 to 27, the military coup overthrew the Yugoslavian Government and on March 29, a general mobilisation was declared. After this, the efforts of the Greek Leadership focused on the reinforcement of the forces in Eastern Macedonia in order to secure the fortified area of Beles-Nestos.

On the other hand, the situation created in Yugoslavia alarmed the Germans, who decided to launch an attack simultaneously against Greece and Yugoslavia on April 6.

**357.** The attack against Greece began at 0515 hrs, on April 6, by the German troops that were deployed along the Greek - Bulgarian borders. The main effort of the Germans was directed against Beles mountain and Rupel pass.

By the evening of April 6, light German forces managed to descend on the valley of Rodopolis and take contact with the Kroussia area, while the forts at Eastern Beles continued to resist. East of Strymonas river and as far as Nestos, the Germans took contact with the main defensive area, without however recording any actual success. Further east, in the area of Xanthi and Komotini, the German troops by-passed Fort Echinos and Nymphaea and moved southwards.

On the following day, April 7, the fight continued with undiminished intensity. The area of Beles-Nestos, despite the occupation of Fort Istimbei and Kelkayia, remained essentially intact. However, the collapse of the Yugoslavian Army and the lack of available forces, to cover the left flank of the area, created a serious danger that the forces deployed in the above area might be cut off from mainland Greece.

On April 8, the third day of the attack, the Germans despite their efforts and the occupation of Fort Popotlivitsa were unable to break through the fortified position. However, the rapid advance of the 2nd Armoured German Division inside the Greek territory through the corridor of Axios river and the attack against Thessaloniki, that was expected to occur on the following day, constituted a danger threat for the EMFAS, that was bound to be captured if it remained on the defensive area.

The withdrawal of its forces towards the ports of Macedonia and their transport by sea, as had been originally decided, was impossible, since there were neither reserves to cover the withdrawal, nor ships required. Under these circumstances and in order to avoid pointless sacrifice, the General Headquarters ordered the EMFAS to capitulate.

The capitulation was signed at 1400 hrs, on April 9, in Thessaloniki, between the Commander of the EMFAS, Lieutenant General Bakopoulos and the Commander of the 2nd German Armoured Division, containing fairly honourable terms for the Greek troops. The hostilities ceased by the same evening, after notifying the units of the capitulation.

**358.** After the occupation of Eastern Macedonia and Thrace and the capitulation of the EMFAS, the German forces crossed Axios river on April 9 and advanced towards Edessa. Simultaneously, other German forces, coming from Yugoslavia entered the Greek territory from the direction of Monastiri, occupied Florina and took contact with the Greek - British forces in the defensive area of Pisoderi-Kirli Derven (Klidi). On the same day, the Germans seized Ahris and established contact with the Italians in the Northern Epirus Front.

The German advance along the axis of Monastiri-Florina-Kozani created a serious threat for the rear of the Kaimaktsalan-Vermio defensive area, that was occupied by the Greek -British 'W' Force, under the command of General Wilson. After this, it was decided to evacuate the above area and to occupy the line of defense Siniatsiko-Vourinos-Olympus.

A battle was conducted in this area on April 13 and 14. Afterwards, because of the gap created in the area of Kleissoura (Kastoria), the Greek - British forces withdrew towards Kalambaka.

The Germans continued their advance southwards, via Grevena and, on April 16, seized Kalambaka. Thus, they succeeded in interposing their forces between the British Expeditionary Corps and the Greek Army that was withdrawing from Albania.

**359.** The British Expeditionary Force, after fierce fighting at the passes of Olympus, withdrew gradually along the axis of Larissa-Lamia-Athens. In order to cover its withdrawal from ports of the mainland of Greece and the Peloponnese towards Crete and Egypt, it occupied the line of Thermopilae-Brallos with strong rear guards, that managed to contain the German columns for two days (April 23 and 24).

The departure of the British Expeditionary Corps from Greece began in the night on April 24 to 25 and ended on May 1, 1941, under extremely adverse conditions. The British forces were transferred to Egypt and Crete.

**360.** The Greek Army that fought in Northern Epirus, was ordered to withdraw towards the defence area in the borders, due to the unfavourable development of the battle in Macedonia.

The WMFAS began its withdrawal in the evening on April 12, 1941, without serious difficulties, along the axis of the Devolis and Aliakmonas valleys. The XIII Division, which had been assigned to cover the gap created in the area of Klissoura, conducted fierce battles on April 15, near Argos Orestiko. After Kastoria had been occupied by the Germans and its withdrawal route had been cut off, the WMFAS directed its divisions towards Epirus via the mountain routes of Pindos.

In the night of April 13, the EFAS withdrawal began as well. Meanwhile the troop morale began to decline and there were a lot of leaks. Nevertheless, for reasons of high national interests, it was expedient that the fight should continue.

By April 20, the situation had become critical. Under these circumstances and without the approval of the General Headquarters, the Commander of the C' Army Corps, Lieutenant General Georgios Tsolakoglou took the initiative and signed a capitulation agreement with the Germans, after communicating first with the Commanders of the A' and B' Army Corps and most Division commanders. The capitulation was signed in the evening on April 20, in Votonosi village in Metsovo. Subsequently, the Commander of the EFAS, Lieutenant General Ioannis Pitsikas considered himself 'resigned' and, on the following day, abandoned the command of the EFAS, which was assumed by Lieutenant General Tsolakoglou.

**361.** After the capitulation, the forced march of the Army continued southwards, in order to arrive in the evening on April 23 south of the line Igoumenitsa-Metsovo and thus to avoid being captured by the Italians.

During the early hours of April 23, the King and the Government departed for Crete. On the same day, the Commander-in-Chief, Alexandros Papagos, resigned.

On April 25, Lieutenant General Tsolakoglou, after assigning the command of the Army in Epirus to Lieutenant General Demestichas, departed for Athens, in order to form a Government.

On May 2, Hitler's decision to grant complete freedom to the Greek officers and soldiers, who were considered prisoners of war until then, was made public. The Greek Large Units, after surrendering their armament, moved towards various areas and disbanded.

Thus ended the last act of the drama, of the Albanian Epic, the epilogue of which was to culminate in the Battle of Crete. The Greek Army had written pages of unsurpassable glory, attracting the admiration of the civilised world. Yet its destiny was to be occupied by the two Great Powers of the Axis.

# PART FOUR

# THE BATTLE OF CRETE

(May 20 to 31, 1941)

# CHAPTER VII

## THE PREPARATIONS AND THE PLANS OF OPERATIONS OF THE ADVERSARIES

### *The Strategic Importance of the Island of Crete*

**362.** The island of Crete lies in the centre of the eastern basin of the Mediterranean, on the cross-roads of the air and sea lines of communication, from east to west and from north to south or vice versa. Thus, it constitutes an excellent base for aeronautical operations in every direction and guarantees to the power that occupies it secures the control of all communications in the Mediterranean. These characteristics lend particular strategic importance to the island.

A natural consequence of this strategic importance was that, since the beginning of the Second World War, Crete was of interest both to the British and Hitler.

**363.** The occupation of Crete by the British, or at least the assurance that it would remain under allied or friendly forces, was of vital importance to them, because it offered them the following advantages:

- Considerable protection to the British bases in Northern Africa against the attacks of the German Airforce, forcing the latter to launch its attacks from the remote airfields of mainland Europe.

- Forward aeronautical base and a base of amphibious operations towards the shores and the islands of the Aegean and the Dodecanese, while, at the same time, it posed a serious threat for the Romanian oil wells.

- Contribution to the security of transportation from the harbours of the Pacific and the Indian Ocean, through the Suez Canal, towards the British bases of the Mediterranean and the Middle East. Given that the greatest part of the re-supply sources of the above British bases came from India, Australia and South Africa, the importance of the occupation or the control of Crete for the British can be easily understood.

Furthermore, Crete was the only free section of the Greek territory with both Greek and British forces and in which the free Greek State still existed, by virtue of the presence of the King, the Government and the national Armed Forces. Consequently, it was extremely important for Greece and Britain, both morally and politically, to hold on to it.

**364.** On the other hand, if Crete were occupied by the Axis, it would offer to its forces the following strategic advantages:
- Capacity for direct airforce threat against the sea and air lines of communication of the Allies and particularly against the British Fleet in the Mediterranean.
-Excellent base of operation towards the Middle East and the Northern Africa area in general.
-Safe Aegean sea lines, provided that Turkey would remain neutral or pro-Axis and free naval communication with the ports of the Black Sea and the Adriatic sea.

**365.** The following communicee of the German General Headquarters, dated June 12, 1941, sums up the strategic importance of the island of Crete for the adversary powers in the Mediterranean area, during the Second World War:
*'... As a powerful naval and airforce stronghold, in close proximity with our sea lines of communication through the Aegean, as a forward base to cover and secure both flanks of the Northern African Front and the British sea lines of communication between Alexandria and Malta, Crete was of equally great importance for the war operations of the adversary in the Eastern Mediterranean, both from the offensive as well as from the defensive aspect. The island had a similar importance, in reverse, for the subsequent operations of the German Military leadership in the Eastern Mediterranean...'*

## The Greek Plans for the Defence of the Island

**366.** In Crete, before the war, the V Division had already been established and was stationed at Hania. The units under its command were the 14th, 43rd and 44th Infantry Regiments at Hania, Rethymno and Iraklio respectively, as well as the V Artillery Regiment at Souda and the Military Hospital of Hania and other Military installation and Services. The transition of the Division from peace to war establishment had been prepared on the basis of the Mobilisation Plan of 1939.

Upon the occupation of Albania by Italy, on April 1939, the threat of war for Greece loomed as an indisputable fact. As a result, the abovementioned Plan IB was drawn up, and among others, foresaw the English-French assistance as a definite development, in the case of an Italian attack.

On the basis of Plan IB and the instructions of the Army General Staff, the Division had drawn the following three plans for the defence of the island:

- Plan No. 1, to cover the mobilisation in case of threat to the island.
- Plan No. 2, to repulse any enemy landing after the termination of the Mobilisation and before the Division was transferred from Crete.
-Plan No. 3, to define the mission of the Military Command of Hania in case the island was attacked after the departure of the Division.

According to Plan No 3 the following units would remain on Crete under the Military Command of Hania: The 44th Infantry Regiment, the 44th Artillery of Escort Platoon, the Base Battalions of Hania, Rethymno and Iraklio, three rifle companies manned by transportation troops from the 44th Infantry Regiment and a Pack Artillery battalion.

**367.** Furthermore, as part of the measures that had been taken by the Garrisons of the islands, by order of the Army General Staff, the Division had deployed the coastal defence troops by the end of May, 1940, while simultaneously activated the sea and air surveillance network.

The troops provided for the coastal defence comprised, in total, three Infantry companies and one Machine-gun platoon.

For the operation of the surveillance network, two centres were established and became active: the Information Centre of Hania (Joint Centre of the Royal Navy and Field Army), which had ten surveillance stations, and the Information Centre of Iraklio (also joint), which had three surveillance stations.

On the naval side, no specific measures were taken for the protection of Crete, due to the lack in defence organisation means (guns, mines, and other equipment) and, most important, because the Government believed that the intervention of the British Fleet in the Mediterranean was assured in conjunction with the overall British assistance.


*Crete under the British Responsibility*


**368.** Since the morning of October 28, the V Division began to mobilise its units and to prepare to be transferred to mainland Greece, so as to be employed in the Albanian Theatre of Operations. That same day, the British Headquarters in the Middle East decided on and ordered the reinforcement of Crete.

On November 4, the Greek Government notified the British Government that it wished to transfer the V Division from Crete, under the condition however, that the island's defence would be undertaken by the British. The proposal was immediately accepted and the responsibility for the defence of the island was assumed by the British.

The transfer of the V Division was carried out from November 18 to 25, using requisitioned Greek ships, under the protection of the Greek and British Fleet. The numbers transferred in total were, 566 officers, 18,662 enlisted men, 687 pack animals and 81 vehicles, without any losses.

**369.** After the departure of the V Division, the command of the Greek forces on the island was assumed by the newly formed Military Command of Hania, under Lieutenant General Ioannis Alexakis. It was subordinate to the A' Military High Command of Athens. The Military Command of Hania had under its command the Depots of Hania, Rethymno and Iraklio. Each Depot had at its disposal an Infantry battalion (of two companies) and a Saint Etienne Machine-gun platoon. On January 1941, in agreement with the British Headquarters in the Middle East, these battalions were also transferred to mainland Greece. Thus, there remained in Crete only the nuclei of the Depots, their strength comprising transit soldiers, and its armament, one thousand Gra rifles, 12 Saint Etienne machine-guns and approximately 40 light machine-guns.

Following the orders of General Headquarters, in December 1940, preparations were made for the organization of militia units. These units were assigned to protect the technical works and the vulnerable points, of the island in general. The strength of the militia was originally 3,000 men, but reduced in February 1941 to approximately 1,500 men, organised in four battalions, one in each Prefecture (Hania, Rethymno, Iraklio and Lasithi). The militia was supposed to be armed by the British, but this never happened. The militia units were subordinate to the Gendarmerie authorities who were also responsible for their training. Tactically they were subordinate to the Military Command of Hania.

During March 1941, the Gendarmerie Academy was transferred to Crete and disembarked at Rethymno, in order to reinforce the units in Crete. Its total strength was 15 officers and about 900 men. Furthermore, during the second fortnight of April 1941, eight recruit battalions were transferred to Crete from the Training Centres of the Peloponnese, their total strength being 85 officers and 4,825 men. These battalions, after their arrival, were designated as Infantry Regiments, temporarily retaining their original title, i.e. the 1st, 2nd, 3rd etc. Their men were recruits from the classes of 1940, 1941 and had received an extremely brief and barely sufficient training.

The armament of all the above Greek units varied. There were between five to twenty cartridges per rifle, while one third of the strength was unarmed.

On April 29, 1941, the Military Academy arrived by motorboats at Kolymbari in Hania, the initiative having been taken by certain officers and Cadets of the Academy. The Military Academy was directly under the command of the Ministry of the Army in Hania and was deployed defensively between the Moni [Monastery] Gonias and the village of Kolymbari.

It is also noted that, at various times 16,000 Italian prisoners (including 576 officers) had been transferred to Crete and were placed in three POW centres in the Prefectures of Hania, Iraklio and Rethymno.

**370.** The British, upon assuming responsibility for the defence, proceeded to organise a fuel depot in the bay of Suda and gradually transfered a very small number of forces for the defence of the island. Thus, by the end of March 1941, the following units had been transfered on Crete: The Headquarters of the 14th Infantry Brigade and the Commander of the Brigade O.H. Titbury, the 156th Light Antiaircraft Battalion, the command of the 52nd Light Antiaircraft Artillery Regiment, the 151st Heavy Antiaircraft Battalion, the 42nd Engineer Company, the 2nd Blackwatch Battalion, the 51st Raiding Force and the 1st Welsh Battalion.

After the German troops entered Bulgaria and the Bulgarian airfields were occupied by German airforce units, the German attack against Greece was regarded as imminent.

This new threat led the British Headquarters to decide that Crete should cease to constitute merely a refuelling base and it should be organised into a naval and airforce base.

On March 29, the Commander of the MNBDO (Mobile Naval Defence Organisation), Major General Weston arrived on the island, in order to examine thoroughly the issue of the island's defence.

In his report, submitted on April 15, 1941, he proposed the serious reinforcement of Crete, with forces and equipment. The General Headquarters of the Middle East agreed on these proposals, nevertheless the situation prevailing in that area did not permit their implementation. The final decision would be made after the retreat of the British forces from mainland Greece.

However, since April 17, when the evacuation of the forces of mainland Greece had been considered, (operation 'Demon'), it was decided that a large section of the retreating British forces should land on Crete.

Thus on April 25, the first substantial British force of approximately 5,000 men arrived in Crete, mainly of the 5th New Zealand Brigade.

During the following days and until April 30, approximately 45,000 men retreated from Greece, to Crete and Egypt. Approximately 25,000 of them remained on Crete. However most of them were unarmed, without any individual items, heavy armament or vehicles.

On April 27, General Wilson, Commander of the British Expeditionary Force in Greece, landed also on Crete, assigned to examine, along with the Senior officers of the Cretan Garrison, the situation from the aspect of the forces required for the defence of the island.

General Wilson, after a briefing on the situation and an examination of the entire matter, reported to the Middle East Headquarters that, the strength of the Field Army should be three brigades, with four battalions each, a motorised battalion and furthermore the strength of the MNBDO for the bay of Suda. He also mentioned the need to provide one additional heavy and one light Antiaircraft Artillery Battalions. The above forces would be sufficient to secure, the vital areas of the island, that is, Iraklio with its airfield, Hania, the Maleme airfield and the bay of Souda.

The proposed forces were considered by General Wilson to be the minimum required for the island's defence and he underlined that the use of less than those would bring disaster, and that it was expedient to come to a decision at once.

### The Arrival of the King and the Government in Crete

**371.** When the King and the Government were convinced that there was no possibility of conducting the struggle in mainland Greece any more, they decided to continue the fight wherever it would be possible, according to the general guide line of the honourable national policy that Greece had adhered to towards its friends and allies.

On April 23, 1941, the King, Prince Petros, the Prime Minister, certain members of Government and the British Ambassador to Athens arrived on Crete by a British hydroplane. The plane touched down in the bay of Souda, which had been bombarded by the German Airforce shortly before.

**372.** The effort of both the King and the Government, since the first hours of their arrival on Crete, was to succeed in arming the Greek Army and the inhabitants of the island, as well as to reinforce the British forces there, particularly the airforce, since there was no fighter-plane unit stationed permanently on Crete.

The Greek Government took the initiative to hold a meeting at Hania, which was attended by British Generals Wilson and Weston, General Skoulas, British Airforce Marshal D' Albiac, Vice Admiral Terl, Captain Bemich, as well as other Greek and British Army officers.

The Greek Prime Minister, as Head of the meeting, in the course of the discussions requested that a British General be assigned the command of the Greek - British forces on the island, that British armament be given to the Greek forces and that their feeding be provided by the British. He also added that he considered the air .support as inadequate. On the following day, a note was delivered to the British Ambassador, in which the Greek views on the British assistance were clearly laid out while, at the same time, the King and the Government, at every opportunity and contact with the British, did not fail to stress the need to reinforce the island's defence.

## The British Preparations

**373.** On April 30, 1941, the Commander-in-Chief in the Middle East, General Wavell arrived on Crete. During a meeting on the same day, he assigned the command of the Greek - British forces on the island to the Commander of the 2nd New Zealand Division, Major General Freyberg, who had arrived on Crete from mainland Greece on the previous day. Furthermore, he added that the German attack upon the island was expected to begin in a few days and that the island had to remain free at all costs. After the meeting General Wavell departed for Egypt.

Until the end of April 1941, no final plans had been drawn yet, nor had any preparations begun for the defence of the island against a serious enemy threat, although Crete had been under British responsibility for the last six months. The island, despite the views of the British Prime Minister, who aspired to see Crete organised as a second Scapa Flow (one of the most important bases of the British Fleet in the Atlantic, on the Orkney isles), was far from being able to defend itself against a strong enemy attack.

Major General Freyberg, upon assuming command of the Greek - British forces on the island, examined the situation immediately and discovered the enormous shortages in armament, ammunition and all kinds of other supplies. On the same day, he also received the intelligence report of April 29, from the British Ministry of Military Affairs, according to which the attack against the island should be regarded as imminent and would be conducted by 3,000-4,000 parachutists and airborne troops, who would be supported by 315 bombers, 60 double-engine fighters, 240 dive bombers and 270 single engine fighters. Furthermore, the enemy would be provided with sufficient naval forces and means, in order to conduct a landing from the sea.

Based on the above information, Major General Freyberg reported immediately to the Commander-in-Chief in the Middle East that his forces were totally inadequate to confront the expected attack and that if the number of fighter aircraft was not increased and the island was not protected from the sea, he wouldn't be able to hope to last long with an army, lacking artillery and inadequately provided with supplies and ammunition.

In reply to General Freyberg's report, the Commander-in-Chief in the Middle East answered that he considered the predictions of the Ministry to be exaggerated, he admitted, however, that there was a possibility of a large scale attack. At the same time, he informed him that, though it would be difficult to offer greater air support, the Fleet of the Mediterranean would be ready to help, if the Germans attacked Crete. In the end, he made it known to the General that, the British Council had expressly ordered that Crete be retained, and that, even if such a decision was revoked, it was doubtful whether the island could be evacuated before the German attack.

**374.** At the same time, Major General Freyberg occupied himself actively in making the most of the forces and the means available to him, awaiting the supply reinforcements he had requested.

Unfortunately, less than half of the supplies, that were originally sent to the island, arrived there, owing to the action of the enemy airforce. Thus, by mid-May, 15,000 tons of army supplies and 3,000 tons of ammunitions, were unloaded, instead of the 27,000 tons of ammunitions that had been sent. The above material included 6 medium and 10 light tanks as well as 49 Italian and French guns of 75 and 100mm calibre. The latter were spoils of war and most of them lacked the necessary equipment and spare parts, while some had no sighting instruments.

Apart from the supplies, the following units and troops landed on Crete:

- MNBDO units, that is, the Staff of the 2nd Antiaircraft Artillery Regiment of the Royal Marines. The A' and C' Heavy Antiaircraft Battalions, with eight three-inch guns each. The X' and Z' Coastal Defence Artillery Battalions with two four-inch guns each. The 23rd Light Antiaircraft Battalion with light guns and a Searchlight Battalion along with the Staff of the II Searchlight Regiment. A Signals company, a Surveillance platoon and a Docks and Transports company.

- The 10th New Zealand Brigade.

- The 2nd Leicester Battalion.
- The 1st Light Battery (four 3.7 inch Howitzer guns).

Meanwhile, the works on the defence of the island continued at a vigorous pace, while great care was being taken to conceal and camouflage the supplies.

On May 16, the Commander of the Crete Forces reported to the Headquarters of the Middle East that he had completed the plan for the defence of Crete and that he was very optimistic.

## The General Disposition of the British-Greek Forces and Missions
### (Sketch-map no. 28, 29, 30, 31)

375. The general disposition of the British-Greek forces on the basis of the importance and vulnerability of the strategic points, the width of the area, the configuration of the terrain and the existing strength was as follows:

- Cretan Forces Headquarters (Major General Freyberg) at the village of Agios Mattheos in Hania.
- Maleme-Agyia Sector

The 2nd New Zealand Division (Brigadier Sir E.Puttick) with its Headquarters near the road junction Alikyanos-Hania and Maleme-Hania. It consisted of the 5th New Zealand Brigade (21, 22, 23, 28 Infantry Battalion and New Zealand Engineer Field Detachment), the 10th New Zealand Brigade (6th, 8th Greek Infantry Regiments, a Joint New Zealand Battalion comprising gunners and soldiers from various services, the 20th New Zealand Battalion[1] and Cavalry Divisional Field Detachment[2]) and the 1st Greek Infantry Regiment[3].

The artillery of the Division comprised the 27th and 28th Artillery Battalions, the 1st Light Battery and platoons from the 156th Light Antiaircraft Battalion, one battery from the 7th Australian Antiaircraft Artillery Battalion and one from the Heavy Antiaircraft Artillery Battalion, the Heavy Coastal Defence Battalion and one battery from the 23rd Antiaircraft Battalion.

The Division had been reinforced with 2 medium tanks, that were placed at the disposal of the 5th Brigade and 10 light tanks from the 3rd Hussars Regiment, which were kept in the zone of the 4th Brigade.

---

[1] Belonging to the 4th New Zealand Brigade
[2] Known as the Detachment of Major Russell
[3] This Regiment was deployed in the Kasteli area of Kissamos and was assigned to defend the area and repulse sea landing or air attack

The boundaries of the Sector were to the west, Tavronitis river, to the east, Kladissos river, to the north, the coast. The southern boundary was not a definite ground line, but depended on the unit boundaries, according to their missions.

- The Hania-Souda Sector

The MNBDO Group (Major General C.E.Westoin) with his Headquarters in Hania. At its disposal there were: the 2nd Greek Infantry Regiment, the Depot Battalion of Hania, the 1st Rangers Battalion, infantry troops from the 16th and 17th Australian Brigades and field troops from the 106th Horse-drawn Artillery Battalion, the 2/2 and 2/3 Australian Artillery Regiments, the 11th Searchlight Regiment and the Northumberland Hussars.

The artillery of the Sector comprised the 'M' Artillery Group (151st Heavy Antiaircraft Artillery Battalion, 129th Light Antiaircraft Artillery Battalion, one platoon from the 156th Light Antiaircraft Artillery Battalion, one platoon from the 7th Light Antiaircraft Artillery battalion and one battery from the 23rd Light Antiaircraft Battalion) and the 'S' Artillery Group (A' Heavy Antiaircraft Artillery Battalion of the Marines, one platoon of the 'C' Heavy Antiaircraft Artillery Battalion, one platoon from the 106th Heavy Artillery Battalion, 15th Artillery regiment minus platoon and the 304th Searchlight Battalion).

The Boundaries of the Sector were: to the west, the rivers Kladissos and Perivolianos, to the north, the coast from Kladissos river to cape Drapanos. The eastern and southern boundaries depended on the power of the MNBDO troops, that were deployed as far as Drapanos and the troops of the 2nd Greek Infantry Regiment, that were deployed in the area Mournies-Perivolia.

- The Rethymno-Georgioupolis Sector

The 19th Australian Brigade (Brigadier G.A.Vasey) with its Headquarters directly to the west of Georgioupolis, which had the Groups of Georgioupolis, Rethymno and the Airfield of Pigi under his responsibility.

The Group of Georgioupolis included the Headquarters of the 19th Australian Brigade, the 2/7 and 2/8 Australian Battalions and one Australian Machine-gun Platoon. The artillery of the Group comprised the 10th Heavy Coastal Artillery Battalion and one 75 mm battery from the 2/3 Australian Artillery Regiment.

The Group of Rethymno included the Depot Battalion of Rethymno and the Greek Gendarmerie Battalion under the orders of the Commander of the 11th Army District, Colonel Stamatis Pothoulakis.

The Pigi Airfield Group included the 4th and 5th Greek Infantry Regiments, the 2/1, 2/11 Australian Battalions and two Australian Machine-gun platoons under the Commander of the 2/1 Australian

Battalion, Lieutenant Colonel Campbell. The artillery of the Group comprised 10 guns (4 were 100mm calibre' and 6 were 75mm calibre ) of the 2/3 Australian Artillery Regiment.

- The Iraklio Sector

The 14th British Brigade (Brigadier B.H.Chappel) with its Headquarters at New Alikarnassos, which had the Groups of Iraklio town and Iraklio airfield (Rousses) under his responsibility.

The Group of Iraklio had the 3rd and 7th Greek Infantry Regiments and the Base Battalion of Iraklio.

The Iraklio Airfield Group had the 2nd Leicester Battalion, the 2nd Blackwatch Battalion, the 2nd York and Lancaster Battalion and the 2/4 Australian Battalion.

The artillery of the Sector comprised the 234th Artillery Battalion (13 guns of 75 and 100 mm calibre), one platoon from the 15th Royal Coastal Defence Artillery Regiment (two 4-inch guns), the 7th Light Antiaircraft Battalion minus three platoons (6 Beaufort guns), one battery from the 156th Light Antiaircraft Royal Artillery Battalion (4 Beaufort guns), 2 platoons from the Heavy Antiaircraft Royal Marine Battalion (four 3-inch guns) and one battery from the 23rd Light Antiaircraft Royal Marine Battalion.

In addition to the above forces, on May 19, the 2nd Argyle and Sutterland Highlanders Infantry Battalion (Scottish unit) and 3 medium tanks landed Crete. The Sector had also been reinforced with 2 medium and 6 light tanks.

- Reserves at the disposal of the Commander of the Forces on Crete.

The 4th New Zealand Brigade (18th and 19th Battalions), deployed in the Sector Malame-Agyia and the 1st Welsh Regiment in the Sector Hania-Souda.

The total number of men of the Greek - British forces on Crete was: 1,512 British officers and 29,977 British soldiers, 474 Greek officers and 10,977 Greek soldiers. Regarding guns and tanks, there were 151 guns (of which 62 were Antiaircraft and 4 Antitank) and 25 tanks (9 medium and 16 light).

Apart from the military units, many other armed civilian teams were organised during the German attack. Some were organised by the British and the Greek Gendarmerie authorities, while others were formed by villagers who came forth spontaneously at the point of conflict or parachutists drop.

There was no Airforce on the island. The very few aircraft that were left, departed, by order of the Commander of Cretan of Forces, on May 19, to the airfields of Egypt.

In conclusion what must be emphasised is that even though the total number of men constituting the Cretan strength sounded impressive, the weapons at their disposal were significantly below the acceptable proportion for all types of armament.

**376.** The abovementioned British-Greek forces allocated in the Maleme, Hania, Rethymno and Iraklio Sectors, were entrusted with the defence of the island, by forbidding the enemy to use its airfields and ports.

In detail, their missions were the following:

- 2nd New Zealand Division, (Maleme-Agyia Sector): To conduct defence within its area, forbidding the enemy to occupy its coast, the Maleme airfield and the valley of Agyia from sea and air.

- MNBDO Group (Hania-Souda Sector): To conduct defence within its area, forbidding the enemy to occupy the town of Hania and the harbour of Souda from sea and air.

- The 19th Australian Brigade (Rethymno-Georgioupolis Sector): To conduct defence within its area, forbidding the enemy to occupy Rethymno, the Airfield of Pigi and Georgioupolis from sea and air.

- The 14th British Brigade (Iraklio Sector): To conduct defence within its area, forbidding the enemy to occupy the town, the airfield and the port of Iraklio from sea and air.

- Reserve (4th New Zealand Brigade minus battalion, plus 1st Welsh Battalion):

To conduct counter-attacks for the 2nd New Zealand Division and the MNBDO Group.

## The German Plans and Preparations
### (Sketch-map no 28)

**377.** On November 12, 1940, Hitler expresses his intentions to occupy mainland Greece, so as to be able to use the German forces against targets in the Eastern Mediterranean.

On December 13, 1940, the Directive No. 20 was issued, by which the mission of the airforce in all phases of the attack against Greece is clearly defined. On April 15, 1941, Air Marshal Alexander Lohr, Commander of the IV German Airforce, to whom the air operations in SE Europe had been assigned, submitted a plan to Marshal Hermann Goering, regarding the occupation of Crete, which had been drawn by Vice Marshal Kurt Student, Commander of the XI Airforce Corps. On the same day, the Army High Command submitted a plan for the occupation of Malta.

As the available forces did not suffice for the implementation of both the above plans, Hitler decided in a meeting on April 20, attended by Air Vice-Marshal Student as well, that the operation for the occupation of Crete should be carried out first.

**378.** Based on the above plan and the decisions of Hitler, the Directive No. 28 was issued on April 25, 1941, under the code name "Fall MERKUR" (Operation "MERCURY"), concerning the operations for the occupation of Crete and the use of the island as an air base against Britain in the Eastern Mediterranean.

The high command of the operation was assigned to the Marshal of the Airforce, Goering, while its tactical preparation was entrusted to the Commander of the IV Air Force, Air Marshal Alexander Lohr. The command of the forces of the XI Airforce Corps, that were to be used in Crete, was assigned to Air Vice Marshal Student. The VIII Airforce Corps, under the command of Air Vice Marshal Von Richthofen would undertake to weaken the defence, before the day of the attack, and would then support the airborne operations and the operations of the land forces. Air Vice Marshal Conrad, Commander of the Transport Airforce of the XI Airforce Corps, was ordered to consider and conduct the transportation of troops and supplies with aircraft. The Commander of the SE Europe Naval forces, Rear Admiral Schuster, was assigned to organise the sea transportation pertaining to the operation, using all means available.

The Italian dictator requested that the Italian Army should take part in the operation, with a strength of a reinforced regiment, that would be operating from the Dodekanese and would land on the eastern shores of the island. This action was finally carried out on May 28, at a time, that is, when the fate of the island had already been decided.

**379.** For the implementation of the operation "MERCURY", the Commander of the German forces of the operation, Air Marshal Alexander Lohr, had the following forces under his command:

- The Staff of the IV Air Force (Kifissia).
- The forces of the XI Airforce Corps, that comprised the 7th Airborne Parachutist Division (three Parachutist regiments), the 5th Mountain Division reinforced with units from the 6th Division, one Paratroopers Assault Regiment and the Transport Airforce of the same Corps with 600 transport aircraft and approximately 100 gliders.
- The VIII Airforce Corps, with 60 reconnaissance aircraft, 280 bombers, 150 dive bombers and 180 fighter of which 90 had a long range capability.
- The Naval Forces of South-eastern Europe.

The total number of forces employed for the assault on Crete amounted to 22,750 men, 1,370 aircraft and 70 vessels for the transportation of landing forces and supplies, supported by a small number of Italian destroyers and motor torpedo boats.

The island would be assaulted by 10,000 paratroopers and 750 men in gliders. Furthermore, 5,000 men would be transported to the occupied airfields and coastal areas by transport planes and 7,000 by ships and other vessels.

The VIII Airforce Corps was allocated to the airfields of Central and Southern Greece, as well as to the airfields of the islands Milos and Karpathos. The airfields of Megara, Topolia, Dadi and Tanagra were used for the transportation of troops, the airfield of Faliro (Elliniko) for the staffs and the one in Korinthos, for the transportation of supplies.

The lack of concrete or metal runways in most of the airfields in mainland Greece, resulted in a thick cloud of dust being raised at every landing or take off. This was damaging to the aircraft engines and caused delays in their departure, owing to the lack of visibility in the take-off runway. During the preparation of the attack, an effort was made to deal with the problem and provisions were made to concentrate fire pumps and other appropriate means.

The estimate was that it would take two weeks to concentrate the personnel and supplies. The Transport units were not in Greece at that time. The 7th Parachutist Division was at the training centres in Germany, with the exception of one of its regiments.

Between May 10 and 12, the airfields and areas of concentration were appointed for each unit. The concentration was terminated by May 16. On May 18 transport aircraft formations landed at the airfield. On the following day, May 19, the distribution of fuel for the operations, to the various airfields, was completed, amounting to approximately 3,535 tons.

**380.** The plan of operations, under the code name "MERCURY", provided for the following, in general:

- Gaining and maintaining air superiority.

- Occupation of the airfields of Crete using paratroopers and gliders with the main effort at Maleme.

- After the occupation of the airfields, landing of airborne mountain troops in order to complete the occupation of the island.

- The troops in Maleme would be reinforced by sea with units that would be transferred from the nearest shores.

- The land forces would be reinforced by sea with a strong echelon of artillery, tanks, vehicles and pack animals.

The airborne troops would operate in three assault groups: Group West, Group Centre and Group East.

The Group West (code name "KOMET"), its strength comprising the Assault Regiment minus two companies, under the command of Major General Eugen Meindl would occupy the Maleme airfield.

The Group Centre (code name "MARS") under the orders of Lt. General Suessmann, Commander of the 7th Airborne Division, divided into two echelons and assigned to occupy the Sectors of Hania-Souda and Rethymno-Pigi airfield, as follows:

The A' Echelon (Commander Colonel Heindrich), that comprised the 3rd Paratrooper Regiment, two companies from the Assault Regiment and various other divisional units, would occupy Hania and Souda.

The B' Echelon (Commander Colonel Sturm), that comprised the 2nd Paratrooper Regiment (minus the II Battalion), would occupy Rethymno and the Pigi airfield.

The Group East (code name "ORION"), its strength comprising the 1st Paratrooper Regiment from the 7th Airborne Division (plus the II/2 Paratrooper Battalion), under the command of Colonel Brauer, would occupy Iraklio along with its airfield (airfield of Rousses).

The above Group would conduct an assault on the island in two waves, in two time steps. The first wave would launch the assault with the "KOMET" Group and the first echelon of the "MARS" Group, at 0800 hrs, on May 20, 1941, against the airfield of Maleme and the area of Hania respectively. The second wave would launch the assault with the B' Echelon of the "MARS" Group and the "ORION" at 1600 hrs on the same day, against the towns and airfield of Rethymno and Iraklio respectively.

The B' Echelon of the "MARS" Group, after the occupation of Rethymnon and the Pigi airfield, would have to move towards Souda so as to link up with the A' Echelon of the same Group.

The "ORION" Group, after the occupation of Iraklio and the airfield of Rousses (Iraklio), would have to seek to link up with the B' Echelon of the "MARS" Group (Rethymno) and send patrols eastwards and southwards. The phasing of the operation in two time steps was imposed by the necessity for a better air support.

On the first day, according to the German plan, the airfield and ports of Hania, Rethymno and Iraklio would be occupied. On the second day, Souda would be occupied. During the same day, units from the 5th Mountain Division, that would be transferred by sea would land on the area of Maleme as well as on other suitable coastal areas, so as to complete the occupation of Crete.

# CHAPTER VIII

# THE CONDUCT OF THE BATTLE - THE COLLAPSE OF THE DEFENCE AND THE EVACUATION OF THE ISLAND OF CRETE

*The German Preparatory Bombardments and their Results*

**381.** The preparation of the German attack for the occupation of Crete had virtually begun since April 16, that is, since the VIII German Airforce Corps had assumed action to destroy or impede the allied vessels sailing in the Eastern Mediterranean. To that end, the ports of Souda and Iraklio had already suffered air attacks.

Since May 14, however, systematic bombardment commenced, according to the German plan. The main targets were the airfields of Malemè, Rethymno (Pigi), and Iraklio (Rousses), the ports of Souda and Iraklio, the Antiaircraft pill boxes and the towns of Hania, Rethymno and Iraklio. At the same time, aircraft that were constantly patrolling, forbade ships to approach the shores of Crete. From May 14 to 18, merchant ships of 36,000 tons capacity were sunk at sea on their way to Crete, as well as the Greek destroyer 'Leon' and the British corvette 'Salvia'.

**382.** As a result of this activity, the ships no longer approached or unloaded their cargo in Souda harbour during the day. The ships approached Crete only at night, sailing in the harbour of Souda at midnight to unload and sailing away on the same night. However, in order to achieve this, it was necessary to use ships that would be able to develop a high speed, as, cruisers and destroyers, so that the demands of the situation (arrival, unloading and departure) could be met within the available limited space of time.

However, the small capacity of these ships -which were not suitable for transportation- and short night, could only barely suffice for unloading approximately 100 tons of supplies, which were naturally insufficient to cover the daily needs that amounted to approximately 600 tons. As a result, the Greek -British forces in Crete were forced to be deprived of large quantities of valuable war supplies, that could not reach their destination.

### The Beginning of the German Airborne Assault
### (May 20, 1941)
### The A' Maleme - Agyia Sector ( 2nd New Zealand Division )
### (Sketch-map no. 29)

**383.** At 0630 hrs, on May 20, bomber and fighter flights of the VIII Air Corps, filled the air space of Maleme, Agyia, Hania and Souda, severely bombing and strafing, mainly the positions of the artillery and the defenders around the Maleme airfield, as well as the town of Hania.

The bombing, that was intensified with the arrival of new aircraft flights, developed into a true barrage of fire. It was made clear, by then, that this activity of the German Airforce, that was greater in intensity, extent and duration than any previous one, aimed at the preparation of an immediate invasion by air.

The Commander of the British-Greek forces in Crete, Major General Freyberg, signalled to the units, at 0730 hrs to be ready to repulse an impending German airborne assault. Indeed, while the fighters were departing after short while, flights of transport 'Junger 52' aircraft and gliders, that were towed, two or three together, filled the air space above the 2nd New Zealand Division Section and the drop of the parachutists began in waves, while the gliders landed on the ground. Simultaneously, the British-Greek troops implemented the defensive plan. The antiaircraft guns hit the transport aircraft and gliders, while the infantry units hit the paratroopers with sustained fire, both in the air and on the ground.

Soon the entire area was turned into a theatre of local deadly conflicts. In time and while the German operation for the occupation of Crete unfolded thoroughly, the local conflicts began to take the definite shape of a tactical operation.

**384.** The airfield of Maleme (5th New Zealand Brigade zone), was the objective of the action of the "KOMET" Group West, that is, the Assault Regiment of Major General Meindl minus two companies (lst and 2nd Company of I Battalion). The landing of the Group began at 0815 hrs and ended at 0915 hrs, with the use of parachutes and more than fifty gliders.

The I Battalion (minus the lst and 2nd Company), the Detachment of Major Koch, landed on the bed of the dry Tavronitis river and east of the village Vlaheronitissa, assigned to neutralise the means of antiaircraft defence in the area and to seize hill 107. ·

The II Battalion landed at the area of Ropaniana village, as a reserve force.

The III Battalion (minus the 9th Company) landed on the south-east of Maleme village, assigned to cut off the airfield of Maleme from the east and to link up with the "MARS" Group, which would be operating towards Hania and Rethymno.

The IV Battalion (minus the 16th Company) landed between the II Battalion and the western bank of Tavronitis river, as a reserve. The Assault Regiment Staff also landed in that area.

The 9th Company of the III Battalion (Braun Detachment) landed south of Tavronitis bridge, assigned to seize and hold it.

The 16th Company of the IV Battalion landed in the area of Sirili village, assigned to operate northwards and to assist the operation of the Koch Detachment towards hill 107.

At 0930 hrs, the Commander of the Assault Regiment, Major General Meindl, also landed at the area west of the river Tavronitis and found the situation as follows:

- The Braun Detachment had already occupied the bridge and had driven a wedge into the adversary front.

- The Koch Detachment had been unable to seize hill 107.

- The III Battalion had almost completely destroyed.

-All British troops in the area of the Maleme airfield had been engaged in the fight.

Based on these assessments, Major General Meindl decided to attack with the troops of the II and IV Battalion, which had not been directly committed to the action, in order to seize hill 107. The attack upon hill 107 was launched from two directions. From the west, via the Tavronitis bridge and from the south, to the direction of Vlaheronitissa village. A fierce fighting followed and by that evening the Germans managed to advance and approach hill 107 from the north-west and the south, at a distance of one thousand meters approximately, while the troops of the Braun Detachment occupied various positions within the area of the airfield.

**385.** After this development, the Commander of the 22nd New Zealand Battalion who had been assigned to defend hill 107, requested the intervention of 5th New Zealand Brigade, at 1700 hrs, by conducting a counter-attack with the 23rd Battalion, according to the provisions of the defence plan. The Brigade replied that the 23rd New Zealand Battalion had already been engaged in combat against the paratroopers in its zone and that its intervention was impossible. Subsequently, the Commander of the

22nd New Zealand Battalion counter-attacked at 1715 hrs, with an Infantry platoon and two tanks, but the attempt failed· and the tanks were destroyed.

At 2200 hrs, a company from the 23rd New Zealand Battalion arrived at the positions of the 22nd New Zealand Battalion, in order to reinforce it. This company was ordered to be deployed defensively on hill 107. The Germans became aware of its movements and fired against it. Though it suffered many losses, the company deployed successfully.

In the meantime, the situation in the area of Maleme airfield was as follows:

- Major General Meindl, in spite of having committed all of his forces, was unable to complete the occupation of the airfield and of hill 107. The German losses were heavy. They lost almost the entire III Battalion, while the Commanders of the I and III Battalions were killed. Major General Meindl himself was wounded, but continued to direct the fight of his Unit. Because of the fatigue and the casualties, the Germans lacked any further offensive capability.

- The 22nd New Zealand Battalion, that carried the weight of the German attack, retained hill 107, but it was doubtful whether it would be able to confront another German attack. Two of its companies had been crushed. The two tanks at its disposal had been destroyed, while the greatest part of the guns and machine-guns it was provided with, had been lost or destroyed. An additional company was expected, as reinforcement, but this had not arrived yet.

The Commander of the 22nd New Zealand Battalion taking into account this situation and expecting a new German attack on the following day, by air as well as by land, decided to withdraw his Battalion to new positions between the 21st and 23rd New Zealand Battalions, that held their ground firmly and had confronted the German parachutists successfully. The 5th New Zealand Brigade, which had been notified, since 2130 hrs, of the Battalion's decision to withdraw, did not forbid it. However it did not notify neither the Division nor the Cretan Forces Command. On the contrary, it gave the Commander of the 22nd New Zealand Battalion complete freedom to act on his own initiative. The withdrawal commenced at midnight and was completed during the same night. All guns in the Battalion zone and the supplies of two Machine-gun platoons were abandoned on site.

Thus, hill 107 and Maleme airfield, that is, the vital ground of the 2nd New Zealand Division and one of the most important strongholds of the Cretan Forces were left at the disposal of the Germans. The latter, expecting a counterattack by the British forces, were established defensively at the positions they had occupied during the course of the day and failed to notice the withdrawal of the 22nd New Zealand Battalion.

**386.** In the area of Kasteli, a force of approximately seventy paratroopers landed at 0800 hrs, under the command of First Lieutenant Moerb. It was part of the II Battalion of the Assault Regiment. This force was successfully confronted and was neutralised at the end of an extremely fierce fighting, conducted by the troops of the lst Greek Infantry Regiment which were in the area. Twenty-eight Germans were taken prisoners, while the rest were killed. The Greek casualties were 57 killed in action and 62 wounded.

**387.** The Cadets of the Military Academy, that had deployed defencively between the monastery of Gonia and the village of Kolymbari in the Rodopos peninsula, were subjected to successive attacks by the troops of the II Assault Battalion, which they were able to repulse successfully, causing serious losses to the attackers. However, due to the casualties and the shortage of ammunition, the Cadets were forced to withdraw on the night of May 20 to 21, towards the area of Deliana village, where they deployed defensively.

**388.** In the area of Agyia (zone of the 10th New Zealand Brigade) the 3rd Parachutist Hunters Regiment of the 7th Parachutist Division and other divisional units, began their assault at 0815 hrs. These units which belonged to the A' Echelon of the "MARS" Group Centre had been assigned to fix strong enemy forces, in order to assist the operation against Maleme airfield, to occupy the town of Hania and finally to seek to link up, with the Group West "KOMET", as soon as possible.

The I and II Para Battalions landed in the area of the Agyia prison, between the 6th and 8th Greek Regiments.

The III Para Battalion landed in the area of Galatas village, near the positions of the Joint New Zealand Battalion.

The Parachutist Engineer Battalion landed on the west of the village Episcopi, near the positions of the 8th Greek Regiment.

The Headquarters of the 7th Para Division landed the south-east of Galatas village. The glider carrying the Division Commander, Major General Sussmann, had crashed near the isle of Aegina and all passengers were killed. Subsequently, the command of the Division was assumed by the Commander of the 3rd Parachutist Regiment, Colonel Heinrich.

A tough fight ensued, which lasted the entire day. The greatest pressure was applied on the 6th Greek Regiment, which occupied the heights south of Galatas and happened to be in the drop zone of the bulk of the German parachutists. This Regiment had been subjected to successive attacks since the very beginning, from all directions, even from within its own positions and had suffered heavy losses. Among the first killed, was the Commander of the Regiment, Lieutenant Colonel Michael Grigoriou, the Deputy Commander, Captain Ioannis Psimoulis, the Commander of the 4th Company, First Lieutenant, Dimitrios Xiroyiannis and many Platoon leaders.

Nevertheless, the Regiment continued its uneven struggle until the early afternoon hours, whereupon it withdrew towards Galatas. Thereafter, it ceased to exist as an organized unit. However, strong sections of the Regiment continued operations effectively until the end of the battle of Crete.

The Germans also suffered heavy losses and, by night on May 20, they had only succeeded in consolidating their positions in the area of the Agyia prison.

**389.** The 4th New Zealand Brigade, which was a reserve at the disposal of the Commander of the Cretan Forces, was placed at the disposal of the 2nd New Zealand Division, at 1100 hrs, on May 20. After neutralising a force of paratroopers of almost company size that landed in its area, it was ordered by the 2nd New Zealand Division to conduct a counter-attack in order to recapture the area of the Agyia prison, within the zone of the 10th New Zealand Brigade. The counter-attack was launched at 1930 hrs with a battalion, which was, however, later immobilised at a distance of one kilometre from the German positions.

### The B' Hania - Souda Sector (MNBDO Group)
### (Sketch-map no. 29)

**390.** In this very area, the Germans operated with the 1st and 2nd Parachutist Companies of the I Battalion of the Assault Regiment, which formed part of the A' Echelon of Group "MARS". These companies had been reinforced with machine-gun teams from the Assault Regiment and formed two detachments which were transported by glider planes.

Their principal mission was to conduct preliminary probing attacks, in order to assist the units of the 3rd Paratrooper Regiment, which would be operating from Agyia towards Hania.

At 0800 hrs on May 20, 1941, the gliders of the one detachment were directed towards Akrotiri. However, due to the fire of the Antiaircraft artillery in the area of Souda, they were prematurely released from towing and were scattered in all directions. Some of them were destroyed upon landing on the ground, whereas the rest became an easy prey for the defending forces. Thus, the detachment was neutralised without managing to accomplish its mission. Its losses were 48 killed in action and 36 wounded.

The other detachment, directly after landing on the north-east of Mournies, attacked the battery of the 234th Battalion and managed to neutralise it. Of the battery men, eight were taken prisoners while the rest were killed on the spot. After a counter-attack, by other troops of that area, the detachment was forced to withdraw to the area of Perivolia village with heavy losses.

**391.** At the end of the day, the situation for the German Commander of the A' Echelon of the "MARS" Group, appeared to be as follows:
- The planned occupation of Hania had not been achieved.
- The raiding troops in the area Hania-Souda had suffered heavy losses and had been unable to achieve their objectives.
- The III Battalion of the 3rd Para Regiment had lost two thirds of its strength, without being able to occupy the area of Galatas.
- The planned link up with the Group West (Assault Regiment) had not been achieved.

Following the above facts and foreseeing a counterattack by the British during the night, the enemy concentrated his forces in the area of Agyia prison where it began to deploy them defensively.

### The C' Rethymno - Georgioupolis Sector (19th Australian Brigade)
(Sketch-map no. 30)

**392.** In the Sector of Rethymno, operated the B' Echelon of the Group "MARS", which comprised the 2nd Para Regiment (minus the II Battalion), under the command of Colonel Sturm. After a severe bombardment at 1600 hrs, by approximately twenty aircrafts the assault of the B' Echelon against that area began at 1615 hrs.

The transport aircraft did not arrive simultaneously above the paratrooper zones, as planned, but their arrival lasted more than two hours. This ruled out the possibility of a tactical surprise against the defenders and deprived the Germans of the ability to take advantage of the bombings that had preceded.

The dropping of parachutists and their supplies was conducted by 161 aircraft in total, as follows:
- The I Para Battalion (minus two companies) landed on the east of the Pigi airfield, assigned to occupy the latter.
- The III Para Battalion landed on the east of Perivolia village, assigned to occupy Rethymno.
- A group from the Staff of the 2nd Para Regiment and a company from the I Para Battalion landed between the village of Platanes and the airfield.

- A company, also from the I Para Battalion, landed at the positions of the 2/11 Australian Battalion and the 4th Greek Infantry Regiment.

**393.** The III Para Battalion, that landed on the east of Perivolia village, attacked immediately against the almost unarmed Depot Battalion, which they dispersed, and then they went on and occupied the villages Perivolia and Kastelakia. Their action towards Rethymno was repulsed by the Greek Gendarmerie Battalion, which counter-attacked, forcing the Germans to withdraw towards the village of Perivolia. There were heavy losses on both sides.

The Para Company, which landed at the positions of the 2/11 Australian Battalion and the 4th Greek Regiment near 'B' hill, suffered heavy losses and dispersed. The 2/11 Australian Battalion had taken more than 80 parachutists prisoners by that same evening.

The I Para Battalion, that landed on the east of the Pigi airfield were deployed at the village of Stavromenos and launched an attack against the strong point of the 'A' hill, which they occupied, threatening directly the airfield.

Subsequently, Lieutenant Colonel Campbell, Commander of the 2/1 Australian Battalion and, at the same time Commander of the Pigi Airfield Group, decided to counter-attack on the following day, in order to mop up his area completely. Although the reinforcement he had requested from the Commander of the Cretan Forces in order to implement his decision was not given, Campbell planned two counterattacks for the following morning, using his own forces.

**394.** Thus, by the night of May 20 to 21, the German paratroopers had occupied the villages Perivolia, Kastelakia and Stavromenos, and 'A' hill.

The German Casualties amounted to one third of their strength, with approximately 400 killed in action and the rest wounded or prisoners, but despite those losses no objective had been seized.

As the Georgioupolis Group had not been subjected to any enemy attack, the Commander of the Cretan Forces gradually transferred the troops of the Group towards Hania during that night and on the following day. They were accompanied by the Headquarters of the 19th Australian Brigade.

## The D' Iraklio Sector (14th British Brigade)
(Sketch-map no. 31)

**395.** In the Iraklio Sector, an attack was launched since 1600 hrs, by the Group East "ORION", that is, the 1st Para Regiment minus one company and the II Para Battalion of the 2nd Para Regiment minus two companies. These companies remained in mainland Greece because their transportation to Crete was not possible. Before the Paratrooper assault, the sector had been severely bombed by approximately fifty aircraft for one hour and serious damages had been caused, mainly to the town of Iraklio.

The parachutists had not been offered any air support during their landing, due to the exhaustion of fuel supplies of the fighter aircrafts. This lack of synchronisation was very important for the development of the landing of the German forces from the very beginning.

The II/1 Para Battalion landed in two echelons, west and south of the airfield, assigned to occupy it. By 2130 hrs, this Battalion had been annihilated by troops from the 2/4 Australian Battalion, the 7th Medium Artillery Regiment and the Blackwatch Battalion. Its casualties were 12 officers and 300 soldiers killed in action and 8 officers and 100 soldiers wounded. Approximately 70 paratroopers, who had survived, concentrated at night on hill 182 (Kopraina), south-east of the airfield, where they deployed defensively.

The III/1 Para Battalion landed in the areas of Therissos, Mastabas, Giofyros, as well as close to the city walls, assigned to occupy Iraklio. During the drop it suffered many losses, but finally managed to concentrate its forces 500 meters west of the city walls.

The II/2 Para Battalion (minus two companies) landed at Gazi, assigned to support the attack of the III/I Para Battalion against the town. However, having been hit a number of times by daring armed civilians, it was forced to deploy defensively.

The I/1 Para Battalion, minus one company, and the command of the Regiment landed in the area of Gournes. Its mission was to cover from the east the troops operating against the airfield and the town of Iraklio. However, it was repeatedly attacked by groups of armed civilians and gendarmes, while concentrating at Gournes as well as during its movement towards the airfield. The Battalion suffered serious losses and its movement was slowed down considerably.

**396.** Colonel Brauer, Commander of the 1st Para Regiment, believed that the airfield would have been taken in the meantime by the II/1 Para Battalion, as planned. He was, therefore, surpised when, upon his arrival near the eastern fringes of the airfield, his Battalion was fired by the Blackwatch Battalion.

Subsequently and despite the enormous losses suffered by his units, he decided to launch an attack during the night of May 20 to 21, against the airfield and the town of Iraklio, with the II/1 and III/1 Para Battalions respectively. The attack against the airfield failed, whereas the attack against Iraklio was not carried out, because the order for its execution did not reach the III/1 Para Battalion.

Thus, the attack of the "ORION" Group against the town of Iraklio failed, with heavy losses on the German side, of approximately 1,000 parachutists.

**397.** In the evening of May 20 (the first day of the German invasion to Crete), the situation, in general, appeared to be as follows for each adversary.

The Commander of the British-Greek Forces on Crete, Major General Freyberg, considered that his forces possessed all airfields and harbours of Crete and was unaware, due to the fact that he was untimely informed of the critical situation that had arisen at Maleme airfield, so that he might intervene at once, in order to secure again the area. Instead, considering the situation at the zone of the 10th New Zealand Brigade (area of Agyia) as critical, at 1100 hrs, of May 20, he placed his reserve (4th New Zealand Brigade) at the disposal of the 2nd New Zealand Division, keeping only the 1st Welsh Battalion as a reserve. Moreover, he transferred the 2/8 Australian Battalion of the 18th Australian Brigade to the area of Hania towards the Mournies area, although there was no serious threat from that direction.

The Commander of the XI German Airforce Corps, Air Marshal Student, considered that no objective had been attained and that the only point at which some success had been recorded, was the Maleme airfield, where forces of the Assault Regiment had established a bridgehead on the east of the Tavronitis bridge. Student was unaware of the fact that the Maleme airfield had essentially been abandoned by the 5th New Zealand Brigade, and that he was only being hit by mortars and artillery fire. Subsequently, he ordered the entire paratrooper reserve to reinforce the Assault Regiment, so as to be able to seize and hold the airfield. Furthermore, he ordered the 5th Mountain Division to move at once, in order to occupy Hania and Souda. The forces operating in the remaining sectors, would continue their fight without any reinforcement, seeking to immobilise and damage the enemy forces as much as possible. The VIII Airforce Corps would support these operations.

Thus, whereas Major General Freyberg was unable to make the right decisions concerning the continuation of the battle, due to inadequate information, the German Command, by assessing accurate by the situation, made the right decisions and issued the appropriate orders.

During the trial of the war criminals, Student reported the following regarding the night of May 20/21:

'That night was crucial for me. If the enemy had attempted an encirclement during the night of the 20th to the 21st, or on the morning of the 21st, then the worn out remains of the Regiment might have been swept away'.

### The Second Day of the German Assault
### ( May 21, 1941 )
### The Maleme - Agyia and Hania - Souda Sectors
(Sketch-map no. 29)

**398.** The Commander of the 5th New Zealand Brigade, at approximately 0200 hrs on May 21, was informed that the 22nd Battalion had finally withdrawn from its positions. Subsequently, he ordered the Commanders of the 21st and 23rd Battalions as well as the 27th Artillery Battalion, to co-operate accordingly and to report to him. They proposed that, the battalions should keep their positions, and the 27th Artillery Battalion should fire against the airfield in order to impede its use by the Germans. The Brigade Commander approved the above proposals. About this decision, the official history of New Zealand relates:

'... This decision, however, was too fateful to pass without comment. For now was the lâst chance to counter-attack to regain the lost positions before the enemy could reorganise and reinforce. The enemy in 23 Battalion area did not exist as an organised force, 21 Battalion had come under no serious pressure, and only 22 Battalion was very much the worse for the previous day's fighting.

No doubt the severity of the last twenty-four hours' experience would make Andrew dubious of the prospects for the success of a counter-attack. But it might have been expected that Leckie himself and Allen would have seen at once the danger of the airfield now open to the enemy and the fact that if counter-attack was to take place it must take place at once. There was still time to get the two relatively fresh battalions organized for attack at daylight, if not before. Together they would have been strong enough to go forward and give the enemy a hard knock at worst, and at best regain Point 107. And 22 Battalion could have taken over the rear.

Here, again, it is to be regretted that Hargest had not made 23 Battalion his advanced HQ the previous day or earlier. As it was, the vital decision had to be taken by his juniors.

There was still time to prepare the two relatively unfatigued Battalions (21st, 23rd) so as to attack during the day, if not sooner. The combined attack of those Battalions would have been sufficiently strong, so that by attacking, under the worst (for them) circumstances, they would inflict a powerful blow against the enemy, and, under the best, they could recapture height 107, with the 22nd New Zealand Battalion undertaking to cover the rear of those Battalions.

Here, it must be noted that it is unfortunate that Harguest (Commander of the 5th New Zealand Brigade) had not established his forward Headquarters at the 23rd Battalion on the previous day or earlier. As the situation had turned out, this decision, which was of vital importance, should have been taken by his subordinates...'

The Commander of the 5th Brigade at approximately 0400 hrs, notified the 2nd New Zealand Division about the situation and proposed the conduct of a counter-attack by the 28th New Zealand Battalion and by one battalion which had to be provided by the Division. The Division Commander agreed on the Brigade's proposal and reported accordingly to the Commander of the Cretan Forces at 1130 hrs. At the same time, he proposed the conduct of a counter-attack, during the night of May 21 to 22, by the 20th and the 28th New Zealand Battalions, which was approved.

**399.** At 0800 hrs, transport aircraft flights dropped a paratrooper company and one and a half company of the Anti-tank Battalion of the 7th Para Division west of Tavronitis river. Colonel Ramcke, the replacement of Major General Meindl who had been wounded, also landed with the above companies. At the same time, two companies from the II Battalion of the 2nd Para Regiment landed near the positions of the 28th New Zealand Battalion. Both companies had been intended for the Iraklio Sector and had remained in Athens, due to inability to transport them during the first day of the attack.

Colonel Ramcke set as first objectives, the completion of the occupation of hill 107 and the destruction of the guns that were firing against the airfield. For that, he ordered the troops, west of Tavronitis river, to move towards hill 107 and the Maleme and Pyrgos villages. The troops moved slowly and cautiously towards their objectives, which they managed to occupy by midday, with the exception of Maleme village which was defended by its population and some New Zealands until 1600 hrs.

The paratroopers that landed at the positions of the 28th New Zealand Battalion, suffered heavy casualties and only 80 of them managed to escape towards Pyrgos village.

**400.** Since 1600 hrs, the 5th Mountain Division troops began to land in the area of the airfield. By 1700 hrs, despite the sustained fire of the British artillery, the landing of the II/100 Mountain Battalion had been completed. The Commander of the 100th Mountain Regiment, Colonel Utz, his Command Post and the last sections of the Battalion disembarked as well. He deployed the II/100 Battalion eastwards, where he considered that the most serious threat lay.

**401.** At 2330 hrs, the British Naval Forces, that were patrolling the sea west of Crete, sunk a large number of German vessels, which had left from Halkis and Piraeus, carrying the III/100 and II/85 Battalions of the 5th Mountain Division. Many men of the III/100 Battalion were drowned and a considerable number of heavy weapons was lost. The vessels which were not sunk, sailed to Milos, where the convoy carrying the II/85 Battalion had also taken shelter.

In the Hania - Souda Sector, no important fighting took place on May 21, apart from the intense action of the German Air Force.

## The B' Rethymno - Georgioupolis Sector
(Sketch-map no. 30)

**402.** On the morning of May 21, the allied forces deployed in the area of the Pigi airfield, launched the two counter-attacks, which had been ordered by Lieutenant Colonel Campbell on the previous day. The first was conducted by the 2/11 Australian Battalion in order to clear the flatland north and east of its positions, as far as the sea, with a simultaneous operation of troops of the 5th Greek Regiment towards the village of ,Platanes. The second was conducted by the 2/1 Australian Battalion in order to recapture the 'A' hill and employed troops of the 5th Greek Regiment aiming at recapturing Stavromenos village, which the Germans had managed to occupy.

The counter-attack of the 2/11 Australian Battalion was successful. Those Germans who were not killed, were taken prisoners, including the Commander of the B' Echelon of the "MARS" Group, Colonel Sturm. The latter had the plans and orders of operation on him, which revealed that the airfield and Rethymno were supposed to have been taken by the Germans since the previous day. The troops of the 5th Greek Regiment seized the village of Platanes and advanced as far as the eastern fringes of Perivolia village.

The 2/1 Australian Battalion recaptured the 'A' hill by midday on May 21, re-positioned the guns and took approximately 60 prisoners. The Germans that survived, took refuge in the village of Stavromenos and barricaded themselves inside the olive oil refinery there, which constituted a stronghold, due to the sturdy construction and the walled enclosure that surrounded it.

The troops of the 5th Greek Regiment overthrew the enemy resistance, and arrived by daybreak before the village of Stavromenos, where they were immobilised. The Greek Commander requested artillery support and one tank, in order to attempt to seize that village. Lieutenant Colonel Campbell did not, however, approve this proposal and ordered that one company should remain at the disposal of the 2/1 Australian Battalion and that the remaining force should retire to its original positions.

**403.** The Germans, who had seized the village Perivolia, launched an attack in the morning upon the town of Rethymno, but were repulsed by the Greek troops and the armed population of the town. At 1715 hrs, following a counter-attack of the II Gendarmerie Company, Kastelakia was recaptured, while the Germans confined themselves to the cemetery of Agios Georgios of Perivolia (village).

The total number of German casualties, by the end of May 21, were 70 men killed in action, 300 wounded and approximately 200 prisoners.

Thus, by the end of May 21, the Germans had occupied two defensive strongholds, the villages Perivolia and Stavromenos. Lieutenant Colonel Campbell decided to launch an attack, on the following day, against these two principal German strongholds.

*The C' Iraklio Sector*
(Sketch-map no. 31)

**404.** The German Airforce since 0900 hrs, began a fierce bombing against Iraklio and the positions of the Greek units. The city walls of Iraklio and the area of the harbour suffered many damages, while the small Greek force that occupied the walls suffered many casualties. At approximately 1000 hrs, the Germans attacked the town of Iraklio from the west, taking advantage of the results of the bombing, and they managed to enter it. Heavy street-fights took place until nightfall, with heavy losses on both sides. In the end, the Germans were forced to withdraw outside the town, to the areas of Tsalikaki and Estavromenos, east of Gazi village.

It is worth noting that the reconnaissance, droppings and bombings of the German Airforce were hindered by the Greek - British troops that used flares and signalling panels with the appropriate panel codes, which had been seized on the German prisoners. Especially in a particular case after a request of the British, the Germans dropped machine-guns, radio transmitters, mortars, food, ammunitions and other supplies onto the British positions.

### The Third Day of the German Attack
### (May 22, 1941)
### The Maleme - Agyia and Hania - Souda Sectors
(Sketch-map no. 29)

**405.** In the Maleme-Agyia Sector the counter-attack of the 20th and 28th New Zealand Battalions in order to recapture Maleme airfield and hill 107 respectively, was launched at approximately 0330 hrs, on May 22, 1941. The counter-attack was supported by three light tanks and one battery, in addition to the guns deployed in the zone of the 5th New Zealand Brigade.

The 20th New Zealand Battalion moved northwards of the Maleme-Hania and the 28th New Zealand Battalion southwards. At the beginning of their advance, both battalions encountered light enemy resistance, which either by-passed or neutralised with few losses. However, upon approaching the village of Pyrgos, they began to encounter much stronger resistance and suffered serious losses. When the first troops came to approximately 1,000 meters east of Pyrgos, it had been already daylight and the enemy airforce had resumed its activity. Under these circumstances it became difficult for the battalions to advance and they were finally forced to withdraw, with heavy losses, to the positions of the 23rd New Zealand Battalion. During the same morning, the 21st New Zealand Battalion also moved westwards and managed to arrive as far as the village of Vlaheronitissa. There, however, it was informed that the attack to recapture Maleme airfield had failed and thus it returned to its original positions.

**406.** The Commander of the Cretan Forces, considering that the occupation of the airfield area by the enemy posed a serious threat, decided at midday, on May 22, to conduct a night counter-attack with the 4th and 5th Brigades, in order to recapture it. However, the counter-attack was not carried out, because there were reports that German troops from the prison of Agyia area were advancing northwards, clearly aiming to cut off the 5th New Zealand Brigade troops from the east, and that the German forces at

Maleme had been reinforced considerably. Furthermore, it was assessed that the 5th New Zealand Brigade troops were unable to assume offensive action. Thus, instead of the counterattack, the Commander of the New Zealand Division proposed to Major General Freyberg to withdraw the 5th New Zealand Brigade eastwards, in order to avoid being cut off.

Subsequently, Major General Freyberg decided to postpone the counter-attack and to withdraw the 5th New Zealand Brigade on a new line eastwards, with the 28th Battalion west of Platania village and the other battalions further to the east. With this new disposition the airfield of Maleme would be at a distance of six kilometres from the British Defence line and only the British Airforce would be able to attack it. There was no such possibility, however, although Major General Freyberg informed Wavell how serious the situation was and requested a strong support by fighters and bombers which would be the only means to reverse the German operations.

**407.** Thus, the initiative passed to the Germans. The troups of the 5th Mountain Division began to arrive at a rate of approximately twelve landings per hour. On the very evening of May 22, more than fifty aircraft landed. By 2000hrs, the I/100, II/100 and I/85 Mountain Battalions, one light battery (6 guns), the 95th Engineer Battalion and sections of the 55th Motorcyclists Battalion had landed together with the Commander of the 3rd Mountain Division, Major General Ringel.

Major General Ringel was appointed commander of the German Forces on Crete, assigned to secure the occupation of the Maleme airfield, to mop up the Souda bay, to relieve the parachutists at Rethymno and to occupy the whole island.

For the implementation of his mission, Major General Ringel organised his forces in three battle groups.

The first group, which comprised the 95th Engineer Battalion under the command of Major Schaette was assigned to secure the airfield of Maleme from the west and the south, by mopping up the areas of Kasteli and Palaeochora.

The second group which comprised the Assault Regiment parachutist forces (two battalions), under the command of the Colonel Ramcke, assigned to secure the airfield from the east and, in co-operation with the third group, to launch an attack against Hania.

The third group which comprised the three battalions of the 5th Mountain Division (the I/100, II/100 and I/85), subordinate to the Commander of the 100th Regiment, Colonel Utz, assigned to continue the action towards the hill Monodendri, in order to eliminate the New Zealand artillery which was firing against the airfield, to establish a liaison with the ˆ ·d Para Regiment and to cut off the coast road to Agia Marina.

**408.** In the Hania-Souda Sector, at 1800hrs on May 22, the Commander of the British-Greek Forces of Crete organised a.group which comprised the 2nd Greek Infantry Regiment and the 2/7 and 2/8 Australian Battalions (of the Georgioupolis group), subordinate to the Commander of the 19th Australian Brigade, Brigadier Vasey, who had remained, after his transfer to the area of Hania, without troops. This Group, as the 19th Australian Brigade, would secure the occupation of the area of Perivolia-Mournies.

The Military Academy was moved on that same day from the village of Deliana towards the village Hosti, attempting to join the British-Greek forces in the area of Hania.

### The B' Rethymno - Georgioupolis Sector
(Sketch-map no. 30)

**409.** The German Airforce since the morning of May 22, began new heavy bombardments throughout the entire zone of the Rethymno Group, so as to relieve the defending paratroopers in that area. As a result, many buildings were destroyed in Rethymno, including the building of the National Bank, in which the Prefect of Rethymno, G. Tsagris, the Chief of Gendarmerie, Lieutenant Colonel Stylianos Minoudakis, who had been working together at that time and several civilians were killed. No other important action was recorded in the Rethymno Sector.

In the Pigi Airfield Group, the 2/11 Australian Battalion conducted a counter-attack to recapture Perivolia village. Although the German positions were bombed by German aircraft, due to their deception using the panel codes which had come into the possession of the Australians, the Battalion was fixed, within a distance of approximately one kilometre from Agios Georgios of Perivolia, where the main German defence had been organised.

Further to the east, a counter attack launched by the 2/1 Australian Battalion in order to recapture the olive oil refinery of Stavromenos village, failed, due to the lack of co-ordination between the Greeks and the Australians forces. After this, the troops withdrew during the night to their original positions.

## The C' Iraklio Sector
### (Sketch-map no. 31)

**410.** In the area of the Iraklio Group, the mopping up of the area continued with patrols, mainly from the 3rd Greek Infantry Regiment and from groups of armed civilians, extending as far as the stream of Giofyros to the west and the village of Arhanes to the south. This operation was terminated successfully before nightfall and no German parachutist remained inside the Greek area. The most important German units (III/1, II/2 Battalions) which had a total strength of 500 paratroopers, were forced to adopt their disposition to defence in the area of Tsalikaki-Estavromenos.

In the area of the Airfield Group the Blackwatch troops mopped up and repulsed the isolated paratrooper centres of resistance on the eastern fringes of the airfield.

On the same day, Greek and British teams burried approximately 1,250 Germans.

## The Fourth and the Fifth Day of the German Attack
### (May 23 and 24, 1941)
## The A' Maleme - Agyia and Hania - Souda Sectors
### (Sketch-map no. 29)

**411.** The withdrawal of the 5th New Zealand Brigade units began at approximately 0630 hrs, on May 23, 1941, and ended at 1000 hrs on the same day. It did not become possible to withdraw the artillery of the Brigade (27th Battalion), since the withdrawal order came to the hands of the Battalion Commander at 0400 hrs, on May 23, with the coming of daylight which led to the abandonment of the guns, which had been "spiked" first, and left behind except for two guns belonging to the C' Battery. The gunners of the Battalion formed an infantry section, which was incorporated into the zone of the 28th New Zealand Battalion.

At approximately 1000 hrs, on May 23, the 5th New Zealand Brigade adopted the following new defensive disposition: The 28th Battalion around Platanias village. Eastwards, the 23rd Battalion and southwards the 21st Battalion. To the south and west of Agia Marina, the 22nd New Zealand Battalion had been deployed and was in the process of reorganisation.

In the meantime, the German troops, continuing their offensive effort, arrived after a fierce fighting, at the line of villages Modio and

Patelari, while a detachment from the 3rd Para Regiment occupied Stalos village.

The presence of German troops in the area of Stalos village and in particular, the German threat appearing from the south created a new unfavourable situation for the 5th New Zealand Brigade. The strength of the Brigade during the four-day fight had been reduced to approximately 600 men, instead of 2,810 it had on May 20.

**412.** The Commander of the 2nd New Zealand Division, taking under consideration the development of the situation in the zone of the 5th New Zealand Brigade as well as the report of the Commander of the l0th New Zealand Brigade that he was not in a position to confront a powerful enemy attack, decided the following:

- The 5th New Zealand Brigade would withdraw eastwards, to the area of Daratsos village, as a reserve.

- The 4th New Zealand Brigade would take over the zone of the l0th New Zealand Brigade, the forces of which had been subordinate to the 4th Brigade.

- The l9th New Zealand Battalion and the Land Detachment of the Divisional Cavalry (Russell Detachment) would remain at their positions.

- The l9th Australian Brigade, which had been subordinate to the 2nd New Zealand Division in the meantime, would extend its line of defence southwards and eastwards.

All the above movements were carried out during the night of May 23 to 24.

**413.** The 24th May was devoted to the establishment and re-organisation of the units, the improvement of positions and the re-supply in ammunition and other equipment.

The Military Academy arrived at the village of Hosti after forced night marches and deployed defensively there.

The 2nd Greek Infantry Regiment launched an attack at approximately 0530 hrs, on May 24, against the German positions in Animbali Tower. The attack lasted until 1700 hrs and then slackened, due to the lack of support and the exhaustion of ammunition of the attacking troops.

Further to the west, the Germans seized the village of Kastelli, as well as the surrounding area, after a fight. The lst Greek Infantry Regiment in the area, after having exhausted its ammunition disbanded in the surrounding villages. Approximately 140 officers and soldiers gradually escaped to the Middle East while those who remained were taken prisoners.

On the night of May 24, the defence line of the New Zealand Division formed an arc, with its right (northern) tip on the coast and the left at Perivolia village and westwards. Further to the south (the Souda-Hania sector) the 2nd Greek Infantry Regiment held the line.

The disposition of the units was the following: The 4th New Zealand Brigade to the north of Daratsos village. The Russell Detachment around Dapia. The 19th Australian Brigade south of the Agyia-Hania road. The 5th New Zealand Brigade, as a reserve, at the triangle formed by Kladissos river and the roads Agyia-Hania and Platanias-Hania.

The casualties of the Division exceeded 20% of its original strength. Its subsequent strength was approximately 5,500 men only.

**414.** The Germans were reinforced, on May 24, with new forces, which were transported by air to the area of Maleme. These were: the III/85 Battalion, the Staff of the 85th Mountain Regiment, the 95th Mountain Reconnaissance Battalion, the I, II Battalions of the 95th Pack Artillery Regiment, the 95th Antitank Artillery Battalion, an Antiaircraft Machinegun company, a Signals unit and a Motorcycle company.

The Commander of the 85th Mountain Regiment, Colonel Cracow, and the III/85 Battalion were directed towards the area of Episcopi Alikyanou, where the I/85 Battalion was also situated.

After these new German reinforcements, the Commander of the German Forces, Major General Ringel, assigned the following missions for the next day, May 25.

- The 85th Mountain Regiment would seize Alikyanos village and the area to the east. Afterwards, it would advance towards Souda and cut off the road Hania-Rethymno.

- The 100th Mountain Regiment and the Assault Regiment would seize Galatas village and the heights to its north.

- The 3rd Para Regiment would move south of the road Agyia-Hania, in close liaison with the 100th Regiment to the north and the 85th Regiment to the south.

- The 95th Engineer Battalion and the 55th Motorcycle Battalion (Schaette Detachment) would continue the mopping-up operations in the areas of Kolymbari, Kasteli of Kissamos, Kandanos and Palaeochora.

- The 93rd Reconnaissance Group and the 95th Antitank Battalion would form a reserve. The attack had been scheduled to occur at 0800 hrs, on May 25, upon Alikyanos and at 1320 hrs, of the same day, upon Galatas.

## The B' Rethymno - Georgioupolis Sector
### (Sketch-map no. 30)

**415.** From 1300 hrs until 2000 hrs, on May 23, Rethymno was heavily bombed. During this bombardment, the barracks and the town hospitals were destroyed, together with other buildings, although the hospitals had visible Red Cross signs on their facades.

An unsuccessful attack was launched by the Rethymno Group against the fortified German forces at Agios Georgios.

In the Airfield Group, there was a three-hour cease-fire between the Germans and the Australians, in order to bury the dead. During this interval, the Commander of the German troops at the village of Stavromenos, asked for the surrender of the Australians, employing the argument that, the German successes at Maleme and Agyia had rendered their position hopeless. Colonel Campbell rejected the proposal.

In the morning of May 24, a Scout company, supported by an Artillery platoon which came from Hania, failed to break through the German positions in the area of Perivolia village and returned to Hania.

At 0800 hrs, on May 24, the German forces in the area of Agios Georgios, attacked the Rethymno Group. This German attack, that lasted until 1400 hrs, was finally repulsed with success by the defending Greek troops of that area and the Germans were forced to return to their line of departure.

## The C' Iraklio Sector
### (Sketch-map no. 31 )

**416.** In the morning of May 23, inhabitants of Iraklio town reported to the Military Commander, Major General Michael Linardakis that relatives of theirs (mostly women and children) had been taken prisoners by the Germans, who used them as a screen during their offensive operations for the occupation of Iraklio.

After this, the Garrison Commander of Iraklio, Major Emmanuel Tsangarakis, was ordered to meet with the Commander of the local German forces. He would request that the women and children should be released, or otherwise he would retaliate against the German prisoners.

The German Commander accepted the Greek proposal, but demanded the surrender of the town within two hours. The Military

Commander of Iraklio rejected the proposal without further discussion and ordered the continuation of the defence 'to the last'.

On May 23 and 24, the town of Iraklio was severely bombed and entire blocks were completely destroyed. The troops supply in bread, food and water became problematic, because of the destruction of the bakeries and the water network. Ammunition was exhausted, while the troops were considerably worn down by the incessant fighting.

Subsequently it was decided the replacement of the Greek troops with British. Thus begun the relief of the Greek troops to the area of Knossos-Spilia for re-organisation, which was carried out during the night of May 24 to 25.

### The Continuation of the German Attack
### (May 25 to 27, 1941)
### The A' Maleme - Agyia and Hania - Souda Sector
### (Sketch-map no. 29)

**417.** At 1400 hrs, on May 25, after a fierce air bombardment, the 100th German Mountain Regiment attacked the village of Galatas and seized it.

During that night, troops from the 23rd New Zealand Battalion, the 6th Greek Infantry Regiment along with armed civilians, managed to re-occupy Galatas village after a hard fight. However, this success was merely of local importance. It simply provided the defenders with a small time gain and nothing more, since the heights to the west and south of the village were still firmly held by the Germans.

The 8th Greek Infantry Regiment and the groups of armed villagers that were fighting on the line Alykianos-Vatolakos, confronted the 85th German Mountain Regiment with success for the whole day of May 25. However, due to lack of ammunition and food, they withdrew south-eastwards. After two days they arrived at Drakones village, where they were informed of the collapse of the Hania-Souda Sector and the withdrawal of those forces to Sfakia. After this, they did not have any escape route, and a lot of men were forced to take refuge in the surrounding mountains, while the Regiment Commander moved to Hania, accompanied by approximately 20 officers and 80 soldiers, and surrendered there to the German authorities, on May 29.

The total casualties of the Regiment were: 2 officers (one of which was the New Zealand liaison), 2 cadets (platoon leaders) and 60 enlisted men killed in action, and 4 officers and about 20 soldiers wounded.

**418.** Meanwhile, on May 25, the II/85 Battalion also landed at Maleme airfield, and linked up with its regiment.

At 2100 hrs, on the same day, the Commander of the German Forces, General Ringel, issued his orders for the next day, which, in general, dictated the continuation of the operation eastwards with the Assault Regiment in the north, the 100th Regiment in the centre and the 3rd Para Regiment south of Galatas.

**419.** The Commander of the British-Greek forces, Major General Freyberg, being unaware, due to lack of communications, of the precise development of the situation, remained under the impression that on the night of May 25, the area was still being held. Nevertheless, he considered that, in case of a break through, the question would no longer be how to hold on to Crete, but, rather, how his troops would survive disaster and captivity.

At midnight on May 25 to 26, he received a report of the Commander of the 2nd New Zealand Division, briefing him on the critical nature of the situation at the Galatas area, as well as about, the decision of the Division Commander to withdraw his troops to a new area west of Kladissos river. Major General Freyberg approved the withdrawal of the Division forces, which was carried out during that same night. At the same time, he ordered the unification of the 2nd New Zealand Division Sector with the Souda Sector, assigning responsibility to the Commander of the MNBDO Group, Major General Weston, as well as the reinforcement of the new line with forces from the Souda Sector. To that end, a new "Brigade" (called Combined Battalion) was organised, from the 1st Welsh Battalion and the Akrotiri Group (1st Rangers Battalion and Northumberland Hussars), under the orders of the 4th New Zealand Brigade Commander. The command of the 4th New Zealand Brigade was assigned to the Commander of the 10th New Zealand Brigade, Colonel Kippenberger, who had been left without troops. The above Joint Brigade would replace the 5th New Zealand Brigade on the evening of May 26. The personnel of the Souda Services, that was not part of the battle force, was ordered to move towards Sfakia.

In the end, however, these command replacements were not carried out. Thus, the Commander of the 4th New Zealand Brigade remained at his position, while Colonel Kippenberger assumed command of the 20th New Zealand Battalion (4th New Zealand Brigade), of which he had also been in command during the fighting in mainland Greece.

At 0200 hrs on May 26, Major General Freyberg reported to the Middle East Headquarters that, he had serious doubts about their ability to hold the Germans on the new line of defence, and at 09:30 hrs of the same day, with a new report he requested permission to evacuate Crete.

**420.** The German attacks against the positions of the 2nd New Zealand Division began on the morning of May 26. After a hard fight, the Germans managed to occupy Efthimi village with the Assault Regiment, Daratso village with the l00th Mountain Regiment and Perivolia and Galaria villages with the 3rd Para Regiment.

During the early night hours, the 3rd Para Regiment arrived at the village of Mournies, thus threatening to envelop the positions of the 2nd New Zealand Division from the south.

Facing this new situation, the Commander of the 2nd New Zealand Division requested that the 5th New Zealand and the l9th Australian Brigades be placed in a new area, east of the Hania-Nerokouros road. The Commander of the Cretan Forces did not approve of that proposal of the Division Commander and ordered that the 5th New Zealand Brigade be relieved by the Combined Battalion, and that the area of Mournies should be secured by the l9th Australian Brigade. The Commander of the 2nd New Zealand Division was not notified of the above decision and being unable to re-establish the liaison which had been cut off, decided to withdraw to the new position, where the Division deployed defensively between 0300 hrs and 0400 hrs on May 27.

The right (north) of the new defensive line was occupied by the l9th Australian Brigade and the left (south) by the 5th New Zealand Brigade.

The Headquarters of the 2nd New Zealand Division and the 4th New Zealand Brigade were established at Stylos village.

The Combined Battalion, under the orders of the Commander of the lst Welsh Battalion was deployed at the previous positions of the 5th New Zealand Brigade, with its flanks left completely without cover.

The Base Battalion of Hania was ordered to move from the town of Hania to the area of Katsifariana, in order to cover the Hania-Souda road from the west.

This was carried out as planned.

**421.** During the same day, the 141st German Mountain Regiment (minus battalion), the remaining troops of the 95th Reconnaissance Group, the heavy weapons of the l00th Mountain Regiment and the rest of the 95th Artillery Regiment landed in the area of Maleme.

The disposition of the German forces, on the night of May 26, was as follows, from north to south: The Assault Regiment, from the coast to the northern fringes of Daratsos village. The l00th Mountain Regiment, from the northern fringes of Daratsos to the Alikyanos-Hania road. The 3rd Para Regiment astride the Alikyanos-Hania road. The 141st Mountain Regiment in the area of the Galaria and Perivolia villages and lastly, the 85th

Mountain Regiment from the Perivolia village to the Ravine of Mourianos river.

On May 27, the German plan provided an attack against Hania with the Assault Regiment, the 100th Mountain Regiment, the 3rd Para Regiment and the 141st Mountain Regiment, aiming at the immobilisation of the British forces. To the south of the 141st Mountain Regiment, would operate the 85th Mountain Regiment towards Stylos and Megala, in order to cut off the retreat routes of the British forces. The 95th Reconnaissance Group would be operating towards Neo Horio, covering the right flank of the whole disposition.

**422.** At approximately 0100 hrs, on May 27 British warships sailed into Souda harbour and the A' and D' Raiding Battalions (750 men approximately) disembarked. The ships sailed, after boarding approximately 930 men, incapable of fighting.

Major General Weston, Commander of the Hania-Souda Sector, deployed a force of 200 men from the A' Raiding Battalion in Souda, in order to protect the town and the docks. The rest of the A' Raiding battalion (of company strength) deployed in the area of Beritiana in order to cover the road to Sfakia and the entire D' Raiding Battalion in the area Hani Babali, in order to hold the Germans in case the defence at Beritiana collapsed.

**423.** On the morning of May 27, the Germans began their attack against the positions of the Combined Battalion with troops from the Assault Regiment and the 100th Mountain Regiment. By that afternoon, the Combined Battalion dispersed. Out of its 1,300 men, 350 fled towards Sfakia, while the rest were either killed or taken prisoners along with their Commander.

Subsequently, the German troops entered Hania at 18:00 hrs. The Mayor surrendered the town to the Commander of the 100th Mountain Regiment.

Further to the south, the 141st Mountain Regiment arrived at the road Hania-Nerokouros, having been delayed for over an hour by the Base Battalion of Hania. There, a fierce counter-attack by the 5th and 19th Brigades forced it to withdraw two kilometres, having lost about 300 men.

**424.** Meanwhile, the Commanders of the above Brigades, having realised that German troops had infiltrated their uncovered southern flank, and that they were running the risk of being cut off, they withdrew their troops, on the night of May 27 to 28, to the areas Stylos and Neo Horio respectively.

The 4th New Zealand Brigade, that had already withdrawn to the area of Stylos village, was ordered at 1000 hrs, on May 27, to move to the valley of Askyfos, in order to repulse possible parachute drops in that area and to cover the road from Vrysses village to Georgioupolis.

The Commander of the German forces, believing that the British were withdrawing towards Rethymno, oriented the bulk of his forces in that direction. Thus, while the Germans were moving towards Rethymno, the British forces of Western Crete, along with the representatives of the Greek Government[1] were directed towards Sfakia.

At 1550 hrs, on May 27, the order of the Commander-in-Chief of the Middle East was received, whereby the evacuation of Crete was approved. Major General Freyberg tried at once to notify the Rethymno Garrison accordingly, but having been unable to communicate with it, requested that it should be informed directly by the Middle East Headquarters. That did not happen.

The Garrison of Iraklio had been directly notified by the Middle East Headquarters.

### The B' Rethymno - Georgioupolis Sector
### (Sketch-map no. 30)

**425.** The Commander of the Airfield Group, Lieutenant Colonel Campbell, decided to launch a final attack on May 26, in order to recapture the village of Stavromenos. The attack was conducted by the 5th Greek Infantry Regiment and Australian troops and was totally successful. One hundred Germans were taken prisoners, including 42 wounded, and considerable quantities of weapons, clothing items and communications equipment were seized.

The Rethymno Group, on both May 25 and May 26, continued to occupy its positions west and south of Perivolia village and to harass the Germans with patrols.

On May 27, the Germans attacked unsuccessfully the Gendarmerie company in the area of Kastelakia.

---

[1]   King George and Prime Minister Emm. Tsouderos had already departed for Alexandria in Egypt on the night of May 23 to 24, from the bay of Agia Roumeli, with the British destroyer 'DECOY'.

## The C' Iraklio Sector
### (Sketch-map no. 31)

**426.** In the morning of May 25, the German airforce resumed the bombing and afterwards, the German forces, west of the town, attacked Iraklio. The attack mainly aimed at engaging as many British units as possible, in order to weaken the Airfield Group, which constituted the main objective. The attack was repulsed by the defending British forces in the area. In the evening on the same day, the German troops moved eastwards, in order to link up with the troops situated on the east of the airfield.

Meanwhile, a British battalion that arrived from Tymbaki, after a fighting, entered the defensive and occupied the positions of the 2nd Leicester Battalion, which became a reserve of the Commander of the 14th British Brigade.

On the same day, the Headquarters of the 2nd Military Command of Crete moved from Spilia to Arhanes, where there existed a telephone centre. On the night of May 25 to 26, the 3rd Greek Regiment arrived for reorganisation and re-supply. The above forces were reorganised into two regiments, of one thousand men each, under the orders of the Commander of the III Military Department, Colonel Papathanassopoulos.

**427.** The German troops that moved eastwards, after bypassing the weak Greek resistance south of Iraklio, attacked, at 0700 hrs on May 26, and seized the hill of Prophitis Elias which had been defended by a platoon of the 2/4 Australian Battalion. A counter-attack to recapture the hill, launched by forces of the 7th Greek Regiment, failed.

Thus, the German forces in the Sector of Iraklio, joined in the area east of the airfield and began to prepare for attack, which was decided to be launched in the evening of May 29. On the following day, May 27, the German forces were reinforced with one additional battalion, which had landed at Gournes and continued the preparations for the attack upon the airfield.

Furthermore, the Commander of the Iraklio Sector did not notify his troops of the evacuation order. Instead, he ordered the conduct of offensive operation, where it was considered necessary, in order to improve the unit positions.

## The Collapse of the Defense and the Evacuation of the Island
### (May 28 until June 1, 1941)
### The A' Maleme - Agyia and Hania - Souda Sectors
(Sketch-map no. 28)

**428.** During the early morning hours of May 28, the Commander of the Cretan Forces, Major General Freyberg, according to the evacuation instructions, received from the Middle East Headquarters, issued an order to Major General Weston, whereby all details concerning the evacuation were being dealt with.

The evacuation would be carried out from the shores of Sfakia and Loutro at the following pace.

| | |
|---|---|
| - On the night of May 28/29 | 1,000 men |
| - On the night of May 29/30 | 6,000 men |
| - On the night of May 30/31 | 3,000 men |
| - On the night of May 31/June 1 | 3,000 men |

General Weston was assigned as commander in charge for the evacuation of all troops from the former Sectors of Maleme-Agyia and Hania-Souda. He issued the necessary orders on the afternoon of May 28.

According to these orders, the 4th New Zealand Brigade would have to retain its positions at the southern entrance of the Askyfos valley until May 29, whereupon it would withdraw to the embarkation coast. The 19th Australian Brigade on the morning of May 29, would have to occupy defence positions on Vitalokoumos hill (2 kms north-east of Sfakia). The Raiding units (A' and D' Battalions) would have to be defensively established in order to cover the road, east of the ravine, at Komitades village. The 5th New Zealand Brigade would have to move to the embarkation areas, except for the 23rd Battalion, which would remain under the command of the 4th Brigade at the positions it already held.

At 2200 hrs, on May 28, four warships sailed into the harbour of Sfakia and approximately 1100 men, including 230 wounded, embarked.

**429.** In the meantime, the Commander of the German Forces in Crete, Major General Ringel, being still unaware of the withdrawal of the British forces southwards, continued to move the bulk of his forces towards Rethymno and only part of the 100th Mountain Regiment advanced southwards, in order to mop up the road to Sfakia.

The 5th New Zealand Brigade continued to move towards the coast, where it concentrated its forces on the morning of May 30. The 4th New Zealand Brigade began to withdraw concurrently with the 23rd Battalion, thus revealing the defence area of the 19th Australian Brigade as well as of one motorised section, that were situated in the north of Imvros village.

At 2230 hrs on May 29, eight warships sailed into Sfakia and approximately 6,000 men, including 550 wounded, embarked. This convoy, that sailed away at 0320 hrs, on May 30, included the Commander of the 2nd New Zealand Division and his Headquarters.

**430.** At 0500 hrs on May 30, German troops from the 100th Mountain Regiment attacked the motorised section north of Imvros village. This section, after delaying the Germans until that afternoon, moved behind the positions of the 19th Australian Brigade. The German troops continued their attack against the 19th Australian Brigade, without success. After this, the Commander of the 100th Mountain Regiment ordered enveloping movements from the mountains and abandoned the frontal attack.

On the night of May 30 to 31, only 2 destroyers sailed into Sfakia, out of the 4 which had set off for the same purpose. They sailed away at 0300 hrs on May 31, with approximately 1,500 men from the 4th and 5th New Zealand Brigades. On two hydroplanes, the representatives of the Greek Government and the Commander of the Cretan Forces, Major General Freyberg, also departed for Egypt. The latter, before leaving, had assigned the command of the entire Cretan Force to Major General Weston.

**431.** During the day, of May 31st, the Germans did not attempt a new attack, but merely harassed with their fire the positions of the 19th Australian Brigade and the A' and D' Raiding Battalions.

At approximately 2320 hrs, 4 warships sailed into Sfakia carrying approximately 4,050 men of the remaining units of the 5th New Zealand Brigade, the 2/8 Australian Battalion, the Commander of the 19th Australian Brigade with his Staff and some Greek and British men from other units.

Meanwhile, Major General Weston gave a written order to Lieutenant Colonel Colvin, whereby, the troops that were unable to leave, were being permitted to capitulate with the Germans. During the same night, Major General Weston and the Commander of the 5th New Zealand Brigade abandoned Crete by hydroplane.

**432.** The troops of the 100th Mountain Regiment became aware, for the first time, that the bulk of the British forces was situated opposite them, on the coast of Sfakia, on the morning of June 1st.

Subsequently, two battalions of the 100th Mountain Regiment advanced towards the coast, supported by the airforce and one gun. However, this action of the Germans was by then pointless, since white flags had been raised and the allied forces that were isolated on the coast, surrendered, except for a few hundreds that fled to the mountains and were hospitably received by the villagers. Until September 1941, 600 men of the entire strength of the British Forces on Crete, fled to the Middle East. The prisoners were driven to prisoner camps, which were organised in the area of Maleme and in the children's summer camps of Hania.

## The B' Rethymno - Georgioupolis Sector
### (Sketch-map no. 30)

**433.** On May 28, the command of the Rethymno Group was informed of the collapse of the defence in the Hania Sector, the withdrawal of the British forces to Sfakia and the departure of the King and the Government from Crete.

This information naturally caused a great decline in the morale of the fighting troops and the population, since new German forces could arrive at the area from the direction of Hania. Subsequently, the view that capitulation was necessary began to prevail, in order to avoid futile loss and destruction.

On the night of May 29 to 30, a German motorised detachment, under the command of Major Witman (Witman Detachment), entered and seized Rethymno without encountering any resistance. Gendarmerie Troops, armed civilian groups and certain groups of soldiers from the Base Battalion deployed east of Rethymno for a final confrontation with the Germans, but were forced to surrender after a brief fighting.

**434.** The Commanders of the 4th and 5th Greek Regiments of the Airfield Group were informed on the evening of May 29, of the collapse of the defence in Western Crete and of the approach of German forces to Rethymno from the direction of Hania, as well as of the Rethymno Group Commander's decision to capitulate. Thus, lacking food and ammunition, they considered that any further fighting would be pointless and the sacrifices futile. Therefore, at 2200 hrs, on May 29, they decided to withdraw to Adele village and Arkadi, respectively. There, the 5th Greek Regiment disbanded, the men who were natives of Crete returned to their villages and the rest were allocated to various communities. The personnel of the 4th Greek Regiment surrendered to the Germans, according to the decision of the Regiment Commander.

The Commander of the Pigi Airfield, Lieutenant Colonel Campbell, being unaware of the order to evacuate the island, issued orders for the continuation of the fight. At midday, on May 30, he finally realised that he was encircled from all directions and that any defence attempt would be futile. Thus, he decided to surrender along with his units. The Commander of the 2/11 Battalion left free choice to his officers and soldiers. Some of them surrendered while others followed him to the mountains where they took refuge. The remainder of the Australian Force surrendered to the Germans along with the Group Commander.

## The C' Iraklio Sector
### (Sketch-map no. 31)

**435.** In the morning of May 28, Brigadier Chapel communicated the order for the evacuation from the harbour of Iraklio, during a meeting with the commanders of the British units (the Greeks were not invited to join them and remained uninformed until the end). By night, the British troops began to move towards the harbour, as planned. At 2330 hrs, 2 cruisers and 6 destroyers sailed in and the British embarked. The ships sailed to Egypt at approximately 0330 hrs, on May 29, without attracting the attention of the Germans.

The Greek troops remained at their positions on May 28, without attempting any action. On the night of May 28 to 29, they were informed of the occupation of Hania and Souda by the Germans and of the flight of the British to Sfakia, while on the morning of May 29, they discovered that the British troops of the Iraklio Sector had also evacuated the area. Subsequently, they decided to call a truce.

On the morning of May 29, German reconnaissance patrols that moved towards the British perimeter encountered no resistance in the town area nor at the airfield. Thus, the German forces moved and seized the airfield and the town of Iraklio, while the German command was established at the barracks of the 43rd Infantry Regiment.

On May 30, Major General Linardakis met, at the camp of the 43rd Infantry Regiment, with the German Commander, Colonel Brauer, in order to sign the truce. At approximately 2215 hrs, he issued orders concerning the deposition and concentration of weapons, except for those troops guarding the Italian prisoners until the latter were delivered to the Germans. These orders were addressed to the army troops and Police Authorities of the Prefecture of Iraklio and Lasithi.

**436.** In the meantime, in the afternoon of that same day, the Witman Detachment also arrived at Iraklio. This Detachment, after encountering the troops of Colonel Brauer in that area, continued its movement and reached Ierapetra by the same evening, where it met with an Italian regiment which had landed there on May 28, from the Dodecanese, by approval of the Commander of the IV Air Force, Air Marshal Lore.

On May 31, the Greek troops were re-located at Peza village. As of June 1, by order of the German Command, two companies were re-stationed at Iraklio, while the remaining strength moved to the plain of Messara, accompanied by a few officers. The other officers remained at Peza and Arhanes and as of June 9 they were transported by motor vehicle to the prison of Maleme and the children's summer camps in Hania, where prisoners from the Cretan forces had been concentrated. From June 20 until the end of November, the Greek prisoners were gradually released. The officers, soldiers and armed civilians, that fled to the mountains, later formed resistance forces throughout Crete, helping the allied struggle with their own struggles and sacrifices.

**437.** Thus, after a ten day struggle, the battle of Crete ended with the German victory. The losses were extremely heavy on both sides and were as follows[1] :

- Greeks: Killed in action (verified) 336 and a large number of wounded and prisoners.

- British: Killed in action 1,742 , wounded 1,737 and prisoners 11,835 . Furthermore, 2 cruisers and 6 destroyers were sunk and more than 2,000 officers and sailors were recorded missing.

- Germans: Killed in action 1,990 , missing 1,955 and a large number of wounded. In total, the casualties of the elite corps of German paratroopers exceeded 8,000 men. Regarding the aircraft 220 of them destroyed completely and approximately 150 were seriously damaged. This discouraged the Germans from daring to attempt another operation of this kind until the end of the war.

### A General Review of the Battle of Crete

**438.** The events related in the two previous chapters (VII and VIII), cover the period from May 20 to June 1, 1941, which is known as the BATTLE OF CRETE. The following constitutes a summary of the above described events.

---

[1]   Brigadier Stylianos Kallonas, 'The Battle of Crete' p. 72.
Publishing Dpt/AGS, 'Military History Topics' p. 361.
L. MCD. G. Stewart, 'The Battle of Crete' Part B', p. 372

With the beginning of the Greek - Italian War, the responsibility for the security of Crete was assumed by Britain, by agreement with the Greek Government, due to the geo-political position and the strategic importance of the island for the British interests in the Middle East. The V Division, which had been stationed at Crete until then, was mobilised and transferred to mainland Greece, where it was employed in the Albanian Theatre of Operations.

**439.** At the end of April 1941, the Command of the British Greek Forces on Crete was assigned to the Commander of the 2nd New Zealand Division, Major General Freyberg. Until then, no final plans had been drawn for the defence of the island and the preparations for the confrontation of a serious enemy invasion had made very little progress, although the German attack was considered to be imminent. The entire military strength of Crete, after being reinforced with forces that were transferred from mainland Greece, consisted of approximately 11,500 Greeks and 31,500 British, but they lacked in armament, since the weapons, ammunition and other supplies were significantly below the acceptable rates. Furthermore, there was no airforce on the island, while the available guns and tanks were totally inadequate.

Upon assuming command of the Cretan Forces, Major General Freyberg examined the situation and requested from the Middle East Commander-in-Chief that, guns, ammunition, and other supplies and equipment should be immediately sent, and air and naval support should be provided. Unfortunately, less than half of the supplies sent to the island arrived there, due to the action of the enemy airforce.

The forces of Crete were allocated to the Maleme, Hania, Rethymno and Iraklio Sectors, based on the importance and vulnerability of the strategic points of the island. Their mission was to defend the island and deny to the enemy the use of its airfields and harbours.

**440.** Hitler had focused his attention on the island of Crete long before Germany manifested its intentions to attack against Greece. He believed that by occupying Crete he would secure a rapid success in the Eastern Mediterranean, and that the attack upon the island ought to be conducted by airborne action.

Thus, on April 25, 1941, the Directive No. 28 was issued, under the code name "MERCURY", regarding the operation to occupy Crete.

The entire German strength engaged in the attack upon Crete amounted to 22,750 men, 1,370 aircraft and 70 ships. The operation was also supported by a small number of Italian destroyers and torpedo boats, while a reinforced Italian regiment, by request of Mussolini, was to land on the coast of the island from the Dodecanese. This operation was eventually carried out in the end of May, when the fate of the island had already been decided.

**441.** The German assault from air upon Crete began on the morning of May 20. After a heavy bombardment, numerous flights of transport aircraft began to drop parachutists in the area of Hania-Maleme. Simultaneously, gliders began to land, carrying airborne troops. A fierce struggle followed, during which the Germans managed to establish a small bridgehead east of Tavronitis river and to place the Maleme airfield and hill 107 under their fire. That hill was the vital area of 2nd New Zealand Division. After this, the New Zealand forces abandoned hill 107 on the night of May 20 to 21 and withdrew further to the south-east.

   In the areas of Rethymno and Iraklio the German attack broke out in the afternoon of the same day. The paratroopers in these areas suffered extremely heavy casualties and were unable to record any success.

**442.** Major General Freyberg, unaware of the critical situation which had arisen in the Maleme Sector, due to untimely briefing by the Commander of the 5th New Zealand Brigade, intervened belatedly to regain control of the area. Thus, the counter-attack, that was launched at 0330 hrs on May 22 in order to recapture Maleme airfield failed.

   After the failure of the above counter-attack and the advance of the German forces, that were constantly reinforced in the north-east, the British-Greek forces in the area withdrew to a new defensive line further east, on the night of May 23 to 24.

   Since that day, the initiative for the operations had been passed to the Germans, while the fate of the island had by then been decided. Nevertheless, hard fighting continued, with the active participation of the islanders, until May 29, whereupon the British forces began to evacuate Crete. The evacuation of the greatest part of the British forces finished at 2320 hrs, on May 31. Those British who remained on the island, as well as the Greek troops there, capitulated to the Germans or sought refuge in mountainous areas, and later fled to the Middle East.

   Thus, after a ten day struggle, the Battle of Crete ended with the German victory, despite the bravery displayed by the British-Greek forces and the stubborn resistance of the Cretan people, whose courage, valour and spirit of self-sacrifice were unsurpassable and attracted the admiration of both the Greeks and all their Allies.

   This victory, was however, very costly and, the Germans did not dare another such operation until the end of the war. Crete, as the Commander of the XI German Corps, Air Vice Marshal Student was forced to admit, became 'the Tomb of the German Parachutists'.

# TABLES

## TABLE I

### Casualties (Killed, Wounded, Missing in action, Prisoners, non combat casualties) during the Greek-Italian and Greek-German War 1940-1941

| Casualties | Regular officers | Officers — Regular officers of the Reserve | Reserve officers | Officers Total | Enlisted Men | Total |
|---|---|---|---|---|---|---|
| Killed in action | 313 | 34 | 342 | 689 | 12,636 | 13,325 |
| Wounded | 476 | 53 | 955 | 1,484 | 61,179 | 62,663[1] |
| Missing | 23 | 2 | 28 | 53 | 1,237[2] | 1,290 |
| Prisoners of war (on the Battle Field) | 60 | 6 | 35 | 101[3] | 2,364[4] | 2,465 |
| | | | | | | |
| Total | 872 | 95 | 1,360 | 2,327 | 77,416 | 79,743 |

Notes
(1) Includes approximately 25, 000 frostbite cases.
(2) Missing soldiers during the Greek-Italian War. There are no substantiated facts on the German - Greek War.
(3) In Germany 14 and in Italy 87
(4) In Germany 59 and in Italy 2, 305.

## TABLE 2

### Formation's Commands and Headquarters during the Greek-Italian and Greek-German War 1940-1941[1]

#### GENERAL HEADQUARTERS

| 28-10-40 | Commander in Chief | LtGen Alexandros Papagos |
|---|---|---|
| | Chief of General HQ | MajGen Paraschos Melissinos |
| | A' Deputy Chief of Gen. HQ | MajGen Ioannis Striber |
| | B' Deputy Chief of Gen. HQ | MajGen Christos Karassos until 11-2-41 |

#### HEADQUARTERS

28-10-40      Athens

---

[1] Occasional voids in the Commands are due to lack of accurate data pertaining to the matter.

## WESTERN  MACEDONIA  FIELD  ARMY  SECTION[1]
### COMMAND

| 28-10-40 | Commander | LtGen Ioannis Pitsikas until 8-3-41 |
| | | LtGen Georgios Tsolakoglou until  17-4-41 |
| | Chief of staff | Col. (INF) Spyridon Georgoulis  until  8-3-41 |
| | | Col (Cav) Athanasios Chryssohoou |

### HEADQUARTERS

| 28-10-40 | Kastoria | 14- 4-41 | Grevena |
| 30- 1-40 | Koritsa | 15- 4-41 | Kastraki  (3kms NW of Kalambaka) |
| 13- 6-41 | Kastoria | 17- 4-41 | Votonossi (6kms W of Metsovo) |

## CENTRAL MACEDONIA FIELD ARMY SECTION [2]
### COMMAND

| 6- 3-41 | Commander | LtGen of the Reserve Ioannis Kotoulas  until 8-4-41 |
| | | MajGen Christos Karassos |
| | Chief of Staff | Col (ARTY) Antonios Peppas  until 19-3-41 |
| | | Col (ARTY) Konst. Papadopoulos |

### HEADQUARTERS

| 6- 3-41 | Kozani | 16-4-41 | Ioannina |
| 9- 4-41 | Perdikas (33kms SE of Florina) | 18-4-41 | Metsovo |
| 14- 4-41 | Kivotos (lOkms SW of Siatista) | | |

## EPIRUS FIELD ARMY SECTION[3]
### COMMAND

| 14-2-41 | Commander | LtGen Markos Drakos until 8-3-41 |
| | | LtGen Ioannis Pitsikas until 20-4-41 |
| | | LtGen Georgios Tsolakoglou |
| | Chief of Staff | Col (ARTY) Konstantinos Platis until 20-4-41 |
| | | Col (ARTY) Konst. Papadopoulos |

---

[1] On 17-4-41 it was renamed as C' Army Corps subordinate to the EFAS.
[2] It began its establishment on 6-3-41.
[3] Established on 14-2-41.

## HEADQUARTERS

14- 2-41     Ioannina

## EASTERN MACEDONIA FIELD ARMY SECTION
### (Kavala Field Army Section until November 1940)
### COMMAND

| | | |
|---|---|---|
| 28-10-40 | Commander | LtGen Markos Drakos until 7-2-41 |
| | | LtGen Konstantinos Bakopoulos |
| | Chief of Staff | Col. (INF ) Kleanthis Boulalas  until 19-12-40 |
| | | Col (ARTY) Theodoros Grigoropoulos until 7-2-41 |
| | | Col (ARTY) Panagiotis Kalogeropoulos |

## HEADQUARTERS

28-10-40     Serres          8-2-41     Thessaloniki

## THRACE FIELD ARMY SECTION[1]
### COMMAND

| | | |
|---|---|---|
| 8- 2-41 | Commander | Reserve LtGen Ioannis Kotoulas until 6-3-41 |
| | Chief of Staff | Col. (ARTY) Antonios Peppas |

## HEADQUARTERS

8- 2-41     Alexandroupolis

## A' ARMY CORPS
### COMMAND

| | | |
|---|---|---|
| 28-10-40 | Commander | LtGen Panagiotis Demestihas until 10-12-40 |
| | | LtGen Georgios Kosmas until 5-3-41 |
| | | LtGen Panagiotis Demestihas |
| | Chief of Staff | Col (INF) Thomas Pentzopoulos until 15-3-41 |
| | | Col (ARTY) Georgios Vagenas |

---

[1] It was established on 8-2-41, from the E' Army High Command. It ceased to exist on 6-3-41, when its units were placed at the disposal of the CMFAS or disbanded .

## HEADQUARTERS

| | | | |
|---|---|---|---|
| 28-10-40 | Athens | 12-12-40 | Delvinaki |
| 5-11-40 | Kalambaka | 23-12-40 | Dervitsani |
| 15-11-40 | Votonossi (6kms W of Metsovon) | 22-04-41 | Elea(Kalpaki) |
| 28-11-40 | Zitsa (17kms SE of Doliana) | 24-04-41 | Philippiada |

## B' ARMY CORPS
### COMMAND

28-10-40     Commander        LtGen Dimitrios Papadopoulos until 5-3-41
MajGen Georgios Bakos
Chief of Staff   Col (INF) Dimitrios Mahas  until 21-3-41
Col (INF) Thrasivoulos Tsakalotos

## HEADQUARTERS

| | | | |
|---|---|---|---|
| 28-10-40 | Larissa | 16-02-41 | Bandiloyia (5kms SE of Premeti) |
| 30-10-40 | Kozani | 7-04-41 | Vassiliko (8kms S of Mertzani bridge) |
| 12-11-40 | Siatista | 19-04-41 | Protopappas (12kms W of Moschopolis) |
| 21-11-40 | Eptahori | | |
| 16-12-40 | Premeti | | |

## C' ARMY CORPS[1]
### COMMAND

28-10-40     Commander     LtGen Georgios Tsolakoglou
Chief of Staff    Col. (Cav) Athanassios Chrissohoou

## HEADQUARTERS

| | | | |
|---|---|---|---|
| 28-10-40 | Thessaloniki | 30-11-40 | Koritsa |
| 31-10-40 | Florina (Skopia) | 12-04-41 | Kastoria |
| 10-11-40 | Kastoria | 13-04-41 | Grevena |
| 27-11-40 | Kristallopigi (30 kms SW of Florina) | | |
| 15-04-41 | Kastraki (3kms NW of Kalambaka) | | |
| 17-04-41 | Votonosi  (6kms  of Metsovo) | | |

---

[1] On 8-3-41 it was renamed as WMFAS and on 17-4-41 renamed again C' Army Corps .

## D' ARMY CORPS[1]
### COMMAND

| | | |
|---|---|---|
| 28-10-40 | Commander | LtGen Georgios Kosmas until 18-11-40 |
| | | MajGen Christos Zoiopoulos until 1-1-41 |
| | | LtGen Konstantinos Bakopoulos until 8-2-41 |
| | Chief of Staff | Col (ARTY) Georgios Vagenas until 17-11-40 |
| | | LtCol (INF) Dimitrios Ploumis until 20-1-41 |
| | | Col (ARTY) Panagiotis Kalogeropoulos |

### HEADQUARTERS

28-10-40    Kavala

## E' ARMY CORPS (Thrace)[2]
### COMMAND

| | | |
|---|---|---|
| 28-10-40 | Commander | LtGen Konstantinos Bakopoulos until 15-12-40 |
| | Chief of Staff | Col (ARTY) Panagiotis Kalogeropoulos |

### HEADQUARTERS

28-10-40    Alexandroupolis

## E' ARMY CORPS (Albanian Theater of Operations)
### (Group 'K' until 15-12-40)[2]
### COMMAND

| | | |
|---|---|---|
| 19-11-40 | Commander | LtGen Georgios Kosmas until 9-12-40 |
| | | LtGen Panagiotis Demestihas 5-03-41 |
| | Chief of Staff | Col (ARTY) Georgios Vagenas |

### HEADQUARTERS

20-11-40 Nestori                              30-1-41 Darda (15 kms SE of Korytsa)
27-11-40 Bobostitsa (6Kms S of Koritsa) 8-2-41 Poptsisti (10 kms NW of Moschopolis)

---

[1] Its Headquarters disbanded on 8-2-41 and its units because subording to the EMFAS.
[2] Its Headquarters disbanded on 8-2-41 and its units became subordinate to the EMFAS.
[2] It ceased to exist on 15-2-41
[3] Group 'K' was established on 19-11-40.

## BOROVA DIVISION GROUP
### (Combat Group from 12-4-41 until 24-4-41)
### COMMAND

12-4-41    Commander    MajGen Christos Zoiopoulos
          Chief of Staff   LtCol (ARTY) Stilianos Manidakis

### HEADQUARTERS

| | | | |
|---|---|---|---|
| 13-4-41 | Stika (11 kms N of Erseka) | 21-4-41 | Konitsa |
| 17-4-41 | Bezani (12kms NE of Erseka) | 22-4-41 | Asprangelos |
| 19-4-41 | Leskoviki | | |

## EMFAS DIVISION GROUP
### COMMAND

28-10-40   Commander           LtGen Panagiotis Dedes
           Chief of Staff        Col (INF) Sotirios Stergiopoulos

### HEADQUARTERS

| | | |
|---|---|---|
| 28-10-40 | Sidirokastron | 10-11-40    Himaros |
| 4-11-40 | Lahanas | |

## I DIVISION
### COMMAND

28-10-40   Commander    MajGen Vasilios Vrahnos
           Chief of Staff   LtCol (ARTY) Michael Spiropoulos   until 20-1-41
                            LtCol (INF) Stefanos Katsimitros

### HEADQUARTERS

| | |
|---|---|
| 28-10-40 | Larissa |
| 1-11-40 | Eptahori |
| 20-11-40 | Fourka (11kms W of Leskoviki) |
| 25-11-40 | Koutsoufliani (26kms SW of Kalambaka) |
| 29-11-40 | Pestani (15 kms E of Premeti) |
| 8-12-40 | Premeti |
| 22-12-40 | Mokritsa (8kms N of Premeti) |
| 31-12-40 | Pakomiti (9kms NW of Premeti) |
| 23-01-41 | Roden (10kms N of Klissoura) |
| 2-04-41 | Sleousa |
| 11-04-41 | Leskoviki |

| | |
|---|---|
| 16-04-41 | Kambassi (6kms NE of Leskoviki) |
| 19-04-41 | Konitsa |
| 21-04-41 | Slati |
| 23-04-41 | Anthohori |
| 26-04-41 | Anilion (S of Metsovo) |
| 30-04-41 | Metsovo |

## II DIVISION
### COMMAND

28-10-40   Commander  MajGen Georgios Lavdas
Col (INF) Dimitrios Christodoulidis  until 20-1-41
LtCol (INF) Georgios Grivas

### HEADQUARTERS

| | | | |
|---|---|---|---|
| 28-10-40 | Athens | 1- 1-41 | Erindi |
| 4-11-40 | Kalambaka | 15- 2-41 | Lambova Major |
| 6-11-40 | Nea Koutsoufliani | 7- 3 -41 | Doukati (7kms NW of Tepeleni) |
| 11-11-40 | Konitsa | 18- 4-41 | Pogonio (Delvinaki) |
| 14-11-40 | Elati | 22- 4-41 | Vissani |
| 17-11-40 | Elafotopos | 23- 4-41 | Hani Kallitheas |
| 7-12-40 | Politsani (7kms S of Premeti) | 25- 4-41 | Avgo |
| 12-12-40 | Doxati | | |

## III DIVISION
### COMMAND

| | | |
|---|---|---|
| 28-10-40 | Commander | MajGen Tilemahos Papadopoulos  until 7-11-40 |
| | | MajGen Georgios Bakos until 5-3-41 |
| | Chief of Staff | Col (INF) Konstantinos Georgantas |
| | | LtCol (INF) Ioannis Theodorou until 4-2-41 |
| | | LtCol (INF) Dimitrios Zafeiropoulos |

### HEADQUARTERS

| | |
|---|---|
| 28-10-40 | Patra |
| 11-11-40 | Agrinio |
| 14-11-40 | Moni  (4kms E of Arta) |
| 19-11-40 | Hani Rovilitsa (S of Ioannina) |
| 8-12-40 | Delvino |
| 12-12-40 | Nivitsa (12kms SW of Tepeleni) |
| 24-12-40 | Koutsi (22kms W of Moschopolis) |
| 20- 1-41 | Borsi (10kms SE of Himara) |
| 18- 3-41 | Kouritesi (E of Himara) |
| 18- 4-41 | Filiates |

| | |
|---|---|
| 23- 4-41 | Paramithia |
| 26- 4-41 | Nikopolis |
| 29- 4-41 | Limin (Arta) |
| 3- 5-41 | Agrinio |
| 5- 5-41 | Patra |

## IV DIVISION
### COMMAND

| | | |
|---|---|---|
| 28-10-40 | Commander | MajGen Leonidas Stergiopoulos until 21-12-40 |
| | | Col (INF) Kleanthis Boulalas |
| | Chief of Staff | LtCol (INF) Athanassios Griveas until 31-1-41 |
| | | LtCol (INF) Antonios Kolliopoulos until 31-3-41 |
| | | LtCol (INF) Sokratis Pavlinos |

### HEADQUARTERS

| | |
|---|---|
| 28-10-40 | Nafplio |
| 10-11-40 | Kastraki (Kalambaka) |
| 25-11-40 | Nea Koutsoufliani |
| 31-11-40 | Vounoplayia |
| 5-12-40 | Ktismata (16kms W of Doliana) |
| 7-12-40 | Doliana |
| 10-12-40 | Gorantzi (8km's SE of Argyrokastro) |
| 24-12-40 | Zouliati (14kms NW of Argyrokastro) |
| 10- 1-41 | Libohovo (12kms SE of Argyrokastro) |
| 17- 3-41 | Loumnitsa (7kms NW of Premeti) |
| 6- 4-41 | Riba |
| 14- 4-41 | Loumnitsa (7kms NW of Premeti) |
| 17- 4-41 | Seperi (valley of Zagorias river) |
| 20- 4-41 | Kato Meropi (15kms NW of Delvinaki) |
| 22- 4-41 | Goritsa (S of Doliana) |
| 24- 4-41 | Philippiada |
| 29- 4-41 | Strevina |
| 8- 5-41 | Nafpaktos |
| 9- 5-41 | Psathopirgos |

## V DIVISION
### COMMAND

| | | |
|---|---|---|
| 28-10-40 | Commander | MajGen Georgios Papastergiou until 25-4-41 |
| | | Col (INF) Dionyssios Papadogonas |
| | | Chief of Staff   LtCol (INF) Ioannis Tzeravinis |

## HEADQUARTERS

| | |
|---|---|
| 28-10-40 | Hania |
| 19- 4-41 | Moni Vela |
| 30-11-40 | Amindeon |
| 21- 4-41 | Zitsa (l7kms SE of Doliana) |
| 7- 12-40 | Korissos (8kms E of Kastoria) |
| 24- 4-41 | Hani Emin Agha |
| 14-12-40 | Biglista (l7kms E of Koritsa) |
| 27- 4-41 | 57km of the road Ioannina-Preveza |
| 19-12-40 | Tepezik |
| 29- 4-41 | 70km of the road Ioannina-Preveza |
| 20- 1-41 | Borova (18 kms N of Leskoviki) |
| 4- 5-41 | Directly N of Lake Amvrakia |
| 27- 1-41 | Koukiari (9kms SE of Klissoura) |
| 14- 5-41 | Nafpaktos |
| 3- 2-41 | Podgrani (9 kms SW of Klissoura) |
| 17-5-41 | Psathopirgos |
| 14-0-41 | Kossina (6 kms NW of Premeti) |

## VI DIVISION
### COMMAND

| | | |
|---|---|---|
| 28-10-40 | Commander | MajGen Nikolaos Markou |
| | Chief of Staff | LtCol (ARTY) Dimitrios Laios until 7-12-40 |
| | | LtCol (Cav.) Konstantinos Stergiou until 17-11-40 |
| | | LtCol (ARTY) Petros Nomikos until 21-3-41 |
| | | LtCol (ARTY) Dimitrios Laios |

## HEADQUARTERS

| | |
|---|---|
| 28-10-40 | Serres |
| 29-10-40 | Sidirokastro |
| 3-02-41 | Amindeo |
| 5-02-41 | Kastoria |
| 9-02-41 | Bitinska (l7kms NE of Korytsa) |
| 27-02-41 | Leskoviki |
| 5-03-41 | Toliari (8kms N of Klissoura) |
| 15-03-41 | Pakomiti |
| 16-04-41 | Rabani (12kms N of Premeti) |
| 19-04-41 | Leskoviki |
| 21-04-41 | Ano Repenia |
| 22-04-41 | Pedini |
| 24-04-41 | Katsika |
| 28-04-41 | Philippiada |
| 5-05-41 | Ioannina |

# VII DIVISION
## COMMAND

| 28-10-40 | Commander | MajGen Christos Zoiopoulos until 19-11-40 |
|---|---|---|
| | | Col (INF) Evangelos Papas until 15-12-40 |
| | | MajGen Christos Zoiopoulos until 8-4-41 |
| | | Col (INF) Evangelos Papas |
| | Chief of Staff | LtCol (ARTY) Stilianos Manidakis |

## HEADQUARTERS

| 28-10-40 | Drama |
|---|---|

# VIII DIVISION
## COMMAND

| 28-10-40 | Commander | MajGen Haralambos Katsimitros |
|---|---|---|
| | Chief of Staff | LtCol (INF) Harilaos Drivas |

## HEADQUARTERS

| 28-10-40 | Ioannina | 9-12-40 | Argirohori |
|---|---|---|---|
| 29-10-40 | Petsali | 7-1-41 | Kardiki |
| 03-11-40 | Protopappas (12kms W of Moschopolis) | 17-04-41 | Dervitsani (6kms SE of Argirokastro) |
| 05-11-40 | Ioannina | 18-04-41 | Kakavia |
| 12-11-40 | Klimatia | 20-04-41 | Kastaniani (15km SW of Doliana) |
| 19-11-40 | Kalpaki Hill | 24-04-41 | Dodoni |
| 30-11-40 | Delvinaki | 28-04-41 | Philippiada |

# IX DIVISION
## COMMAND

| 28-10-40 | Commander | MajGen Christos Zigouris |
|---|---|---|
| | Chief of Staff | Res. Maj (INF) Alkiviadis Bourdaras |

## HEADQUARTERS

| 28-10-40 | Kastoria | 14-04-41 | Staritsa |
|---|---|---|---|
| 06-11-40 | Nestori | 16-04-41 | Anthiro |
| 11-11-40 | Polianemo (20kms W of Koritsa) | 20-04-41 | Metsovo |
| 21-11-40 | Hotsisti | 23-04-41 | Koutsoufliani (16kms SW of Kalambaka) |
| 26-11-40 | Koritsa | 26-04-41 | Ambelohori |

| | | | | |
|---|---|---|---|---|
| 06-12-40 | Soviani | | 01-05-41 | Gorgopotamos |
| 15-12-40 | Maliki (15 kms N of Koritsa) | | 5-05-41 | Kifissohori |
| 23-12-40 | Derdousia | | | |

## X DIVISION
### COMMAND

| | | |
|---|---|---|
| 28-10-40 | Commander | MajGen Christos Kitsos until 18-11-40 |
| | | MajGen of the Reserve Georgios Dromazos until 13-12-40 |
| | | MajGen Panaghiotis Gazis |
| | Chief of Staff | LtCol (ARTY) Michael Nikolaidis |

### HEADQUARTERS

| | |
|---|---|
| 28-10-40 | Veria |
| 4-11-40 | Xino Nero |
| 8-11-40 | Nestori |
| 20-11-40 | Slimnitsa |
| 26-11-40 | Liavdari (6kms SE of Moschopolis) |
| 4- 12-40 | Moschopolis |
| 26-12-40 | Poptsisti (lOkms NW of Moschopolis) |
| 29- 1-41 | Vrebska |
| 11- 3-41 | Poptsisti (lOkm Moschopolis) |
| 14- 4-41 | Nestori |
| 15- 4-41 | Avgerinos (23kms NE of Konitsa) |
| 19- 4-41 | Metsovo |
| 23- 4-41 | Trigona |
| 25- 4-41 | Kalomira |
| 5- 5-41 | Kifissohori |

## XI DIVISION
### COMMAND

| | | |
|---|---|---|
| 28-10-40 | Commander | Col (ARTY) Georgios  Kotsalos until 14-11-40 |
| | | MajGen of the Reserve  Nikolaos Tsipouras until 29-12-40 |
| | | Col (Cav. ) Sokratis Dimaratos |
| | Chief of Staff | LtCol (ARTY) Alexandros Spirakis until 17-3-41 |
| | | LtCol (INF) Spiros Stathopoulos |

### HEADQUARTERS

| | | | |
|---|---|---|---|
| 28-10-40 | Thessaloniki | 25-12-40 | Giorgiova |
| 2-11-40 | Kozani | 10-01-41 | Visotska |
| 9-11-40 | Grevena | 20-01-41 | Greptska (20kms SW of  Premeti) |
| 14-11-40 | Argos Orestiko | 2-02-41 | Slatina |
| 16-11-40 | Enoe  (Ano Fteria) | 5-02-41 | Nivitsa  (l2kms SW of  Tepeleni) |

| | | | |
|---|---|---|---|
| 20-11-40 | Agios Zaharias | 1-04-41 | Toliari (8 kms N of Klissoura) |
| 28-11-40 | Vonitsa (7kms NW of Erseka) | 11-04-41 | Kossina (6 kms NW of Premeti) |
| 6-12-40 | Liouarassa | | |
| 18-12-40 | Trebitska (26 kms NE of Premeti) | 12-04-41 | Metsovo |

## XII  DIVISION (CMFAS)
### COMMAND

| | | |
|---|---|---|
| 28-10-40 | Commander | MajGen Anastasios Roussopoulos until 21-12-40 |
| | | MajGen Napoleon Batas until 24-1-41 |
| | | Col (INF) Anastassios Kalis until 4-3-41 |
| | | Col (INF) Georgios Karambatos |
| | Chief of Staff | Lt Col (INF) Nikolaos Spendos until 17-1-41 |
| | | Maj (INF) Elias Hartokollis until 9-2-41 |
| | | Lt Col (INF) Alexandros Georgiou until 29-3-41 |
| | | Res. Lt Col (INF) Haralambos Manolopoulos |

### HEADQUARTERS

| | | | |
|---|---|---|---|
| 28-10-40 | Komotini | 5-04-41 | Grevena |
| 07-03-41 | Sofular (l6kms NE of Kozani) | 16-04-41 | Melissi |
| 03-04-41 | Xino Nero | 17-04-41 | Kastritsi |
| 13-04-41 | Siatista | | |

## XIII  DIVISION
### COMMAND

| | | |
|---|---|---|
| 28-10-40 | Commander | MajGen Georgios Razis until 18-11-40 |
| | | MajGen Sotirios Moutoussis |
| | Chief in Staff | Maj (ARTY) Alexandros Yiotis until 2-12-40 |
| | | LtCol (INF) Spyros Sakellaropoulos until 2-2-41 |
| | | LtCol (INF) Sotirios Anagnostopoulos from 16-2-41 |

### HEADQUARTERS

| | | | |
|---|---|---|---|
| 28-10-40 | Alexandroupolis | 16-4-41 | Skalohori (4kms S of Argos Orestiko) |
| 12-11-40 | Florina | 17-4-41 | Pendalofo |
| 14-11-40 | Vatohori (20kms NW of Kastoria) | 18-4-41 | Prosvoron (37 kms W of Konitsa) |
| 27-11-40 | Podgoriyie (22kms N of Koritsa) | 19-4-41 | Vovoussa |
| 27-12-40 | Grambovitsa | 21-4-41 | Chrissovitsa |
| 13-04-41 | Biglista (l7kms E of Koritsa) | 23-4-41 | Metsovo |
| 15-04-41 | Argos Orestiko | | |

## XIV DIVISION
### COMMAND

28-10-40  Commander  MajGen Konstantinos Papakonstantinou
          Chief of Staff  LtCol (INF) Georgios Frangiadakis until 2-3-41
          LtCol (ARTY) Dionyssios Chrysanthakopoulos

### HEADQUARTERS

28-10-40  Xanthi                     24-2-41  Sidirokastro

## XV DIVISION (former IV Infantry Brigade)[1]
### COMMAND

28-10-40  Commander       MajGen Agamemnon Metaxas until 21-12-40
                          Col (INF) Panagiotis Spiliotopoulos

          Chief of Staff  LtCol (ENGR) Arhimidis Argiropoulos

### HEADQUARTERS

| | |
|---|---|
| 28- 10-40 | Florina |
| 14- 11-40 | Pili (4kms E of Greek Albanian borders) |
| 24- 11-40 | Bitinska |
| 7- 12-40 | Flaki |
| 15- 12-40 | Frateri |
| 9- 01-41 | Topoyianni |
| 24- 01-41 | Vinokazit |
| 14- 02-41 | Kaitsa |
| 5- 04-41 | Pakomiti (9kms NW of Premeti) |
| 13- 04-41 | Rambani (12kms N of Premeti) |
| 16- 04-41 | Hotova (7kms N of Premeti) |
| 18- 04-41 | Leskoviki |
| 20- 04-41 | Hani Bourazani (3kms SE of the Mertzani bridge) |
| 22- 04-41 | Ano Reveni |
| 23- 04-41 | Bizani |
| 26- 04-41 | Pantanassa |
| 3- 05-41 | Agrinio |

---

[1]  It was reorganized as XV Infantry Division on 6-11-40.

## XVI DIVISION (former XVI Infantry Brigade)[1]
### COMMAND

| 28-10-40 | Commander | Col (INF) Konstantinos Georgantas until 1-1-41 |
| | | MajGen Agamemnon Metaxas |
| | Chief of Staff | Maj (INF) Konstantinos Anagnostopoulos until 22-1-41 |
| | | LtCol (INF) Georgios Kostarelos |

### HEADQUARTERS

| 28-10-40 | Lamia | 5-04-41 | Voditsa (7kms NW of Erseka) |
| 09-11-40 | Larissa | 17-04-41 | Borova (18kms N of Leskoviki) |
| 27-11-40 | Kivotos (10kms SW of Siatista) | 20-04-41 | Leskoviki |
| 12-10-40 | Amindeo | 21-04-41 | Konitsa |
| 17-12-40 | Skopia (6kms S of Florina) | 4-04-41 | Artsista (9kms NW of Doliana) |
| 24-01-41 | Bitinska (17kms NE of Korytsa) | 27-04-41 | Halkiades |
| 04-02-41 | Lieskovo | 05-05-41 | Agrinio |
| 12-02-41 | Postenani (5kms NW of Leskoviki) | | |

## XVII DIVISION
### COMMAND

| 28-10-40 | Commander | MajGen Panagiotis Bassakidis until 22-12-40 |
| | | MajGen Anastassios Roussopoulos |
| | Chief of Staff | LtCol (ARTY) Gerassimos Lamaris |

### HEADQUARTERS

| 28-10-40 | Thessaloniki |
| 5-11-40 | Gida (Alexandria) |
| 16-11-40 | Kozani |
| 24-11-40 | Dipotamia (9kms NW of Nestori) |
| 27-11-40 | Podgoriyie (22kms N of Koritsa) |
| 11-12-40 | Sovgiani (18kms SE of Pogradetz) |
| 5-12-40 | Lesnitsa (8kms SE of Pogradetz) |
| 18-12-40 | Zeblac (13kms NE of Koritsa) |
| 11-02-41 | Erseka |
| 16-02-41 | Leskoviki |
| 20-03-41 | Kossina (6kms NW of Premeti) |
| 31-03-41 | Roden (10kms N of Klissoura) |
| 15-04-41 | Kossina (6kms NW of Premeti) |
| 17-04-41 | Darthesi |
| 20-04-41 | Vassiliko (8kms S of Mertzani bridge) |
| 23-04-41 | Ioannina |
| 4-05-41 | Agrinio |

---

[1] It organized into Division on 2-12-40.

## XVIII  DIVISION [1]
### COMMAND

| | | |
|---|---|---|
| 24-12-40 | Commander | MajGen Leonidas Stergiopoulos |
| | Chief of Staff | LtCol (ARTY) Sotirios Kassimis |

### HEADQUARTERS

| | |
|---|---|
| 11-02-40 | Vyronia (10kms W of Sidirokastron) |
| 7-04-41 | Himaros |

## 19th MOTORIZED DIVISION[2]
### COMMAND

| | | |
|---|---|---|
| 24-2-41 | Commander | MajGen Nikolaos Lioubas |
| | Chief of Staff | Col (ARTY) Vassilios Assimakis |

### HEADQUARTERS

| | |
|---|---|
| 24-01-41 | Athens |
| 26-02-41 | Larissa |
| 06-03-41 | Katerini |
| 29-03-41 | Kilkis |
| 08-04-41 | Lahanas |
| 09-04-41 | Elliniko |

## 20th DIVISION[3]
### COMMAND

| | | |
|---|---|---|
| 12-02-41 | Commander | MajGen Christos Karassos until 8-4-41 |
| | | Col (INF) Miltiadis Papakonstantinou |
| | Chief of Staff | Maj (Cav) Petros Nikolopoulos |

### HEADQUARTERS

| | |
|---|---|
| 01-03-41 | Skopia |
| 05-03-41 | Proti (Florina) |
| 06-04-41 | Kato Grammatiko (17kms E of Amyndaeon) |

---

[1] It began to be established in Vironia on 11-12-40
[2] It began to be established in the area of Athens on 24-1-41.
[3] It began to be established in the area of Florina on 12-2-41.

| | |
|---|---|
| 12-04-41 | Vogatsiko |
| 15-04-41 | Tsotili |
| 17-04-41 | Monahiti˙ |
| 21-04-41 | Ardomitsa (7kms E of Ioannina) |

## CAVALRY DIVISION
### COMMAND

| | | |
|---|---|---|
| 28-10-40 | Commander | MajGen Georgios Stanotas |
| | Chief of Staff | LtCol (Cav) Solon Ghikas |

### HEADQUARTERS

| | | | |
|---|---|---|---|
| 28-10-40 | Langadas | 27-12-40 | Limni |
| 07-11-40 | Vovoussa (34kms NE of Ioannina) | 22-02-41 | Bitinska |
| 14-11-40 | Elefthero | 27-03-41 | Zeblac |
| 19-11-40 | Konitsa | 09-04-41 | Vatohori (20kms N of Kastoria) |
| 15-11-40 | Strani | 16-04-41 | Skalohori |
| | | | (4kms S of Argos Orestiko) |
| 14-12-40 | Trapezitsa | 20-04-41 | Metsovo |

## V INFANTRY BRIGADE[1]
### COMMAND

| | | |
|---|---|---|
| 28-10-40 | Commander | Col (INF) Anastassios Kalis |
| | Chief of Staff | Maj of the Reserve(ARTY)  Dimitrios Zanglis |

### HEADQUARTERS

| | |
|---|---|
| 28-10-40 | Larissa |
| 29-10-40 | Nestori |
| 06-11-40 | Likorrahi  (27 kms NE of Konitsa) |
| 26-11-40 | Borova  (18kms N of Leskoviki) |
| 07-12-40 | Frasseri (16kms NE of Premeti) |
| 26-12-40 | Rambani (12kms N of Premeti) |
| 02- 0l-41 | Mokritsa (8kms N of Premeti) |

## 21st INFANTRY BRIGADE[1]
### COMMAND

| | | |
|---|---|---|
| 22-03-41 | Commander | Col (INF) Christos Dedes |
| | Chief of Staff | Maj (INF) Elias Hartokollis |

---

[1]   Began to be established on 23-3-41

## HEADQUARTERS

| | |
|---|---|
| 22-03-41 | Biglista (17kms E of Korytsa) |
| 09-04-41 | Aetos (10kms SW of Amyndeon) |
| 13-04-41 | Melissotopos (12kms NE of Kastoria) |
| 15-04-41 | Aposkepos (4kms N of Kastoria) |
| 20-04-41 | Metsovo |
| 23-04-41 | Kalambaka |

## NESTOS BRIGADE[1]
### COMMAND

| | | |
|---|---|---|
| 05-03-41 | Commander | Col (INF) Anastassios Kalis |
| | Chief of Staff | LtCol (INF) Georgios Frangiadakis |

### HEADQUARTERS

| | | | |
|---|---|---|---|
| 05-03-41 | Xanthi | 07-04-41 | Makrihori |

## EVROS BRIGADE[2]
### COMMAND

| | | |
|---|---|---|
| 08-02-41 | Commander | MajGen of the Reserve Georgios Zissis |
| | Chief of Staff | Maj (INF) Konstantinos Rotas |

### HEADQUARTERS

| | |
|---|---|
| 08-02-41 | Soufli |

## ALEXANDROUPOLIS BRIGADE[3]
### COMMAND

| | | |
|---|---|---|
| 08-02-41 | Commander | MajGen of the Reserve Georgios Margaris |

### HEADQUARTERS

| | |
|---|---|
| 08-02-41 | Alexandroupolis |

---

[1] Was established on 8-2-41.

[2] It ceased to exist on 7-3-41. Its units were placed under the XII Division.

[3] It began to be established in Xanthi on 5-3-41.

## CAVALRY BRIGADE[1]
### COMMAND

| 28-10-40 | Commander | Col Cav. Sokratis Dimaratos |
| | Chief of Staff | LtCol (Cav) Konstantinos Georgiou |

### HEADQUARTERS

| 28-10-40 | Thessaloniki |
| 01-11-40 | Afhenas Skourtza (Pindos) |
| 03-11-40 | Kirkouri |
| 06-11-40 | Kergoli |
| 10-11-40 | Samarina (20 kms NE of Konitsa) |
| 16-11-40 | Fourka (ll kms W of Leskoviki) |
| 25-11-40 | Borova (18kms N of Leskoviki) |
| 03-12-40 | Kessibasi |
| 07-12-40 | Frasseri (16kms NE of Premeti) |
| 24-12-40 | Konitsa |

## MILITARY HIGH COMMAND OF CRETE
### COMMAND

| 20-05-41 | Commander | MajGen Ahilleas Skoulas |
| | Chief of Staff | LtCol Polidoros Klados |

### HEADQUARTERS

| 20-05-41 | Hania |
| 28-05-41 | Nerokourou |

## 1st MILITARY COMMAND (HANIA)[2]
### COMMAND

| 20-05-41 | Commander | MajGen Nikolaos Gagaras |
| | Chief of Staff | Maj (Cav) Apostolos Vahlas |

### HEADQUARTERS

| 20-05-41 | Hania | 28-05-41 | Nerokourou |

---

[1] On 1-1-41 it was incorporated to the Calavary Division.

[2] It was established on 9-5-41.

## 2nd MILITARY COMMAND (IRAKLIO)[1]
### COMMAND

| | | |
|---|---|---|
| 20-05-41 | Commander | MajGen Michael Linardakis |
| | Chief of Staff | Maj (Cav) Athanassios Doumbiotis |

### HEADQUARTERS

| | |
|---|---|
| 20-05-41 | Iraklio |
| 23-05-41 | Arhanes |

## BRITISH EXPEDITIONARY FORCE
### COMMAND

| | |
|---|---|
| 27-03-41 | Commander Gen Sir H.M. Wilson |

### HEADQUARTERS

| | |
|---|---|
| 27-03-41 | Athens |
| 18-04-41 | Thiva |
| 05-04-41 | Tsaritsani (Elassona) |
| 25-04-41 | Miloi |

## 1st AUSTRALIAN ARMY CORPS
### COMMAND

| | | |
|---|---|---|
| 27-03-41 | Commander | LtGen Sir T.A. Blamey |

### HEADQUARTERS

| | |
|---|---|
| 27-03-41 | Athens |
| 11-04-41 | Elassona |
| 18-04-41 | Soubassi (Larissa) |
| 20-04-41 | Livadia |
| 23-04-41 | Mandra |

## 2nd NEW ZEALAND DIVISION
### COMMAND

| | | |
|---|---|---|
| 27-03-41 | Commander | LtGen Lord Freyberg until 30-4-41[2] |
| | | Brig Sir E. Pattick |

[1] It was established on 9-5-41.
[2] Since the same day he had been appointed Commander of the British-Greek forces on Crete.

## HEADQUARTERS

| | |
|---|---|
| 27-03-41 | Athens |
| 06-04-41 | Ganohori (N of Katerini) |
| 11-04-41 | Dolihi (N of Elassona) |
| 18-04-41 | Nea Karia (S of Larissa) |
| 20-04-41 | Longos (S of Volos) |
| 29-04-41 | Crete |

## 6th AUSTRALIAN DIVISION
### COMMAND

| | | |
|---|---|---|
| 27-03-41 | Commander | MajGen Sir I. Mackay |

## HEADQUARTERS

| | |
|---|---|
| 27-03-41 | Athens |
| 06-04-41 | Servia |
| 11-04-41 | Perdikas (33 kms SE of Florina) |
| 20-04-41 | Agia Marina |
| 24-04-41 | Livadia |
| 16-04-41 | Nikea (S of Larissa) |

## 1st BRITISH ARMOURED BRIGADE
### COMMAND

| | | |
|---|---|---|
| 27-03-41 | Commander | Brig Charringdon |

## HEADQUARTERS

| | |
|---|---|
| 27-03-41 | Edessa |
| 13-04-41 | Komano (Ptolemaida) |
| 14-04-41 | Grevena |
| 18-04-41 | Atalanti |
| 21-04-41 | Thiva |

## BRITISH FORCES IN CRETE
### COMMAND

| | | |
|---|---|---|
| 20-05-41 | Commander | LtGen Lord Freyberg until 28- 5-41<br>MajGen E.C. Weston |

## HEADQUARTERS

| | |
|---|---|
| 20-05-41 | Agios Mattheos (Hania) |
| 27-05-41 | Askifou (Sfakia) |
| 28-05-41 | Sfakia |

## 2nd NEW ZEALAND DIVISION[1]
### COMMAND

| | | |
|---|---|---|
| 20-05-41 | Commander | Brig Sir E. Puttick |

## HEADQUARTERS

| | | | |
|---|---|---|---|
| 20-05-41 | Alikianos (Hania) | 28-05-41 | Askifou (Sfakia) |
| 26-05-41 | Mournies | 29-05-41 | Sfakia |

## 4th NEW ZEALAND BRIGADE
### COMMAND

| | | |
|---|---|---|
| 20-05-41 | Commander | Brig L.M. Ingliss |

## HEADQUARTERS

| | | | |
|---|---|---|---|
| 20-05-41 | Efthimi (Hania) | 30-05-41 | Sfakia |
| 27-05-41 | Askifou (Sfakia) | | |

## 5th NEW ZEALAND BRIGADE
### COMMAND

| | | |
|---|---|---|
| 20-05-41 | Commander | Brig J. Hargest |

## HEADQUARTERS

| | | | |
|---|---|---|---|
| 20-05-41 | Platanias (Hania) | 30-05-41 | Sfakia |
| 27-05-41 | Stilos (Hania) | | |

---

[1] Comprising the 4th,5th and 10th New Zealand Brigades.

# 10th NEW ZEALAND BRIGADE[1]
## COMMAND

20-05-41       Commander       Col H.K. Kippenberger

## HEADQUARTERS

20-05-41       Ayia (Hania)

# MNBDO[2]
## COMMAND

20-05-41       Commander       MajGen C.E. Weston [3]

## HEADQUARTERS

20-05-41       Hania

# 19th AUSTRALIAN BRIGADE
## COMMAND

20-05-41       Commander       Brig G.A. Vasey

## HEADQUARTERS

| | | | |
|---|---|---|---|
| 20-05-41 | Georghioupolis | 30-5-41 | Sfakia |
| 27-05-41 | Neo Horio (Hania) | | |

# 14th BRITISH BRIGADE
## COMMAND

20-05-41       Commander       Brig B.H. Chappel

## HEADQUARTERS

20-05-41       Nea Alikarnassos (Iraklio)

---

[1] This Brigade was disbanded on 26-10-41.
[2] MOBILE NAVAL BASE DEFENSE ORGANIZATION
[3] This unit was disbanded on 26-5-41 and MajGen Weston was appointed Commander of the forces in the Sectors of Maleme and Suda which were unified.

## LIST OF ABBREVIATIONS

| | |
|---|---|
| A'AC | A' Army Corps |
| AA | Antiaircraft |
| AAHC | Army Aviation High Command |
| AC | Army Corps |
| Adm | Admiral |
| AFGS | Air Force General Staff |
| AGS | Army General Staff |
| AirMA | Air Marshal |
| AirVMA | Air Vice Marshal |
| ANZAC | Australian-New Zealand Corps |
| AT | Antitank |
| B'AC | B' Army Corps |
| BAF | Bombardment Aviation Command |
| BrigGen | Brigadier General |
| C'AC | C' Army Corps |
| CAirMA | Chief Air Marshal |
| Capt | Captain |
| Capt (Cav) | Cavalry Captain |
| CFH | Cretan Forces Headquarters |
| CMFAS | Central Macedonia Field Army Section |
| Col | Colonel |
| D'AC | D' Army Corps |
| DivGr | Division Group |
| DivGr"K" | Division Group "K" |
| E'AC | E' Army Corps |
| EFAS | Epirus Field Army Section |
| EMFAS | Eastern Macedonia Field Army Section |
| Gen | General |
| GH | General Headquarters |
| GHC | Greek High Command |
| HAGS | Hellenic Army General Staff |
| HQ | Headquarters |
| InfBtn. | Infantry Battalion |
| InfRegt. | Infantry Regiment |
| KFAS | Kavala Field Army Section |
| L. U. | Large Unit (Formation) |
| LoN | League of Nations |
| Lt | Lieutenant |
| LtCol | Lieutenant Colonel |
| LtGen | Lieutenant General |
| Maj | Major |
| MajGen | Major General |
| MHD | Military History Division |
| MNBDO | Mobile Naval Base Defense Organization |
| NAHC | Naval Aviation High Command |
| NGS | Navy General Staff |
| POW | Prisoner of War |
| RAdm | Rear Admiral |
| TFAS | Thrace Field Army Section |
| VAdm | Vice Admiral |
| WMFAS | Western Macedonia Field Army Section |

# MAIN NAMES IN ALPHABETICAL ORDER

### -A-

Alevizatos Tzanis (Major) 79
Alexakis Ioannis (Lieutenant General) 250
Alfieri (Italian Ambassador to Berlin) 113
Allen (Brigadier General) 227
Anfuzo (Head of the personal office of Italian Foreign Minister Ciano) 20
Antoneski (Prime Minister of Rumania) 7
Argyropoulos (Ambassador) 170

### -B-

Badoglio (Marshal) 111,112
Bakopoulos Konstantinos (Lieutenant General) 32,178,179,183,196,198,245
Bakos Georgios (Major General) 76,149,154
Bartai (Minister) 146
Basiakos Sotirios (Lieutenant Colonel) 110
Bassakidis Panaghiotis (Major General) 68
Bemich (Captain) 253
Bennini (Italian Deputy Minister of Albanian affairs) 21
Beyetis (Colonel) 91
Blamey (Lieutenant General) 227
Blamey (Major General) 185
Boeme (General) 207
Bonnini (General) 29
Brauer (Colonel) 261,271,293
Brauhitz von (General) 145

### -C-

Campell (Lieutenant Colonel) 256,270,275,276,283,288,292
Cavallero (Colonel) 112
Cavallero (General) 129,134,135,136,144,146,151,159,164
Chapel (Brigadier) 257,293
Charrington (Brigadier General) 186
Chrisohoou Athanasios (Colonel) 233
Churchill Winston (British Prime Minister) 49,175,230
Ciano Count (Foreign Minister of Italy) 6,11,20,21,22,102, 113, 145, 146
Colvin (Lieutenant Colonel) 291
Conrad (Air Vice Marshal) 259
Cracow (Colonel) 282
Cunningham (Admiral) 173
Cvetkovitch 164

-R-

-S-

**-Y-**

**-Z-**

Picture 2

Picture 3
The arrival of the reserves on the day of the declaration of the Greek - Italian War

Picture 4
The Mother's Amulet

Picture 5
Soldiers set off by train to the front

Picture 6

Picture 7
Scene of national elation during the first days of the war

Picture 8
Greek Observation Post at the Albanian Theatre of Operations

"Εφοδος μέ έφ' ὅπλου λόγχη.

Picture 9
Infantry in action

Picture 10
Infantry Team during combat

Picture 11
Battery in action

Picture 12

Picture 13
Transportation of supplies to the Albanian Theatre of Operations

Picture 14
Women from Epirus carry ammunition and other supplies to the front line

Picture 15
Heroic inhabitants of Epirus open the way through the snow

Picture 16
Typical means of transportation of the Greek Army

Picture 17
New Year Day at the front

Picture 18
Italian Troops undermine the road 'Kakavia - Argyrokastro'

Picture 19
Italian tank - Spoils of the Victors

Picture 20
View of Klissoura

Picture 21
Mount Kourvelessi covered with snow

Picture 22
First Aid Station at the Albanian Theatre of Operations

Picture 23
Evacuating the wounded from the front-line

Picture 24
Evacuating wounded men on a mule

Μεταφορά τραυματιών αποσπάσματος Δαβάκη

Picture 25
Inhabitants of Pindos evacuating the wounded

Picture 26
Meals to the Italian Prisoners of War

Picture 27
Italian POWs at a military hospital in Athens

Picture 28
Mussolini observing the Italian "Primavera" (Spring) attack

Picture 29
View of the 'greatly' fought for height no. 731

Picture 30
Permanent pillbox on the fortification line of Eastern Macedonia

Picture 31
Permanent observation post on the fortification line of Eastern Macedonia

Picture 32
Anti-aircraft pillbox at Fort Rupel

Picture 33
Camouflazed pillbox on the fortification line

345

Picture 34
Pillbox and antitank obstacle on the fortification line

Picture 35
Antitank obstacle in front of Fort Partaluska

Picture 36
Advance of German Armoured Unit to Larissa

Picture 37
German motorcyclists moving on the railway line Thessaloniki - Larissa

Picture 38
Destroyed bridge over the river Aliakmonas, on the road  Thessaloniki - Larissa

Picture 39
Blowing up of the bridge of the Isthmus of Corinth, by the British

Picture 40
Scene from the surrendering of the city of Athens

Picture 41
Field-Marshal Brauchitsch with the Italian General Celoso at the Acropolis

Picture 42
German parachutists boarding an aircraft for Crete

Picture 43
Scene from the German invasion on Crete

Picture 44
Dropping of German parachutists on Crete

Picture 45
Destroyed German glider on Crete

Picture 46
Memorial to a Greek Soldier, at Kalpaki (Elea)

Picture 47
Memorial to a Greek Woman of Pindos at Fourka, Konitsa

Picture 48
Memorial at Fort Rupel

Picture 49
Memorial at Fort Lisse

Picture 50
Memorial at Forts of Kato Nevrokopi (Lisse heights)

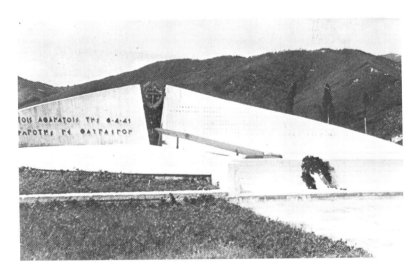

Picture 51
Memorial at Fort Nymphaea

Picture 52
Memorial to the fallen cadets

Picture 53
Memorial to the fallen in the Battle of Crete (Iraklio)